# THE EUROPEAN UNION

THIRD EDITION

# THE EUROPEAN UNION

## Readings on the Theory and Practice of European Integration

edited by

Brent F. Nelsen
Alexander Stubb

BOULDER
LONDON

Published in the United States of America in 2003 by
Lynne Rienner Publishers, Inc.
1800 30th Street, Boulder, Colorado 80301
www.rienner.com



**Library of Congress Cataloging-in-Publication Data**
The European Union : readings on the theory and practice of European integration / Brent F. Nelsen and Alexander Stubb, editors—third edition.
p. cm.
Includes index.
ISBN 978-1-58826-231-8 (alk. paper)
1. European federation. 2. European Union. 3. Europe—Economic integration. I. Nelsen, Brent F. II. Stubb, Alexander C-G.

JN15.E889 2003
341.242'2—dc21

2003043221

Printed and bound in the United States of America

The paper used in this publication meets the requirements of the American National Standard for Permanence of Paper for Printed Library Materials Z39.48-1992.

5 4

*To our children,*
*Kirsten, Evan, and Derek Nelsen*
*and Emilie Stubb*

# Contents

## PART 2 EARLY CURRENTS IN INTEGRATION THEORY



## PART 3 CURRENT DEBATES IN INTEGRATION THEORY

# Preface

This book records a conversation among political leaders and scholars about the possibility, purpose, and process of unifying Europe. European politicians, from the close of World War II, have been articulating a vision of a united Europe and taking practical steps to achieve it. Academics over the same period have also been known to prescribe a course of action for Europe, but more often than not, have confined themselves to describing and explaining the process and progress of integration. The conversation has never been one-way: officials have sometimes taken their cues from theoretical work done by scholars, and scholars have often allowed political notions to inform their theoretical reflections. Nor has the conversation proceeded without its heated debates. Some of the heat has come from scholars—particularly the federalists among them—who look for greater progress toward integration from the politicians; some has come from policymakers who lament the abstract nature of much of the scholarly work (a familiar refrain). Most of the conversational heat, however, comes from internal debates. European politicians have disagreed deeply over the nature and purpose of postwar integration, and scholars have divided over everything from the best method of integration, to who controls integration, to what the European Union actually is. This book looks at this conversation over time and allows students to enter the debate that continues to shape contemporary Europe.

We have structured the third edition of this book like its predecessors. The first part concentrates on the visions articulated by politicians and policymakers. We include in Part 1 the writings and speeches of the men and women who have shaped the European Union (and its predecessors) over more than half a century of integration. In addition, this part contains the vision-casting portions of the Union's basic treaties. New to this section is the preamble to the Treaty of Nice—which is a bit thin on vision—as well as a compilation of statements made by political leaders in the run-up to the European Convention. As the last selection in this part demonstrates, the new constitutional process in Europe has suddenly brought the "vision thing" back into fashion.

The second part of the current edition remains, with only minor modifications, the same as the second edition. The classical theories of integration—federalism, functionalism, transactionalism, neofunctionalism, intergovernmentalism, economic theory—are all represented by their most prominent exponents. Many of these theories echo views expressed by the policymakers of Part 1; all of them have their contemporary advocates. No student of European integration can understand contemporary theory without a firm grasp of the classical approaches.

Finally, the all-new third part of the book, which explores recent trends in integration theory, presents us—as always—with our greatest challenge. We desire—given the constraints of space, permission fees, and an unavoidable time lag—to include the most significant works representing the most important contemporary theoretical developments. Our choices are always agonizingly difficult, but have been made harder by the apparent fragmentation of the field. The decline of "grand theory" has multiplied schools of thought. Certainly neofunctionalism, intergovernmentalism, and (less often) federalism continue to be represented in the best journals, but the proliferation of "institutionalisms" of various stripes; the rise of the "governance approach," which incorporates almost any approach to politics not connected to international relations; and the radical challenge of "constructivism" and "reflectivism" (a distinction of doubtful significance), not to mention the many approaches not easily labeled, make it very difficult to discern the most significant trends. But discern we must.

We have chosen to highlight developments in three areas. First, we present four pieces that can be loosely labeled "grand theory" (a label some in this group explicitly reject) representing federalism, neofunctionalism, intergovernmentalism, and rational choice institutionalism. Second, we offer three examples of the governance approach to EU politics. These chapters do not address the "why" and "how" of integration, but instead assume Europe is significantly integrated and focus on how such a complex system governs its citizens. The approach represents a shift in perception. Governance scholars see the EU as enough like other domestic systems of government to treat it not as a system of nation states but as a—more or less—"normal" polity. Finally, we introduce a constructivist perspective to the debate. Although constructivism has yet to demonstrate that it is able to go toe-to-toe with the grand theories of integration, it certainly has the potential to reorder the academic discussion. Constructivism—a label that unfortunately covers a wide variety of approaches—is usually grounded in a deep critique of the underlying methodology of most integration studies. It intersects at some points with transactionalism and neofunctionalism, but for the most part it rejects the materialist basis of all rationalist theories (i.e., that actors make choices based on rational calculations of material benefit), and thus critiques most work done on integration. If constructivism continues to gain popularity, the main cleavage in integration studies may soon be between rationalists and constructivists.

European integration remains controversial. Policymakers still argue over what European unity means, and the scholars still argue over how to explain it. We trust this book will introduce readers to the conversation and open a door to their participation.

. . .

As always, readers need to be aware of several protocols we employed when constructing the book. First, the introductions preceding each chapter set the context and summarize the argument of the following selection. The prologues are designed to amplify the dialogue between the authors of the texts. They should not substitute for a broader discussion of the historical or theoretical contexts, nor should they replace a close reading of each piece. Second, we have abridged each selection. Centered bullets mark significant abridgments; less significant abridgments (i.e., less than a paragraph) are marked with ellipses; very minor abridgments go unmarked; brackets [ ] mark editors' additions; and all notes are omitted (to save space and confusion caused by editing). We have taken great care to preserve the core—and much more—of each author's argument, but readers should consider the original sources before making definitive (i.e., published) statements about the selections reprinted here.

. . .

The first edition of this reader was conceived and executed at Furman University (Greenville, South Carolina). The third edition, like the second, is a cyber-age product of cross-Atlantic e-mail exchanges. It is also a collaborative effort between the world of scholarship and the world of policymaking. With one of us firmly planted in the academy and one of us straddling the university-government divide, the book represents—we trust—the sensibilities of both.

We, of course, take full responsibility for the final product, but we could not have put this book together without the help of both

European and American friends and colleagues. In determining the content of the third edition we took valuable advice from Elizabeth Bomberg, James Guth, Paulette Kurzer, Leon Lindberg, Gary Marks, Janne Haaland Matlary, John Peterson, Helen Wallace, and William Wallace. Helen Greer, Margaret Crisp, Jeremy Uecker, and Vera Kotrschal provided valuable secretarial help. Klaudia Kruszynska and Elizabeth McNeill chased down countless books and articles during the research phase of this book. Finally, without Lynne Rienner and Sally Glover of Lynne Rienner Publishers, this book would never have made it to press.

Generous financial support for this project came from the Duke Endowment and the Knight Foundation, via Furman University's Research and Professional Growth and Furman Advantage Programs. And as with previous editions, emotional support and personal sacrifices were generously offered by our long-suffering families. Their love and support provide the foundation on which we stand.

*—Brent F. Nelsen and Alexander Stubb*

# PART 1

# Visions of a United Europe

# 1 The Ventotene Manifesto

ALTIERO SPINELLI AND ERNESTO ROSSI

*Visions of a united Europe have their roots in the political unity of ancient Rome and the ideological solidarity of medieval Christendom. In the twentieth century these visions grew to maturity in the harsh climate of modern war. When the Allies began to turn back Hitler's armies, Europeans of many political persuasions began arguing for a united Europe as a means of eliminating the possibility of war and preserving European civilization. The resistance movements fighting fascist occupation were especially vocal in their criticism of the nation-state system and their support for a unified Europe. Leading the way was a small group of left-wing intellectuals from the Italian Resistance Movement who illegally launched their drive for a federated Europe from a political internment center on the island of Ventotene.*

*Altiero Spinelli (1907–1986), a former communist and future academic and politician (see Chapter 13), and Ernesto Rossi (1897–1967), an anti-fascist journalist, in consultation with several other prisoners, drafted what came to be known as the Ventotene Manifesto in June 1941. Ada Rossi smuggled the Manifesto to the Italian mainland, where the underground press published it in late 1941.*[1] *In August 1943 Spinelli founded the European Federalist Movement, which adopted the Manifesto as its political program.*

*The Manifesto is ultimately a call to action. It begins with a critique of totalitarianism and its causes, then proceeds to call for a movement of workers and intellectuals to seize the opportunity offered by the war to create a "European Federation" equipped to provide security and social justice for all Europeans. The section of the*

Reprinted with permission from *Documents on the History of European Integration*, Vol. 1: *Continental Plans for European Union, 1939–1945*, ed. Walter Lipgens (Berlin: Walter de Gruyter, 1985), pp. 471–484. Notes omitted.

*Manifesto reprinted below—which appeared under the heading "Post-war Duties: European Unity"—assesses the coming postwar crisis and asserts that a European Federation would easily solve "the multiple problems which poison international life on the continent." Finally, the authors sketch the outline of a federal state that controls the armed forces of Europe, its economy, and its internal security, while leaving the states with sufficient autonomy to develop the political life of their people.*

*The version reproduced here is the 1981 Rome translation with further English clarifications inserted in brackets.*

. . .

Germany's defeat would not automatically lead to the reformation of Europe according to our ideal of civilization.

In the brief, intense period of general crises (during which the fallen governments lie broken, during which the popular masses anxiously await a new message and are, meanwhile, like molten matter, burning, susceptible of being poured into new moulds, capable of welcoming the guidance of serious internationalists), the classes which were most privileged under the old national systems will attempt, underhandedly or violently, to quench the thirst, the sentiments, the passions groping towards internationalism, and they will ostentatiously [obstinately] begin to reconstruct the old state organ. And it is probable that the English leaders, perhaps in agreement with the Americans, will attempt to push things in this direction, in order to restore the policy of the balance of power, in the apparent immediate interests of their empire.

. . .

If this purpose were to be reached [achieved], the reaction would have won. In appearance, these states might well be broadly democratic and socialistic; [but] it would only be a question of time before power returned into the hands of the reactionaries. National jealousies would again develop, and [each] state would again express its satisfaction at its own existence in its armed strength. In a more or less brief space of time the most important duty would be to convert populations into armies. Generals would again command, the monopoly holders would again draw profits from autarchy, the bureaucracy would continue to swell, the priests would keep the masses docile. All the initial conquests would shrivel into nothing, in comparison to the necessity of once more preparing for war.

The question which must first be resolved, and if it is not then any other progress made up to that point is mere appearance, is that of the abolition of the division of Europe into national, sovereign states.

The collapse of the majority of the states of the continent under the German steam-roller has already placed the destinies of the European populations on common ground: either all together they will submit to Hitler's dominion, or all together they will enter a revolutionary crisis after his fall, and they will not find themselves adamantly distinct in solid, state structures.

The general spirit today is already far more [better] disposed than it was in the past to a federal reorganization of Europe. The hard experience of the last decades has opened the eyes even of those who would not see, and has matured many circumstances favorable to our ideal.

All reasonable men recognize that it is impossible to maintain a balance of power among European states with militarist Germany enjoying equal conditions, nor can Germany be broken up into pieces once it is conquered. We have seen a demonstration that no country within Europe can stay on the sidelines to naught. The uselessness, even harmfulness, of organizations like the League of Nations has been demonstrated: they pretend to guarantee an international law without a military force capable of imposing its decisions respecting the absolute sovereignty of the member states. The principle of non-intervention turned out to be absurd. According to it each population was left free to choose the despotic government it thought best, as if the constitution of each of the single states were not a question of vital interest for all the other European nations.

The multiple problems which poison international life on the continent have proved to be insoluble: tracing boundaries through areas inhabited by mixed populations, defence of alien minorities, seaports for landlocked countries, the Balkan question, the Irish problem, and so on. All matters which would find easy solutions in the European Federation.

. . .

And, once the horizon of the Old Continent is passed beyond, and all the peoples who make up humanity embrace in a grand vision of their common participation it will have to be recognized that European Federation is the single conceivable guarantee that relationships with American and Asiatic peoples can exist on the basis of peaceful cooperation; this while awaiting a more distant future, when the political unity of the entire globe becomes a possibility.

The dividing line between progressive and reactionary parties no longer follows the formal line of greater or lesser democracy, or of more or less socialism to be instituted; rather the division falls along the line, very new and substantial, that separates the party members into two groups. The first is made up of those who conceive of the essential purpose and goal of struggle as the ancient one, that is, the conquest of national political power—and who, although involuntarily, play into the hands of reactionary forces, letting the incandescent lava of popular passions set in the old moulds, and this allowing old absurdities to arise once again. The second are those who see as the main purpose the creation of a solid international state; they will direct popular forces toward this goal, and having won national power, use it first and foremost as an instrument for achieving international unity.

With propaganda and action, seeking to establish in every possible way the agreements and links among the single [similar] movements which are certainly being formed in the various countries, the foundation must be built now for a movement that knows how to mobilize all forces for the birth of the new organism which will be the grandest creation, and the newest, that has occurred in Europe for centuries; in order to constitute a steady federal state, that will have at its disposal a European armed service instead of national armies; to break decisively economic autarchies, the backbone of totalitarian regimes; [an organism] that will have sufficient means to see that its deliberations for the maintenance of common order are executed in the single federal states, while each state will retain the autonomy it needs for a plastic articulation and development of political life according to the particular characteristics of its people.

If a sufficient number of men in European countries understand this, then victory is shortly to be [will soon be] in their hands, because the situation and the spirit [people's minds] will be favourable to their work. They will have before them [as their adversaries] parties and factions that have already been disqualified by the disastrous experience of the last twenty years. It will be the moment of new men: the movement for a free and united Europe.

## ■ NOTE

1. Walter Lipgens, *Documents on the History of European Integration, Vol. 1: Continental Plans for European Union 1939–1945*, ed. Walter Lipgens (Berlin: Walter de Gruyter, 1985), pp. 471–73.

# 2 The Tragedy of Europe

WINSTON S. CHURCHILL

*Calls for a united Europe—like that of the Ventotene Manifesto—drew the attention of a wide range of political leaders and activists. Many were young idealists or politicians with limited influence; no leaders of undeniable political stature raised a strong voice in favor of a federated Europe—that is, until Winston Churchill (1874–1965) spoke from a platform in Zurich.*

*Churchill, the great wartime prime minister of Britain, found himself leader of the Conservative opposition in Parliament after Labour's victory in the 1945 general election. Despite his removal from office, Churchill remained a key architect of the postwar world by identifying the dangers facing the West and articulating a clear strategy for defending western interests and values.*

*Churchill's speech at Zurich University on 19 September 1946 profoundly influenced the shape of postwar Europe. He began this speech with the refrain common to all the postwar integrationists: Europe must unite before war destroys the continent, its glorious civilization, and perhaps much of the rest of the world. He called specifically for a "United States of Europe" led by Europe's former antagonists, France and Germany, but he did not outline a detailed program for achieving unity. Rather, he argued simply and powerfully for Europe to adopt an ideal to guide its future. Interestingly, Churchill seems to exclude Britain from his grand European project, thus reflecting an ambiguity toward Europe that remains strong in Britain today.*

---

*Churchill's stature forced European leaders to take his Zurich call seriously. His efforts eventually led to the Hague Congress of May 1948 and the creation of the Council of Europe in 1949, both milestones in European integration.*

I wish to speak to you today about the tragedy of Europe. This noble continent, comprising on the whole the fairest and the most cultivated regions of the earth, enjoying a temperate and equable climate, is the home of all the great parent races of the western world. It is the fountain of Christian faith and Christian ethics. It is the origin of most of the culture, arts, philosophy, and science both of ancient and modern times. If Europe were once united in the sharing of its common inheritance, there would be no limit to the happiness, to the prosperity and glory which its three or four hundred million people would enjoy. Yet it is from Europe that have sprung that series of frightful nationalistic quarrels, originated by the Teutonic nations, which we have seen even in this twentieth century and in our lifetime, wreck the peace and mar the prospects of all mankind.

And what is the plight to which Europe has been reduced? Some of the smaller states have indeed made a good recovery, but over wide areas a vast quivering mass of tormented, hungry, care-worn and bewildered human beings gape at the ruins of their cities and homes, and scan the dark horizons for the approach of some new peril, tyranny or terror. Among the victors there is a babel of jarring voices; among the vanquished a sullen silence of despair. That is all that Europeans, grouped in so many ancient states and nations, that is all that the Germanic Powers have got by tearing each other to pieces and spreading havoc far and wide. Indeed, but for the fact that the great Republic across the Atlantic Ocean has at length realized that the ruin or enslavement of Europe would involve their own fate as well, and has stretched out hands of succor and guidance, the Dark Ages would have returned in all their cruelty and squalor. They may still return.

Yet all the while there is a remedy which, if it were generally and spontaneously adopted, would as if by a miracle transform the whole scene, and would in a few years make all Europe, or the greater part of it, as free and as happy as Switzerland is today. What is this sovereign remedy? It is to re-create the European Family or as much of it as we can, and provide it with a structure under which it can dwell in peace, in safety and in freedom. We must build a kind of United States of Europe. In this way only will hundreds of millions of toilers be able to regain the simple joys and hopes which make life worth living. The process is simple. All that is needed is the resolve of hundreds of millions of men and women to do right instead of wrong and gain as their reward blessing instead of cursing.

Much work has been done upon this task by the exertions of the Pan-European Union which owes so much to Count Coudenhove-Kalergi and which commanded the services of the famous French patriot and statesman, Aristide Briand. There is also that immense body of doctrine and procedure, which was brought into being amid high hopes after the first world war, as the League of Nations. The League of Nations did not fail because of its principles or conceptions. It failed because these principles were deserted by those states who had brought it into being. It failed because the governments of those days feared to face the facts, and act while time remained. This disaster must not be repeated. There is therefore much knowledge and material with which to build; and also bitter dear-bought experience.

I was very glad to read in the newspapers two days ago that my friend President Truman had expressed his interest and sympathy with this great design. There is no reason why a regional organization of Europe should in any way conflict with the world organization of the United Nations. On the contrary, I believe that the larger synthesis will only survive if it is founded upon coherent natural groupings. There is already a natural grouping in the Western Hemisphere. We British have our own Commonwealth of Nations. These do not weaken, on the contrary they strengthen, the world organization. They are in fact its main support. And why should there not be a European group which could give a sense of enlarged patriotism and common citizenship to the distracted peoples of this turbulent and mighty continent and why should it not take its rightful place with other great groupings in shaping the destinies of men? In order that this should be accomplished there must be an act of faith in which millions of families speaking many languages must consciously take part.

We all know that the two world wars through which we have passed arose out of the vain passion of a newly-united Germany to play the dominating part in the world. In this last struggle crimes and massacres have been committed for which there is no parallel since the invasions of the Mongols in the fourteenth century and no equal at any time in human history. The guilty must be punished. Germany must be deprived of the power to rearm and make another aggressive war. But when all this has been done, as it will be done, as it is being done, there must be an end to retribution. There must be what Mr. Gladstone many years ago called "a blessed act of oblivion." We must all turn our backs upon the horrors of the past. We must look to the future. We cannot afford to drag forward across the years that are to come the hatreds and revenges which have sprung from the injuries of the past. If Europe is to be saved from infinite misery, and indeed from final doom, there must be an act of faith in the European family and an act of oblivion against all the crimes and follies of the past.

Can the free peoples of Europe rise to the height of these resolves of the soul and instincts of the spirit of man? If they can, the wrongs and injuries which have been inflicted will have been washed away on all sides by the miseries which have been endured. Is there any need for further floods of agony? Is it the only lesson of history that mankind is unteachable? Let there be justice, mercy and freedom. The peoples have to will it, and all will achieve their hearts' desire.

I am now going to say something that will astonish you. The first step in the re-creation of the European family must be a partnership between France and Germany. In this way only can France recover the moral leadership of Europe. There can be no revival of Europe without a spiritually great France and a spiritually great Germany. The structure of the United States of Europe, if well and truly built, will be such as to make the material strength of a single state less important. Small nations will count as much as large ones and gain their honor by their contribution to the common cause. The ancient states and principalities of Germany, freely joined together for mutual convenience in a federal system, might each take their individual place among the United States of Europe. I shall not try to make a detailed program for hundreds of millions of people who want to be happy and free, prosperous and safe, who wish to enjoy the four freedoms of which the great President Roosevelt spoke, and live in accordance with the principles embodied in the Atlantic Charter. If this is their wish, they have only to say so, and means can certainly be found, and machinery erected, to carry that wish into full fruition.

But I must give you a warning. Time may be short. At present there is a breathing space. The cannon have ceased firing. The fighting has stopped; but the dangers have not stopped. If we are to form the United States of Europe or whatever name or form it may take, we must begin now.

In these present days we dwell strangely and precariously under the shield and protection of the atomic bomb. The atomic bomb is still only in the hands of a state and nation which we know will never use it except in the cause of right and freedom. But it may well be that in a few years this awful agency of destruction will be widespread and the catastrophe following from its use by several warring nations will not only bring to an end all that we call civilization, but may possibly disintegrate the globe itself.

I must now sum up the propositions which are before you. Our constant aim must be to build and fortify the strength of [the United Nations]. Under and within that world concept we must re-create the European family in a regional structure called, it may be, the United States of Europe. The first step is to form a Council of Europe. If at first all the states of Europe are not willing or able to join the union, we must nevertheless proceed to assemble and combine those who will and those who can. The salvation of the common people of every race and of every land from war or servitude must be established on solid foundations and must be guarded by the readiness of all men and women to die rather than submit to tyranny. In all this urgent work, France and Germany must take the lead together. Great Britain, the British Commonwealth of Nations, mighty America, and I trust Soviet Russia—for then indeed all would be well—must be the friends and sponsors of the new Europe and must champion its right to live and shine.

# 3 The Schuman Declaration

ROBERT SCHUMAN

*Efforts in the 1940s to realize Churchill's vision of a united Europe led to increased economic and political cooperation but did not yield anything like a United States of Europe. European leaders needed a new strategy to achieve such a goal. On 9 May 1950, Robert Schuman (1886–1963), France's foreign minister, outlined a plan to unite under a single authority the coal and steel industries of Europe's bitterest enemies, France and Germany. The purpose of the plan, which was developed by Jean Monnet, was to begin building a peaceful, united Europe one step at a time. European governments would start with two industries essential to the making of war, coal and steel, then add other economic and political sectors until all major decisions were taken at a European level. This would create, in Schuman's words, a "de facto solidarity" that would ultimately make war between France and Germany "materially impossible." The practical approach of Schuman and Monnet won favor on the European continent; France, Germany, Italy, and the Benelux countries eventually responded by creating the European Coal and Steel Community in 1952.*

World peace cannot be safeguarded without the making of creative efforts proportionate to the dangers which threaten it.

The contribution which an organized and living Europe can bring to civilization is indispensable to the maintenance of peaceful relations. In taking upon herself for more than 20 years the role of champion of a united Europe, France has always had as her essential

---

aim the service of peace. A united Europe was not achieved and we had war.

Europe will not be made all at once, or according to a single plan. It will be built through concrete achievements which first create a *de facto* solidarity. The coming together of the nations of Europe requires the elimination of the age-old opposition of France and Germany. Any action taken must in the first place concern these two countries.

With this aim in view, the French government proposes that action be taken immediately on one limited but decisive point. It proposes that Franco-German production of coal and steel as a whole be placed under a common High Authority, within the framework of an organization open to the participation of the other countries of Europe.

The pooling of coal and steel production should immediately provide for the setting up of common foundations for economic development as a first step in the federation of Europe, and will change the destinies of those regions which have long been devoted to the manufacture of munitions of war, of which they have been the most constant victims.

The solidarity in production thus established will make it plain that any war between France and Germany becomes not merely unthinkable, but materially impossible. The setting up of this powerful productive unit, open to all countries willing to take part and bound ultimately to provide all the member countries with the basic elements of industrial production on the same terms, will lay a true foundation for their economic unification.

This production will be offered to the world as a whole without distinction or exception, with the aim of contributing to raising living standards and to promoting peaceful achievements.

In this way, there will be realized simply and speedily that fusion of interests which is indispensable to the establishment of a common economic system; it may be the leaven from which may grow a wider and deeper community between countries long opposed to one another by sanguinary divisions.

By pooling basic production and by instituting a new High Authority, whose decisions will bind France, Germany and other member countries, this proposal will lead to the realization of the first concrete foundation of a European federation indispensable to the preservation of peace.

. . .

# 4 Preambles to the Treaties Establishing the European Communities (Treaties of Paris and Rome)

*In Rome on 25 March 1957, the six member countries of the European Coal and Steel Community (ECSC) signed treaties establishing the European Economic Community (EEC) and the European Atomic Energy Community (EURATOM). These two treaties are often called the "Treaties of Rome" (the ECSC treaty was signed in Paris). The EEC treaty is also sometimes referred to as the "Treaty of Rome."*

*The preambles to each of the three original treaties reflect the founders' vision for building, through economic integration, "an ever closer union among the peoples of Europe." The deep desire for peace on the Continent runs through each of the preambles and links them to the visions articulated by Spinelli and Rossi, Churchill, Schuman, Monnet, and many others. But the documents also represent a subtle shift in emphasis away from peace to economic prosperity as the driving motive for unity. We can detect the shift in the Schuman Declaration and its parallel, the preamble to the ECSC treaty, but it becomes more evident in the preamble to the EEC treaty, where "economic and social progress" seems to take precedence over preserving and strengthening "peace and liberty." European leaders, while mindful of the dangers of violent conflict in Western Europe, were becoming more concerned with the material improvement of life on a peaceful continent.*

---

## ■ EUROPEAN COAL AND STEEL COMMUNITY

. . .

CONSIDERING that world peace can be safeguarded only by creative efforts commensurate with the dangers that threaten it,

CONVINCED that the contribution which an organized and vital Europe can make to civilization is indispensable to the maintenance of peaceful relations,

RECOGNIZING that Europe can be built only through practical achievements which will first of all create real solidarity, and through the establishment of common bases for economic development,

ANXIOUS to help, by expanding their basic production, to raise the standard of living and further the works of peace,

RESOLVED to substitute for age-old rivalries the merging of their essential interests; to create, by establishing an economic community, the basis for a broader and deeper community among peoples long divided by bloody conflicts; and to lay the foundations for institutions which will give direction to a destiny henceforward shared,

HAVE DECIDED to create a European Coal and Steel Community.

. . .

## ■ EUROPEAN ECONOMIC COMMUNITY

. . .

DETERMINED to lay the foundations of an ever closer union among the peoples of Europe,

RESOLVED to ensure the economic and social progress of their countries by common action to eliminate the barriers which divide Europe,

AFFIRMING as the essential objective of their efforts the constant improvement of the living and working conditions of their peoples,

RECOGNIZING that the removal of existing obstacles calls for concerted action in order to guarantee steady expansion, balanced trade and fair competition,

ANXIOUS to strengthen the unity of their economies and to ensure their harmonious development by reducing the differences existing between the various regions and the backwardness of the less favored regions,

DESIRING to contribute, by means of a common commercial policy, to the progressive abolition of restrictions on international trade,

INTENDING to confirm the solidarity which binds Europe and the overseas countries and desiring to ensure the development of their prosperity, in accordance with the principles of the Charter of the United Nations,

RESOLVED by thus pooling their resources to preserve and strengthen peace and liberty, and calling upon the other peoples of Europe who share their ideal to join in their efforts,

HAVE DECIDED to create a European Economic Community.

. . .

## ■ EUROPEAN ATOMIC ENERGY COMMUNITY

. . .

RECOGNIZING that nuclear energy represents an essential resource for the development and invigoration of industry and will permit the advancement of the cause of peace,

CONVINCED that only a joint effort undertaken without delay can offer the prospect of achievements commensurate with the creative capacities of their countries,

RESOLVED to create the conditions necessary for the development of a powerful nuclear industry which will provide extensive energy resources, lead to the modernization of technical processes and contribute, through its many other applications, to the prosperity of their peoples,

ANXIOUS to create the conditions of safety necessary to eliminate hazards to the life and health of the public,

DESIRING to associate other countries with their work and to cooperate with international organizations concerned with the peaceful development of atomic energy,

HAVE DECIDED to create a European Atomic Energy Community (EURATOM).

. . .

# 5 A Ferment of Change

Jean Monnet

*Jean Monnet (1888–1979) was the "father of Europe." No single individual influenced the shape of the European Union more than this French civil servant and diplomat. Monnet convinced Robert Schuman to propose the European Coal and Steel Community and became the first president of its High Authority. Monnet convinced Johan Willem Beyen and Paul-Henri Spaak to propose EURATOM and the EEC, and then established the influential Action Committee for a United States of Europe to pressure governments to accept the proposals. Monnet worked hard, and eventually successfully, to enlarge the Community by adding Britain, Ireland, and Denmark. And shortly before his death, Monnet persuaded EC governments to turn their regular summits into the European Council.*[1]

*Monnet was a pragmatic government official who quite naturally developed a strategy for uniting Europe that looked much like the step-by-step functionalism of David Mitrany (see Chapter 14). Monnet argued that problems of insecurity and human need in the world—and in Europe in particular—required radical changes in the way people thought. Nations, he believed, should adopt common rules governing their behavior and create common institutions to apply these rules. Such a strategy, even if applied on a small scale, would create a "silent revolution in men's minds" that would change the way people thought and acted. For Monnet, the European Communities of the early 1960s demonstrated that small collective steps set off "a chain reaction, a ferment where one change induces another." This ferment, he asserted, would not lead to another nineteenth-century–style great power—although a united Europe would be able to shoulder an equal burden*

---

Reprinted with permission from *Journal of Common Market Studies*, 1(1)(1962):203–211. 

*of leadership with the United States—nor would it be confined to Europe. Integration was a process that may have started in Europe but would soon have to include the broader West, then the rest of the world, if humanity was to "escape destruction."*

This century has probably changed the manner of life more for every one of us than all the thousands of years of man's progress put together. In the past, men were largely at the mercy of nature. Today in our industrial countries of the Western world and elsewhere, we are acquiring an unprecedented mastery over nature. Natural resources are no longer a limitation now that we control more and more forms of energy and can use raw materials in more and more ways. We are entering the age of abundance where work, as we know it, will only be one of many human activities. For the first time we in the West are witnessing the emergence of a truly mass society marked by mass consumption, mass education and even mass culture.

We are moving, in the West, from a society where privilege was part of nature to one where the enjoyment of human rights and human dignity are common to all. Unfortunately, two-thirds of mankind have not shared in this process.

And now, on the very eve of creating unprecedented conditions of abundance, we are suddenly faced with the consequences of our extraordinary mastery over the physical forces of nature. Modern medicine is steadily increasing our prospects of life, so that the population of the world is increasing fantastically fast. This revolution is creating new explosive pressures of all kinds in the world. At the same time, science is repeatedly creating new powers of destruction. This faces us with the greatest threat humanity has ever had to deal with. The issue today is no longer peace or war, but the triumph or destruction of civilized life.

We cannot assume that we shall avoid such destruction. We have only to look back on the last fifty years to see how constant the risk of upheaval has become. No region of the world has escaped violence. One-third of mankind has become Communist, another third has obtained independence from colonialism, and even among the remaining third nearly all countries have undergone revolutions or wars. True, atomic bombs have made nuclear war so catastrophic that I am convinced no country wishes to resort to it. But I am equally convinced that we are at the mercy of an error of judgment or a technical breakdown, the source of which no man may ever know.

We are then in a world of rapid change, in which men and nations must learn to control themselves in their relations with others.

This, to my mind, can only be done through institutions; and it is this need for common institutions that we have learnt in Europe since the war.

We are used to thinking that major changes in the traditional relations between countries only take place violently, through conquest or revolution. We are so accustomed to this that we find it hard to appreciate those that are taking place peacefully in Europe even though they have begun to affect the world. We can see the communist revolution, because it has been violent and because we have been living with it for nearly fifty years. We can see the revolution in the ex-colonial areas because power is plainly changing hands. But we tend to miss the magnitude of the change in Europe because it is taking place by the constitutional and democratic methods which govern our countries.

Yet we have only to look at the difference between 1945 and today to see what an immense transformation has been taking place under our very eyes, here in what used to be called the old world. After the war, the nations of continental Europe were divided and crippled, their national resources were depleted and, in most of them, the peoples had little faith in the future. During the last fifteen years, these countries have lost their empires. It might have been expected they would be further depressed by what many considered the loss of past greatness and prestige.

And yet, after all these upheavals, the countries of continental Europe, which have fought each other so often in the past and which, even in peacetime, organized their economies as potential instruments of war, are now uniting in a Common Market which is laying the foundations for political union. Britain is negotiating to enter this European Community and by this very fact changing the tradition of centuries. And now the President of the United States is already asking Congress for powers to negotiate with the enlarged European Common Market.

To understand this extraordinary change in all its basic simplicity, we must go back to 1950, only five years after the war. For five years, the whole French nation had been making efforts to re-create the bases of production, but it became evident that to go beyond recovery towards steady expansion and higher standards of life for all, the resources of a single nation were not sufficient. It was necessary to transcend the national framework.

The need was political as well as economic. The Europeans had to overcome the mistrust born of centuries of feuds and wars. The governments and peoples of Europe still thought in the old terms of victors and vanquished. Yet, if a basis for peace in the world was to be established, these notions had to be eliminated. Here again, one had to go beyond the nation and the conception of national interest as an end in itself.

We thought that both these objectives could in time be reached if conditions were created enabling these countries to increase their resources by merging them in a large and dynamic common market; and if these same countries could be made to consider that their problems were no longer solely of national concern, but were mutual European responsibilities.

Obviously this could not be done all at once. It was not possible to create a large dynamic market immediately or to produce trust between recent enemies overnight. After several unsuccessful attempts, the French Government through its Foreign Minister, M. Robert Schuman, proposed in 1950 what many people today would regard as a modest beginning but which seemed very bold at the time; and the parliaments of France, Germany, Italy and Benelux voted that, for coal and steel, their countries would form a single common market, run by common institutions administering common rules, very much as within a single nation. The European Coal and Steel Community was set up. In itself this was a technical step, but its new procedures, under common institutions, created a silent revolution in men's minds. It proved decisive in persuading businessmen, civil servants, politicians and trade unionists that such an approach could work and that the economic and political advantages of unity over division were immense. Once they were convinced, they were ready to take further steps forward.

In 1957, only three years after the failure of the European Army, the six parliaments ratified the Treaty of Rome which extended the Common Market from coal and steel to an economic union embracing all goods. Today, the Common Market, with its 170 million people that will become 225 million when Britain joins, is creating in Europe a huge continental market on the American scale.

The large market does not prejudge the future economic systems of Europe. Most of the Six have a nationalized sector as large as the British and some also have planning procedures. These are just as compatible with private enterprise on the large market as they are within a single nation. The contribution of the Common Market is to create new opportunities of expansion for all the members, which make it easier to solve any problems that arise, and to provide the rest of the world with prospects of growing trade that would not exist without it. In Europe, an open society looking to the future is replacing a defensive one regretting the past.

The profound change is being made possible essentially by the new method of common action which is the core of the European Community. To establish this new method of common action, we adapted to our situation the methods which have allowed individuals to live together in society: common rules which each member is committed to respect, and common institutions to watch over the application of these rules. Nations have applied this method within their frontiers for centuries, but they have never yet been applied between them. After a period of trial and error, this method has become a permanent dialogue between a single European body, responsible for expressing the view of the general interest of the Community, and the national governments expressing the national views. The resulting procedure for collective decisions is something quite new and, as far as I know, has no analogy in any traditional system. It is not federal because there is no central government; the nations take their decisions together in the Council of Ministers. On the other hand, the independent European body proposes policies, and the common element is further underlined by the European Parliament and the European Court of Justice.

This system leads to a completely changed approach to common action. In the past, the nations felt no irrevocable commitment. Their responsibility was strictly to themselves, not to any common interest. They had to rely on themselves alone. Relations took the form either of domination if one country was much stronger than the others, or of the trading of advantages if there was a balance of powers between them. This balance was necessarily unstable and the concessions made in an agreement one year could always be retracted the next.

But in the European Communities, common rules applied by joint institutions give each a responsibility for the effective working of the Community as a whole. This leads the nations, within the discipline of the Community, to seek a solution to the problems themselves, instead of trading temporary advantages. It is this method which explains the dramatic change in the relations of Germany with France and the other Common Market countries. Looking forward to a common future has made them agree to live down the feuds of the past. Today people have almost forgotten that the Saar was ever a problem and yet from 1919 to 1950 it was a major bone of contention between France and Germany. European unity has made it seem an anachronism. And today, at French invitation, German troops are training on French soil.

. . .

We have seen that Europe has overcome the attitude of domination which ruled state policies for so many centuries. But quite apart from what this means for us in the old continent, this is a fact of world importance. It is obvious that countries and peoples who are overcoming this state of mind between themselves will bring the same mentality to their relations with others, outside Europe. The new method of action developed in Europe replaces the efforts at domination of nation states by a constant process of collective adaptation to new conditions, a chain reaction, a ferment where one change induces another.

Look at the effect the Common Market has already had on world tariffs. When it was set up, it was widely assumed the member countries would want to protect themselves and become, as some put it, an inward-looking group. Yet everything that has happened since has shown this view to be wrong. The Six have reduced the tariffs between themselves and towards other countries faster than expected. Now President Kennedy proposes America and Europe should cut tariffs on manufactures by half, and the Common Market will certainly welcome it. This leads to a situation where tariffs throughout the major trading areas of the world will be lower than they have ever been.

These changes inside and outside Europe would not have taken place without the driving force of the Common Market. It opens new prospects for dealing with problems the solution of which was becoming increasingly urgent. I am thinking of world agriculture in a more and more industrial civilization; of links between the new and the long-established industrial regions, and in particular of the need for growing trade between Japan and the United States and Europe together.

Naturally, increasing trade will also benefit the Commonwealth. The prospect of Britain's future entry into the Common Market has already made the Continent more aware than ever before of the problems of the Commonwealth. Clearly, for countries whose major need is to obtain more capital for development, the fact that Britain is part of a rapidly developing Europe holds great promise of future progress.

Similarly, problems are arising that only Europe and the United States together have the resources to deal with. The need to develop policies of sustained growth, which in large part depend on maintaining international monetary stability, is an example. Increasing the aid of the West to the underdeveloped areas on a large scale is another. Separately, the European nations have inevitably taken divergent views of aid policies. But tomorrow, the nations of Europe by acting together can make a decisive contribution. The necessary precondition of such a partnership between America and Europe is that Europe should be united and thus be able to deploy resources on the same scale as America. This is what is in the course of happening today.

That we have begun to cooperate on these affairs at the Atlantic level is a great step forward. It is evident that we must soon go a good deal further towards an Atlantic Community. The creation of a united Europe brings this nearer by making it possible for America and Europe to act as partners on an equal footing. I am convinced that ultimately, the United States too will delegate powers of effective action to common institutions, even on political questions. Just as the United States in their own day found it necessary to unite, just as Europe is now in the process of uniting, so the West must move towards some kind of union. This is not an end in itself. It is the beginning on the road to the more orderly world we must have if we are to escape destruction.

The discussions on peace today are dominated by the question of disarmament. The world will be more and more threatened by destruction as long as bombs continue to pile up on both sides. Many therefore feel that the hopes for peace in the world depend on as early an agreement on armaments as possible, particularly an agreement on nuclear arms. Of course we must continue to negotiate on these questions. But it is too simple to hope the problems that arise out of philosophic conflicts could be settled without a change in the view which people take of the future. For what is the Soviet objective? It is to achieve a Communist world, as Mr. Khrushchev has told us many times. When this becomes so obviously impossible that nobody, even within a closed society, can any longer believe it—when the partnership of America and a United Europe makes it plain to all that the West may change from within but that others cannot change it by outside pressures, then Mr. Khrushchev or his successor will accept the facts, and the conditions will at last exist for turning so-called peaceful coexistence into genuine peace. Then at last real disarmament will become possible.

Personally, I do not think we shall have to wait long for this change. The history of European unification shows that when people become convinced a change is taking place that creates a new situation, they act on their revised estimate before that situation is established. After all, Britain has asked to join the Common Market before it was complete. The President of the United States is seeking powers to negotiate with the European Community on steps to an Atlantic partnership even before Britain has joined. Can we not expect a similar phenomenon in the future relations with the Soviet Union?

What conclusions can we draw from all these thoughts?

One impression predominates in my mind over all others. It is this: unity in Europe does not create a new kind of great power; it is a method for introducing change in Europe and consequently in the world. People, more often outside the European Community than within, are tempted to see the European Community as a potential nineteenth-century state with all the overtones of power this implies. But we are not in the nineteenth century, and the Europeans have built up the European Community precisely in order to find a way out of the conflicts to which the nineteenth-century power philosophy gave rise. The natural attitude of a European Community based on the exercise by nations of common responsibilities will be to make these nations also aware of their responsibilities, as a Community, to the world. In fact, we already see this sense of world responsibilities developing as unity in Europe begins to affect Britain, America and many other areas of the world. European unity is not a blueprint, it is not a theory, it is a process that has already begun, of bringing peoples and nations together to adapt themselves jointly to changing circumstances.

European unity is the most important event in the West since the war, not because it is a new great power, but because the new institutional method it introduces is permanently modifying relations between nations and men. Human nature does not change, but when nations and men accept the same rule and the same institutions to make sure that they are applied, their behavior towards each other changes. This is the process of civilization itself.

## ■ NOTE

1. Richard Mayne, "Gray Eminence," in *Jean Monnet: The Path to European Unity*, ed. Douglas Brinkley and Clifford Hackett (New York: St. Martin's Press, 1991), 114–116.

# 6 A Concert of European States

CHARLES DE GAULLE

*Charles de Gaulle (1890–1970), French Resistance leader and first president of France's fifth republic, was above all a French nationalist. His overriding objective after the humiliation of World War II was to reestablish France as a great power, free from domination by the superpowers and once again the source of western civilization's cultural and spiritual strength. De Gaulle's vision of France profoundly shaped his vision of Europe, and differed markedly from the views held by the founders of the European Communities, most noticeably Jean Monnet.*

*De Gaulle believed in European unity, but he criticized the supranational vision of Europe as unrealistic and undesirable. He argued instead for a "concert of European states" where national governments coordinated their policies extensively but did not give up their rights as sovereign entities to a European "superstate." De Gaulle's unwillingness to concede France's right to control its vital affairs led to the 1965 crisis in the Communities and eventually the Luxembourg Compromise, which in practice gave every member state the right to veto Community decisions (although it has officially been invoked only a handful of times). In effect, the Six were forced to accept de Gaulle's vision of an intergovernmental Europe.*

War gives birth and brings death to nations. In the meantime, it never ceases to loom over their existence. For us French, the develop-

---

From "Europe," in *Memoirs of Hope: Renewal and Endeavor,* trans. Terence Kilmartin (Simon and Schuster, 1971). Reprinted with permission from Georges Borchardt, Inc., and the Orion Publishing Group.

ment of our national life, our political regimes and our world position from 1815 to 1870 was determined by the hostile coalition which united the nations of Europe against the Revolution, the dazzling victories and then the downfall of Napoleon, and finally the disastrous treaties which sanctioned so many battles. Thereafter, during the forty-four years of the "armed truce," it was our defeat, our secret desire to avenge it, but also the fear that a united Germany might inflict another on us, that dominated our actions at home and abroad. Although the gigantic effort put forth by our people in the First World War opened the way to renewal, we closed it upon ourselves by failing to consolidate our military victory, by forgoing the reparations which would have provided us with the means of industrializing our country and thus compensating for our enormous human and material losses, and, finally, by withdrawing into a passive strategic and foreign policy which left Europe a prey to Hitler's ambitions. Now, in the aftermath of the last conflict in which she had all but perished, on what premises was France to base her progress and her actions?

The first of these premises was that, in spite of everything, she was alive, sovereign and victorious. That was undoubtedly a marvel. Who would have thought that, after suffering an unparalleled disaster, after witnessing the subjection of her rulers to the authority of the enemy, after undergoing the ravages of the two greatest battles of the war and, in the meantime, prolonged plundering by the invader, after enduring the systematic abasement inflicted on her by a regime founded on surrender and humiliation, she would ever heal the wounds inflicted on her body and her soul? Who would not have sworn that her liberation, if it was to come, would be due to foreigners alone and that they would decide what was to become of her at home and abroad? Who, in the almost total extinction of her resistance, had not condemned as absurd the hope that one day the enemy would surrender to her at the same time as to her allies? Nevertheless, in the end she had emerged from the struggle with her frontiers and her unity intact, in control of her own affairs, and in the ranks of the victors. There was nothing, therefore, to prevent her now from being what she intended to be and doing what she wished to do.

This was all the more true because, for the first time in her history, she was unhampered by any threat from her immediate neighbors. Germany, dismembered, had ceased to be a formidable and domineering power. Italy regretted having turned her ambitions against us. The alliance with England, preserved by Free France, and the process of decolonization which had removed old grievances, ensured that the wind of mistrust no longer blew across the English

Channel. Bonds of affection and common interest were bringing a serene France and a pacified Spain closer together across the Pyrenees. And what enmities could possibly spring up from the friendly lands of Belgium, Luxembourg, Holland or neutral Switzerland? Thus we were relieved of the state of constant tension in which dangerous neighbors once held us and which gravely hampered our activities.

It is true that, while France had lost her special vocation of being constantly in danger, the whole world was now haunted by the permanent fear of global conflict. Two empires, the American and the Soviet, now became giants in comparison with the old powers, confronted each other with their forces, their hegemonies and their ideologies. Both were in possession of nuclear armaments which could at any moment shake the entire world, and which made each of them omnipotent protectors in their respective camps. This perilous balance was liable to tip over eventually into limitless war unless it evolved into a general *détente*. For France, reduced in wealth and power by the conflicts in which she had been engaged over the past two centuries, dangerously exposed by her geographical position at the edge of the Old World and facing the New, mortally vulnerable by reason of her size and population, peace was obviously of vital importance. And, as it happened, circumstances now ordained that she should appoint herself its champion. For she was in the singular position of having no claims on what others possessed while they had nothing to claim from her, and of harboring no grievances on her own behalf against either of the giants, for whose peoples she cherished a traditional friendship confirmed by recent events, while they felt an exceptional attachment to her. In short, if there was a voice that might be listened to and a policy that might be effective with a view to setting up a new order to replace the Cold War, that voice and that policy were pre-eminently those of France. But only on condition that they were really her own and that the hand she held out in friendship was free.

At the same time, France now enjoyed a vast fund of interest and trust among peoples whose future was in gestation but who refused to pay allegiance to either of the rival dominations. China, endowed with such reserves of manpower and resources that limitless possibilities were open to her for the future; Japan, re-creating an independent world role on the basis of economic strength; India, at grips with problems of subsistence as vast as her size, but ultimately destined to turn towards the outside world; a great number of old and new states in Africa, Asia and Latin America which accepted aid from either or both of the two camps for the immediate needs of their development, but refused to align themselves—all these now looked by choice towards France. True, until she had completed the process of decolonization, they bitterly criticized her, but the criticisms soon ceased when she had liberated her former possessions. It remained for her to exploit the potential of respect, admiration and prestige which existed in her favor over a large part of the globe provided that, as the world expected of her, she served the universal cause of human dignity and progress.

Thus the same destiny which had enabled France to survive the terrible crisis of the war, offered to her afterwards, in spite of all she had lost over the past two centuries in terms of relative power and wealth, a leading international role which suited her genius, responded to her interests and matched her means. I was naturally determined that she should play this role, the more so since I believed that the internal transformation, the political stability and the social progress without which she would unquestionably be doomed to disorder and decline demanded that she should once again feel herself invested with world responsibility. Such was my philosophy. What was my policy to be as regards the practical problems that faced our country abroad?

Apart from that of Algeria and our colonies, which was for us to settle on our own, these problems were of such scope and range that their solution would be a very lengthy undertaking, unless a new war should chance to come and cut the Gordian knots tied by the previous one. Hence a sustained and continuous policy was required to deal with them, and this was precisely what, in contrast to the unending shifts and changes of the past, our new institutions made possible.

But what exactly were these problems? First of all there was Germany, divided into three by the existence of a parliamentary republic in the West, a Communist dictatorship in the East, and a special status for Berlin, a prey to the internal strains imposed by this state of affairs and the principal pawn in the rivalry between the two camps. There was Europe, impelled by reason and sentiment towards unification after the terrible convulsions which had torn it apart but radically divided by the Iron Curtain, the Cold War and the enforced subjection of its eastern half to Soviet domination. There was the organization imposed on the Atlantic alliance, which amounted to the military and political subordination of Western Europe to the United States of America. There was the problem of aid for the development of the Third World, which was used by Washington and Moscow as a battleground for their rivalry. There were crises in the East, in Africa, in Asia and in Latin America, which the rival interventions of the two giants rendered chronic and incurable. And there were the international institutions in which the two opposing camps polarized judgments on all subjects and prohibited impartiality.

In each of these fields, I wanted France to play an active part. In this poor world which deserved to be handled gently and each of whose leaders was weighed down with grave difficulties, we had to advance step by step, acting as circumstances demanded and respecting the susceptibilities of all. I myself had struck many a blow in my time, but never at the pride of a people nor at the dignity of its leaders. Yet it was essential that what we did and said should be independent of others. From the moment of my return to power, that was our rule—such a complete change of attitude on the part of our country that the world political scene was suddenly and profoundly transformed.

It is true that the Eastern camp at first confined itself to watching to see what new attitude emerged in Paris. But our Western partners, among whom up till then official France had submissively taken its place under the hegemony known as Atlantic solidarity, could not help being put out. However, they would eventually resign themselves to the new situation. It must be said that the experience of dealing with de Gaulle which some of them had had during the war, and all of them after it, meant that they did not expect this Republic to be as easy to handle as the previous one. Still, there was a general feeling in their chancelleries, their parliaments and their newspapers that the ordeal would be a brief one, that de Gaulle would inevitably disappear after a while, and that everything would then be as it had been before. On the other hand, there was no lack of people in these countries, especially among the masses, who were not at all displeased by France's recovery and who felt a certain satisfaction, or envy perhaps, when they saw her shaking off a supremacy which weighed heavily on the whole of the Old World. Added to this were the feelings which foreign crowds were kind enough to entertain for me personally and which, each time I came in contact with them, they demonstrated with a fervor that impressed their governments. On the whole, in spite of the annoyance that was felt, the malicious remarks that were made, the unfavorable articles and aggressive caricatures that proliferated, the outside world would soon accommodate itself to a France who was once more behaving like a great power, and henceforth would follow her every action and her every word with an attention that had long been lacking.

I was to find rather less resignation in what was said and written in quarters which had hitherto been looked upon as the fountainhead of French political thought. For there it had long been more or less taken for granted that our country should take no action that was not dictated to it from outside. No doubt this attitude of mind dated from the time when the dangers which threatened France forced her continually to seek support from abroad, and when the instability of the political regime prevented the government from taking upon itself the risks of major decisions. Even before the First World War, in its alliance with Russia, the Third Republic had had to undertake to respect the Treaty of Frankfurt and let St. Petersburg lead the way rather than Paris. It is true that, during the long battle subsequently fought on our soil in alliance with the English, the Belgians and finally the Americans, the leading role and then the supreme command fell to the French, who in fact provided the principal effort. But was it not primarily the Anglo-Saxons' cry of "Halt!" that brought the sudden cessation of hostilities on 11 November 1918, at the very moment when we were about to pluck the fruits of victory? Were not the wishes and promises of the American President the dominant factor in the Treaty of Versailles, which admittedly restored Alsace and Lorraine to us but left the enemy's unity, territory and resources intact? And afterwards, was it not to gratify the wishes of Washington and London that the government in Paris surrendered the guarantees we had secured and renounced the reparations which Germany owed us in exchange for specious schemes offered to us by America? When the Hitlerian threat appeared and the Führer ventured to move his troops into the Rhineland, and preventive or repressive action on our part would have been enough to bring about his retreat and discomfiture at a time when he was still short of armaments, did not our ministers remain passive because England failed to take the initiative? At the time of the Austrian Anschluss, then the dismemberment and annexation of Czechoslovakia by the Reich, from whence did French acquiescence stem if not from the example of the English? In the surrender of Vichy to the invader's law and in the "collaboration" designed to make our country participate in a so-called European order which in fact was purely Germanic, was there not a trace of this long inurement to satellite status? At the same time, even as I strove to preserve France's sovereign rights in relation to our allies while fighting the common enemy, whence sprang the reprobation voiced by even those closest to me, if not from the idea that we should always give way?

After so many lessons, it might have been thought that once the war was over, those who claimed to lead public opinion would be less inclined towards subordination. Far from it: for the leading school of thought in each political party, national self-effacement had become an established and flaunted doctrine. While for the Communists it was an absolute rule that Moscow is always right, all the old party formations professed the doctrine of "supranationalism," in other words France's submission to a law that was not her own. Hence the support for "Europe" seen as an edifice in which technocrats forming an "executive" and parliamentarians assuming legislative powers—the great majority of both being foreigners—would have the authority to decide the fate of the French people. Hence, too, the passion for the Atlantic organization which would put the security and therefore the policy of our country at the disposal of another. Hence, again, the eagerness to submit the acts of our government to the approval of international organizations in which, under a semblance of collective deliberation, the authority of the protector reigned supreme in every field, whether political, military, economic, technical or monetary, and in which our representatives would never dare to say "we want" but simply confine themselves to "pleading France's cause." Hence, finally, the constant fury aroused among the party-political breed by my actions in the name of an independent nation.

Nevertheless, I was to find no lack of support. Emotionally, I would have the backing of the French people, who, without being in the least inclined to arrogance, were determined to preserve their own identity, all the more so because they had nearly lost it and because others everywhere were ardently affirming theirs, whether in terms of sovereignty, language, culture, production or even sport. Whenever I expressed myself in public on these matters I felt a quiver of response. Politically, the organization which had been formed to follow me above and beyond all the old parties, and which had had a numerous and compact group elected to parliament, was to accompany me through thick and thin. Practically, I would have a stable government at my side, whose Prime Minister was convinced of France's right and duty to act on a world scale, and whose Foreign Minister displayed in his field an ability which few have equalled in the course of our arduous history.

Maurice Couve de Murville had the required gifts. Amid a welter of interlocking problems and tangled arguments he was immediately able to distinguish the essential from the accessory, so that he was clear and precise in matters which others deliberately made as obscure and ambiguous as possible. He had the experience, having dealt with many of the issues of the day and known most of the men in command in the course of a distinguished career. He had the confidence, certain as he was that the post to which I had nominated him would be his for a long time. He had the manner, being skillful at making contact by listening, observing and taking note, and then excelling, at the critical moment, in the authoritative formulation of a position from which he would never be deflected. He had the necessary faith, convinced as he was that France could survive only in the first rank of nations, that de Gaulle could put her back there, and that nothing in life was more important than working towards this goal.

This was what we were aiming for in the vast arena of Europe. I myself had always felt, and now more than ever, how much the nations which peopled it had in common. Being all of the same white race, with the same Christian origins and the same way of life, linked to one another since time immemorial by countless ties of thought, art, science, politics and trade, it was natural that they should come to form a whole, with its own character and organization in relation to the rest of the world. It was in pursuance of this destiny that the Roman emperors reigned over it, that Charlemagne, Charles V and Napoleon attempted to unite it, that Hitler sought to impose upon it his crashing domination. But it is a fact of some significance that not one of these federators succeeded in inducing the subject countries to surrender their individuality. On the contrary, arbitrary centralization always provoked an upsurge of violent nationalism by way of reaction. It was my belief that a united Europe could not today, any more than in previous times, be a fusion of its peoples, but that it could and should result from a systematic *rapprochement*. Everything prompted them towards this in an age of proliferating trade, international enterprises, science and technology which know no frontiers, rapid communications and widespread travel. My policy therefore aimed at the setting up of a concert of European states which in developing all sorts of ties between them would increase their interdependence and solidarity. From this starting point, there was every reason to believe that the process of evolution might lead to their confederation, especially if they were one day to be threatened from the same source.

In practice this led us to put the European Economic Community into effect; to encourage the Six to concert together regularly in political matters; to prevent certain others, in particular Great Britain, from dragging the West into an Atlantic system which would be totally incompatible with a European Europe, and indeed to persuade these centrifugal elements to integrate themselves with the Continent by changing their outlook, their habits and their customers; and finally to set an example of *détente* followed by understanding and cooperation with the countries of the Eastern bloc, in the belief that beyond all the prejudices and preconceptions of ideology and propaganda, it was peace and progress that answered the needs and desires of the inhabitants of both halves of an accidentally divided Europe.

At the heart of the problem and at the center of the continent lay Germany. It was her destiny to be the keystone of any European edifice, and yet her misdeeds had contributed more than anything else to tearing the Old World apart. True, now that she was sliced into three segments, with the forces of her conquerors stationed in each, she was no longer a direct threat to anyone. But how could the memory of her ambition, her audacity, her power and her tyranny be effaced from people's memories—an ambition which only yesterday had unleashed a military machine capable of crushing with one blow the armies of France and her allies; an audacity which, thanks to Italy's complicity, had carried her armies as far as Africa and the Nile basin; a power which, driving across Poland and Russia with Italian, Hungarian, Bulgarian and Rumanian aid, had reached the gates of Moscow and the foothills of the Caucasus; a tyranny whose reign had brought oppression, plunder and crime wherever the fortune of war took the German flag? Henceforth, every precaution must be taken to prevent Germany's evil genius from breaking loose again. But how could a real and lasting peace be built on foundations that were unacceptable to this great people? How could a genuine union of the continent be established without Germany being a part of it? How could the age-old threat of ruin and death be finally dispelled on either side of the Rhine as long as the old enmity remained?

On the all-important question of Germany's future, my mind was made up. First of all, I believed that it would be unjust and dangerous to revise the *de facto* frontiers which the war had imposed on her. This meant that the Oder-Neisse line which separates her from Poland should remain her definitive boundary, that nothing should remain of her former claims in respect of Czechoslovakia, and that a new Anschluss in whatever form must be precluded. Furthermore, the right to possess or to manufacture atomic weapons—which in any case she had declared her intention to renounce—must in no circumstances be granted to her. This being so, I considered it essential that she should form an integral part of the organized system of cooperation between states which I envisaged for the whole of our continent. In this way the security of all nations between the Atlantic and the Urals would be guaranteed, and a change brought about in circumstances, attitudes and relationships which would doubtless ultimately permit the reunion of the three segments of the German people. In the meantime, the Federal Republic would have an essential role to play within the Economic Community and, should it ever materialize, in the political concert of the Six. Finally, I intended that France should weave a network of preferential ties with Germany, which would gradually lead the two peoples towards the mutual understanding and appreciation to which their natural instinct prompts them when they are no longer using up their energies in fighting each other.

. . .

Cooperation between the two former enemies [France and Germany] was a necessary but by no means a sufficient precondition for organized European cooperation. It is true that, judging merely by the spate of speeches and articles on the subject, the unification of our Continent might well appear to be a matter as simple as it was foreordained. But when the realities of needs, interests and preconceptions came into play, things took on an altogether different aspect. While fruitless bargaining with the British showed the fledgling Community that good intentions are not enough to reconcile the irreconcilable, the Six found that even in the economic sphere alone the adjustment of their respective positions bristled with difficulties which could not be resolved solely in terms of the treaties concluded to that end. It had to be acknowledged that the so-called executives installed at the head of common institutions by virtue of the delusions of integration which had prevailed before my return, were helpless when it came to making and enforcing decisions, that only governments were in a position to do this, and then only as a result of negotiations carried out in due form between ministers or ambassadors.

In the case of the European Coal and Steel Community, for example, once it had used up the birthday presents bestowed upon it by its member states, none of them, be it said, for our benefit—French relinquishment of coke from the Ruhr, deliveries of coal and iron to Italy, financial subventions to the Benelux mines—the High Authority, although vested with very extensive theoretical powers and considerable resources, was soon overwhelmed by the problems presented by competing national requirements. Whether it was a matter of fixing the price of steel, or regulating fuel purchases from outside, or converting the collieries of the Borinage, the areopagus enthroned in Luxembourg was powerless to legislate. The result was a chronic decline in that organization, whose prime mover, Jean Monnet, had moreover resigned the presidency.

At the same time, in the case of EURATOM, there seemed an irremediable disparity between the situation of France, equipped for some fifteen years past with an active Atomic Energy Commissariat, provided with numerous installations and already engaged in precise and far-reaching programs of research and development, and that of the other countries which, having done nothing on their own account, now wanted to use the funds of the common budget to obtain what they lacked by placing orders with American suppliers.

Lastly, in the case of the Economic Community, the adoption of the agricultural regulations in conjunction with the lowering of industrial tariffs raised obstacles which the Brussels Commission was unable to overcome on its own. It must be said that in this respect the spirit and terms of the Treaty of Rome did not meet our country's requirements. The industrial provisions were as precise and explicit as those concerning agriculture were vague. This was evidently due to the fact that our negotiators in 1957, caught up in the dream of a supranational Europe and anxious at any price to settle for something approaching it, had not felt it their duty to insist that a French interest, no matter how crucial, should receive satisfaction at the outset. It would, therefore, be necessary either to obtain it *en route*, or to liquidate the Common Market. Meanwhile, determined though it was to have its way in the end, the French government was able to allow the machinery of the Treaty of Rome to be set in motion thanks to the recovery of our balance of payments and the stabilization of the franc. In December 1958 it announced that it would implement the inaugural measures which were scheduled for New Year's Day, in particular a 10 percent tariff cut and a 20 percent quota increase.

Once initiated, the implementation of the Common Market was to give rise to a vast outgrowth of not only technical but also diplomatic activity. For, irrespective of its very wide economic scope, the operation proved to be hedged about with specifically political intentions calculated to prevent our country from being its own master. Hence, while the Community was taking shape, I was obliged on several occasions to intervene in order to repel the threats which overshadowed our cause.

The first arose from the original ambivalence of the institution. Was its objective—in itself momentous enough—the harmonization of the practical interests of the six states, their economic solidarity in face of the outside world and, if possible, their cooperation in foreign policy? Or did it aim to achieve the total fusion of their respective economies and policies in a single entity with its own government, parliament and laws, ruling in every respect its French, German, Italian, Dutch, Belgian and Luxembourg subjects, who would become fellow citizens of an artificial motherland, the brainchild of the technocrats? Needless to say, having no taste for make believe, I adopted the former conception. But the latter carried all the hopes and illusions of the supranational school.

For these champions of integration, the European executive was already alive and kicking: it was the Commission of the Economic Community, made up, admittedly, of representatives nominated by the six states but, thereafter, in no way dependent on them. Judging by the chorus of those who wanted Europe to be a federation, albeit without a federator, all the authority, initiative and control of the exchequer which are the prerogatives of government in the economic sphere must in future belong to this brigade of experts, not only within the Community but also—and this could be indefinitely extensible—from the point of view of relations with other countries. As for the national ministers, who could not as yet be dispensed with in their executive capacity, they had only to be summoned periodically to Brussels, where they would receive the Commission's instructions in their specialized fields. At the same time, the mythmongers wanted to exhibit the Assembly in Strasbourg, consisting of deputies and senators delegated by the legislatures of the member countries, as a "European parliament" which, while having no effective power, provided the Brussels "executive" with a semblance of democratic responsibility.

Walter Hallstein was the Chairman of the Commission. He was ardently wedded to the thesis of the superstate, and bent all his skillful efforts towards giving the Community the character and appearance of one. He had made Brussels, where he resided, into a sort of capital. There he sat, surrounded with all the trappings of sovereignty, directing his colleagues, allocating jobs among them, controlling several thousand officials who were appointed, promoted and remunerated at his discretion, receiving the credentials of foreign ambassadors, laying claim to high honors on the occasion of his official visits, concerned above all to further the amalgamation of the Six, believing that the pressure of events would bring about what he envisaged. But after meeting him more than once and observing his activities, I felt that although Walter Hallstein was in his way a sincere European, he was first and foremost a German who was ambitious for his own country. For in the Europe that he sought lay the framework in which his country could first of all regain, free of charge, the respectability and equality of rights which the frenzy and defeat of Hitler had cost it, then acquire the preponderant influence which its economic strength would no doubt earn it, and finally ensure that the cause of its frontiers and its unity was backed by a powerful coalition in accordance with the doctrine to which, as Foreign Minister of the Federal Republic, he had formerly given his name. These factors did not alter my esteem and regard for Walter Hallstein, but the goals I was pursuing on behalf of France were incompatible with such projects.

The fundamental divergence between the way the Brussels Commission conceived its role and my own government's insistence, while looking to the Commission for expert advice, that important measures should be subordinated to the decisions of the individual states, nurtured an atmosphere of latent discord. But since the Treaty specified that during the inaugural period no decision was valid unless unanimous, it was enough to enforce its application to ensure that there was no infringement of French sovereignty. So during this period the institution took wing in what was and must remain the economic sphere without being subjected to any mortal political crisis, in spite of frequent clashes. Moreover, in November 1959, at the initiative of Paris, it was decided that the six foreign ministers should meet at three-monthly intervals to examine the overall situation and its various implications and to report back to their own governments, which would have the last word if the need arose. It may be imagined that ours did not allow itself to be led.

But it was not only from the political angle that the newfledged Community had to undergo the truth test. Even in the economic sphere two formidable obstacles, secreting all kinds of contradictory interests and calculations, threatened to bar its way. These were, of course, the external tariff and agriculture, which were closely bound up with each other. True, on signing the Treaty, our partners had seemed to accept that common taxes should be imposed upon foreign goods as customs duties were reduced within the Community. But although they all recognized in principle that this procedure was essential to their solidarity, some of them were nonetheless irked by it because it deprived them of trade facilities which had hitherto been intrinsic to their existence. They therefore wanted the common external tariff to be as low as possible and in any case so elastic that their habits would not be disturbed. The same countries, for the same reasons, were in no hurry to see the Six take upon themselves the consumption and, therefore, the cost of continental farm products, nearly half of which happened to be French. For instance, Germany, nearly two-thirds of whose food was imported cheaply from outside the Community in exchange for manufactured goods, would have liked to see a Common Market for industrial goods only, in which case the Federal Republic would inevitably have had an overwhelming advantage. This was unacceptable to France. We therefore had to put up a fight in Brussels.

The battle was long and hard. Our partners, who bitterly regretted our having changed Republics, had been counting on us once again to sacrifice our own cause to "European integration," as had happened successively with the Coal and Steel Community, in which all the advantages went to others at our expense; with EURATOM, for which our country put up practically the entire stake without a *quid pro quo,* and, moreover, submitted her atomic assets to foreign supervision; and with the Treaty of Rome, which did not settle the agricultural question which was of paramount importance to ourselves. But now France was determined to get what she needed, and in any case her demands were consistent with the logic of the Community system. So her requirements were eventually met.

In May 1960, at our urgent insistence, the Six agreed to establish the external tariff and to adopt a timetable for the decisions to be taken on agricultural policy. In December of the same year, while urging an acceleration of the process of lowering customs barriers between them, they agreed that all imports of foodstuffs from elsewhere should be liable to an enormous financial levy at the expense of the purchasing state. And in January 1962 they adopted the decisive resolutions.

For at this date, now that the first phase of application was completed, it had to be decided whether or not, in pursuance of the terms of the Treaty, to proceed to the second phase, a kind of point of no return, involving a 50 percent reduction in customs duties. We French were determined to seize the opportunity to tear aside the veil and induce our partners to make formal commitments on what we regarded as essential. When they proved reluctant to give way, and indeed showed signs of some disquieting reservations, I judged that now or never was the moment to take the bull by the horns. Our ministers in Brussels, Couve de Murville, Baumgartner and Pisani, made it quite clear that we were prepared to withdraw from the Community if our requirements were not met. I myself wrote in similar terms to Chancellor Adenauer, whose government was our principal antagonist in this matter, and repeated it by formal telegram on the evening of the final debate. Feeling ran high in the capitals of the Six. In France, the parties and most of the newspapers, echoing foreign opinion, were disturbed and scandalized by the attitude of General de Gaulle, whose intransigence was threatening "the hopes of Europe." But France and common sense prevailed. During the night of 13–14 January 1962, after some dramatic exchanges, the Council of Ministers of the six states formally decided to admit agriculture into the Common Market, laid down then and there a broad basis for its implementation, and made the necessary arrangements to establish the agricultural regulations on the same footing and at the same time as the rest. Whereupon the implementation of the Treaty was able to enter its second phase.

But how far could it go, in view of the difficulties which the British were doing their utmost to raise, and the tendency of our five partners to submit to their influence? It was not surprising that Great Britain should be radically opposed to the whole venture, since by virtue of her geography, and therefore her policy, she has never been willing to see the Continent united or to merge with it herself. In a sense it might almost be said that therein lay the whole history of Europe for the past eight hundred years. As for the present, our neighbors across the Channel, adapted to free trade by the maritime nature of their economic life, could not sincerely agree to shut themselves up behind a continental tariff wall, still less to buy their food dear from us rather than import it cheap from everywhere else, for example the Commonwealth. But without the common tariff and agricultural preference, there could be no valid European Community. Hence at the time of the preliminary studies and discussions that led up to the Treaty of Rome, the London government, which was represented at the outset, had soon withdrawn. Then, with the intention of undermining the project of the Six, it had proposed that they should join a vast European free trade area with itself and various others. Things had reached this stage when I returned to power.

As early as 29 June 1958, Prime Minister Harold Macmillan had come to see me in Paris. In the midst of our friendly discussions which touched upon a great many topics, he suddenly declared with great feeling: "The Common Market is the Continental System all over again. Britain cannot accept it. I beg you to give it up. Otherwise, we shall be embarking on a war which will doubtless be economic at first but which runs the risk of gradually spreading into other fields." Ignoring the overstatement, I tried to pacify the English premier, at the same time asking him why the United Kingdom should object to seeing the Six establish a system of preference such as existed inside the Commonwealth. Meanwhile, his minister, Reginald Maudling, was actively engaged inside the so-called Organization for European Economic Cooperation, to which Britain belonged, in negotiations which were keeping the Six in suspense, and delaying the launching of the Community by proposing that the latter should be absorbed and, consequently, dissolved in a free trade area. Harold Macmillan wrote me a number of very pressing letters in an effort to obtain my compliance. But my government broke the spell, and made it clear that it would not agree to anything which did not include the common external tariff and an agricultural arrangement. London then appeared to abandon its policy of obstruction and, suddenly changing course, set up its own European Free Trade Association, with the Scandinavians, Portugal, Switzerland and Austria. At once, our Brussels partners dropped all their hesitations and set about launching the Common Market.

But the match had merely been postponed. In the middle of 1961 the British returned to the offensive. Having failed from without to prevent the birth of the Community, they now planned to paralyze it from within. Instead of calling for an end to it, they now declared that they themselves were eager to join, and proposed examining the conditions on which they might do so, "provided that their special relationships with the Commonwealth and their associates in the free trade area were taken into consideration, as well as their special interests in respect of agriculture." To submit to this would obviously have meant abandoning the Common Market as originally conceived. Our partners could not bring themselves to do so. But, on the other hand, it was beyond their power to say "No" to England. So, affecting to believe that the squaring of the circle was a practical proposition, they proceeded to discuss a series of projects and counter-projects in Brussels with the British minister, Edward Heath, which threw nothing but doubt on the future of the Community. I could see the day approaching when I should either have to remove the obstruction and put an end to the tergiversation, or else extricate France from an enterprise which had gone astray almost as soon as it had begun. At all events, as could have been foreseen, it was now clear to all that in order to achieve the unification of Europe, individual states are the only valid elements, that when their national interest is at stake nothing and nobody must be allowed to force their hands, and that cooperation between them is the only road that will lead anywhere.

In this respect what is true of economics is even truer of politics. And this is no more than natural. What depths of illusion or prejudice would have to be plumbed in order to believe that European nations forged through long centuries by endless exertion and suffering, each with its own geography, history, language, traditions and institutions, could cease to be themselves and form a single entity? What a perfunctory view is reflected in the parallel often naively drawn between what Europe ought to do and what the United States have done, when the latter was created from nothing in a completely new territory by successive waves of uprooted colonists? For the Six in particular, how was it conceivable that their external aims should suddenly become identical when their origins, situations and ambitions were so very different? In the matter of decolonization, which France was about to bring to a conclusion, what part could her neighbors play? If, from time immemorial, it had been in her nature to accomplish "God's work," to disseminate freedom of thought, to be a champion of humanity, why should it *ipso facto* become the concern of her partners? Germany, balked by defeat of her hopes of supremacy, divided at present and suspected by many of seeking her revenge, was now a wounded giant. By what token should her wounds automatically be shared by others? Given the fact that Italy, having ceased to be an annex of the Germanic or the French empires, and thwarted of her Balkan ambitions, remained a peninsular power confined to the Mediterranean and naturally located within the orbit of the maritime nations, why should she throw in her lot with the Continentals? By what miracle would the Netherlands, which had always owed its livelihood to shipping and its independence to overseas resources, allow itself to be swallowed up by the land powers? How could Belgium, hard put to it to maintain the juxtaposition of Flemings and Walloons in a single entity ever since a compromise between rival powers had turned her into a State, genuinely devote herself to anything else? With Luxembourg lying at the center of the territorial arrangements which had succeeded the rivalries of the two great countries bordering on the Moselle, what major concern could its people have other than the survival of Luxembourg?

On the other hand, while recognizing that each of these countries had its own national personality which it must preserve, there was no reason why they should not organize concerted action in every sphere, arrange for their ministers to meet regularly and their Heads of State or Government periodically, set up permanent organs to discuss politics, economics, culture and defense, have these subjects debated in the normal way by an assembly of delegates from their respective parliaments, acquire the taste and habit of examining together problems of common interest, and as far as possible adopt a united attitude towards them. Linked with what was already being practiced in the economic sphere in Brussels and Luxembourg, might not this general cooperation lead to a European policy as regards progress, security, influence, external relations, aid to the developing countries, and finally and above all as regards peace? Might not the grouping thus formed by the Six gradually attract the other states of the Continent into joining in on the same terms? And perhaps in this way, by opposing war, which is the history of men, that united Europe which is the dream of the wise might ultimately be achieved.

. . .

In the course of a press conference on 5 September [1960], after saying that "to build Europe, which means to unite Europe, is an essential aim of our policy," I declared that to this end it was necessary "to proceed, not on the basis of dreams, but in accordance with realities. Now, what are the realities of Europe? What are the pillars on which it can be built? The truth is that those pillars are the states of Europe . . . states each of which, indeed, has its own genius, history and language, its own sorrows, glories and ambitions; but states that are the only entities with the right to give orders and the power to be obeyed." Then, while recognizing "the technical value of certain more or less extranational or supranational organisms," I pointed out that they were not and could not be politically effective, as was proved by what was happening at that very moment in the European Coal and Steel Community, EURATOM and the Brussels Community. I insisted that, "although it is perfectly natural for the states of Europe to have specialist bodies available to prepare and whenever necessary to follow up their decisions, those decisions must be their own." Then I outlined my plan: "To arrange for the regular cooperation of the states of Western Europe in the political, economic and cultural spheres, as well as that of defense, is an aim that France deems desirable, possible and practical. . . . It will entail organized, regular consultations between the governments concerned and the work of specialist bodies in each of the common domains, subordinated to those governments. It will entail periodic deliberations by an assembly made up of delegates of the national parliaments. It must also, in my view, entail as soon as possible a solemn European referendum, in order to give this new departure for Europe the popular backing which is essential to it." I concluded: "If we set out on this road . . . links will be forged, habits will be developed, and, as time does its work, it is possible that we will come to take further steps towards European unity."

. . .

# 7 Preamble to the Single European Act

*Representatives of the twelve members of the European Community signed the Single European Act (SEA) in February 1986 and saw it implemented in July 1987. The SEA, the first major revision of the Treaties of Rome, brought together in one "single" act a treaty on European cooperation in the area of foreign policy and institutional and procedural reforms (such as the increased use of qualified majority voting and the introduction of the cooperation procedure) designed to facilitate the completion of the Single Market. The SEA, while not universally recognized as significant at the time, marked a milestone in the attempt by Community leaders to bury the legacy of Charles de Gaulle and "relaunch" Europe. The success of the SEA in facilitating the Single Market opened the way for further institutional reforms in the early 1990s.*

*The preamble to the SEA differs significantly from its predecessors. Gone is the vision of a united Europe as an alternative to war. In its place is a vision of an evolving European Union ready to act in the world as a single entity to protect the common interests of its members, promote democracy and human rights, contribute to the "preservation of international peace," and "improve the economic and social situation in Europe." The preamble assumed the European Communities now resembled a sovereign entity more than a mere collection of individual states, an evolution the signatories believed corresponded to the "wishes of the democratic peoples of Europe."*

. . .

---

Reprinted with permission from *Treaties Establishing the European Communities (ECSC, EEC, EAEC), Single European Act, Other Basic Instruments*, abridged edition (Office for Official Publications of the European Communities, 1987). 

MOVED by the will to continue the work undertaken on the basis of the Treaties establishing the European Communities and to transform relations as a whole among their States into a European Union, in accordance with the Solemn Declaration of Stuttgart of 19 June 1983,

RESOLVED to implement this European Union on the basis, firstly, of the Communities operating in accordance with their own rules and, secondly, of European Cooperation among the Signatory States in the sphere of foreign policy and to invest this union with the necessary means of action,

DETERMINED to work together to promote democracy on the basis of the fundamental rights recognized in the constitutions and laws of the Member States, in the Convention for the Protection of Human Rights and Fundamental Freedoms and the European Social Charter, notably freedom, equality and social justice,

CONVINCED that the European idea, the results achieved in the fields of economic integration and political cooperation, and the need for new developments correspond to the wishes of the democratic peoples of Europe, for whom the European Parliament, elected by universal suffrage, is an indispensable means of expression,

AWARE of the responsibility incumbent upon Europe to aim at speaking ever increasingly with one voice and to act with consistency and solidarity in order more effectively to protect its common interests and independence, in particular to display the principles of democracy and compliance with the law and with human rights to which they are attached, so that together they may make their own contribution to the preservation of international peace and security in accordance with the undertaking entered into by them within the framework of the United Nations Charter,

DETERMINED to improve the economic and social situation by extending common policies and pursuing new objectives, and to ensure a smoother functioning of the Communities by enabling the institutions to exercise their powers under conditions most in keeping with Community interests,

WHEREAS at their Conference in Paris from 19 to 21 October 1972 the Heads of State or of Government approved the objective of the progressive realization of Economic and Monetary Union,

HAVING REGARD to the Annex to the conclusions of the Presidency of the European Council in Bremen on 6 and 7 July 1978 and the Resolution of the European Council in Brussels on 5 December 1978 on the introduction of the European Monetary System (EMS) and related questions, and noting that in accordance with that

Resolution, the Community and the Central Banks of the Member States have taken a number of measures intended to implement monetary cooperation,

HAVE DECIDED to adopt this Act.

. . .

# 8 A Family of Nations

MARGARET THATCHER

*Margaret Thatcher served as Britain's prime minister from 1979 to 1990. During her eleven years in office, she attempted to reduce the role of government in British society, particularly the economy. Her distrust of big government extended to the institutions of the European Community, which she considered a threat to prosperity in Europe and her policy successes in Britain. While prime minister, Thatcher raised the ire of most EC leaders by working tirelessly and unapologetically for Britain's particular interests and by resisting, often alone, most attempts to expand the powers of EC institutions. After her elevation to the House of Lords, she furthered her reputation as a virulent Euroskeptic by leading a small group of parliamentarians in a loud but unsuccessful fight to block Britain's ratification of the Maastricht treaty in 1993.*

*Prime Minister Thatcher outlined her views on European integration in a speech at the College of Europe in Bruges, Belgium, on 20 September 1988. There she placed Britain firmly in Europe but rejected the notion that "Europe" meant the absorption of Britain—and all the other member states—into a single, bureaucratized European "superstate." The European Community, she argued, would succeed only if each member state was allowed to maintain its own identity. Her vision of Europe as a "family of nations"—which mirrors de Gaulle's—represents well the traditional British approach to integration, but challenges the federalist vision of the founders and continental builders of the Community. For this reason, Margaret Thatcher's Bruges speech proved highly controversial.*

---

Mr Chairman, you have invited me to speak on the subject of Britain and Europe. Perhaps I should congratulate you on your courage. If you believe some of the things said and written about my views on Europe, it must seem rather like inviting Genghis Khan to speak on the virtues of peaceful coexistence!

I want to start by disposing of some myths about my country, Britain, and its relationship with Europe. And to do that I must say something about the identity of Europe itself. Europe is not the creation of the Treaty of Rome. Nor is the European idea the property of any group or institution. We British are as much heirs to the legacy of European culture as any other nation. Our links to the rest of Europe, the continent of Europe, have been the dominant factor in our history. For three hundred years we were part of the Roman Empire and our maps still trace the straight lines of the roads the Romans built. Our ancestors—Celts, Saxons and Danes—came from the continent. Our nation was—in that favorite Community word—"restructured" under Norman and Angevin rule in the eleventh and twelfth centuries. This year we celebrate the three hundredth anniversary of the Glorious Revolution in which the British crown passed to Prince William of Orange and Queen Mary. Visit the great churches and cathedrals of Britain, read our literature and listen to our language: all bear witness to the cultural riches which we have drawn from Europe—and other Europeans from us.

We in Britain are rightly proud of the way in which, since Magna Carta in 1215, we have pioneered and developed representative institutions to stand as bastions of freedom. And proud too of the way in which for centuries Britain was a home for people from the rest of Europe who sought sanctuary from tyranny. But we know that without the European legacy of political ideas we could not have achieved as much as we did. From classical and medieval thought we have borrowed that concept of the rule of law which marks out a civilized society from barbarism. And on that idea of Christendom—for long synonymous with Europe—with its recognition of the unique and spiritual nature of the individual, we still base our belief in personal liberty and other human rights.

Too often the history of Europe is described as a series of interminable wars and quarrels. Yet from our perspective today surely what strikes us most is our common experience. For instance, the story of how Europeans explored and colonized and—yes, without apology—civilized much of the world is an extraordinary tale of talent, skill and courage.

We British have in a special way contributed to Europe. Over the centuries we have fought to prevent Europe from falling under the dominance of a single power. We have fought and we have died for her freedom. Only miles from here in Belgium lie the bodies of 120,000 British soldiers who died in the First World War. Had it not been for that willingness to fight and to die, Europe would have been united long before now—but not in liberty, not in justice. It was British support to resistance movements throughout the last War that helped to keep alive the flame of liberty in so many countries until the day of liberation. It was from our island fortress that the liberation of Europe itself was mounted. And still today we stand together. Nearly 70,000 British servicemen are stationed on the mainland of Europe. All these things alone are proof of our commitment to Europe's future.

The European Community is one manifestation of that European identity. But it is not the only one. We must never forget that east of the Iron Curtain peoples who once enjoyed a full share of European culture, freedom and identity have been cut off from their roots. We shall always look on Warsaw, Prague and Budapest as great European cities. Nor should we forget that European values have helped to make the United States of America into the valiant defender of freedom which she has become.

This is no arid chronicle of obscure facts from the dust-filled libraries of history. It is the record of nearly two thousand years of British involvement in Europe, cooperation with Europe and contribution to Europe, a contribution which today is as valid and as strong as ever. Yes, we have looked also to wider horizons—as have others—and thank goodness for that because Europe never would have prospered and never will prosper as a narrow-minded, inward-looking club.

The European Community belongs to all its members. It must reflect the traditions and aspirations of all its members. And let me be quite clear. Britain does not dream of some cozy isolated existence on the fringes of the European Community. Our destiny is in Europe, as part of the Community. That is not to say that our future lies only in Europe. But nor does that of France or Spain or indeed any other member.

The Community is not an end in itself. Nor is it an institutional device to be constantly modified according to the dictates of some abstract intellectual concept. Nor must it be ossified by endless regulation. The European Community is the practical means by which Europe can ensure the future prosperity and security of its people in a world in which there are many other powerful nations and groups of nations. We Europeans cannot afford to waste our energies on internal disputes or arcane institutional debates. They are no substitute for effective action. Europe has to be ready both to contribute in full measure to its own security and to compete commercially and industrially, in a world in which success goes to the countries which encourage individual initiative and enterprise, rather than to those which attempt to diminish them.

This evening I want to set out some guiding principles for the future which I believe will ensure that Europe does succeed, not just in economic and defence terms but also in the quality of life and the influence of its peoples.

My first guiding principle is this: willing and active cooperation between independent sovereign states is the best way to build a successful European Community. To try to suppress nationhood and concentrate power at the center of a European conglomerate would be highly damaging and would jeopardize the objectives we seek to achieve. Europe will be stronger precisely because it has France as France, Spain as Spain, Britain as Britain, each with its own customs, traditions and identity. It would be folly to try to fit them into some sort of identikit European personality.

Some of the founding fathers of the Community thought that the United States of America might be its model. But the whole history of America is quite different from Europe. People went there to get away from the intolerance and constraints of life in Europe. They sought liberty and opportunity; and their strong sense of purpose has, over two centuries, helped create a new unity and pride in being American—just as our pride lies in being British or Belgian or Dutch or German.

I am the first to say that on many great issues the countries of Europe should try to speak with a single voice. I want to see us work more closely on the things we can do better together than alone. Europe is stronger when we do so, whether it be in trade, in defense, or in relations with the rest of the world. But working more closely together does not require power to be centralized in Brussels or decisions to be taken by an appointed bureaucracy. Indeed, it is ironic that just when those countries such as the Soviet Union, which have tried to run everything from the center, are learning that success depends on dispersing power and decisions away from the center, some in the Community seem to want to move in the opposite direction. We have not successfully rolled back the frontiers of the state in Britain, only to see them reimposed at a European level, with a European superstate exercising a new dominance from Brussels.

Certainly we want to see Europe more united and with a greater sense of common purpose. But it must be in a way which preserves the different traditions, parliamentary powers and sense of national pride in one's own country; for these have been the source of Europe's vitality through the centuries.

My second guiding principle is this: Community policies must tackle present problems in a practical way, however difficult they may be. If we cannot reform those Community policies which are patently wrong or ineffective and which are rightly causing public disquiet, then we shall not get the public's support for the Community's future development.

. . .

My third guiding principle is the need for Community policies which encourage enterprise. If Europe is to flourish and create the jobs of the future, enterprise is the key. The basic framework is there: the treaty of Rome itself was intended as a Charter for Economic Liberty. But that is not how it has always been read, still less applied.

The lesson of the economic history of Europe in the 1970s and 1980s is that central planning and detailed control don't work, and that personal endeavor and initiative do. That a state-controlled economy is a recipe for low growth; and that free enterprise within a framework of law brings better results. The aim of a Europe open to enterprise is the moving force behind the creation of the Single European Market by 1992. By getting rid of barriers, by making it possible for companies to operate on a Europewide scale, we can best compete with the United States, Japan and the other new economic powers emerging in Asia and elsewhere. And that means action to free markets, action to widen choice, action to reduce government intervention. Our aim should not be more and more detailed regulation from the center: it should be to deregulate and to remove the constraints on trade.

. . .

My fourth guiding principle is that Europe should not be protectionist. The expansion of the world economy requires us to continue the process of removing barriers to trade, and to do so in the multilateral negotiations in the GATT [General Agreement on Tariffs and Trade]. It would be a betrayal if, while breaking down constraints on trade within Europe, the Community were to erect greater external protection. We must ensure that our approach to world trade is consistent with the liberalization we preach at home.

We have a responsibility to give a lead on this, a responsibility which is particularly directed towards the less developed countries.

They need not only aid; more than anything they need improved trading opportunities if they are to gain the dignity of growing economic strength and independence.

. . .

I believe it is not enough just to talk in general terms about a European vision or ideal. If we believe in it, we must chart the way ahead and identify the next steps. That is what I tried to do this evening.

This approach does not require new documents: they are all there, the North Atlantic Treaty, the Revised Brussels Treaty, and the Treaty of Rome, texts written by far-sighted men. However far we may want to go, the truth is that we can only get there one step at a time.

What we need now is to take decisions on the next steps forward rather than let ourselves be distracted by Utopian goals. Utopia never comes, because we know we should not like it if it did. Let Europe be a family of nations, understanding each other better, appreciating each other more, doing more together but relishing our national identity no less than our common European endeavor.

Let us have a Europe which plays its full part in the wider world, which looks outward not inward, and which preserves that Atlantic Community—that Europe on both sides of the Atlantic—which is our noblest inheritance and our greatest strength.

# 9 A Necessary Union

Jacques Delors

*Jacques Delors assumed the presidency of the Commission of the European Community in January 1985 and served for ten years. Prior to his appointment to the Commission, he was elected to the European Parliament (1979) and served as minister of finance (1981–1984) in France. Delors's energetic and visionary leadership contributed significantly to the revival of the Community in the 1980s and early 1990s. Under his watch the Community took several significant steps, including the creation of the Single Market and the European Economic Area; expansion to Portugal, Spain, Austria, Finland, and Sweden; and negotiation and implementation of the Single European Act and the Maastricht treaty.*

*On 17 October 1989, one year after Margaret Thatcher made her Bruges speech, Jacques Delors traveled to the same spot and offered an alternative vision. His purpose was to convince the Community to seize the moment afforded by history and take a dramatic leap toward federalism. World events, particularly those in the East, and global interdependence necessitated the strengthening of Community institutions and the expansion of the "joint exercise of sovereignty." But true federalism, he asserted, included the principle of subsidiarity: "never entrust to a bigger unit anything that is best done by a smaller one." Subsidiarity, he argued in response to Margaret Thatcher, made federalism the savior of pluralism, diversity, patriotism, and national identity in Europe. Indeed, the rejection of federalism, he warned, would mean the return of ugly nationalism.*

*Two years later, in Maastricht, EC leaders heeded Delors's Bruges call.*

I am speaking to you today at the invitation of your Rector, Professor Lukaszewski, as the College of Europe celebrates its fortieth birthday. European integration has had its ups and downs over those forty years, its high seasons of hope and progress and its long winters of despondency and stagnation. But here, in Bruges, faith in the European ideal has never wavered. . . .

It is a happy coincidence that this year your College has chosen to pay tribute to Denis de Rougemont, an all too little-known figure, whose lifework and writings are a precious legacy. I would like to speak in more personal terms of Denis de Rougemont, I never had the good fortune to work with him, but I would like to tell you why I think so much of him, why I draw on his intellectual and political contribution.

First of all, as a militant European, I, like many others, am carrying on the work he began in his time. He was an ardent federalist. For him federalism was a many-splendored thing; he saw it as a method, an approach to reality, a view of society. I often find myself invoking federalism as a method, with the addition of the principle of subsidiarity. I see it as a way of reconciling what for many appears to be irreconcilable: the emergence of a United Europe and loyalty to one's homeland; the need for a European power capable of tackling the problems of our age and the absolute necessity to preserve our roots in the shape of our nations and regions; and decentralization of responsibilities, so that we never entrust to a bigger unit anything that is best done by a smaller one. This is precisely what subsidiarity is about.

[I speak] as a personalist, a disciple of Emmanuel Mounier, whose influence will, I am convinced, revive as Europeans become aware of the quandaries of frenzied individualism, just as, for some years now, they have been rejecting collectivism and, in its attenuated form, the benevolent State.

. . .

Denis de Rougemont believed in what I would call working from the bottom up, rebuilding from below, from small entities rooted naturally in a solidarity of interests and a convergence of feeling. That is of course essential, but it is not enough. Others, and I am one of them, must at the same time work from the top down, viewing the paths of integration from above. Otherwise the small streams of solidarity will never converge to form a wide river.

And de Rougemont abhorred power. Let me quote him again: "My philosophy comes down to this: power is the authority one would wield over others; freedom is the authority one can wield over oneself." Although I would not deny the philosophical value of this statement, I would beg to disagree with it from a political standpoint.

Politically speaking, power is not necessarily the obverse of freedom. Neither the European Community—nor the peoples and nations that form it—will truly exist unless it is in a position to defend its values, to act on them for the benefit of all, to be generous. Let us be powerful enough to command respect and to uphold the values of freedom and solidarity. In a world like ours, there is no other way.

I would link power with the necessity I have so often invoked to promote the revitalization of European integration. Today I would like to get power working for the ideal. Where would necessity take us had we no vision of what we want to achieve? And, conversely, what impact can an ideal have without the resolve and the means to act? The time has come, I feel, to reconcile necessity and the ideal.

We can do so by drawing on our own experiences, on our national heritages, and on the strength of our institutions. Let me underline the importance of this at a time when people can appreciate the limits of any action implemented with national resources alone. Our present concerns—be it the social dimension or the new frontier represented by economic and monetary union—offer a golden opportunity for the joint exercise of sovereignty, while respecting diversity and hence the principles of pluralism and subsidiarity.

There is a need for urgency, for history does not wait. As upheavals shake the world, and the other "Europe" in particular, our reinvigorated Community must work for increased cohesion and set objectives commensurate with the challenges thrown down by history.

History is only interested in the far-sighted and those who think big, like Europe's founding fathers. They are still with us today in the inspiration they provided and the legacy they left.

By "thinking big," I mean taking account of worldwide geopolitical and economic trends, the movement of ideas and the development of the fundamental values which inspire our contemporaries. The founding fathers wanted to see an end to internecine strife in Europe. But they also sensed that Europe was losing its place as the economic and political center of the world. Their intuition was confirmed before our very eyes, to the point in the 1970s when we had to choose between survival and decline. I shocked many people at that time by constantly arguing this point. Gradually, though, the need for a quantum leap became apparent and created a climate in which a single European market by 1992 could be accepted as an objective. The same dynamism led to revision of the Treaty of Rome—the Single Act—and to what is known as the Delors package, in other words the financial reforms necessary to pay for our ambitious plans. Necessity woke Europe from its slumbers.

By "far-sighted," I mean being simultaneously capable of drawing on our historical heritage and looking to the future. Futurology has a part to play but so has a code of ethics for the individual, society and the human adventure. This, frankly, is what we most lack today. I can say, with both feet on the ground, that the theory of the bogeyman-nation has no place in the life of our Community if it wants to be a Community worthy of the name. The inevitable conflicts of interest between us must be transcended by a family feeling, a sense of shared values. These include the enhancement of personality through mutual knowledge and exchange. The younger generation is very conscious of this new horizon. It rejects isolation, it wants to experience other ideas, to explore new territory. The time has come, my friends, to revive the ideal.

To get there, however, we must take the path of necessity. At a time when the Community is being courted by some, threatened by others; at a time when there are those who, with scant regard for the mortar which already binds us, advocate a headlong dash in the name of a greater Europe, or offer us as an ultimate reference nothing more than the laws of the market; to these we must say that our Community is the fruit not only of history and necessity, but also of political will.

Let us consider necessity for a moment. Since the turn-around of 1984–85 our achievements are there for all to see. The threat of a decline is receding. Businessmen and manufacturers are more aware of this than politicians, many of whom still underestimate the way in which the gradual achievement of the single European market and common policies have supported national efforts to adapt to the new world economic order. Yet all we need to do to see how far we have come is look beyond our frontiers: Europe is once again a force to be reckoned with and is arousing interest everywhere: in America, in Asia, in Africa, in the North and in the South.

Then there is political will. I know that the term has sometimes been abused, as a sort of incantation, but it is precisely political will that led first six, then nine, ten, twelve countries to decide to unite their destiny, with their eyes wide open. The contract binding them is clear, involving both rights and obligations.

Last of all, history. The Twelve cannot control history but they are now in a position to influence it once again. They did not want Europe to be cut in two at Yalta and made a hostage in the Cold War. They did not, nor do they, close the door to other European countries willing to accept the terms of the contract in full.

The present upheavals in Eastern Europe are changing the nature of our problems. It is not merely a matter of when and how all the countries of Europe will benefit from the stimulus and the advantages of a single market. Our times are dominated by a new mercantilism and our young people expect something better of us. Are we going to turn away?

Make no mistake about it. Behind triumphant nationalism and excessive individualism, ethics are making a comeback in the wake of scientific progress. How far, for example, are we prepared to allow genetic manipulation to go? We need a code of ethics for man, we need to promote our concept of the individual and his integrity. Nature, whether pillaged or neglected, strikes back with disturbances and upheavals. So we also need a code of ethics governing the relationship between man and nature. With millions of young people knocking in vain on the door of adult society, not least to find their place in the world of work, with millions of pensioners—still in the prime of life—cut off from any real role in society, we must ask ourselves what kind of society are we building. A society in which the door is always closed?

Europe has always been the continent of doubt and questioning, seeking a humanism appropriate to its time, the cradle of ideas which ultimately encircle the globe. The time has come to return to ideals, to let them penetrate our lives. Let us continue to consider, in everything we do in the field of politics, economics and social and cultural life, what will enable every man, every woman, to achieve their full potential in an awareness not only of their rights, but also of their obligations to others and to society as a whole. We must sustain our efforts to create a humane society in which the individual can blossom through contact and cooperation with others.

Of course any reference to humanism is bound to unleash a debate among Europeans. People will hold conflicting views, but a synthesis will emerge to the benefit of democracy and Europe itself. For the Community is a concept charged with significance. "Where there is no big vision, the people perish," as Jean Monnet said, making this saying of President Roosevelt's [and Prov. 29:18] his own.

In this respect we are engaged in a unique adventure. We are creating a model, admittedly by reference to inherited principles, but in circumstances so extraordinary that the end result will be unique, without historical precedent. We owe much to the strength of our institutions because our Community is a Community based on the rule of law. And the condition for success is the joint, transparent exercise of sovereignty.

Let us consider the strength of our institutions for a moment, beginning with legitimacy. Without legitimacy—as earlier attempts to unite nations have shown—no progress, no permanence is possible.

In the Community the progress of history is there for all to see. We have the Treaty duly ratified by all national parliaments, an expression of national will. The Court of Justice plays a vital role in dealing with differences of interpretation. The European Council—now institutionalized—allows Heads of State and Government to monitor progress, to pinpoint delays and failures to honor the contract that unites and binds us, to provide impetus and to make good any deficiencies. A new development is that the Commission now presents a balance sheet at each meeting of what has been accomplished and what remains to be done. The Commission takes the European Council's pronouncements very seriously and does not hesitate to remind the Twelve of undertakings given. In this way the Community is demonstrating more and more clearly that it has little in common with organizations that produce worthy resolutions that are rarely if ever acted upon.

. . .

Many envy us our Community based on the rule of law and this explains its growing influence. What a model our institutions, which allow every country irrespective of its size to have its say and make its contribution, offer the nations of Eastern Europe. They, and many other nations besides, admire the practical, forward-looking application of pluralist democracy within our borders. In the circumstances how can anyone expect us to accept absorption into a larger, looser structure along intergovernmental lines? We would be abandoning a bird in the hand for two in the bush. It would be a tragic mistake for Europe.

Despite the success of our Community based on the rule of law, disputes about sovereignty continue. We need to face the issues squarely.

A dogmatic approach will get us nowhere. It will merely complicate the difficult discussions that lie ahead and make it even harder to remove the remaining obstacles on the road to the single European market and 1992.

The facts speak for themselves. Each nation needs to consider how much room for manoeuvre it genuinely has in today's world. The growing interdependence of our economies, the internationalization of the financial world, the present or growing influence of the main protagonists on the world stage—all point to a dual conclusion. Firstly, nations should unite if they feel close to each other in terms of geography, history, values—and also necessity. Secondly—and ideally at the same time—cooperation should develop at world level to deal with such matters as international trade, the monetary system, underdevelopment, the environment and drugs. The two are complementary rather than concurrent. Because in order to exist on a global level and to influence events, not only the trappings of power are needed, but also a strong hand—that is, a capacity for generosity which is essential to any great undertaking. Europe has little clout as yet, although, as I have said, our economic performance is impressing our partners and reassuring our own people. It is quite clear that the fault lies in the deliberately fostered fiction of full national sovereignty and hence of the absolute effectiveness of national policies.

. . .

The Commission has no intention of getting embroiled in insidious tactical manoeuvering designed to lead the member states in a direction they do not wish to take. Let me repeat that our Community is a community based on the rule of law, where we work by the book with complete openness. Indeed, this is the first rule for success. Everyone must acknowledge this in good faith. If I turn to the principles of federalism in a bid to find workable solutions, it is precisely because they provide all the necessary guarantees on pluralism and the efficiency of the emergent institutional machinery. Here, there are two essential rules:

1. the rule of autonomy, which preserves the identity of each member state and removes any temptation to pursue unification regardless;
2. the rule of participation, which does not allow one entity to be subordinated to another, but on the contrary, promotes cooperation and synergy, on the basis of the clear and well-defined provisions contained in the Treaty.

This is the starting point for an original experiment which resists comparison with any other models, such as the United States of America, for instance. I have always shied away from such parallels, because I know that our task is to unite old nations with strong traditions and personalities. There is no conspiracy against the nation state. Nobody is being asked to renounce legitimate patriotism. I want not only to unite people, as Jean Monnet did, but also to bring nations together. As the Community develops, as our governments emphasize the need for a people's Europe, is it heresy to hope that all Europeans could feel that they belong to a Community which they see as a second homeland? If this view is rejected, European integration will founder and the specter of nationalism will return to haunt us, because the Community will have failed to win the hearts and minds of the people, the first requirement for the success of any human venture.

The success of the Community is such that it is attracting interest from all quarters. It cannot ignore this without abandoning its claim to a universal dimension. But here again the question of "what should be done" is inseparable from the question of "how do we go about it."

History will not wait for the Single Act to work through the system. It is knocking at our door even now.

. . .

Communist Europe is exploding before our eyes. Gorbachev has launched Perestroika and Glasnost. Poland and Hungary are carrying out political reforms, ushering in an era of greater freedom and democracy. East Germany totters as tens of thousands of its people flee to the West. The virus of freedom has reached Leipzig and East Berlin.

As early as 1984 François Mitterrand, in a speech to the European Parliament, voiced his presentiment of a radical new departure in Europe. "It is clear," he said, "that we are moving away from the time when Europe's sole destiny was to be shared out and divided up by others. The two words 'European independence' now sound different. This is a fact that our century, which is nearing its end, will, I am sure, remember."

As many European leaders have already stressed, it is our Community, a Community based on the rule of law, a democratic entity and a buoyant economy, that has served as the model and the catalyst for these developments. The West is not drifting eastward, it is the East that is being drawn towards the West. Will the Community prove equal to the challenges of the future? This is the question we should ask ourselves today, whether we mean helping the countries of Eastern Europe to modernize their economies—a precondition for the success of political reforms—or getting to grips with the German question when the time comes—in other words, extending the right of self-determination to everyone.

I have no doubt that if we refuse to face up to these new challenges, not only will we be shirking our responsibilities but the Community will disintegrate, stopped in its tracks by the weight of unresolved contradictions. When I look around me now, as these events unfold, I see too much despondency, too much defeatist thinking, too much willingness paralyzed by passive acquiescence. . . . How are we to find a solution except by strengthening the federalist features of the Community which, to paraphrase Hans-Dietrich Genscher, offer the best possible guarantee of survival to all concerned? There, I am quite sure, lies the only acceptable and satisfactory solution to the German question.

How are we to shoulder our international responsibilities and at the same time pave the way for the emergence of a greater Europe, except by pressing ahead with European integration? Only a strong, self-confident Community, a Community which is united and determined, can truly hope to control that process.

The pace of change is gathering momentum and we must try to keep up. If our institutions are to adapt to the new situation, we cannot afford to shilly-shally about economic and monetary union. There is no question of shortening the time we need to test wide-ranging cooperation and move on to successive stages. That would be unrealistic. But time is running out for the political decision which will generate the dynamism necessary for success and lead to the creation of institutions with the capacity to face up to the demands imposed by our international responsibilities.

. . .

I have always favored the step-by-step approach—as the experiment we are embarked upon shows. But today I am moving away from it precisely because time is short. We need a radical change in the way we think of the Community and in the way we act on the world stage. We need to overcome whatever resistance we encounter. If only to adapt the instruments we already have, so that we can, for example, inject more substance into the Lomé Convention or make a success of our aid program for Poland and Hungary. We need to give countries that depend on exports for survival more access to our markets to prevent them plunging deeper into debt. We need financial instruments which will help these countries to adapt and modernize their economies.

I am concerned that we will never achieve all this with our present decision-making procedures. Thanks to the Single Act the Council, Parliament and the Commission are a more efficient institutional troika than they were a few years ago. But this is not enough to enable us to keep pace with events.

For the honor of your generation and mine, I hope that in two years' time we will be able to repeat the very words which another great European, Paul-Henri Spaak, spoke at the signing of the Treaty of Rome: "This time the people of the West have not lacked daring and have not acted too late."

It is time, then, for a new political initiative. The Commission is ready for it and will play its full part in pointing the way. It will propose answers to the questions raised by another quantum leap: who takes the decisions; how do the various levels of decision making intermesh (subsidiarity again!); who puts decisions into practice; what resources will be available; what will it mean in terms of democracy?

There is no doubt that we are living in exciting times, but they are dangerous times too. The Community is faced with the challenge of making a telling contribution to the next phase of our history.

As I stand before a predominantly young audience, I find myself dreaming of a Europe which has thrown off the chains of Yalta, a Europe which tends its immense cultural heritage so that it bears fruit, a Europe which imprints the mark of solidarity on a world which is far too hard and too forgetful of its underdeveloped regions.

I say to these young people: If we can achieve this Europe you will be able to stretch yourselves to the utmost, you will have all the space you need to achieve your full potential. For you are being invited to play your part in a unique venture, one which brings peoples and nations together for the better, not for the worse. It will bring you back to your philosophical and cultural roots, to the perennial values of Europe. But you will need to give of yourselves and insist that those who govern you display boldness tempered with caution, a fertile imagination and a clear commitment to making the Community a necessity for survival and an ideal towards which to work.

# 10 Preamble to the Treaty on European Union (The Maastricht Treaty)

*Several factors, including the success of the Single Market program and the collapse of communism, increased momentum for integration as the European Community entered the 1990s. In December 1990, the member states opened negotiations to complete economic and monetary union, reform EC institutions, and expand Community competence in foreign and security policy. Final negotiations took place in December 1991 in Maastricht, The Netherlands, and the Maastricht treaty was signed there on 7 February 1992. Ratification seemed certain until Danish voters rejected the treaty on 2 June 1992 and opened a debate in Europe over the merits of integration. Public dissatisfaction with the complex treaty combined with a currency crisis and a severe economic recession to sap popular and elite enthusiasm for the European project. Nevertheless, all twelve countries finally ratified the treaty, which came into force in late 1993.*

*The preamble to the Maastricht treaty reflects the essence of Jacques Delors's thinking: the need to construct a new Europe out of a formerly divided continent requires a leap to a new stage of integration through the creation of a European Union. The institutions of the Union will have responsibility for issue areas previously reserved for national governments. But respect for Europe's core values, increased accountability, and faithful application of the principle of subsidiarity will, according to the treaty, preserve democracy and diversity within the new Europe.*

---

. . .

RESOLVED to mark a new stage in the process of European integration undertaken with the establishment of the European Communities,

RECALLING the historic importance of the ending of the division of the European continent and the need to create firm bases for the construction of the future Europe,

CONFIRMING their attachment to the principles of liberty, democracy and respect for human rights and fundamental freedoms and the rule of law,

DESIRING to deepen the solidarity between their peoples while respecting their history, their culture and their traditions,

DESIRING to enhance further the democratic and efficient functioning of the institutions so as to enable them better to carry out, within a single institutional framework, the tasks entrusted to them,

RESOLVED to achieve the strengthening and the convergence of their economies and to establish an economic and monetary union including, in accordance with the provisions of this Treaty, a single and stable currency,

DETERMINED to promote economic and social progress for their peoples, within the context of the accomplishment of the internal market and of reinforced cohesion and environmental protection, and to implement policies ensuring that advances in economic integration are accompanied by parallel progress in other fields,

RESOLVED to establish a citizenship common to nationals of their countries,

RESOLVED to implement a common foreign and security policy including the eventual framing of a common defence policy, which might in time lead to a common defence, thereby reinforcing the European identity and its independence in order to promote peace, security and progress in Europe and in the world,

REAFFIRMING their objective to facilitate the free movement of persons, while ensuring the safety and the security of their peoples, by including provisions on justice and home affairs in this Treaty,

RESOLVED to continue the process of creating an ever closer union among the peoples of Europe, in which decisions are taken as closely as possible to the citizen in accordance with the principle of subsidiarity,

IN VIEW of further steps to be taken in order to advance European integration,

HAVE DECIDED to establish a European Union.

. . .

# 11 Preamble to the Treaty of Nice Amending the Treaty on European Union (The Nice Treaty)

*The European Union (EU) is constantly revising its fundamental law. For nearly two decades the Union has been either preparing, negotiating, or ratifying a new treaty. The Amsterdam treaty (which did not have a preamble) incorporated a range of new policy areas into the EU and transferred areas of justice and home affairs to the community area (the first pillar). The member states, however, proved unable to reach a compromise on their original objective: the institutional changes required for enlargement. Their later attempt to address this deficiency by hammering out an agreement on, among other things, the size of the Commission and the reweighting of votes in the Council of Ministers resulted in the Treaty of Nice. Unfortunately, the success of the negotiations was—to be charitable—limited.*

*The infamous European Council of Nice (December 2000) lasted a total of four days and three nights. The Nice treaty was signed on 26 February 2001. The Irish "pulled a Denmark" and voted against the new treaty in a referendum in the summer of 2001. After a second Irish referendum brought a positive result, the treaty finally entered into force on 1 February 2003.*

*The preamble to the Treaty of Nice, as can be seen below, demonstrates a total lack of vision. Paradoxically, however, the minimalist result seemed to inspire most of the European leaders to outline new, high-flying visions that included the necessity for a European constitution (see Chapter 12). Thus, the failure of Nice became a catapult for a constitutional debate on Europe, and, perhaps for that reason, history books will remember Nice more for what it started than for what it achieved.*

. . .

RECALLING the historic importance of the ending of the division of the European continent,

DESIRING to complete the process started by the Treaty of Amsterdam of preparing the institutions of the European Union to function in an enlarged union,

DETERMINED on this basis to press ahead with the accession negotiations in order to bring them to a successful conclusion, in accordance with the procedure laid down in the Treaty on European Union,

HAVE RESOLVED to amend the Treaty on European Union, the Treaties establishing the European Communities and certain related acts.

. . .

# 12 Reflections on a Constitution for Europe

JOSCHKA FISCHER, JACQUES CHIRAC, TONY BLAIR, AND PAAVO LIPPONEN

*Debating the future of the European Union (EU) became a popular sport among European political leaders in the months before the Nice Summit. German foreign minister Joschka Fischer kicked off an unusual conversation in Berlin on 12 May 2000 that eventually included virtually every head of state and government, foreign minister, and minister of Europe of both member and candidate states. All of the contributions to the debate had one thing in common: each offered a reflection on a constitution for Europe—an unimaginable idea only a few months before.*

*Joschka Fischer, French president Jacques Chirac, British prime minister Tony Blair, and Finnish prime minister Paavo Lipponen delivered the speeches excerpted in this chapter in the short span of a year. The speeches came against the backdrop of the new European single currency—the euro—and the Union's triple challenge of enlargement, democratic legitimacy, and its role in the world. All of the speakers could agree on the challenges facing Europe; they divided, however, on how to meet them.*

*Fischer's stunning speech called for a "European Federation," complete with a bicameral parliament and a responsible executive. The new federation, he argued, must be based on a constitution that describes a clear division of competences between the European and national governments. One month later, Jacques Chirac (a French Gaullist) countered Fischer's call for federation in a speech before the German Bundestag. Chirac was less willing than Fischer to give up national sovereignty to a European Federation, but did support a new constitution. In addition, he called for an intergovernmental "pioneer group," driven by France and Germany, to push the integration process forward. Tony Blair followed the mainly intergovernmental line of Chirac in his contribution by stating that he wanted Europe to become a superpower, but not a superstate, and suggested the formation of a new parliamentary chamber to represent national parliaments. Paavo Lipponen, often seen as the champion of small states (together with Belgian prime minister Guy Verhofstadt), extolled the virtues of the existing "Community Method" in his speech at the College of Europe, but suggested ways of strengthening democratic legitimacy. He was the first prime minister to suggest that the next Intergovernmental Conference (IGC) should be prepared by a convention.*

*The speeches and the European Council of Laeken under the Belgian presidency led to the inauguration of the European Convention in February 2002, chaired by former French president Valéry Giscard d'Estaing. The aim of the convention was to provide a blueprint for a European constitution, which many hoped would be approved by an IGC. At the convention, the topics discussed in the speeches—a constitution, competences, fundamental rights of EU citizens, the role of national parliaments, a common European defense, and more—which were so shocking at the time, became almost second nature. While the success of the convention is still to be determined, one thing is certain: Joschka Fischer's speech at Humboldt University opened an unprecedented public debate and paved the way for a European constitution.*

## From Confederacy to Federation—Thoughts on the Finality of European Integration

JOSCHKA FISCHER

Fifty years ago almost to the day, Robert Schuman presented his vision of a "European Federation" for the preservation of peace. This heralded a completely new era in the history of Europe. European integration was the response to centuries of a precarious balance of powers on this continent, which again and again resulted in terrible hegemonic wars culminating in the two World Wars between 1914 and 1945. The core of the concept of Europe after 1945 was and still is a rejection of the European balance-of-power principle and the hegemonic ambitions of individual states that had emerged following the Peace of Westphalia in 1648, a rejection which took the form of

---

Speech given at Humboldt University in Berlin, 12 May 2000. Reprinted with permission.

closer meshing of vital interests and the transfer of nation-state sovereign rights to supranational European institutions.

Fifty years on, Europe, the process of European integration, is probably the biggest political challenge facing the states and peoples involved, because its success or failure, indeed even just the stagnation of this process of integration, will be of crucial importance to the future of each and every one of us, but especially to the future of the young generation. And it is this process of European integration that is now being called into question by many people; it is viewed as a bureaucratic affair run by a faceless, soulless Eurocracy in Brussels—at best boring, at worst dangerous.

. . .

Quo vadis Europa? is the question posed once again by the history of our continent. And for many reasons the answer Europeans will have to give, if they want to do well by themselves and their children, can only be this: onwards to the completion of European integration. A step backwards—even just standstill or contentment with what has been achieved—would exact a fatal price of all EU member states and of all those who want to become members; it would exact a fatal price, above all, of our people. . . .

. . .

Enlargement will render imperative a fundamental reform of the European institutions. Just what would a European Council with thirty heads of state and government be like? Thirty presidencies? How long will Council meetings actually last? Days, maybe even weeks? How, with the system of institutions that exists today, are thirty states supposed to balance interests, take decisions and then actually act? How can one prevent the EU from becoming utterly untransparent, compromises from becoming stranger and more incomprehensible, and the citizens' acceptance of the EU from eventually hitting rock bottom?

Question upon question, but there is a very simple answer: the transition from a union of states to full parliamentarization as a European Federation, something Robert Schuman demanded 50 years ago. And that means nothing less than a European Parliament and a European government, which really do exercise legislative and executive power within the Federation. This Federation will have to be based on a constituent treaty.

I am well aware of the procedural and substantive problems that will have to be resolved before this goal can be attained. For me, however, it is entirely clear that Europe will only be able to play its due role in global economic and political competition if we move forward courageously. The problems of the 21st century cannot be solved with the fears and formulae of the 19th and 20th centuries.

Of course, this simple solution is immediately criticized as being utterly unworkable. Europe is not a new continent, so the criticism goes, but full of different peoples, cultures, languages and histories. The nation-states are realities that cannot simply be erased, and the more globalization and Europeanization create superstructures and anonymous actors remote from the citizens, the more the people will cling on to the nation-states that give them comfort and security.

Now I share all these objections, because they are correct. That is why it would be an irreparable mistake in the construction of Europe if one were to try to complete political integration against the existing national institutions and traditions rather than by involving them. Any such endeavor would be doomed to failure by the historical and cultural environment in Europe. Only if European integration takes the nation-states along with it into such a Federation—only if their institutions are not devalued or even made to disappear—will such a project be workable despite all the huge difficulties. In other words: the existing concept of a federal European state replacing the old nation-states and their democracies as the new sovereign power shows itself to be an artificial construct which ignores the established realities in Europe. The completion of European integration can only be successfully conceived if it is done on the basis of a division of sovereignty between Europe and the nation-state. Precisely this is the idea underlying the concept of "subsidiarity," a subject that is currently being discussed by everyone and understood by virtually no one.

So what must one understand by the term "division of sovereignty"? As I said, Europe will not emerge in a political vacuum, and so a further fact in our European reality is therefore the different national political cultures and their democratic publics, separated in addition by linguistic boundaries. A European Parliament must therefore always represent two things: a Europe of the nation-states and a Europe of the citizens. This will only be possible if this European Parliament actually brings together the different national political elites and then also the different national publics.

In my opinion, this can be done if the European Parliament has two chambers. One will be for elected members who are also members of their national parliaments. Thus there will be no clash between national parliaments and the European Parliament, between the nation-state and Europe. For the second chamber a decision will have to be made between the Senate model, with directly elected senators from the member states, and a chamber of states along the lines of Germany's

Bundesrat. In the United States, every state elects two senators; in our Bundesrat, in contrast, there are different numbers of votes.

Similarly, there are two options for the European executive, or government. Either one can decide in favor of developing the European Council into a European government, i.e., the European government is formed from the national governments, or—taking the existing Commission structure as a starting-point—one can opt for the direct election of a president with far-reaching executive powers. But there are also various other possibilities between these two poles.

. . .

[T]hree reforms—the solution of the democracy problem and the need for fundamental reordering of competences both horizontally, i.e. among the European institutions, and vertically, i.e. between Europe, the nation-state and the regions—will only be able to succeed if Europe is established anew with a constitution. In other words: through the realization of the project of a European constitution centered around basic, human and civil rights, an equal division of powers between the European institutions and a precise delineation between European and nation-state level. The main axis for such a European constitution will be the relationship between the Federation and the nation-state. Let me not be misunderstood: this has nothing whatsoever to do with a return to renationalization, quite the contrary.

The question which is becoming more and more urgent today is this: can this vision of a Federation be achieved through the existing method of integration, or must this method itself, the central element of the integration process to date, be cast into doubt?

In the past, European integration was based on the "Monnet method" with its communitarization approach in European institutions and policy. This gradual process of integration, with no blueprint for the final state, was conceived in the 1950s for the economic integration of a small group of countries. Successful as it was in that scenario, this approach has proved to be of only limited use for the political integration and democratization of Europe. Where it was not possible for all EU members to move ahead, smaller groups of countries of varying composition took the lead, as was the case with Economic and Monetary Union and with Schengen.

Does the answer to the twin challenge of enlargement and deepening, then, lie in such a differentiation, an enhanced cooperation in some areas? Precisely in an enlarged and thus necessarily more heterogeneous Union, further differentiation will be inevitable. . . .

However, increasing differentiation will also entail new problems: a loss of European identity, of internal coherence, as well as the danger of an internal erosion of the EU, should ever larger areas of intergovernmental cooperation loosen the nexus of integration. Even today a crisis of the Monnet method can no longer be overlooked, a crisis that cannot be solved according to the method's own logic.

So if the alternative for the EU in the face of the irrefutable challenge posed by eastern enlargement is indeed either erosion or integration, and if clinging to a federation of states would mean standstill with all its negative repercussions, then, under pressure from the conditions and the crises provoked by them, the EU will at some time within the next ten years be confronted with this alternative: will a majority of member states take the leap into full integration and agree on a European constitution? Or, if that doesn't happen, will a smaller group of member states take this route as an avant-garde, i.e., will a center of gravity emerge comprising a few member states which are staunchly committed to the European ideal and are in a position to push ahead with political integration? The questions then would simply be: When will be the right time? Who will be involved? And will this center of gravity emerge within or outside the framework provided by the treaties? One thing at least is certain: no European project will succeed in future either without the closest Franco-German cooperation.

Given this situation, one could imagine Europe's further development far beyond the coming decade in two or three stages. First the expansion of reinforced cooperation between those states that want to cooperate more closely than others, as is already the case with Economic and Monetary Union and Schengen. . . . [Secondly], one possible interim step on the road to completing political integration could then later be the formation of a center of gravity. Such a group of states would conclude a new European framework treaty, the nucleus of a constitution of the Federation. On the basis of this treaty, the Federation would develop its own institutions, establish a government, which within the EU should speak with one voice on behalf of the members of the group on as many issues as possible, a strong parliament and a directly elected president. . . . The last step will then be completion of integration in a European Federation. Let's not misunderstand each other: closer cooperation does not automatically lead to full integration, either by the center of gravity or straight away by the majority of members. Initially, enhanced cooperation means nothing more than increased intergovernmentalization under pressure from the facts and the shortcomings of the "Monnet Method." The steps towards a constituent treaty—and precisely that will be the precondition for full integration—require a deliberate political act to reestablish Europe.

This is my personal vision for the future: from closer cooperation towards a European constituent treaty and the completion of Robert Schuman's great idea of a European Federation. This could be the way ahead!

## Our Europe

JACQUES CHIRAC

. . .

I would like, here in Berlin, to scout out the way, tell you what I firmly believe, offer you some ideas for the way forward [for the European Union].

First of all, I believe that the European Union's enlargement is a great ambition, one which is both legitimate and necessary. It is under way. It will be difficult, for both the candidate countries and member states. But tomorrow we shall be thirty or more represented in Brussels, in Strasbourg and Luxembourg. That's an achievement! For peace and democracy, entrenched on our continent and making our joint venture wholly meaningful. For the candidate countries, buttressed in their fight for freedom by the hope of joining us. For the Union itself which, as a result, will become stronger, politically and economically.

But, for all that, the obligation is clear. The enlargement won't go ahead regardless. We shall not allow the unraveling of the European enterprise to which you [the Germans] and we [the French], with our partners, have devoted so much determination and energy for almost half a century. And which, in return has brought us so much, not just peace, but also economic success and thus social progress. Which has proved, for us all, tremendously empowering. Our Union won't be quite the same tomorrow. But it won't be diluted, nor will it take a backward step. It will be our responsibility to ensure this. I believe too that the pace of European construction can't be decreed. It is to a large extent dictated by the increase in the strength of the feeling, among our peoples, of identity and of belonging to Europe, of their wish to live together in a mutually supportive community. And I am confident since this feeling is growing stronger and stronger, especially among the young.

---

Speech to the German Bundestag, Berlin, 27 June 2000. Reprinted with permission.

Finally, I believe it is necessary to provide an informed background to the debate on the nature of the Union. It's misrepresenting the truth to say that, on one side, there are those who are defending national sovereignty and, on the other, those who are selling it off. Neither you nor we are envisaging the creation of a super European State which would supplant our national states and mark the end of their existence as players in international life. Our nations are the source of our identities and our roots. The diversity of their political, cultural and linguistic traditions is one of our Union's strengths. For the peoples who come after us, the nations will remain the first reference points.

Envisaging their extinction would be as absurd as denying that they have already chosen to exercise jointly part of their sovereignty and that they will continue to do so, since that is in their interest. Yes, the European Central Bank, the Luxembourg Court of Justice and qualified majority voting are elements of a common sovereignty. It is by accepting these areas of common sovereignty that we shall acquire new power and greater influence. So, please, let's stop anathemizing and over-simplifying and at last agree that the Union's institutions are, and will remain original and specific!

But let's recognize too that they can be improved and that the forthcoming major enlargement has to be the opportunity for us to think more deeply about our institutions. With this in mind, I would like us to be able to agree on some principles.

First of all, the need to make the European Union more democratic. The task of building Europe has, to a large extent, been solely that of leaders and elite. It is time our peoples once more became the sovereigns of Europe. Democracy in Europe must be more dynamic, particularly through the European parliament and the national parliaments.

Then, to clarify, but without setting it in stone, the division of responsibilities between the different levels of the European system. Say who does what in Europe, bearing in mind the need for the answers to be provided at the best level, the one closest to the problems. In short, at last apply the principle of subsidiarity.

We must also ensure that, in the enlarged Europe, the capacity for forward momentum remains. There must constantly be the possibility of opening up new avenues. For this, and as we have done in the past, the countries which want to integrate further, on a voluntary basis and on specific projects, must be able to do so without being held up by those who, and it is their right, don't wish to go so fast.

Finally, there's the Europe as a world power that we so want to see—this Europe, one which is a strong player on the international stage, has to have strong institutions and an effective and legitimate decision-making mechanism, i.e., one in which majority voting is the rule and which reflects the relative weights of the member states.

These are the main guidelines which, I believe, must govern the process of remolding the EU's institutions. The face of the future Europe has still to be shaped. It will depend on the debate and the negotiations. And, of course and above all, on the will of our peoples. But we can already, at this stage, map out the route.

After the Intergovernmental Conference [of 2000], the end of the year will see the opening of what I would describe as the "great transition" period at the end of which the EU's institutions and borders will have to have been stabilized. During this period, we will have to work on three major projects at one and the same time.

Firstly, of course, the enlargement. It will take a good few years to conclude the accession negotiations and ensure the successful integration of the new member states. Then there's the deepening of the policies, on the initiative of those countries I was talking about just now and which wish to go further or faster. Together with Germany and France, they could form a "pioneer group." This group would blaze the trail, by making use of the new enhanced cooperation procedure defined by the IGC and forging, if necessary, cooperation in spheres not covered by the Treaty, but without ever undermining the Union's coherence and *acquis*.

This is, of course, how the composition of the "pioneer group" will emerge. Not on an arbitrary basis, but through the will of the countries which decide to participate in all the spheres of enhanced cooperation. Thus, starting next year, I would like the "pioneer group" to be able to set to work *inter alia* on improving the coordination of economic policies, strengthening the defense and security policy and increasing the effectiveness of the fight against organized crime.

Should these states conclude a new treaty together and give themselves sophisticated institutions? I don't believe so. This, we should realize, would add an additional level to a Europe which already has plenty! And let's avoid setting Europe's divisions in stone when our sole objective is to maintain a capacity for forward momentum. Instead, we should envisage a flexible cooperation mechanism, a secretariat tasked with ensuring the consistency of the positions and policies of the members of this pioneer group, which should, of course, remain open to all those wishing to join it.

Thus, in this transition period, Europe will continue to move forward while the preparations are being made for the reshaping of the institutions. Indeed, and this is the third project, I propose that, immediately after the Nice Summit, we launch a process which, going beyond the IGC, will enable us to address the other institutional issues facing Europe.

Firstly, to reorganize the treaties to make their presentation more coherent and easier for people to understand. Then, clearly define the division of responsibilities—you emphasized this and were right to do so—between Europe's various levels. We could also, in the framework of this process, ponder the issue of the Union's ultimate geographical limits, clarify the nature of the Charter of Fundamental Rights which, I hope, we shall have adopted in Nice and, finally, prepare the necessary institutional adjustments, as regards both the executive and the Parliament, to strengthen the effectiveness and democratic control of our Union.

This preparatory discussion will have to be conducted openly, with the participation of governments and citizens, through their representatives in the European Parliament and national Parliaments. The candidate countries will of course have to take part in it. There are several possible ways of organizing, ranging from a Committee of Wise Men to an approach modeled on the Convention which is drafting our Charter of Fundamental Rights.

And at the end of these discussions, which will very probably take some time, the governments, then the peoples would be called on to give their verdict on a text which we will then be able to establish as the first "European Constitution." But if the European enterprise is to prosper, it is the Franco-German friendship that we must first seek constantly to deepen. Our innumerable and so familiar areas of cooperation, the close political dialogue between our institutions at all levels, the fertile interchange between our cultures, the exchanges among young people thanks to our thousands of twinning arrangements and language courses—all have forged a unique, irreversible and irreplaceable bond.

. . .

## What Sort of Europe?

TONY BLAIR

. . .

Today I want to ask: Europe, yes, but what sort of Europe?

The trouble with the debate about Europe's political future is

Speech to the Polish Stock Exchange, 6 October 2000. Reprinted with permission.

that if we do not take care, we plunge into the thicket of institutional change, without first asking the basic question of what direction Europe should take.

To those who say the need for change in Europe's institutions is driven by the impression Europe is slowing down, I must say I find that bizarre. Monetary union is currently the most ambitious economic enterprise in the world. We have just begun to fashion a common defense policy. And we are now set to reunify Europe and expand it with up to 13 new members and in the longer term more. We are hardly short of challenges.

Neither do I see any profit in pitting the European institutions against intergovernmental cooperation. We need a strong Commission able to act independently, with its power of initiative: first because that protects smaller states; and also because it allows Europe to overcome purely sectional interests. All governments from time to time, Britain included, find the Commission's power inconvenient but, for example, the single market could never be completed without it. The European Parliament is a vital part of the checks and balances of the EU. The Commission and the Council have different but complementary roles.

The need for institutional change does not derive either from a fear that Europe is immobile or that it is time to upset the delicate balance between Commission and governments; it derives from a more fundamental question.

The most important challenge for Europe is to wake up to the new reality: Europe is widening and deepening simultaneously. There will be more of us in the future, trying to do more. The issue is: not whether we do this, but how we reform this new Europe so that it both delivers real benefits to the people of Europe, addressing the priorities they want addressed; and does so in a way that has their consent and support.

There are two opposite models so far proposed. One is Europe as a free trade area, like NAFTA [North American Free Trade Agreement] in North America. This is the model beloved by British Conservatives. The other is the classic federalist model, in which Europe elects its Commission President and the European Parliament becomes the true legislative European body and Europe's principal democratic check.

. . .

A limited vision of Europe does not remotely answer the modern demands people place on Europe. The difficulty, however, with the view of Europe as a superstate, subsuming nations into a politics dominated by supranational institutions, is that it too fails the test of the people.

There are issues of democratic accountability in Europe—the so-called democratic deficit. But we can spend hours on end, trying to devise a perfect form of European democracy and get nowhere. The truth is, the primary sources of democratic accountability in Europe are the directly elected and representative institutions of the nations of Europe—national parliaments and governments. That is not to say Europe will not in future generations develop its own strong demos or polity, but it hasn't yet.

And let no-one be in any doubt: nations like Poland, who struggled so hard to achieve statehood, whose citizens shed their blood in that cause, are not going to give it up lightly. We should celebrate our diverse cultures and identities, our distinctive attributes as nations.

Europe is a Europe of free, independent sovereign nations who choose to pool that sovereignty in pursuit of their own interests and the common good, achieving more together than we can achieve alone. The EU will remain a unique combination of the intergovernmental and the supranational.

Such a Europe can, in its economic and political strength, be a superpower; a superpower, but not a superstate.

. . .

So let me turn to the changes I believe are part of delivering that direction.

First, we owe it to our citizens to let them know clearly what policies and laws are being enacted in their name. The European Council, bringing together all the Heads of Government, is the final court of appeal from other Councils of Ministers unable to reconcile national differences.

That is a vital role. But the European Council should above all be the body which sets the agenda of the Union. Indeed, formally in the Treaty of Rome, that is the task given to it. We now have European Council meetings every three months. And in truth they do, for example, in areas like the Luxembourg summit on jobs, the Lisbon summit on economic reform, the Peortschach summit on defense, develop the future political direction of Europe. I would like to propose that we do this in a far more organized and structured way.

Just as governments go before their electorates and set out their agenda for the coming years, so must the European Council do the same. We need to do it in all the crucial fields of European action: economic, foreign policy, defense, and the fight against cross-border crime. I am proposing today an annual agenda for Europe, set by the European Council.

The President of the Commission is a member of the European

Council, and would play his full part in drawing up the agenda. He would then bring a proposal for Heads of Government to debate, modify and endorse. It would be a clear legislative, as well as political, program setting the workload of individual Councils. The Commission's independence as guardians of the treaty would be unchanged. And the Commission would still bring forward additional proposals where its role as guardian of those treaties so required. But we would have clear political direction, a program and a timetable by which all the institutions would be guided.

We should be open too to reforming the way individual Councils work, perhaps through team presidencies that give the leadership of the Council greater continuity and weight; greater use of elected chairs of Councils and their working groups; and ensuring that the Secretary-General of the Council, Javier Solana, can play his full role in the development of foreign and defense policy. For example, when Europe is more than 25 members, can we seriously believe that a country will hold the Presidency only every 12 or 13 years? But two or three countries together, with a mix of large and small states, might make greater sense. In future we may also need a better way of overseeing and monitoring the Union's program than the three monthly European Councils.

Second, there is an important debate about a Constitution for Europe. In practice I suspect that, given the sheer diversity and complexity of the EU, its constitution, like the British constitution, will continue to be found in a number of different treaties, laws and precedents. It is perhaps easier for the British than for others to recognize that a constitutional debate must not necessarily end with a single, legally binding document called a Constitution for an entity as dynamic as the EU.

What I think is both desirable and realistic is to draw up a statement of the principles according to which we should decide what is best done at the European level and what should be done at the national level, a kind of charter of competences. This would allow countries too, to define clearly what is then done at a regional level. This Statement of Principles would be a political, not a legal document. It could therefore be much simpler and more accessible to Europe's citizens.

I also believe that the time has now come to involve representatives of national parliaments more on such matters, by creating a second chamber of the European Parliament. A second chamber's most important function would be to review the EU's work, in the light of this agreed Statement of Principles. It would not get involved in the day-to-day negotiation of legislation—that is properly the role of the existing European Parliament. Rather, its task would be to help implement the agreed statement of principles, so that we do what we need to do at a European level, but also so that we devolve power downwards. Whereas a formal Constitution would logically require judicial review by a European constitutional court, this would be political review by a body of democratically elected politicians. It would be dynamic rather than static, allowing for change in the application of these principles without elaborate legal revisions every time.

Such a second chamber could also, I believe, help provide democratic oversight at a European level of the common foreign and security policy.

Efficient decision making, even with these changes, will be harder in an enlarged European Union. In the long run, I do not believe that a Commission of up to 30 members will be workable. The present intergovernmental conference must and will address the size of the Commission. More radical reform is not possible this time round in view of the worries of some states. I simply give my view that, in the end, we shall have to revisit this issue and streamline considerably. Reweighting votes in the Council has also become a democratic imperative which this current intergovernmental conference must resolve.

Efficient decision making in an enlarged Union will also mean more enhanced cooperation. I have no problem with greater flexibility or groups of member states going forward together. But that must not lead to a hard core; a Europe in which some member states create their own set of shared policies and institutions from which others are in practice excluded. Such groups must at every stage be open to others who wish to join.

We need to get the political foundations of the European Union right. These foundations are rooted in the democratic nation state. Efficiency and democracy go together. . . . We are building a Europe of equal partners served by institutions which need to be independent but responsive and accountable. We want a Europe where there are national differences, not national barriers, where we hold many of our policies in common, but keep our distinct, separate identities.

The European Union is the world's biggest single economic and political partnership of democratic states. That represents a huge opportunity for Europe and the peoples of Europe. And as a Union of democracies, it has the capacity to sustain peace in our continent, to deliver unprecedented prosperity and to be a powerful force for democratic values in the rest of the world.

Our task, with the help of the new democracies about to join the EU, is to shape a responsive European Union—in touch with the people, transparent and easier to understand, strengthened by its nations and regions—a European Union whose vision of peace is matched by its vision of prosperity. A civilized continent united in defeating brutality and violence. A prosperous continent united in extending opportunities to all. A continent joined together in its belief in social justice. A superpower, but not a superstate. An economic powerhouse through the completion of the world's biggest single market, the extension of competition, an adaptable and well-educated workforce, the support for businesses large and small. A civilized continent through common defense, the strength of our values, the pursuit of social justice, the rich diversity of our cultures.

The countries represented here today have suffered more than most in the cause of freedom. I want you, as soon as possible, to share in the European Union's success, and to join as equal partners, as, amid the new reality I have outlined, a new Europe is built.

## In Defense of the Community Method

PAAVO LIPPONEN

. . .

In recent months we have seen the beginnings of a real debate on the future of Europe. . . . The debate has started and we should not try to avoid it.

I propose to give you today my vision on the future of the European Union. I do not pretend to have all the answers, and I do not claim to be inventing the wheel all over again. On the contrary, I want to try to bring some realism to the ongoing debate about the future of the Union. I want to do this, because at times I feel that a debate about the future emerges when we do not seem to know what we want to do with the present.

My message today is simple: there are many things we can do better with the existing rules, but in the long run we will need radical changes. We need a change from a bureaucratic top-down approach to a bottom-up philosophy of direct public involvement. . . .

. . .

The EU is a Union of states and a Union of peoples. In our *sui generis* decision-making structure the Council reflects the principle of equality

---

Speech given at the College of Europe, Bruges, Belgium, 10 November 2000. Reprinted with permission.

between the member states. The composition of the European Parliament is a reflection of the population spread of the member states. Today, most decisions are made through co-decision between the Council and the European Parliament. I am of the opinion that any option for re-weighting of the votes is valid as long it fulfils a basic principle: a qualified majority vote must be supported by at least half of the member states and at least half of the population. Whatever changes we deem to be necessary concerning the numbers, the key is to ensure that the fundamental principles of equality and respect of the national integrity of all member states, large or small, are preserved.

The institutional balance of the European Union is not static. The constant changes are reflected in the debate about the future of the Union, the ongoing IGC [2000] as well as in the day-to-day work in the institutions. The institutional framework is molded through these large and small decisions. It could be argued that the past years have witnessed a strengthening of the European Parliament, a weakening of the Commission and a tendency towards intergovernmentalism.

The cornerstone of the institutional structure is an effective and impartial Commission, a responsible European Parliament and an efficient Council. This is the combination that guarantees the interests of the Union as a whole.

. . .

The debate about the future of the Union has indicated that some member states would be prepared to deepen the integration process outside the current institutional framework, on the basis of the intergovernmental method. This is an alarming trend. The intergovernmental method is often inefficient, lacks transparency and leads to the domination of some over others. It is also a potentially destabilizing factor because strong institutions are less prone to pressure from political changes and crises in the member states.

The community method has brought enormous benefits through the single market and the EMU [Economic and Monetary Union]. A commitment to the community method should be the foundation of the future Union as well. The key role of an initiator belongs to the Commission, which also serves as a guardian of the treaties. If the role of the Commission is weakened, who is going to guarantee that rules are being adhered to and commitments made together are being met by all member states?

. . .

A fundamental debate about the future of the EU emerges at regular intervals. The debate usually highlights the tension between intergovernmentalism and the community method. It is also linked to the broader picture of the EU's *finalité*. If we were first to define what we want, it might be easier to establish how we can achieve it. I am, however, the first one to admit, that in a changing world this might be an impossible task. Developing a Union that is responsive to change and challenges will always be a continuous process.

. . .

In short, I think the European Union has two fundamental problems: firstly, alienation from the people which is due to lack of democratic legitimacy, lack of transparency and too much bureaucracy; and secondly, an incapability to adapt to a changing world.

Neither one of these problems can be solved with a traditional top-down approach. European co-operation must have a strong social content that is supportive of basic rights, equal opportunities and non-discrimination. But, deeper integration reflected as a change in the text of the treaties does not in itself bring the Union closer to the citizens. Most of the practical work towards fulfilling the goals of social dimension is done, and it should be, at the local level and with direct involvement of the citizens.

. . .

I am afraid that the present tendency towards intergovernmentalism threatens, not only the institutional balance and clarity of rules, but basically the equality of member states, European citizens and European companies. Also a proliferating flexibility can lead to structures that are discriminating and even designed to benefit certain countries.

We must make the interests of the people, beginning with equality, as the starting point of our institutional analysis. From such an approach, also taking into account safeguarding the interests of member countries large and small, we can establish certain principles for the future architecture of the Union.

The Union is about pooling sovereignty on a supranational level in order to find common solutions to common problems. For this reason it is widely considered that policies like those relating to the internal market, international trade, the common currency, foreign and security policy, external borders and security in the Union and the global environment are best dealt with on the EU level. By the same token I believe that many other things—such as culture, education and basic social security—are best dealt with on the national and regional levels. In addition there are a lot of economic, employment and social policy issues that need to be coordinated in the Union.

A clear definition of competences and the principle of subsidiarity are also of fundamental importance. The deeper our integration, the more important it is to fix competences. Otherwise a bureaucracy will develop in Brussels that is even more overblown than today.

For any institutional structure we need a decision-making system that is as simple as possible, democratic, efficient and transparent. Fundamentally, our institutions must enjoy democratic legitimacy.

With these principles and tools in our hands we should approach what is coming, a process of developing the Union's institutions, eventually at a constitutional conference. For this we need an open and analytical debate on various alternatives.

A constitution for the Union should produce an institutional structure that would permanently secure the equality of member states by transforming the Council. This would rid us of permanent haggling with the weighting of votes in Council. The Parliament would represent democratic legitimacy from an equally fundamental point of view as a directly elected body with considerable powers. The Commission should enjoy the confidence of the Parliament, with a President with powers to appoint members of the Commission. And in this institutional setup, just like in national decision-making, all aspects of civil society should be involved.

Let me be clear, I am an advocate of good and sensible governance with an efficient and democratic institutional system. A Union based on the principles of decentralization and a clear division of competence would serve that purpose.

Any moves towards a European constitution need to be solidly anchored in the public.

The basic philosophy of the so-called Monnet method is that integration in one area leads to pressure to integrate in another. The Monnet method has worked well in relation to economic integration.

The problem, however, is that the Monnet method does not reflect the reality of day-to-day European politics. Should Jean Monnet live today I think he would agree with me when I say that strong institutions need an even stronger legitimacy. The EU cannot be run as a functionalist, elite-driven project, which is bureaucratically managed on the basis of a top-down philosophy. We need to seek alternative approaches.

For me transparency is not only about "access to documents," efficiency is not only about qualified majority, and democracy is not only reflected within the borders of the nation state. They are all part and parcel of the broader decision-making structure. They mean direct involvement in all phases of decision-making and implementation. They mean active engagement in the day-to-day politics of European integration.

A good starting point for shifting toward a bottom-up approach would be to change the way in which we revise the treaties. In the past fifteen years we have prepared, negotiated or ratified a treaty. The problem is that many of the IGCs are detached from the public sphere and proceed on the basis of a lowest common denominator. Last minute deals are struck so that everyone can bring something home.

The integration proccss has now reached a stage in which this approach should be changed. On the European level we are dealing with issues that touch all aspects of society. This means that the preparatory phase should be as broad as possible. We need to take the fundamental decisions together, not only among governments.

I would like to finish by outlining a concrete proposal on how we should proceed in the coming years. I propose the following steps. Firstly, we must finish the Intergovernmental Conference in Nice with ambitious results and restate our commitment to enlargement through our readiness to accept new member states in 2003. Secondly, I think that we should define a preliminary agenda for the future in Nice. The agenda I propose is limited and it is important that we leave it open ended. My suggestion is that this agenda deals with at least the following issues: 1) legal status of fundamental rights, 2) a political guideline on the division of competences, 3) restructuring of the treaties, 4) a re-examination of the institutional balance, and 5) the principles of good governance. The agenda should also contain deliberations that aim at strengthening of the European Union as an international actor.

Thirdly, I think the Swedish and Belgian Presidencies could draw up a preliminary timetable and establish some clear working methods.

Fourthly, I suggest that any future European agenda should be prepared on a broad basis by a Convention that should include the governments and national parliaments of the member states and the candidate states and the EU institutions and representatives. We need broad involvement because we are now dealing with things that are close to the core of national sovereignty. Let the Convention participate in the process of drawing up a basic constitution.

Finally, after the preparatory process for a constitution has been finished we should convene an IGC to negotiate and finalize the document.

The quest for peace, security and prosperity in the whole of Europe has guided the Union to the eve of the next enlargement. The benefits of economic and political integration should be available to all. Uniting the continent means also to strengthen the fundamental principles of democracy, human rights and the rule of law. These principles are prerequisites for prosperity and citizens' participation not only in Europe, but globally.

While preparing the Union for enlargement and reforming it we should respect the fact that we are all equally good Europeans. Citizens and institutions of member states should have equal rights and possibilities within the Union and should also be able to participate in its development regardless of where they live or are based. The real value of integration is in the abolition of dividing lines in Europe. We are not putting up new barriers or creating clubs—we are in the process of unifying the continent.

# PART 2

## Early Currents in Integration Theory

# 13 Altiero Spinelli and the Strategy for the United States of Europe

SERGIO PISTONE

*Integration theory describes and explains the process of unifying separate nation-states. Early theories of integration also contained a strong prescriptive element. Thus, Altiero Spinelli (Chapter 1), founder of the European Federalist Movement, Italian deputy, member of the European Parliament, and ardent federalist, was dedicated not just to understanding the integration process, but even more to the actual uniting of Europe. Spinelli criticized the slow, and in his view, undemocratic process that characterized postwar integration in Europe. He longed for a revolutionary leap to a federal state.*

*Spinelli elaborated his federalist vision of European integration in the years after the Ventotene Manifesto. His goal, like most federalists, was a new Europe composed of individual states that had ceded their sovereignty to common democratic institutions. What made his brand of federalism more than just a description of a European Federation, however, was his strategy for achieving a united Europe, here summarized by his associate, Sergio Pistone (University of Turin). In Spinelli's view, overcoming resistance from national governments required a popular pan-European movement that demanded a U.S.-style constitutional convention. This constituent assembly would command such democratic legitimacy that national governments would have to accede to its wishes and ratify the new European con-*

---

*stitution. Spinelli believed that only a dramatic leap to federalism would succeed in unifying Europe; functionalism's step-by-step approach would never create institutions strong enough to solve major problems and democratic enough to respond to the people.*

*Spinelli eventually saw the directly elected European Parliament (EP) as a possible constituent assembly and, as a member of parliament, set about writing a new constitution for Europe. Shortly before his death he saw this document passed by the EP as the Draft Treaty on European Union (1984). Although the Draft Treaty was not ratified by the member states, many of the ideas contained in it found their way into the Maastricht and Amsterdam treaties. More significant, Spinelli's dream of a constitutional process—if not a constituent assembly—has been recently realized. The question is: would he have approved of the process and the results?*

What distinguishes Spinelli's approach to European federalism from that of its former supporters is his commitment to turn it into an active movement with a political program. That is why his ideas about a campaign strategy for the United States of Europe, which he had always considered as a first stage in the process of unifying the whole world, are amongst the most important, if not the most important contributions to federalism. To illustrate the essential elements of these ideas is, in my view, a contribution to a clearer understanding of the problems of the struggle for European unification (still in progress), but also to help in the fight for world unity (now in its initial stages).

For the purposes of synthesis, my case will follow a logical rather than chronological course. In other words I will not trace the origins of Spinelli's strategic concepts, but the basic theses that emerged from his ideas and actions. In my view these boil down to three:

1. The autonomous nature of the movement for the European federation;
2. The European Constituent Assembly;
3. The exploitation of the contradictions of the functional approach to European unification.

The arguments in favor of the autonomy of the movement for the European federation stem from the belief that the national democratic governments are, simultaneously, the means and the obstacles to European unification.

They are the means because unification can only be achieved as a result of freely arrived at decisions by democratic governments. This implies the rejection of two other ways forward. Spinelli rejects any attempts to unite Europe by force, as Hitler tried, and against which European federalists fought in the Resistance during the Second World War. As a matter of principle he also rejects unification by illegal and violent means from below, because the federalist struggle takes place in Western Europe within democratic political systems which provide legal means for even the most radical change. Moreover such unification stems from the historical development of European democracy.

Whilst European unification can only be achieved by the free decisions of democratic national governments, by their very nature they represent obstacles to its attainment. As a direct consequence of the Second World War, which led to the collapse of the European nation states, they are obliged to face the alternative of "either unite or perish." Yet, at the same time, they are inclined to reject a genuine European federation involving the irreversible transfer of substantial parts of their sovereignty to a supranational authority.

With regard to this obstacle one must clarify Spinelli's important distinction between the permanent agents of executive power, such as diplomats, civil servants and the military, and those who wield political power temporarily, such as heads of governments and their ministers. The strongest opposition to the transfer of sovereignty usually comes from the former because they would suffer immediate and substantial loss of power and status. After all, the permanent agents of executive power were originally created to put into effect the unfettered sovereignty of the state, and they thus became the natural defenders of nationalist traditions. For the latter, wielders of temporary power, the situation is rather more complex for three reasons: (1) without permanent positions of power they have much greater opportunities of playing a role within a wider European political framework; (2) they represent democratic parties with international programs which usually include support for a European federation; (3) they are in direct touch with public opinion which, in countries suffering from the decline and crisis of the nation state, is generally favorable to European unification. This distinction is of great importance, as we shall see later, in considering procedures for the creation of institutions for European unity. Nevertheless, there remains the fact that democratic national governments, by the very nature of their structures, are unfavorably inclined towards federal unification. In the absence of ulterior reasons they are only likely to favor the type of unification which does not involve the irrevocable transfer of power.

A direct consequence springs from these structural problems: namely, that an essential condition for exercising pressure on governments and political parties in favor of genuine federal unification is the existence of an independent movement for a European federation, which is able to persuade them in favor of action they would not, otherwise, take readily on their own.

According to Spinelli, the basic features of such a movement must be:

1. it should not be a political party, but an organization aimed at uniting all supporters of a European federation, irrespective of their political beliefs or social background. This is because a political party seeking national power to achieve European unification would be fatally weakened by intending to transfer to supranational institutions substantial parts of the national power for which it would be competing;
2. it has to be a supranational organization uniting all federalists beyond their national allegiance, so as to imbue them with a supranational loyalty and enable them to organize political action at European level;
3. it must seek to establish direct influence on public opinion, outside national electoral campaigns, which would help it to exert effective pressure on the European policies of governments. One should remember that these have been the guiding principles of the Italian European Federalist Movement from its inception in 1943, even when Spinelli ceased to be its leader and continued to cooperate with the MFE [European Federalist Movement] as an ordinary member, while working in the European Commission or Parliament.

The existence of a European federal movement with these characteristics represents for Spinelli merely a subjective condition for effective federalist action. There is, however, also need for objective conditions for a successful struggle, such as those provided by crises within national political systems.

During periods of relative stability of national political systems, when governments appear able to deal with the principal political, economic or social problems, the movement for a European federation is unable to influence national governments effectively, because public opinion tends to support the latter and their policies. Only at times of acute crisis, when governments are unable to cope and this fact is generally evident, will public opinion be able to share the federalist point of view. At such times the federalist movement ought to be able to mobilize support for federal solutions and persuade governments in favor of them. Spinelli was always convinced that such crises were bound to arise because we are living during a historically critical stage for nation states which, after periods of relative and apparent stability, will be subject to intense crises of their political systems. And this is also true for policies of European unification based on the maintenance of absolute national sovereignty, because intergovernmental cooperation does not provide adequate means for facing such crises, which stem from an irreversible decline of national power of European states.

I will now deal with the second main theme of Spinelli's strategy—the concept of a European constituent assembly.

The fact that national governments are simultaneously the means and the obstacles to the federal unification of Europe carries important implications for the procedure needed to establish European institutions: if one wants federal institutions then one must proceed by way of a constituent assembly and not by the use of intergovernmental or diplomatic conferences.

In other words, Spinelli was always convinced that the creation of European institutions, being entrusted to representatives of national governments, and diplomats in particular, or if they have the last word over the constituent procedure, cannot bring about federal solutions, because the tendency of all such diplomatic negotiations will be the maintenance of absolute national sovereignty at the expense of effective unification. In contrast, in a constituent assembly, composed of people representing public opinion, a favorable attitude towards federal institutions is likely to be incomparably stronger than nationalist tendencies. This is for a number of reasons: (1) the great majority of public opinion (especially in countries first committed to European unification) is in favor of genuine unification and its representatives have to take account of this; (2) the parties and the principal democratic political trends have an international orientation which, by its very nature, would be favorable to a European federation, and would, therefore, back the creation of transnational groups within a European assembly working to strengthen pro-European attitudes; (3) those representing public opinion, unlike the diplomats, do not hold positions of power which are directly dependent on the maintenance of absolute national sovereignty.

Thus, in the event of a critical situation, the pre-eminent task of the movement for a European federation will be to persuade governments (which, at such moments, are susceptible to persuasion by the federalists) to initiate a constituent democratic procedure under which the ultimate responsibility for proposing the nature of the European institutions will be entrusted to the representatives of public opinion, and whose draft of the European constitution will then be directly submitted for ratification to the appropriate constitution organs of the member states, without being subjected to prior diplomatic negotiations.

The concept of a constituent European assembly was patterned by Spinelli on the way the first federal constitution in history was drawn up, namely that of the American constitution, worked out by the Philadelphia Convention in 1787. The example of Philadelphia which, according to him, should provide the model for a European constituent procedure contains three essential elements:

1. governments of individual states have the basic responsibility for initiating the process by conferring the constituent mandate upon the convention, but refrain from interfering in its deliberations;
2. the convention acts by majority votes in drawing up the constitution;
3. the ratification of the constitution is entrusted to the appropriate constitutional organs of individual states, and it comes into force once ratified by a majority of them (in the American case it required ratification by 9 out of the 13 states).

Throughout his federalist campaign Spinelli never ceased to press for the adoption of a constituent procedure on these lines. One needs to stress that for him the essence lay not in the form but the substance of the procedure, namely to give the last word on the constitutional project to a parliamentary assembly. During the various stages of his campaign he proposed various forms of political action, each adapted to prevailing circumstances, to advance the constituent procedure:

1. a constituent assembly elected by universal suffrage with the sole mandate of drawing up a European constitution;
2. the transformation of the consultative parliamentary assembly into a constituent one, either by its own action or by mandate conferred upon it by national governments;
3. by the direct election of a European parliament with a specific constituent mandate;
4. by a popular referendum which would confer the constituent mandate upon the European parliament.

But the substance remained unchanged.

Spinelli's constituent concept stemmed from his belief that the functional approach to European unification will not achieve profound and irreversible unity. He never shared the conviction of the supporters of the functional approach that one can integrate selected sectors of national activity without a federalist constitutional framework from the very start. And this for two fundamental reasons:

1. by refusing to start with a supranational authority of a democratic character, the principle of the national veto is retained (even with a formal acceptance of majority voting). This would deprive European institutions of the capacity to overcome special interests that arise from the exercise of unfettered national sovereignty, and to ensure the supremacy of the common European interest;
2. the chaos and inefficiency which result from the lack of common management of the interdependent economies of modern states and of their foreign and defense policies.

One needs to recognize, however, that Spinelli accepted that unification could start with effective supranational powers being first confined to economic issues, while postponing their immediate adoption in matters of foreign and security policies (as provided in the draft treaty for European Union). And this from the consideration that convergence in the latter sectors was already being influenced by American leadership. But he always stressed the need for genuine federal institutions which would ensure the ultimate extension of supranational powers from economic to defense and foreign policies. That is why he never ceased to insist on the constitutional approach, in place of the functional one, by calling for a federal constitution from the start, obtained by a democratic constituent procedure.

Spinelli's criticism of the functional method was not confined to a dialectical and doctrinaire preference for the constitutional approach. First he was clearly aware that the functional approach stemmed largely from the contradictory nature of the attitudes of national governments to European unification. As objective historical circumstances force them to face the need for supranational unification, whilst they resist giving up their sovereignty, it is natural that they prefer an approach that postpones indefinitely the establishment of an authentic supranational authority. At the same time he recognized that the functional approach could assist the constitutional process by exposing, due to its inadequacy, the contradictions of the former, that could be exploited in the course of the federalist struggle.

These contradictions boil down to two. The first stems from the precariousness and inefficiency of functional unification. Functional institutions established by the unanimous decisions of national governments have shown themselves to be weak and incapable of acting decisively at critical moments when particularly grave problems face them. As a consequence, positive results obtained in more favorable circumstances tend to be compromised or abandoned in time of crisis. This leads to the disappointment of expectations in the development of European integration and can lead to support for federal solutions. The second contradiction stems from the democratic deficit which arises when important responsibilities and powers are transferred to the supranational level without subjecting them to effective democratic control. This causes uneasiness among political parties and to democratically sensitive public opinion which can be thus influenced to favor the concept of supranational democracy. Spinelli's federalist campaign had always aimed at exploiting these contradictions in order to initiate the democratic constituent procedure.

. . .

# 14 A Working Peace System

DAVID MITRANY

*David Mitrany (1888–1975) was a Romanian-born academic who spent most of his adult life in Britain and the United States. During World War II, Mitrany—who had been profoundly influenced by the radical intellectual currents of interwar London—thought seriously about the shape of the postwar world and how to prevent future wars. The result of his reflection was a pamphlet entitled* A Working Peace System, *which he published in the summer of 1943, two years before the end of the war. In this pamphlet, Mitrany argued for a transformation of the way people think about international relations, particularly the prevention of war. His "functional alternative" aimed at world, not European, unity. Nevertheless, it had a profound effect on European activists and early integration theorists, especially the neofunctionalists (see Chapters 16 and 17).*

*Mitrany saw the division of the world into "competing political units" as the root of international conflict. A world federal government, he argued, would eliminate these divisions but would be impossible to establish given the modern "disregard for constitutions and pacts" and continuing nationalism. Mitrany called, instead, for a functional approach that would "overlay political divisions with a spreading web of international activities and agencies, in which and through which the interests and life of all the nations would be gradually integrated." Functional integration would be rational, pragmatic, technocratic, and flexible; it would deliberately blur national and international, public and private, and political and nonpolitical distinctions. As functional agencies were formed and joined, national divisions would become less and less important. Ultimately, a central*

Reprinted from *A Working Peace System* (Quadrangle Books, 1966).  Notes omitted.

*authority might coordinate the various agencies, but such a government would not be necessary to successful international relations, and might not be desirable. Here Mitrany parted with many other functionalists (such as Monnet) and the neofunctionalists who believed federal institutions were essential to the success of functional integration. Mitrany was far less sanguine about the value of the state and its institutions, reflecting an anarchic streak that led him to distrust political authority.*

## ■ THE GENERAL PROBLEM

The need for some new kind of international system was being widely canvassed before the Second World War, in the measure in which the League of Nations found itself frustrated in its attempts to prevent aggression and to organize peace. Some blamed this failure on the irresponsibility of small states; others rather the egoism of the Great Powers. Still others imputed the League's failure more directly to weaknesses in its own constitution and machinery: the proper ingredients were there, but the political dosage was inadequate. It was especially among those who held this view that the idea of a wide international federation began to be embraced as a new hope.

Federation seemed indeed the only alternative to a League tried so far for linking together a number of political units by democratic methods. It would mean an association much closer than was the League, and its advocacy therefore takes it for granted that the League failed because it did not go far enough. In what way would federation go further? Federation would be a more intensive union of a less extensive group; the constitutional ties would be closer. Second, certain activities would be more definitely and actively tied together. More definite common action is clearly the end; the formal arrangements which the federalists put in the forefront would be merely a necessary adjunct, to ensure the reliable working of the federal undertakings. And that is as it should be for, leaving formal arguments aside, it is plain that the League failed not from overstrain but from inanition. It might have done more about sanctions, but that would not have been enough. Even if the League's action for "security" had been more fearless, that would not by itself have sufficed to give vitality to an international system that was to last and grow. To achieve that end, such a system must in some important respects take over and coordinate activities hitherto controlled by the national state, just as the state increasingly has to take over activities which until now have been carried on by local bodies; and like the state, any new international authority could under present conditions not be merely a police authority.

We realize now that the League failed because, whatever the reasons, it could not further that process of continuous adjustment and settlement which students of international affairs call "peaceful change." But they themselves, taking the form for the substance, all too often thought of it mainly as a matter of changing frontiers. We shall have to speak of this again, but what peaceful change should mean, what the modern world, so closely interrelated, must have for its peaceful development, is some system that would make possible automatic and continuous social action, continually adapted to changing needs and conditions, in the same sense and of the same general nature as any other system of government. Its character would be the same for certain purposes; only the range would be new. It is in that sense that the League's work has in truth been inadequate and ineffective, as one may readily see if one reflects whether a change of frontiers now and then would really have led to a peaceful and cooperative international society.

A close federation is supposed to do just what the League proved unable to do, and in a set and solid way. But to begin with, can we take a system which has worked well in one field and simply transplant it to another, so much wider and more complex? Federations have still been national federations; the jump from national states to international organization is infinitely more hazardous than was the jump from provincial units to national federations. None of the elements of neighborhood, of kinship, of history are there to serve as steps. The British Empire is bound closely by old ties of kinship and history, but no one would suggest that there is among its parts much will for federation. Yet apart from this matter of whether the federal idea has any great prospects, there is the more important question whether it would have any great virtues in the international sphere. If the evil of conflict and war springs from the division of the world into detached and competing political units, will it be exorcised simply by changing or reducing the lines of division? Any political reorganization into separate units must sooner or later produce the same effects; any international system that is to usher in a new world must produce the opposite effect of subduing political division. As far as one can see, there are only two ways of achieving that end. One would be through a world state which would wipe out political divisions forcibly; the other is the way discussed in these pages, which would rather overlay political divisions with a spreading web of international activities and agencies, in which and through which the interests and life of all the nations would be gradually integrated. That is the fundamental change to which any effective international system must aspire and contribute: to make international government coextensive with international activities. A League would be too loose to be able to do it; a number of sectional federations would, on the contrary, be too tight to be welded into something like it. Therefore when the need is so great and pressing, we must have the vision to break away from traditional political ideas, which in modern times have always linked authority to a given territory, and try some new way that might take us without violence toward that goal. The beginnings cannot be anything but experimental; a new international system will need, even more than national systems, a wide freedom of continuous adaptation in the light of experience. It must care as much as possible for common needs that are evident, while presuming as little as possible upon a global unity which is still only latent and unrecognized. As the late John Winant well said in a lecture at Leeds in October 1942: "We must be absolute about our principal ends (justice and equality of opportunity and freedom), relative and pragmatic about the mechanical means used to serve those ends."

The need for a pragmatic approach is all the greater because we are so clearly in a period of historical transition. When the state itself, whatever its form and constitution, is everywhere undergoing a deep social and political sea-change, it is good statesmanship not to force the new international experiments into some set familiar form, which may be less relevant the more respectable it seems, but to see above all that these experiments go with and fit into the general trend of the time.

When one examines the general shape of the tasks that are facing us, one is, to begin with, led to question whether order could be brought into them by the device of formal written pacts. Why did written constitutions, declarations of rights, and other basic charters play such a great role during the nineteenth century? The task of that time, following the autocratic period, was to work out a new division of the sphere of authority, to determine new relationships between the individual and the state, to protect the new democracy. These relationships were meant to be fixed and final, and they had to rest on general principles, largely of a negative character. It was natural and proper that all that should be laid down in formal rules, meant to remain untouched and permanent. In much the same way the new nation state was in world society what the new citizen was in municipal society; and with the increase in their number, the liberal growth in international trade and cultural and social intercourse, the resulting international rules and a host of written treaties and pacts sought, like the national constitutions, to fix the formal relationship between the sovereign individual states and their collectivity; which in this case also was expected to be fixed and final, with international law as a gradually emerging constitution for that political cosmos.

Viewed in this light, the Covenant of the League is seen to have continued that nineteenth-century tradition. It was concerned above all with fixing in a definite way the formal relationship of the member states and in a measure also of non-members, and only in a very secondary way with initiating positive common activities and action. The great expectation, security, was a vital action, but a negative one; its end was not to promote the active regular life of the peoples but only to protect it against being disturbed. Broadly one might say that the Covenant was an attempt to universalize and codify the rules of international conduct, gradually evolved through political treaties and pacts, and to give them general and permanent validity. It was neither unnatural nor unreasonable to follow up that nineteenth-century trend and try to steady international relations by bringing them within the framework of a written pact, one provided with set rules for its working. But when it came to going beyond that, the League could not be more or do more than what its leading members were ready to be and do, and they were ready to do but little in a positive way. It was indeed characteristic of the post-Armistice period 1918–19 that even the victors hastened to undo their common economic and other machinery, such as the Allied Shipping Control, which had grown and served them well during the war. And that was at a time when within each country government action and control were spreading fast, causing many a private international activity also to be cut down or cut off. In other words, the incipient common functions, as well as many old connections, were disbanded in the international sphere at the very time when a common constitution was being laid down for it. It was that divorce between life and form that doomed the League from the outset, and not any inadequacy in its written rules.

Hence it is pertinent to ask: Would another written pact, if only more elaborate and stringent, come to grips more closely with the problems of our time? Let us by way of a preliminary answer note two things: First, the lusty disregard for constitutions and pacts, for settled rules and traditional rights, is a striking mark of the times. In the pressure for social change no such formal ties are allowed to stand in the way, either within the several countries or between them. It is a typical revolutionary mood and practice. If it does not always take the outward form of revolution, that is because the governments themselves act as spearheads of the trend, and not only in countries ruled by dictatorships. Those who lead in this rush for social change pride themselves indeed on their disregard for forms and formalities. The appeal which communism, fascism, and nazism had for youth in particular and for the masses in general lies in no small degree in that political iconoclasm. At the turn of the nineteenth century the radical masses were demanding settled rules and rights, and Napoleon could play the trump card of constitutional nationalism against the autocratic rulers. Now the masses demand social action without regard to established "rights," and the totalitarian leaders have been playing the strong card of pragmatic socialism against constitutional democracy.

That universal pressure for social reform, in the second place, has utterly changed the relation of nationalism to internationalism, in a way that could be promising if rightly used. In constitution-making there was a parallel between the two spheres, but nothing more, for they belonged politically to different categories. The nineteenth-century nationalism rested mainly on cultural and other differential factors, and the creation of the nation state meant inevitably a breaking up of world unity. A cosmopolitan outlook spread rapidly, but the nations at the same time balked at international political organization and control, and they could justify that refusal by seemingly good principle. At present the new nationalism rests essentially on social factors; these are not only alike in the various countries, thus paradoxically creating a bond even between totalitarian groups, but often cannot make progress in isolation. At many points the life of the nation state is overflowing back into that common world which existed before the rise of modern nationalism. At present the lines of national and international evolution are not parallel but converging, and the two spheres now belong to the same category and differ only in dimensions.

In brief, the function of the nineteenth century was to restrain the powers of authority; that led to the creation of the "political man" and likewise of the "political nation," and to the definition through constitutional pacts of their relation to the wider political group. The Covenant (and the Locarno and Kellogg pacts) was still of that species essentially, with the characteristic predominance of rules of the "thou shall not" kind. The function of our time is rather to develop and coordinate the social scope of authority, and that cannot be so defined or divided. Internationally it is no longer a question of defining relations between states but of merging them—the workday sense of the vague talk about the need to surrender some part of sovereignty. A constitutional pact could do little more than lay down certain elementary rights and duties for the members of the new community. The community itself will acquire a living body not through a written act of faith but through active organic development. Yet there is in this no fundamental dispute as to general principles and ultimate aims. The only question is, which is the more immediately practicable and promising way: whether a general political framework should be provided formally in advance, on some theoretical pattern, or left to grow branch by branch from action and experience and so find its natural bent.

## ■ THE FUNCTIONAL ALTERNATIVE

Can these vital objections be met, and the needs of peace and social advance be satisfied, through some other way of associating the nations for common action? The whole trend of modern government indicates such a way. That trend is to organize government along the lines of specific ends and needs, and according to the conditions of their time and place, in lieu of the traditional organization on the basis of a set constitutional division of jurisdiction and of rights and powers. In national government the definition of authority and the scope of public action are now in a continuous flux, and are determined less by constitutional norms than by practical requirements. The instances are too many and well known to need mentioning; one might note only that while generally the trend has been toward greater centralization of services, and therefore of authority, under certain conditions the reverse has also occurred, powers and duties being handed over to regional and other authorities for the better performance of certain communal needs. The same trend is powerfully at work in the several federations, in Canada and Australia, and especially in the United States, and in these cases it is all the more striking because the division of authority rests on written constitutions which are still in being and nominally valid in full. Internationally, too, while a body of law had grown slowly and insecurely through rules and conventions, some common activities were organized through ad hoc functional arrangements and have worked well. The rise of such specific administrative agencies and laws is the peculiar trait, and indeed the foundation, of modern government.

A question which might properly be asked at the outset in considering the fitness of that method for international purposes is this: Could such functions be organized internationally without a comprehensive political framework? Let it be said, first, that the functional method as such is neither incompatible with a general constitutional framework nor precludes its coming into being. It only follows Burke's warning to the sheriffs of Bristol that "government is a practical thing" and that one should beware of elaborating constitutional forms "for the gratification of visionaries." In national states and federations the functional development is going ahead without much regard to, and sometimes in spite of, the old constitutional divisions. If in these cases the constitution is most conveniently left aside, may not the method prove workable internationally without any immediate and comprehensive constitutional framework? If, to cite Burke again, it is "always dangerous to meddle with foundations," it is doubly dangerous now. Our political problems are obscure, while the political passions of the time are blinding. One of the misfortunes of the League experiment was that a new institution was devised on what have proved to be outworn premises. We might also recollect that of the constitutional changes introduced in Europe after the First World War, fine and wise though they may have been, none has survived even a generation. How much greater will that risk of futility be in Europe after the Second World War, when the split within and between nations will be much worse than in 1919? We know now even less about the dark historical forces which have been stirred up by the war, while in the meantime the problems of our common society have been distorted by fierce ideologies which we could not try to bring to an issue without provoking an irreconcilable dogmatic conflict. Even if an action were to be to some extent handicapped without a formal political framework, the fact is that no obvious sentiment exists, and none is likely to crystallize for some years, for a common constitutional bond.

In such conditions any pre-arranged constitutional framework would be taken wholly out of the air. We do not know what, if anything, will be in common—except a desperate craving for peace and for the conditions of a tolerable normal life. The peoples may applaud declarations of rights, but they will call for the satisfaction of needs. That demand for action could be turned into a historic opportunity. Again we might take to heart what happened to the U.S. in 1932–33 and think of what chances the Roosevelt administration would have to have had to achieve unity, or indeed to survive, if instead of taking immediate remedial action it had begun by offering constitutional reforms—though a common system was already in being. A timid statesman might still have tried to walk in the old constitutional grooves; Mr. Roosevelt stepped over them. He grasped both the need and opportunity for centralized practical action. Unemployment, the banking collapse, flood control, and a hundred other problems had to be dealt with by national means if they were to be dealt with effectively and with lasting results.

The significant point in that emergency action was that each and every problem was tackled as a practical issue in itself. No attempt was made to relate it to a general theory or system of government. Every function was left to generate others gradually, like the functional subdivision of organic cells; and in every case the appropriate authority was left to grow and develop out of actual performance. Yet the new functions and the new organs, taken together, have revolutionized the American political system. The federal government has become a national government, and Washington for the first time is really the capital of America. In the process, many improvements in the personnel and machinery of government have come about, and many restrictive state regulations have melted away. More recently there has been heard the significant complaint that the ties between cities and their states are becoming looser, while those with the national government become ever stronger. No one has worked to bring this about, and no written act has either prescribed it or confirmed it. A great constitutional transformation has thus taken place without any changes in the Constitution. There have been complaints, but the matter-of-course acceptance has been overwhelming. People have gladly accepted the service when they might have questioned the theory. The one attempt at direct constitutional revision, to increase and liberalize the membership of the Supreme Court, was bitterly disputed and defeated. Yet that proposal involved in effect much less of a constitutional revolution than has the experiment of the Tennessee Valley Authority. The first would not have ensured any lasting change in the working of the American government, whereas the second has really introduced into the political structure of the United States a new regional dimension unknown to the Constitution.

In many of its essential aspects—the urgency of the material needs, the inadequacy of the old arrangements, the bewilderment in outlook—the situation at the end of the Second World War will resemble that in America in 1933, though on a wider and deeper scale. And for the same reasons the path pursued by Mr. Roosevelt in 1933 offers the best, perhaps the only, chance for getting a new international life going. It will be said inevitably that in the United States it was relatively easy to follow that line of action because it was in fact one country, with an established Constitution. Functional arrangements could be accepted, that is, because in many fields the federal states had grown in the habit of working together. That is no doubt true, but not the most significant point of the American experiment; for that line was followed not because the functional way was so easy but because the constitutional way would have been so difficult. Hence the lesson for unfederated parts of the world would seem to be this: If the constitutional path had to be avoided for the sake of effective action even in a federation which already was a working political system, how much less promising must it be as a starting mode when it is a matter of bringing together for the first time a number of varied, and sometimes antagonistic, countries? But if the constitutional approach, by its very circumspectness, would hold up the start of a working international system, bold initiative during the period of emergency at the end of the war might set going lasting instruments and habits of a common international life. And though it may appear rather brittle, that functional approach would in fact be more solid and definite than a formal one. It need not meddle with foundations; old institutions and ways may to some extent hamper reconstruction, but reconstruction could begin by a common effort without a fight over established ways. Reconstruction may in this field also prove a surer and less costly way than revolution. As to the new ideologies, since we could not prevent them we must try to circumvent them, leaving it to the growth of new habits and interests to dilute them in time. Our aim must be to call forth to the highest possible degree the active forces and opportunities for cooperation, while touching as little as possible the latent or active points of difference and opposition.

There is one other aspect of the post-war period which has been much discussed and has a bearing on this point, and which helps to bring out the difference in outlook between the two methods contrasted here. Much has been heard of a suggestion that when the war ends we must have first a period of convalescence and that the task of permanent reorganization will only come after that. It is a useful suggestion, insofar as it may help to clear up certain practical problems. But it could also be misleading and even dangerous if the distinction were taken to justify either putting off the work of international government or differentiating between the agencies by which the new international activities are to be organized, into nurses for convalescence and mentors for the new life. A clean division in time between two such periods in any case is not possible, for the period of convalescence will be different for different activities and ends; but, above all, except for such direct and exceptional consequences of the war as demobilization and the rebuilding of damaged areas, the needs of society will be the same at once after the war as later on. The only difference will be the practical one of a priority of needs, the kind of difference which might be brought about by any social disturbance—an epidemic or an earthquake or an economic crisis—and the urgency of taking action. For the rest, one action and period will merge into the other, according to circumstances. Seed and implements will be as urgent for ensuring the food supply of Europe and Asia as the actual distribution of relief, and indeed more urgent if the war should end after a harvest. Again, both relief and reconstruction will depend greatly on the speedy reorganization and proper use of transport, and so on.

Both circumstances point again to the advantage of a functional practice and to the disadvantage, if not the impossibility, of a comprehensive attempt at political organization. To obtain sufficient agreement for some formal general scheme would, at best, not be possible without delay; at the same time, action for relief and reconstruction will have to start within the hour after the ceasefire. The alternatives would be, if a comprehensive constitutional arrangement is desired and waited for, either to put the immediate work in the hands of temporary international agencies or to leave it to the individual states. The one, in fact, would prepare for the other. Except in matters of relief—the distribution of food, fuel, and clothing and also medical help—*ad hoc* temporary agencies could have no adequate authority or influence; all of what one might call the society-building activities, involving probably considerable planning and reorganization within and between the several countries, would fall upon the individual states again, as in 1919, when they competed and interfered rather than cooperated with each other, to the loss of them all. Yet it is vital that international activity should be from the outset in the same hands and move in the same direction after the war as later; otherwise the chances of building up an international system would be gravely prejudiced. It is certain that one of the chief reasons for the failure of the League was that it was given a formal authority and promissory tasks for the future, while the immediate, urgent, and most welcome tasks of social reconstruction and reform were left to be attended to by national agencies. Later efforts to retrieve that mistake only led to a series of barren economic conferences, as by that time the policy of each country was set hard in its own mold. It is inevitable with any scheme of formal organization that the national states should have to re-start on their own, and natural therefore that refuge should be sought in the idea of a period of convalescence while the full-fledged scheme is worked out and adopted. But functional authorities would not need such political hospitalization, with its arbitrary and dangerous division of stages; they would merely vary, like any other agency anywhere and at any time, the emphasis of their work in accordance with the changing condition of their task, continuing to control and organize transport, for instance, after they had rebuilt it, and in the same way taking each task in hand with a plan and authority for continuing it. The simple fact is that all the re-starting of agriculture and industry and transport will either be done on some pre-arranged common program or it will have to be done, for it could not wait, on disjointed local plans; it will be done either by pre-established international agencies or it will have to be done by local national agencies—and the agencies which will act in the supposed convalescence period will also be those to gather authority and acceptance unto themselves.

. . .

## The Broad Lines of Functional Organization

The problem of our generation, put very broadly, is how to weld together the common interests of all without interfering unduly with the particular ways of each. It is a parallel problem to that which faces us in national society, and which in both spheres challenges us to find an alternative to the totalitarian pattern. A measure of centralized planning and control, for both production and distribution, is no longer to be avoided, no matter what the form of the state or the doctrine of its constitution. Through all that variety of political forms there is a growing approximation in the working of government, with differences merely of degree and of detail. Liberal democracy needs a redefinition of the public and private spheres of action. But as the line of separation is always shifting under the pressure of fresh social needs and demands, it must be left free to move with those needs and demands and cannot be fixed through a constitutional re-instatement. The only possible principle of democratic confirmation is that public action should be undertaken only where and when and insofar as the need for common action becomes evident and is accepted for the sake of the common good. In that way controlled democracy could yet be made the golden mean whereby social needs might be satisfied as largely and justly as possible, while still leaving as wide a residue as possible for the free choice of the individual.

That is fully as true for the international sphere. It is indeed the only way to combine, as well as may be, international organization with national freedom. We have already suggested that not all interests are common to all, and that the common interests do not concern all countries in the same degree. A territorial union would bind together some interests which are not of common concern to the group, while it would inevitably cut asunder some interests of common concern to the group and those outside it. The only way to avoid that twice-arbitrary surgery is to proceed by means of a natural selection, binding together those interests which are common, where they are common, and to the extent to which they are common. That functional selection and organization of international needs would extend, and in a way resume, an international development which has been gathering strength since the latter part of the nineteenth century. The work of organizing international public services and activities was taken a step further by the League, in its health and drug-control work, in its work for refugees, in the experiments with the transfer of minorities and the important innovations of the League loan system, and still more through the whole activity of the ILO [International Labour Organisation]. But many other activities and interests in the past had been organized internationally by private agencies—in finance and trade and production, etc., not to speak of scientific and cultural activities. In recent years some of these activities have been brought under public national control in various countries; in totalitarian countries indeed all of them. In a measure, therefore, the present situation represents a retrogression from the recent past: the new turn toward self-sufficiency has spread from economics to the things of the mind; and while flying and wireless were opening up the world, many old links forged by private effort have been forcibly severed. It is unlikely that most of them could be resumed now except through public action, and if they are to operate as freely as they did in private hands they cannot be organized otherwise than on a nondiscriminating functional basis.

What would be the broad lines of such a functional organization of international activities? The essential principle is that activities would be selected specifically and organized separately—each according to its nature, to the conditions under which it has to operate, and to the needs of the moment. It would allow, therefore, all freedom for practical variation in the organization of the several functions, as well as in the working of a particular function as needs and conditions alter. Let us take as an example the group of functions which fall under communications, on which the success of post-war reconstruction will depend greatly. What is the proper basis for the international organization of *railway* systems? Clearly it must be European, or rather *continental*, North American, and so on, as that gives the logical administrative limit of coordination. A division of the Continent into separate democratic and totalitarian unions would not achieve the practical end, as political division would obstruct that necessary coordination; while British and American participation would make the organization more cumbersome without any added profit to the function. As regards shipping, the line of effective organization which at once suggests itself is *international*, or intercontinental, but not universal. A European union could not solve the problem of maritime coordination without the cooperation of America and of certain other overseas states.

*Aviation* and *broadcasting*, a third example in the same group, could be organized effectively only on a *universal* scale, with perhaps subsidiary regional arrangements for more local services. Such subsidiary regional arrangements could in fact be inserted at any time and at any stage where that might prove useful for any part of a function. Devolution according to need would be as easy and natural as centralization, whereas if the basis of organization were political every such change in dimension would involve an elaborate constitutional re-arrangement. Similarly, it could be left safely to be determined by practical considerations whether at the points where functions cross each other—such as rail and river transport in Europe and America—the two activities should be merely coordinated or put under one control.

These are relatively simple examples. The functional coordination of production, trade, and distribution evidently would be more complex, especially as they have been built up on a competitive basis. But the experience with international cartels, with the re-organization of the shipping, cotton, and steel industries in England, not to speak of the even wider and more relevant experience with economic coordination in the two world wars—all shows that the thing can be done and that it has always been done on such functional lines. No fixed rule is needed, and no rigid pattern is desirable for the organization of these working functional strata.

A certain degree of fixity would not be out of place, however, in regard to more *negative* functions, especially those related to law and order, but also to any others of a more formal nature which are likely to remain fairly static. Security, for instance, could be organized on an interlocking regional basis, and the judicial function likewise, with a hierarchy of courts, as the need may arise—the wider acting as courts of appeal from the more local courts. Yet, even in regard to security, and in addition to regional arrangements, the elasticity inherent in functional organization may prove practicable and desirable, if only in the period of transition. Anglo-American naval cooperation for the policing of the seas may prove acceptable for a time, and it would cut across physical regions. Agreement on a mineral sanction would of necessity mean common action by those countries which control the main sources; and other such combinations might be found useful for any particular task in hand. That is security only for defense; security arrangements were conceived usually on a geographical basis because they were meant to prevent violence, and that would still be the task of sanctions, etc., based on some regional devolution. But in addition there is a growing functional devolution in the field of social security in connection with health, with the drug and white slave traffic, with crime, etc. In all that important field of social policing it has been found that coordination and cooperation with the police of other countries on functional lines, varying with each task, was both indispensable and practicable. There is no talk and no attempt in all this to encroach upon sovereignty, but only a detached functional association which works smoothly and is already accepted without question.

However that may be, in the field of more *positive* active functions—economic, social, cultural—which are varied and ever changing in structure and purpose, any devolution must, like the main organization, follow functional lines. Land transport on the Continent would need a different organization and agencies should the railways after a time be displaced by roads; and a Channel tunnel would draw England into an arrangement in which she does not at present belong, with a corresponding change in the governing organ.

Here we discover a cardinal virtue of the functional method—what one might call the virtue of technical self-determination. The functional *dimensions*, as we have seen, determine its appropriate *organs*. It also reveals through practice the nature of the action required under given conditions, and in that way the *powers* needed by the respective authority. The function, one might say, determines the executive instrument suitable for its proper activity, and by the same process provides a need for the reform of the instrument at every stage. This would allow the widest latitude for variation between functions, and also in the dimension or organization of the same function as needs and conditions change. Not only is there in all this no need for any fixed constitutional division of authority and power, prescribed in advance, but anything beyond the original formal definition of scope and purpose might embarrass the working of the practical arrangements.

## □ *The Question of Wider Coordination*

The question will be asked, however, in what manner and to what degree the various functional agencies that may thus grow up would have to be linked to each other and articulated as parts of a more comprehensive organization. It should be clear that each agency could work by itself, but that does not exclude the possibility of some of them or all being bound in some way together, if it should be found needful or useful to do so. That indeed is the test. As the whole sense of this particular method is to let activities be organized as the need for joint action arises and is accepted, it would be out of place to lay down in advance some formal plan for the coordination of various functions. Coordination, too, would in that sense have to come about functionally. Yet certain needs and possibilities can be foreseen already now, though some are probable and others only likely, and it may help to round off the picture if we look into this aspect briefly.

1. *Within the same group* of functions probably there would have to be coordination either simply for technical purposes or for wider functional ends, and this would be the first stage toward a wider integration. To take again the group concerned with communications—rail, road, and air transport in Europe would need *technical* coordination in regard to timetables, connections, etc. They may need also a wider *functional* coordination if there is to be some distribution of passenger and freight traffic for the most economic performance—whether that is done by a superior executive agency or by some arbitral body, perhaps on the lines of the Federal Commerce Commission in America. Sea and air traffic across the Atlantic or elsewhere, though separately organized, probably would also benefit from a similar type of coordination. Again, various mineral controls, if they should be organized separately, would need some coordination, though this arbitrary grouping of "minerals" would be less to the point that the coordination of specific minerals and other products with possible substitutes—of crude oil with synthetic oil, of crude rubber with synthetic rubber, and so on.

2. The next degree or stage might be, if found desirable, the coordination of *several groups* of functional agencies. For instance, the communications agencies may not only work out some means of acting together in the distribution of orders for rolling stock, ships, etc., but they could or should work in this through any agencies that may have come into being for controlling materials and production, or through some intermediary agency as a clearinghouse. There is no need to prescribe any pattern in advance, or that the pattern adopted in one case should be followed in all the others.

3. The coordination of such working functional agencies with any *international planning* agencies would present a third stage, and one that brings out some interesting possibilities, should the ideas for an international investment board or an international development commission, as an advisory organ, come to fruition. One can see how such a development commission might help to guide the growth of functional agencies into the most desirable channels, and could watch their inter-relations and their repercussions. And an investment board could guide, for instance, the distribution of orders for ships, materials, etc., not only according to the best economic use but also for the purpose of ironing out cyclical trends. It could use, ac-

cording to its nature, its authority or its influence to make of such orders a means additional to international public works, etc., for dealing with periods or pockets of unemployment. Coordination of such a general kind may in some cases amount almost to arbitration of differences between functional agencies; regional boards or councils like those of the Pan-American Union might be used to adjust or arbitrate regional differences.

4. Beyond this there remains the habitual assumption, as we have already said, that international action must have some overall *political authority* above it. Besides the fact that such a comprehensive authority is not now a practical possibility, it is the central view of the functional approach that such an authority is not essential for our greatest and real immediate needs. The several functions could be organized through the agreement, given specifically in each case, of the national governments chiefly interested, with the grant of the requisite powers and resources; whereas it is clear, to emphasize the previous point, that they could not allow such organizations simply to be prescribed by some universal authority, even if it existed. For an authority which had the title to do so would in effect be hardly less than a world government; and such a strong central organism would inevitably tend to take unto itself rather more authority than that originally allotted to it, this calling in turn for the checks and balances which are used in federal systems, but which would be difficult to provide in any loose way. If issues should arise in any functional system which would call either for some new departure or for the reconsideration of existing arrangements, that could be done only in council by all the governments concerned. Insofar as it may be desired to keep alive some general view of our problems, and perhaps a general watch over the policies of the several joint agencies, some body of a representative kind, like the League Assembly or the governing body of the ILO, could meet periodically, perhaps elected by proportional representation from the assemblies of the member states. Such an assembly, in which all the states would have a voice, could discuss and ventilate general policies, as an expression of the mind and will of public opinion; but it could not actually prescribe policy, as this might turn out to be at odds with the policy of governments. Any line of action recommended by such an assembly would have to be pressed and secured through the policy-making machinery of the various countries themselves.

These, then, are the several types and grades of coordination which might develop with the growth of functional activities. But there is, finally, in the political field also the problem of security, admittedly a crucial problem, for on its being solved effectively the successful working of the other activities will depend. At the same time, the general discussion of functional organization will have served to bring out the true place and proportion of security, as something indispensable but also as something incapable by itself of achieving the peaceful growth of an international society. It is in fact a separate function like the others, not something that stands in stern isolation, overriding all the others. Looking at it in this way, as a practical function, should also make it clear that we would not achieve much if we handled it as a one-sided, limited problem—at present too often summed up in "German aggression." German aggression was a particularly vicious outgrowth of a bad general system, and only a radical and general change of the system itself will provide continuous security for all. In this case also it would be useful to lay down some formal pledges and principles as a guiding line, but the practical organization would have to follow functional, perhaps combined with regional, lines. That is all the more necessary as we know better now how many elements besides the purely military enter into the making of security. The various functional agencies might, in fact, play an important role in that wide aspect of security; they could both watch over and check such things as the building of strategic railways or the accumulation of strategic stocks in metals or grains. Possibly they could even be used, very properly and effectively, as a first line of action against threatening aggression, by their withholding services from those who are causing the trouble. They could apply such preventive sanctions more effectively than if this were to wait upon the agreement and action of a number of separate governments; and they could do so as part of their practical duties, and therefore with less of the political reactions caused by political action.

### *Representation in Controls*

One aspect likely to be closely examined is that of the structure of the functional controls, and here again the initial difficulty will be that we shall have to break away from attractive traditional ideas if we are to work out the issue on its merits. It is not in the nature of the method that representation on the controlling bodies should be democratic in a political sense, full and equal for all. Ideally it may seem that all functions should be organized on a worldwide scale and that all states should have a voice in control. Yet the weight of reality is on the side of making the jurisdiction of the various agencies no wider than the most effective working limits of the function; and while it is understandable that all countries might wish to have a voice in control, that would be really to hark back to the outlook of political sovereignty. In no functional organization so far have the parties interested had a share in control as "by right" of their separate existence—neither the various local authorities in the London Transport Board, nor the seven states concerned in the TVA [Tennessee Valley Authority]. And in any case, in the transition from power politics to a functional order we could be well satisfied if the control of the new international organs answered to some of the merits of each case, leaving it to experience and to the maturing of a new outlook to provide in time the necessary correctives.

. . .

## ■ THROUGH FUNCTIONAL ACTION TO INTERNATIONAL SOCIETY

### □ *The Way of Natural Selection*

One cannot insist too much that such gradual functional developments would not create a new system, however strange they might appear in the light of our habitual search for a unified formal order. They would merely rationalize and develop what is already there. In all countries social activities, in the widest sense of the term, are organized and reorganized continually in that way. But because of the legalistic structure of the state and of our political outlook, which treat national and international society as two different worlds, social nature, so to speak, has not had a chance so far to take its course. Our social activities are cut off arbitrarily at the limit of the state and, if at all, are allowed to be linked to the same activities across the border only by means of uncertain and cramping political ligatures. What is here proposed is simply that these political amputations should cease. Whenever useful or necessary the several activities would be released to function as one unit throughout the length of their natural course. National problems would then appear, and would be treated, as what they are—the local segments of general problems.

. . .

### □ *Epilogue*

Peace will not be secured if we organize the world by what divides it. But in the measure in which such peace-building activities develop and succeed, one might hope that the mere prevention of conflict, crucial as that may be, would in time fall to a subordinate place in the scheme of international things, while we would turn to what are the real tasks of our common society—the conquest of poverty and of disease and of ignorance. The stays of political federation were needed when life was more local and international activities still loose. But now our social interdependence is all-pervasive and all-embracing, and if it be so organized the political side will also grow as part of it. The elements of a functional system could begin to work without a general political authority, but a political authority without active social functions would remain an empty temple. Society will develop by our living it, not by policing it. Nor would any political agreement survive long under economic competition, but economic unification would build up the foundation for political agreement, even if it did not make it superfluous. In any case, as things are, the political way is too ambitious. We cannot start from an ideal plane but must be prepared to make many attempts from many points, and build things and mend things as we go along. The essential thing is that we should be going together, in the same direction, and that we get into step now.

. . .

Cooperation for the common good is the task, both for the sake of peace and of a better life, and for that it is essential that certain interests and activities should be taken out of the mood of competition and worked together. But it is not essential to make that cooperation fast to a territorial authority, and indeed it would be senseless to do so when the number of those activities is limited, while their range is the world. "Economic areas do not always run with political areas," wrote the *New York Times* (February 26, 1943) in commenting on the Alaska Highway scheme, and such cross-country cooperation would simply make frontiers less important. "Apply this principle to certain European areas and the possibilities are dazzling." If it be said that all that may be possible in war but hardly in peace, that can only mean that practically the thing is possible but that we doubt whether in normal times there would be the political will to do it. Now, apart from everything else, the functional method stands out as a solid touchstone in that respect. Promissory covenants and charters may remain a headstone to unfulfilled good intentions, but the functional way is action itself and therefore an inescapable test of where we stand and how far we are willing to go in building up a new international society. It is not a promise to act in a crisis, but itself the action that will avoid the crisis. Every activity organized in that way would be a layer of peaceful life; and a sufficient addition of them would create increasingly deep and wide strata of peace—not the forbidding peace of an alliance, but one that would suffuse the world with a fertile mingling of common endeavor and achievement.

This is not an argument against any ideal of formal union, if that should prove a possible ultimate goal. It is, above all, a plea for the creation now of the elements of an active international society. Amidst the tragedy of war one can glimpse also the promise of a broader outlook, of a much deeper understanding of the issues than in 1918. It is because the peoples are ready for action that they cannot wait. We have no means and no standing to work out some fine constitution and try to impose it in time upon the world. But we do have the standing and the means to prepare for immediate practical action. We do not know what will be the sentiments of the peoples of Europe and of other continents at the end of the war, but we do know what their needs will be. *Any* political scheme would start a disputation; *any* working arrangement would raise a hope and make for confidence and patience.

The functional way may seem a spiritless solution—and so it is, in the sense that it detaches from the spirit the things which are of the body. No advantage has accrued to anyone when economic and other social activities are wedded to fascist or communist or other political ideologies; their progeny has always been confusion and conflict. Let these things appear quite starkly for what they are, practical household tasks, and it will be more difficult to make them into the household idols of "national interest" and "national honor." The ideological movements of our time, because of their indiscriminate zeal, have sometimes been compared to religious movements. They may be, but at their core was not a promise of life hereafter. The things which are truly of the spirit—and therefore personal to the individual and to the nation—will not be less winged for being freed in their turn from that worldly ballast. Hence the argument that opposes democracy to totalitarianism does not call the real issue. It is much too simple. Society is everywhere in travail because it is everywhere in transition. Its problem after a century of laissez faire philosophy is to sift anew, in the light of new economic possibilities and of new social aspirations, what is private from what has to be public; and in the latter sphere what is local and national from what is wider. And for that task of broad social refinement a more discriminating instrument is needed than the old political sieve. In the words of a statement by the American National Policy Committee, "Part of the daring required is the daring to find new forms and to adopt them. We are lost if we dogmatically assume that the procedures of the past constitute the only true expression of democracy."

# 15 Political Community and the North Atlantic Area

KARL W. DEUTSCH ET AL.

*In the 1950s, with memories of World War II still fresh and the Cold War threatening to burn hot, the issue of war and peace in Europe remained vital. European politicians were busy abolishing war between France and Germany by laying the foundation for a united Europe. In the meantime, U.S. social scientists, many of them immigrants from the Continent, began systematically studying the European integration process to discover what propelled it and whether it would actually ensure peace.*

*One of these academics, a 1938 German-Czech refugee named Karl W. Deutsch (1912–1992), helped revolutionize the study of international relations by introducing scientific and quantitative methods. While at the Massachusetts Institute of Technology (he later taught at Yale and Harvard), he and seven of his colleagues applied their new social scientific skills to "the study of possible ways in which men someday might abolish war." The result of this study was* Political Community and the North Atlantic Area *(1957). The work did not focus on the new supranational institutions of Europe, but rather examined ten historical cases of integration to see if lessons could be applied to an area that included Western Europe, Canada, and the United States. After comparing these cases, they concluded that successful integration required a sense of community—a "we-feeling"—among the populations of the integrating territories, a core political*

Reprinted with permission from *Political Community and the North Atlantic Area: International Organization in the Light of Historical Experience.*  Notes omitted.

*area around which this community could coalesce, and a rise in administrative capabilities to meet the challenge of an enlarged domain. To meet these requirements for an "amalgamated security-community," Deutsch and his colleagues argued that the integrating territories must share a common set of values and that the communication and transactions between them must expand in numerous ways. This was their key insight: integration was a learning process that took place over a long period of extensive and sustained contact between people from the politically relevant strata of society. They were skeptical of the functionalists' claim (see Chapter 14) that integrating government tasks one step at a time would lead to more successful amalgamation, but they did confirm that functionalism had succeeded in the past.*

*Deutsch's transactionalist approach to integration was largely overshadowed by the rise of neofunctionalism (see Chapter 16) in the late 1950s and early 1960s, but recently Deutsch has attracted attention from a new generation of scholars impressed by his prescient insights. His relevance seems to grow as the European Union enlarges to the east and the question of who is a "European" increases in importance.*

## ■ THE PROBLEM

We undertook this inquiry as a contribution to the study of possible ways in which men someday might abolish war. From the outset, we realized the complexity of the problem. It is difficult to relate "peace" clearly to other prime values such as "justice" and "freedom." There is little common agreement on acceptable alternatives to war, and there is much ambiguity in the use of the terms "war" and "peace." Yet we can start with the assumption that war is now so dangerous that mankind must eliminate it, must put it beyond serious possibility. The attempt to do this may fail. But in a civilization that wishes to survive, the central problem in the study of international organization is this: How can men learn to act together to eliminate war as a social institution?

This is in one sense a smaller, and in another sense a larger, question than the one which occupies so many of the best minds today: how can we either prevent or avoid losing "the next war"? It is smaller because there will, of course, be no chance to solve the long-run problem if we do not survive the short-run crisis. It is larger because it concerns not only the confrontation of the nations of East and West in the twentieth century, but the whole underlying question of relations between political units at any time. We are not, therefore, trying to add to the many words that have been written directly concerning the East-West struggle of the 1940–1950's. Rather, we are seeking new light with which to look at the conditions and processes of long-range or permanent peace, applying our findings to one contemporary problem which, though not so difficult as the East-West problem, is by no means simple: peace within the North Atlantic area.

Whenever a difficult political problem arises, men turn to history for clues to its solution. They do this knowing they will not find the whole answer there. Every political problem is unique, of course, for history does not "repeat itself." But often the reflective mind will discover situations in the past that are essentially similar to the one being considered. Usually, with these rough parallels or suggestive analogies, the problem is not so much to find the facts as it is to decide what is essentially the same and what is essentially different between the historical facts and those of the present.

. . .

We are dealing here with political communities. These we regard as social groups with a process of political communication, some machinery for enforcement, and some popular habits of compliance. A political community is not necessarily able to prevent war within the area it covers: the United States was unable to do so at the time of the Civil War. Some political communities do, however, eliminate war and the expectation of war within their boundaries. It is these that call for intensive study. We have concentrated, therefore, upon the formation of "security-communities" in certain historical cases. The use of this term starts a chain of definitions, and we must break in here to introduce the other main links needed for a fuller understanding of our findings.

> A SECURITY-COMMUNITY is a group of people which has become "integrated."
>
> By INTEGRATION we mean the attainment, within a territory, of a "sense of community" and of institutions and practices strong enough and widespread enough to assure, for a "long" time, dependable expectations of "peaceful change" among its population.
>
> By SENSE OF COMMUNITY we mean a belief on the part of individuals in a group that they have come to agreement on at least this one point: that common social problems must and can be resolved by processes of "peaceful change."

> By PEACEFUL CHANGE we mean the resolution of social problems, normally by institutionalized procedures, without resort to large-scale physical force.

A security-community, therefore, is one in which there is real assurance that the members of that community will not fight each other physically, but will settle their disputes in some other way. If the entire world were integrated as a security-community, wars would be automatically eliminated. But there is apt to be confusion about the term "integration."

In our usage, the term "integration" does not necessarily mean only the merging of peoples or governmental units into a single unit. Rather, we divide security-communities into two types: "amalgamated" and "pluralistic."

> By AMALGAMATION we mean the formal merger of two or more previously independent units into a single larger unit, with some type of common government after amalgamation. This common government may be unitary or federal. The United States today is an example of the amalgamated type. It became a single governmental unit by the formal merger of several formerly independent units. It has one supreme decision-making center.
>
> The PLURALISTIC security-community, on the other hand, retains the legal independence of separate governments. The combined territory of the United States and Canada is an example of the pluralistic type. Its two separate governmental units form a security-community without being merged. It has two supreme decision-making centers. Where amalgamation occurs without integration, of course a security-community does not exist.
>
> Since our study deals with the problem of ensuring peace, we shall say that any political community, be it amalgamated or pluralistic, was eventually SUCCESSFUL if it became a security-community—that is, if it achieved integration—and that it was UNSUCCESSFUL if it ended eventually in secession or civil war.

Perhaps we should point out here that both types of integration require, at the international level, some kind of organization, even though it may be very loose. We put no credence in the old aphorism that among friends a constitution is not necessary and among enemies it is of no avail. The area of practicability lies in between.

Integration is a matter of fact, not of time. If people on both sides do not fear war and do not prepare for it, it matters little how long it took them to reach this stage. But once integration has been reached, the length of time over which it persists may contribute to its consolidation.

It should be noted that integration and amalgamation overlap, but not completely. This means that there can be amalgamation without integration, and that there can be integration without amalgamation. When we use the term "integration or amalgamation" in this book, we are taking a short form to express an alternative between integration (by the route of either pluralism or amalgamation) and amalgamation short of integration. We have done this because unification movements in the past have often aimed at both of these goals, with some of the supporters of the movements preferring one or the other goal at different times. To encourage this profitable ambiguity, leaders of such movements have often used broader symbols such as "union," which would cover both possibilities and could be made to mean different things to different men.

. . .

## ■ THE INTEGRATIVE PROCESS: SOME GENERAL CHARACTERISTICS

For purposes of exposition, we have divided our findings into two parts: first, general changes in our way of thinking about political integration; and second, specific findings about the background conditions and the dynamic characteristics of the integrative process. . . . [W]e we shall first discuss our general findings. Our more specific findings will follow in later sections. . . .

### □ *Reexamining Some Popular Beliefs*

To begin with, our findings have tended to make us increasingly doubtful of several widespread beliefs about political integration. The first of these beliefs is that modern life, with rapid transportation, mass communications, and literacy, tends to be more international than life in past decades or centuries, and hence more conducive to the growth of international or supranational institutions. Neither the study of our cases, nor a survey of more limited data from a larger number of countries, has yielded any clear-cut evidence to support this view. Nor do these results suggest that there has been inherent in modern economic and social development any unequivocal trend toward more internationalism and world community.

. . .

Another popular belief that our findings make more doubtful is that the growth of a state, or the expansion of its territory, resembles a snowballing process, or that it is characterized by some sort of bandwagon effect, such that successful growth in the past would accelerate the rate of growth or expansion of the amalgamated political community in the future. In this view, as villages in the past have joined to make provinces, and provinces to make kingdoms, so contemporary states are expected to join into ever-larger states or federations. If this were true, ever larger political units would appear to be the necessary result of historical and technological development. Our findings do not support this view. While the successful unification of England facilitated the later amalgamation of England and Wales, and this in turn facilitated the subsequent amalgamation of England and Wales with Scotland in the union of the two kingdoms, the united kingdom of Britain did not succeed in carrying through a successful and lasting amalgamation with Ireland. Nor could it retain its political amalgamation with the American colonies. These seceded from the British Empire in 1776 to form the United States; and Ireland seceded in effect in the course of the Anglo-Irish civil war of 1918–1921. The unity of the Habsburg monarchy became increasingly strained in the course of the nineteenth century and was followed by disintegration in the twentieth; and so was the more limited union of the crowns of Norway and Sweden.

. . .

Another popular notion is that a principal motive for the political integration of states has been the fear of anarchy, as well as of warfare among them. According to this view, men not only came to look upon war among the units concerned as unpromising and unattractive, but also as highly probable. For they came to fear it acutely while believing it to be all but inevitable in the absence of any strong superior power to restrain all participants. Consequently, according to this theory, one of the first and most important features of a newly-amalgamated security-community was the establishment of strong federal or community-wide laws, courts, police forces, and armies for their enforcement against potentially aggressive member states and member populations. Beliefs of this kind parallel closely the classic reasoning of Thomas Hobbes and John Locke; and some writers on federalism, or on international organization, have implied a stress on legal institutions and on the problem of coercing member states. Our findings suggest strong qualifications for these views. The questions of larger-community police forces and law enforcement, and of the coercion of member states, turned out to be of minor importance in the early stages of most of the amalgamated security-communities we studied.

. . .

This stress on the supposed importance of the early establishment of common laws, courts, and police forces is related to the suggestion that it is necessary to maintain a balance of power among the member states of a larger union or federation, in order to prevent any one state from becoming much stronger than the others. There is much to be said for this point of view: if a member state is far stronger than all the rest together, its political elite may well come to neglect or ignore the messages and needs of the population of the smaller member units, and the resulting loss of responsiveness may prevent integration or destroy it. The evidence from our cases suggests, however, that not merely amalgamation, but also responsiveness and integration can all be achieved and maintained successfully without any such balance of power among the participating states or political units. Neither England within the United Kingdom, nor Prussia in Germany after 1871, nor Piedmont in Italy for some time after 1860, was balanced in power by any other member or group of members, yet each of the larger political communities achieved integration.

. . .

## □ *General Findings*

Among our positive general findings, the most important seems to us that both amalgamated security-communities and pluralistic security-communities are practicable pathways toward integration. In the course of our research, we found ourselves led by the evidence to attribute a greater potential significance to pluralistic security-communities than we had originally expected. Pluralistic security-communities turned out to be somewhat easier to attain and easier to preserve than their amalgamated counterparts. . . .

*The strengths of pluralism.* The somewhat smaller risk of breakdown in the case of pluralistic security-communities seems indicated by an examination of the relative numbers of successes and failures of each type of security-community. We can readily list a dozen instances of success for each type. . . .

On the other hand, we find a sharp contrast in the number of failures for each type. We have found only one case of a pluralistic security-community which failed in the sense that it was followed by actual warfare between the participants, and it is doubtful whether a pluralistic security-community existed even in that case: this was the relationship of Austria and Prussia within the framework of the German Confederation since 1815. . . .

On balance, therefore, we found pluralistic security-communities to be a more promising approach to the elimination of war over large areas than we had thought at the outset of our inquiry.

But this relative superiority of a pluralistic security-community as a more easily attainable form of integration has limited applications. It worked only in those situations in which the keeping of the peace among the participating units was the main political goal overshadowing all others. This goal has been the main focus of our study. In our historical cases, however, we found that men have often wanted more: they have wanted a political community that would not merely keep the peace among its members but that would also be capable of acting as a unit in other ways and for other purposes. In respect to this capacity to act—and in particular, to act quickly and effectively for positive goals—amalgamated security-communities have usually been far superior to their pluralistic counterparts. In many historical cases, men have preferred to accept the somewhat greater risk of civil war, or of war among the participating units, in order to insure this greater promise of joint capacity for action. It is only today, in the new age of nuclear weapons, that these risks and gains must be reevaluated. Now a pluralistic security-community may appear a somewhat safer device than amalgamation for dealing with man's new weapons.

*The thresholds of integration.* Our second general finding concerns the nature of integration. In our earliest analytical scheme, we had envisaged this as an all-or-none process, analogous to the crossing of a narrow threshold. On the one side of this threshold, populations and policy-makers considered warfare among the states or political units concerned as still a serious possibility, and prepared for it; on the other side of the threshold they were supposed to do so no longer. . . .

Somewhat contrary to our expectations, however, some of our cases taught us that integration may involve a fairly broad zone of transition rather than a narrow threshold; that states might cross and recross this threshold or zone of transition several times in their relations with each other; and that they might spend decades or generations wavering uncertainly within it.

Thus we found that states could maintain armed forces which were potentially available for warfare against each other, but which were not specifically committed to this purpose. The American state militias from 1776 to 1865 and the forces of the Swiss cantons from the thirteenth to the nineteenth centuries seem to have been available for such purposes if the political temper of their respective communities had warranted such employment, as it did on a few occasions. It would thus be extraordinarily difficult to say just in which year warfare between the Protestant and Catholic cantons ceased to be a practical political possibility after 1712, or when it again became temporarily a practical possibility between 1815 and 1847; or just when integration within the United States was lost in the period between 1820 and 1861, and warfare between North and South became a substantial possibility.

. . .

The threshold of integration thus turned out to be far broader, and far less easy to discern, in our historical cases than we had envisaged at the outset. Not only the approach toward integration, but the very act of crossing the integration threshold, have turned out to be much lengthier and more uncertain processes than had been expected.

*Communication and the sense of community.* Integration has proved to be a more continuous process than our earliest analytical scheme had suggested; but it continues to be characterized by important thresholds. Within this framework of our revised general concept of integration, we have arrived at a somewhat deeper understanding of the meaning of "sense of community." It appears to rest primarily on something other than verbal assent to some or many explicit propositions. The populations of different territories might easily profess verbal attachment to the same set of values without having a sense of community that leads to political integration. The kind of sense of community that is relevant for integration, and therefore for our study, turned out to be rather a matter of mutual sympathy and loyalties; of "we-feeling," trust, and mutual consideration; of partial identification in terms of self-images and interests; of mutually successful predictions of behavior, and of cooperative action in accordance with it—in short, a matter of a perpetual dynamic process of mutual attention, communication, perception of needs, and responsiveness in the process of decision-making. "Peaceful change" could not be assured without this kind of relationship.

. . .

*Growth around core areas.* As such a process of integrative behavior, sense of community requires some particular habits of political behavior on the part of individuals and some particular traditions and institutions on the part of social groups and of political units, such as provinces or states.

These habits, in turn, are acquired by processes of social learning. People learn them in the face of background conditions which change only slowly, so that they appear at any moment as something given—as political, economic, social, or psychological facts that must be taken for granted for the purposes of short-range politics. The speed and extent of this learning of habits of integrative political behavior are then influenced in each situation by these background conditions, as well as by the dynamics of the particular political process—the particular movement toward integration. Some of our more specific findings deal with the importance of certain background conditions in each area studied, while others deal with the successive stages of the integrative political process that occurred.

The outcome, then, of the integrative process among any particular group of countries depends on the interplay of the effects of background conditions with moving political events. One aspect of this interplay deserves to be singled out for particular attention. It is the matter of political, economic, and social capabilities of the participating political units for integrative behavior.

Generally, we found that such integrative capabilities were closely related to the general capabilities of a given political unit for action in the fields of politics, administration, economic life, and social and cultural development. Larger, stronger, more politically, administratively, economically, and educationally advanced political units were found to form the cores of strength around which in most cases the integrative process developed.

Political amalgamation, in particular, usually turned out to be a nuclear process. It often occurred around single cores, as in the case of England, Piedmont, Prussia, and Sweden. Each of these came to form the core of a larger amalgamated political community (even though the Norwegian-Swedish union turned out to be transitory). . . .

*The need for rising capabilities.* The extent of integrative capabilities which already existed in the individual political units at the beginning of a major drive toward amalgamation thus turned out to be very important for the future development of the process. But another step was no less important: the further increase of these capabilities in the course of the movement toward amalgamation. The presence or absence of growth in such capabilities played a major role in every integrative process we studied, and particularly in every case of an amalgamation movement.

Generally, amalgamation did not come to pass because the government of the participating units had become weaker or more inefficient; nor did it come to pass because men had been forced to turn away from these increasingly incapable organizations to the building of a larger and less decrepit common government. Rather, amalgamation occurred after a substantial increase in the capabilities of at least some of the participating units, or sometimes of all of them. Examples are the increase in the capabilities of the American colonies before 1789, and in the capabilities of Prussia before 1871. The increase in the capabilities of the political organizations or governments of the individual states, cantons, principalities, and the like, formed a major element in the dynamic political process leading to amalgamation in each instance.

Such capabilities relevant to integration were of two broad kinds. One was related to the capacity to act of a political unit—such as its size, power, economic strength, administrative efficiency, and the like. The other kind was related to the ability of a unit to control its own behavior and to redirect its own attention. More accurately, this means the ability of its political decision-makers and relevant political elites to redirect and control their own attention and behavior so as to enable rulers to receive communications from other political units which were to be their prospective partners in the integrative process. It means, further, the ability to give these messages from other political units adequate weight in the making of their own decisions, to perceive the needs of the populations and elites of these other units, and to respond to them quickly and adequately in terms of political or economic action. The first kind of capabilities—those related to the capacity to act and to overcome external obstacles—are closely linked to what we often call power; the second kind are linked to what we propose to call responsiveness.

. . .

*The race between capabilities and loads.* Another set of data we found to be of crucial importance pertained to the burdens thrown upon the tangible and intangible resources of political units by the requirements of establishing or maintaining either an amalgamated or a pluralistic security-community. Such loads or burdens, as we have called them, were of many kinds. They included military or financial burdens, drains on manpower or wealth; the burden of risk from political or military commitments; costs of social and economic readjustments, such as at the establishment of a customs union; and similar burdens of a material kind. But they also included intangible burdens upon government, which could be visualized as somewhat similar to traffic loads of vehicles at a road intersection or of messages at a telephone exchange. In the cases of crossroads or switchboards, the flow of vehicles or messages requires more than a certain volume of material facilities for its accommodation; it also requires a certain number of decisions which must be made in a limited amount of time by the traffic officer who controls traffic at the intersection, or by the persons or apparatus that control the flow of calls through the telephone exchange.

It is this burden, imposed by the traffic load of messages and signals upon the attention-giving and decision-making capabilities of the persons or organizations in control, that has close parallels in the burden of government upon rulers. It is a burden upon the attention-giving, information-processing, and decision-making capabilities of administrators, political elites, legislatures, or electoral majorities. Thus the failure of the British Parliament to respond quickly and adequately to the disastrous Irish famine of 1846 was not caused primarily by any lack of material or financial resources to provide relief. Rather, the failure was one of adequate attention, perception, and decision-making to meet the burdens of responsibility which the Parliament had taken upon itself under the terms of Anglo-Irish union. It was nonetheless a failure that was to have far-reaching effects upon the future of Anglo-Irish relations.

Political amalgamation in general tended to increase the load of demands upon the material resources and the decision-making capabilities of governments, since decisions for larger areas and populations had to be made by fewer central institutions. The success or failure of amalgamation, then, depended in considerable part upon the relationship of two rates of change: the growing rate of claims and burdens upon central governments as against the growing—in some instances, the insufficiently growing—level of capabilities of the governmental institutions of the amalgamated political community. The load of communications, demands, and claims upon the capabilities of government was also growing from independent causes—such as the increasing complexity of economic life, the increasing level of popular expectations in terms of living standards, social opportunities, and political rights, and the increasing political activity of previously passive groups and strata. Hence the outcome of the race between the growth of loads and capabilities sometimes remained precarious for a longer period, or it changed from one period to another.

. . .

## ■ THE IMPORTANCE OF BACKGROUND CONDITIONS

In general, our cases have left us impressed with the importance of certain background conditions for the success or failure of the integrative process. The influence of background conditions appears to be larger, and the opportunities for decisive action by political leaders or movements appear to be somewhat more limited, than we had thought at the beginning of our study.

To be sure, we found that the importance of a few background conditions had been somewhat overrated. Certain conditions which had often been considered as essential for the establishment of an amalgamated security-community turned out to be helpful to that end but not essential to it. Such helpful but nonessential conditions included previous administrative and/or dynastic union; ethnic or linguistic assimilation; strong economic ties; and foreign military threats. While all of these turned out to be helpful to integration, none of them appeared to be essential since each of them was absent in the successful establishment of at least one amalgamated security-community.

. . .

## ■ SOME ESSENTIAL REQUIREMENTS FOR THE ESTABLISHMENT OF AMALGAMATED SECURITY-COMMUNITIES

A number of conditions appear to be essential, so far as our evidence goes, for the success of amalgamated security-communities—that is, for their becoming integrated. None of these conditions, of course, seems to be by itself sufficient for success; and all of them together may not be sufficient either, for it is quite possible that we have overlooked some additional conditions that may also be essential. Nonetheless, it does seem plausible to us that any group of states or territories which fulfilled all the essential conditions for an amalgamated security-community which we have been able to identify should also be at least on a good part of the way to successful amalgamation.

### □ *Values and Expectations*

The first group of essential conditions deals with motivations for political behavior, and in particular with the values and expectations held in the politically relevant strata of the political units concerned. In regard to values, we found in all our cases a compatibility of the main values held by the politically relevant strata of all participating units. Sometimes this was supplemented by a tacit agreement to deprive of political significance any incompatible values that might remain.

. . .

Values were most effective politically when they were not held merely in abstract terms, but when they were incorporated in political institutions and in habits of political behavior which permitted these values to be acted on in such a way as to strengthen people's attachment to them. This connection between values, institutions, and habits we call a "way of life," and it turned out to be crucial. In all our cases of successful amalgamation we found such a distinctive way of life—that is, a set of socially accepted values and of institutional means for their pursuit and attainment, and a set of established or emerging habits of behavior corresponding to them. To be distinctive, such a way of life has to include at least some major social or political values and institutions which are different from those which existed in the area during the recent past, or from those prevailing among important neighbors. In either case, such a way of life usually involved a significant measure of social innovation as against the recent past.

Putting the matter somewhat differently, we noted in our cases that the partial shift of political habits required in transferring political loyalties from the old, smaller political units, at least in part, to a new and larger political community has only occurred under conditions when also a great number of other political and social habits were in a state of change. Thus we find that the perception of an American people and an American political community, as distinct from the individual thirteen colonies, emerged between 1750 and 1790. This occurred at the same time as the emergence of a distinct American way of life clearly different from that of most of the people of Great Britain or French Canada. This way of life had been developing since the beginnings of colonial settlement in the seventeenth century, but had undergone accelerated change and development in the course of the American Revolution and its aftermath. . . .

In regard to expectations, we found that in all our cases amalgamation was preceded by widespread expectations of joint rewards for the participating units, through strong economic ties or gains envisaged for the future. By economic ties, we mean primarily close relations of trade permitting large-scale division of labor and almost always giving rise to vested interests. It was not necessary, however, for such strong economic ties to exist prior to amalgamation. . . . Only a part of such expectation had to be fulfilled. A "down payment" of tangible gains for a substantial part of the supporters of amalgamation soon after the event, if not earlier, seems almost necessary. . . .

Some noneconomic expectations also turned out to be essential. In all our cases of successful amalgamation we found widespread expectations of greater social or political equality, or of greater social or political rights or liberties, among important groups of the politically relevant strata—and often among parts of the underlying populations—in the political units concerned.

### □ *Capabilities and Communication Processes*

Values and expectations not only motivate people to performance, but the results of this performance will in turn make the original values and expectations weaker or stronger. Accordingly, we found a number of essential conditions for amalgamation which were related to the capabilities of the participating units or to the processes of communication occurring among them. The most important of these conditions was an increase in the political and administrative capabilities of the main political units to be amalgamated. Thus the amalgamation of Germany was preceded by a marked increase in the political and administrative capabilities of Prussia from 1806 onward, and by a lesser but still significant increase in the corresponding capabilities of Bavaria and of other German states. . . .

Another essential condition for amalgamation, closely related to the increase in capabilities, is the presence of markedly superior economic growth, either as measured against the recent past of the territories to be amalgamated, or against neighboring areas. Such superior economic growth did not have to be present in all participating units prior to amalgamation, but it had to be present it least in the main partner or partners vis-à-vis the rest of the units to be included in the amalgamated security-community. . . .

Another essential requirement for successful amalgamation was the presence of unbroken links of social communication between the political units concerned, and between the politically relevant strata within them. By such unbroken links we mean social groups and institutions which provide effective channels of communication, both horizontally among the main units of the amalgamated security-community and vertically among the politically relevant strata within them. Such links thus involve always persons and organizations.

. . .

[A final] essential condition, related to the preceding one, is the broadening of the political, social, or economic elite, both in regard to its recruitment from broader social strata and to its continuing connections with them. An example of such a broadening of the elite was the emergence of a new type of political leader among the landowners of Virginia, such as George Washington, who retained the respect of his peers and at the same time also knew, well before the American Revolution, how to gain the votes of poorer farmers and frontiersmen at the county elections in Virginia. . . .

### □ *Mobility of Persons*

Another condition present in all our cases of successful amalgamation was the mobility of persons among the main units, at least in the politically relevant strata. It is quite possible that this condition, too, may be essential for the success of amalgamation. In any event, our cases have persuaded us that the mobility of persons among the main political units of a prospective amalgamated security-community should be given far more serious consideration than has often been the case. Full-scale mobility of persons has followed every successful amalgamated security-community in modern times immediately upon its establishment. . . .

### □ *Multiplicity and Balance of Transactions*

We also found that it was not enough for a high level of communications and transactions to exist only on one or two topics, or in one or two respects, among two or more political units if their amalgamation was to be successful. Rather it appeared that successfully amalgamated security-communities require a fairly wide range of different common functions and services, together with different institutions and organizations to carry them out. Further, they apparently require a multiplicity of ranges of common communications and transactions and their institutional counterparts. . . .

Two other conditions may well turn out to be essential for the success of amalgamation, but these will have to be investigated further. The first of them is concerned with the balance in the flow of communications and transactions between the political units that are to be amalgamated, and particularly with the balance of rewards between the different participating territories. It is also concerned with the balance of initiatives that originate in these territories or groups of population, and finally with the balance of respect—or of symbols standing for respect—between these partners. In the course of studying cases of successful amalgamation, we found that it was apparently important for each of the participating territories or populations to gain some valued services or opportunities. It also seemed important that each at least sometimes take the initiative in the process, or initiate some particular phase or contribution; and that some major symbol or representative of each territory or population should be accorded explicit respect by the others. . . .

The second condition follows from the preceding one. It was not essential that the flow of rewards, of initiatives, or of respect should balance at any one moment, but it seems essential that they should balance over some period of time. Sometimes this was accomplished by alternating flows or by an interchange of group roles. Territories which received particular prestige, or material benefits, at one time might become sources of benefits for their partners at another; or territories whose political elites found themselves ranged with a majority on one political issue might find themselves in a minority on another, without any one particular division between majorities and minorities becoming permanent. . . .

### □ *Mutual Predictability of Behavior*

A final condition that may be essential for the success of amalgamation may be some minimum amount of mutual predictability of behavior. Members of an amalgamated security-community—and, to a lesser extent, of a pluralistic security-community—must be able to expect from one another some dependable interlocking, interchanging, or at least compatible behavior; and they must therefore be able, at least to that extent, to predict one another's actions. Such predictions may be based on mere familiarity. . . . While familiarity appears to have contributed successfully to the growth of mutual trust in some of our cases, such as that between Scottish Highlanders and Lowlanders, and later between Scots and Englishmen, or between German, French, and Swiss during much of the eighteenth century, we found in a number of our cases that mutual predictability of behavior was eventually established upon a firmer basis.

This firmer basis was the acquisition of a certain amount of common culture or of common group character or "national character." In this manner, an increasing number of Germans in the German states, of Italians in the Italian principalities, and of Americans in the American colonies, came to feel that they could understand their countrymen in the neighboring political units by expecting them, by and large, to behave much as they themselves would behave in similar situations; that is to say, they came to predict the behavior of their countrymen in neighboring political units on the basis of introspection: by looking into their own minds they could make a fairly good guess as to what their neighbors would do, so they could trust them or at least understand them, to some extent much as they would trust or understand themselves. The extent of mutual predictability of behavior, however, seems to have varied from case to case, and it also seems to have varied with the particular political elites or relevant strata concerned. That some mutual predictability of political behavior is an essential condition for an amalgamated security-community seems clear from our cases; but the extent of such predictability must remain a matter for further research.

### *Summary*

Altogether we have found nine essential conditions for an amalgamated security-community: (1) mutual compatibility of main values; (2) a distinctive way of life; (3) expectations of stronger economic ties or gains; (4) a marked increase in political and administrative capabilities of at least some participating units; (5) superior economic growth on the part of at least some participating units; (6) unbroken links of social communication, both geographically between territories and sociologically between different social strata; (7) a broadening of the political elite; (8) mobility of persons, at least among the politically relevant strata; and, (9) a multiplicity of ranges of communication and transaction. And we have found indications that three other conditions may be essential: (10) a compensation of flows of communications and transactions; (11) a not too infrequent interchange of group roles; and, (12) considerable mutual predictability of behavior.

. . .

## BACKGROUND CONDITIONS CONDUCIVE TO DISINTEGRATION

Several conditions were found present in all cases of disintegration of amalgamated political communities which we studied, and they appear likely to promote disintegration wherever they occur. This does not mean, however, that they are sufficient by themselves to produce disintegration. We have found these conditions also present in some cases where disintegration did not follow but where other factors favoring integration were present in particular strength. The establishment and preservation of amalgamated security-communities thus turned out to depend upon a balance of favorable and adverse conditions. Amalgamation does not seem likely to be established, or to persist, except in the presence of the nine essential conditions for amalgamation which we listed earlier in this chapter; but even in their presence, the disintegrative conditions which we shall discuss below could prevent, destroy, or at least endanger an amalgamated security-community.

In our earlier general discussion, we have described integration as a process depending upon a balance between political loads upon a government, and its capabilities for maintaining amalgamation, or its capabilities for maintaining integration within a pluralistic security-community. In accordance with this general view, we may group the disintegrative conditions in our cases under two headings: conditions that increased the burdens upon amalgamated governments, and conditions that reduced the capability of such governments to cope with the burdens put upon them.

One of the outstanding conditions that tended to destroy amalgamated security-communities by placing excessive burdens upon them was the effect of excessive military commitments. Common armies with light burdens and conspicuous gains in prestige or privileges, or short wars of similar character, were helpful, though not essential, to the deeper integration of a political community; but heavy military burdens with few conspicuous gains over the *status quo* tended to have the opposite effect.

. . .

Another condition which tended to increase greatly the load upon governments, and thus tended to disintegrate amalgamated security-communities, was a substantial increase in political participation on the part of populations, regions, or social strata which previously had been politically passive. Such a substantial increase in political participation meant in each case that the needs, wishes, and pressures of additional social strata or regions had to be accommodated within an old system of political decision-making that might be—and often was—ill-suited to respond to them adequately and in time. . . .

A further disintegrative condition related to this rise in political participation is the increase in ethnic or linguistic differentiation. Another aspect of the same condition is a rise in the political awareness of such differentiation as already may exist. Both of these are likely to be a consequence of the rise in political participation among groups that are already thus differentiated, in language and culture, from the predominant nationality or regional-cultural group within the political community in question. . . .

Another group of disintegrative conditions tends to weaken or destroy amalgamated security-communities by reducing the capabilities of their governments and political elites for adequate and timely action or response. One such condition in our cases appeared to be any prolonged economic decline or stagnation, leading to economic conditions comparing unfavorably with those in neighboring areas.

Another disintegrative condition of this kind was the relative closure of the established political elite. This tended to promote the rise of frustrated counter-elites, somewhat in Pareto's sense, among ethnic or cultural out-groups, or in outlying regions.

Another disintegrative condition, related to the foregoing, was the excessive delay in social, economic, or political reforms which had come to be expected by the population—reforms which sometimes had already been adopted in neighboring areas.

. . .

## ■ SPECIAL FEATURES OF PLURALISTIC SECURITY-COMMUNITIES

In regard to the problem of a pluralistic security-community, we found that its attainment would be favored by any conditions favorable to the success of an amalgamated security-community, and that it was sometimes hindered by conditions or processes harmful to the latter. Pluralistic security-communities sometimes succeeded, however, under far less favorable conditions than the success of an amalgamated government would have required; and they sometimes survived unfavorable or disintegrative processes which would have destroyed an amalgamated political community.

. . .

Of the twelve conditions that appeared to be essential for the success of an amalgamated security-community, or at least potentially so, only two or possibly three were found to be very important for a pluralistic security-community as well. The first of these was the compatibility of major values relevant to political decision-making. The second was the capacity of the participating political units or governments to respond to each other's needs, messages, and actions quickly, adequately, and without resort to violence. . . . A third essential condition for a pluralistic security-community may be mutual predictability of behavior; this appears closely related to the foregoing. But the member-states of a pluralistic security-community have to make joint decisions only about a more limited range of subject matters, and retain each a far wider range of problems for autonomous decision-making within their own borders. Consequently the range and extent of the mutual predictability of behavior required from members of a pluralistic security-community is considerably less than would be essential for the successful operation of an amalgamated one.

. . .

Altogether, our findings in the field of background conditions tend to bring out the great and potentially restrictive importance of these conditions for the establishment and preservation of amalgamated security-communities. Further, our findings tend to bring out the very considerable potentialities of pluralistic security-communities for overcoming even partially unfavorable background situations.

## ■ POLITICAL INTEGRATION AS A DYNAMIC PROCESS

The transition from background to process is fluid. The essential background conditions do not come into existence all at once; they are not established in any particular fixed sequence; nor do they all grow together like one organism from a seed. Rather, it appears to us from our cases that they may be assembled in almost any sequence, so long only as all of them come into being and take effect. Toward this end, almost any pathway will suffice. As each essential condition is fulfilled, it is added, one by one or a few at a time, as strands are added to a web, or as parts are put together on an assembly line.

So long as this assembling of conditions occurs very slowly, we may treat the status of each condition and the status of all of them together at any one time as a matter of stable, seemingly unchanging background. Indeed, in our historical cases they were so considered, as practically unchanged or slow-changing situations, by most of their contemporaries. But as the last of the conditions in each sequence are added to those whose attainment was assembled previously, the tempo of the process quickens. Background and process now become one. A multiplicity of ranges of social communication and transaction was a background condition for amalgamation, but the rapid adding of new ranges of such communications and transactions is a process. Moreover, it is a process that may become accelerated as a by-product of other processes of political and social change. A balance of flows of transactions between the different units eligible for amalgamation is another of the necessary background conditions for amalgamation. This is particularly true in regard to a balance of initiatives, of rewards, and of respect. But substantial progress toward the establishment of some such balance may be a matter of political process, or else a political process directed toward the attainment of amalgamation may produce a better balance of transaction flows as one of its by-products.

. . .

## ■ THE ISSUE OF FUNCTIONALISM AS A PATHWAY TO AMALGAMATION

Our finding that the bringing together of the necessary background conditions for amalgamation in our cases resembled an assembly-line process suggests indirectly an answer to an old question: does merging of one or more governmental functions among two or more political units promote progress toward later over-all amalgamation of their governments? Or, on the contrary, does what we shall call functional amalgamation impede such over-all amalgamation by inadequate performance of the few already amalgamated functions? Does it take the wind from the sails of the movement for full-scale amalgamation by making the few already amalgamated functions serve adequately the main needs which had supplied most of the driving power for the over-all amalgamation movement?

Before we answer this question, we must say exactly what we mean by functionalism. As we are using the term here, it includes all cases of partial amalgamation, where some governmental functions are delegated by the participating units on a low or a high level of decision-making. Whether a particular function or institution is so important that its pooling with another government would have the effect of over-all amalgamation rather than partial—and thus take it out of the field of functionalism—depends on the importance of this particular function or institution in the domestic politics of the participating units.

. . .

How helpful, then, has functionalism been? We have found, first of all, that over-all amalgamation can be approached functionally and by steps, with successful over-all amalgamation at the end. This occurred in the cases of Germany with the Zollverein (of which, significantly, Austria was not a member); the United States with the common administration of Western lands under the Articles of Confederation; the Swiss cantons since the fourteenth century, and the common citizenship between Geneva, Bern, and Fribourg, and later other Swiss cantons from the sixteenth century onward; finally, between England and Wales and England and Scotland before the union of crowns preceding full amalgamation. In all these cases amalgamation eventually was successful. But functional amalgamation was also proposed and rejected among the Italian states in the 1840's, and eventually amalgamation was achieved without its aid. Moreover, functional amalgamation took place in at least three of our cases that were eventually unsuccessful: there was the union of crowns between Austria, Bohemia, and Hungary from 1526 onward; there was the union of crowns between Norway and Sweden in 1814; and there were various forms of partial amalgamation between England and Ireland before 1801.

These examples are taken from a sample collection of historical cases and situations in which instances of successful amalgamation outnumber the unsuccessful ones by more than two to one. From this it should be clear that the historical evidence in favor of functionalism is quite inconclusive.

It seems safest to conclude that the issue of functionalism has been greatly overrated. Functionalism, it appears, is a device that has been widely used both in successful and in unsuccessful movements toward amalgamation, somewhat as functional devolution and decentralization have been used in successful and in unsuccessful attempts at secession. The outcome in all such situations seems mostly to have been the result of other conditions and other processes—depending largely on whether functionalism mainly was associated with experiences of joint rewards or of joint deprivations—with functionalism in itself doing little to help or to harm. . . . Perhaps the most that can be said for functionalism as an approach to integration is that it seems less hazardous than any sudden attempt at over-all amalgamation.

. . .

# 16 The Uniting of Europe

Ernst B. Haas

*Ernst B. Haas (1925–2003), an immigrant born in Frankfurt, was among the U.S. social scientists applying behavioral methods to international relations in the 1950s. In 1958 he published a book entitled* The Uniting of Europe: Political, Social, and Economic Forces, 1950–1957, *in which he used the European Coal and Steel Community as a case study in an attempt to dissect the "actual 'integration process'. . . to derive propositions about its nature." Haas recognized that functional integration was taking place in Europe, but that functionalism as a theory had failed to explain why decisionmakers chose to integrate in some areas and not others. Functionalism needed a theory of politics, which Haas provided.*

*Haas first defined political integration as "the process whereby political actors in several distinct national settings are persuaded to shift their loyalties, expectations and political activities toward a new center, whose institutions possess or demand jurisdiction over the pre-existing national states." Then he drew on democratic theory, systems theory, group theory, and a host of other approaches to produce a scientifically rigorous explanation for European political integration that he also believed held predictive power. This neofunctionalist approach (here introduced by Haas in the preface to* The Uniting of Europe *and described in greater detail by Leon Lindberg in Chapter 17) views the integration process as group driven. Federal institutions are established because important political groups see tangible benefits from joint governance in specific areas. The integration process pushes forward when federal institutions affect the interests of groups*

---

Reprinted from *The Uniting of Europe: Political, Social, and Economic Forces, 1950–1957* (Stanford University Press, 1958).  Notes omitted. Used with permission of Peter M. Haas.

*that respond by organizing across national boundaries and pushing for more integration. Thus integration in one area spills over into another when groups perceive it in their interest.*

*Haas wrote prolifically on integration in the 1960s and early 1970s as the acknowledged leader of the neofunctionalist school. Neofunctionalism, while no longer as dominant as it was in the 1960s, is still very influential. And Ernst Haas is still widely read.*

"United Europe" is a phrase meaning many things to many men. To some it implies the creation of a full-fledged federation of the independent states of Western Europe, either the Six of "Schumania" or the Fifteen of the Council of Europe. To others the phrase means no more than the desirability of creating a loose concert or confederation. Some see in it the guarantee for future greatness, a political, economic and cultural renaissance for the Old Continent, about to be eclipsed by the United States, the Soviet world, and perhaps the Arab-Asians. But others identify it with the death of cherished patterns of national uniqueness. Even government policy, on both sides of the Atlantic, sometimes hesitates between endorsing the creation of a new center of economic and political power and fearing the evolution of a high-tariff region or of institutionalized "third force" sentiments. One must add the still lively controversy over whether economic or military unification, or both, is possible without prior or simultaneous political federation. The arguments over the merits and types of unification have continued since the end of World War II; they are unlikely to be exhausted soon.

But for the political scientist the unification of Europe has a peculiar attraction quite irrespective of merits and types. He may see in it, as I do, an instance of voluntary "integration" taking place before his eyes, as it were under laboratory conditions. He will wish to study it primarily because it is one of the very few current situations in which the decomposition of old nations can be systematically analyzed within the framework of the evolution of a larger polity—a polity destined, perhaps, to develop into a nation of its own. Hence, my purpose is not the evaluation of the virtues and drawbacks of a United Europe in terms of European, American, national, international, free-enterprise, or welfare-state values. Nor is it an analysis of the advantages of federation over intergovernmental cooperation, economic over military unity. My aim is merely the dissection of the actual "integration process" in order to derive propositions about its nature. Hence, I focused my analysis on selected groups, institutions and ideologies which have already been demonstrated to act as unifying agents in political systems clearly "integrated" by any applicable standard. Further, I confined the analysis to the impact of the one organization whose powers, functions and composition make it *a priori* capable of redirecting the loyalties and expectations of political actors: the European Coal and Steel Community. My study, then, attempts to advance generalizations about the processes by which political communities are formed among sovereign states, and my method is to select specific political groups and institutions, to study their reactions to a new species of "federal" government, and to analyze the impact of that government in terms of the reactions caused. On the assumption that "integration" is a two-way process in which the central institutions affect and are affected by the subject groups, the Coal and Steel Community is to serve as a case study illustrating the effects on the totality of interactions.

. . .

The essential conclusions may be briefly summarized. The initiation of a deliberate scheme of political unification, to be accepted by the key groups that make up a pluralistic society, does not require absolute majority support, nor need it rest on identical aims on the part of all participants. The European Coal and Steel Community was initially accepted because it offered a multitude of different advantages to different groups. Acceptance of a federal scheme is facilitated if the participating state units are already fragmented ideologically and socially. Moreover, the acceptance of such a scheme is considerably eased if among the participating industrial, political, or labor groups there is a tradition, however vague, of mutual consultation and of rudimentary value sharing. A helpful, but by no means indispensable, condition is the existence of an external threat, real or imagined.

Once established, the central institution will affect political integration meaningfully only if it is willing to follow policies giving rise to expectations and demands for more—or fewer—federal measures. In either case, the groups concerned will organize across national state boundaries in order to be able to influence policy. If the central institution, however, fails to assert itself in any way so as to cause strong positive or negative expectations, its impact on unity will be as small as the integrative role of such technically powerful international administrative unions as the Danube Commissions or the Universal Postal Union. As far as the industrial groups—business and labor—are concerned, they tend to unite beyond their former national confines in an effort to make common policy and obtain common benefits. Thus perhaps the chief finding is that group pressure will spill over into the federal sphere and thereby add to the integrative impulse. Only industries convinced that they have nothing to gain from integration will hold out against such pressures. But industrial sectors initially opposed to integration for a variety of motives do change their attitude and develop strong positive expectations if they feel that certain common problems can be more easily met by a federal authority. More commonly still, groups are likely to turn to the federal authority for help in the solution of purely national problems if the local government proves uncooperative. Groups with strong initial positive expectations do not necessarily turn against the principle of integration if their hopes are disappointed: they merely intensify their efforts to obtain the desired advantages on the federal level, thus integrating themselves into organizations less and less dependent on and identified with the national state. Political parties, if allowance is made for their varying ideologies and constituencies, tend to fall into the same pattern. National governments, operating in the nexus of all these forces, may on occasion attempt to sidestep, ignore, or sabotage the decisions of the federal authority. The study of the Coal and Steel Community shows, however, that governments also recognize a point beyond which such evasions are unprofitable, and that in the long run they tend to defer to federal decisions, lest the example of their recalcitrance set a precedent for other governments.

After five years of activity, the pattern of supranational pressure and counter-pressure has become apparent: groups, parties, and governments have reassessed and reformulated their aims in such a way that the drive for a United Europe has become the battle cry of the Left. The "sinistration" of federalism has been accomplished in the recognition of trade unions and Socialist parties that their version of the welfare state and of peace can rationally be achieved only in a federated Western Europe. Perhaps the most salient conclusion we can draw from the community-building experiment is the fact that major interest groups as well as politicians determine their support of, or opposition to, new central institutions and policies on the basis of a calculation of advantage. The "good Europeans" are not the main creators of the regional community that is growing up; the process of community formation is dominated by nationally constituted groups with specific interests and aims, willing and able to adjust their aspirations by turning to supranational means when this course appears profitable.

Our study thus substantiates the pluralistic thesis that a larger political community can be developed if the crucial expectations, ideologies, and behavior patterns of certain key groups can be successfully refocussed on a new set of central symbols and institutions. Yet this conclusion also begs the question of the generality of the process laid bare. Can larger political communities be created on this basis in all sections of the world, in all ages, irrespective of the specific powers initially given to the central authority? I suggest that the value of this case study is confined to the kind of setting which reproduces in essence the physical conditions, ideologies, class structure, group relations, and political traditions and institutions of contemporary Western Europe. In short, I maintain that these findings *are* sufficiently general in terms of the socio-political context to serve as propositions concerning the formation of political communities—*provided* we are dealing with (1) an industrialized economy deeply enmeshed in international trade and finance, (2) societies in which the masses are fully mobilized politically and tend to channel their aspirations through permanent interest groups and political parties, (3) societies in which these groups are habitually led by identifiable elites competing with one another for influence and in disagreement on many basic values, and (4) societies in which relations among these elites are governed by the traditions and assumptions of parliamentary (or presidential) democracy and constitutionalism. It may well be that the specific economic conditions under which the European coal and steel industries operate act as additional factors limiting the possibility of generalizing. Monopolistic competition and the prevalence of private ownership are such factors, though isolated pockets of nationalized industry exist in the total industrial complex. It may also be true that the impact of an overwhelmingly powerful external economic center acts as a limiting condition. Economic integration in Europe might have been much slower if the governments had been compelled to come to grips with investment, currency and trade questions—decisions which were in effect spared them by the direct and indirect role of United States economic policy. Hence, I would have little hesitation in applying the technique of analysis here used to the study of integration under NATO, the Scandinavian setting, the Organization for European Economic Co-operation, or Canadian-United States relations. I would hesitate to claim validity for it in the study of regional political integration in Latin America, the Middle East, or South-East Asia.

. . .

# 17 Political Integration: Definitions and Hypotheses

LEON N. LINDBERG

*Leon Lindberg (University of Wisconsin–Madison), one of Haas's students at the University of California–Berkeley, helped define and advance neofunctionalism with the publication of three books in the 1960s and early 1970s. In the first chapter of* The Political Dynamics of European Economic Integration *(1963), Lindberg illustrates early neofunctionalism's systematic approach to explaining integration, as well as its enthusiasm for a European project that promised to "move beyond the nation-state as a basic framework for action." Lindberg first draws on Haas to define "political integration," then goes on to identify conditions for integration. The central roles played by political actors are key to Lindberg's view of the integration process. New central institutions, for instance, help "precipitate unity"; political groups "restructure their expectations and activities" in response to integration; and member states must possess "the will to proceed" if integration is to continue. Also important is the role of "spillover," which propels integration forward as cooperation in one area spills over into other areas. Lindberg does not argue that spillover is inevitable (and thus integration, once started, will proceed indefinitely), but he does display a faith in its power that is not yet tempered by Charles de Gaulle and the Luxembourg compromise.*

*Neofunctionalism proved fertile and flexible in the 1960s and early 1970s. Numerous scholars in international relations and comparative politics applied their considerable energies to dissecting the*

---

Reprinted from *The Political Dynamics of European Economic Integration* by Leon N. Lindberg (Stanford University Press, 1963).  Notes omitted.

*integration process. Several empirical and theoretical problems cropped up along the way, but creative thinkers modified neofunctionalism to settle most of the issues. By 1970, the theory was rigorously specified but very complex—hardly the elegant model of the early 1960s. Problems with the theory continued to mount in the early 1970s, and in 1975 Ernst Haas declared regional integration theory (read neofunctionalism) "obsolescent." Most neofunctionalists took Haas's hint and moved on to other theories of international political economy, such as interdependence theory and regime theory. But neofunctionalism did not die, as we shall see in Part 3.*

The Europe that gave birth to the idea of the nation state appears to be well on the way to rejecting it in practice. The Treaty establishing the European Economic Community (EEC), signed in Rome on 25 March 1957, represents the latest in a series of steps designed to break down the bastions of European national separatism. Its six signatories, France, Germany, Italy, Belgium, the Netherlands, and Luxembourg, were already members of the European Coal and Steel Community (ECSC), whose foundation in 1952 had created a common market restricted to coal and steel. The experience with this first effort at sector integration led ultimately to the creation of the EEC as well as the European Atomic Energy Community (EURATOM):

> It soon became evident that integration by sectors could only yield limited results. Its restricted scope, unconnected with the other parts of the economic and financial system, ruled out any large-scale activities and made it impossible to achieve an overall equilibrium. To sweep away from Europe protectionism and economic nationalism with their resulting high production costs, high costs of living and economic stagnation, a different approach was required, a wide attack in more than one dimension as it were; it must have the depth of integration and the wide scope of a freeing of trade. This approach was provided first by the Beyen Plan and then by the Spaak Report, which marked the first step towards the Common Market.

The EEC has as its primary goal the creation of an area in which goods, people, services, and capital will be able to circulate freely. To achieve this, a customs union is created, but a customs union in which attention is devoted not only to barriers between states, but to economic, financial, and social reactions that may take place in the member states. The main purpose is the abolition of trade barriers, tariffs, and quotas, which is to be accomplished more or less automatically during a twelve- to fifteen-year transition period, divided into three four-year stages. A series of targets is assigned to each stage, and these relate not only to progress in removal of trade barriers, but also to parallel measures of economic and social alignment. This process is to be accompanied by the establishment of a common external tariff, within which an alignment of the several economies is to go on in order to adjust differences in price and working conditions, and in productive resources. Advancement from one stage to another is dependent upon achieving these respective targets. All this is to be supervised by institutions specially set up by the Treaty.

The economic and social significance of these developments is certainly far-reaching—one need only read the newspapers to confirm this. For the political scientist, too, they are of consuming interest, for here he can observe the actual processes whereby political actors move beyond the nation state as a basic framework for action, appearing finally to realize the oft-proclaimed "fact" of the international interdependence of nations. Forces are at work in Western Europe that may alter the nature of international relations, as well as offer promise of a fuller and more prosperous life for the inhabitants of the region.

The stated goal of the EEC is the creation of a customs union and ultimately the achievement of a significant measure of economic integration. The fundamental motivation is political. It is, in the words of the Treaty, to establish "an ever closer union among the European peoples." Our concern will be with the political *consequences* of economic integration. We shall try to measure the extent to which the creation of the EEC and the activities which take place in its framework give rise to the phenomenon of political integration. Whereas in terms of commercial policy the establishment of the EEC is "already the most important event of this century," its vast political significance is still only a potential.

## ■ POLITICAL INTEGRATION

What, then, do we mean by political integration? Some writers define it as a *condition,* and others as a *process.* In the works of Karl W. Deutsch, integration refers to the probability that conflicts will be resolved without violence. The central concept is that of a "security-community," which is "a group of people which has become integrated": that is, they have attained "within a territory . . . a 'sense of community' and . . . institutions and practices strong enough and widespread enough to assure, for a 'long' time, dependable expectations of 'peaceful change' among its population." Integration may come about through several types of security-communities, "amalgamated" or "pluralistic," implying respectively either the presence or the absence of any real central decision-making institutions or delegations of national autonomy. In either case, integration is achieved when the states concerned cease to prepare for war against each other.

Similarly, North, Koch, and Zinnes list six criteria in terms of which one can consider integration: the probability of violence given a conflict situation (same as Deutsch); the frequency of conflicts between any given number of organizations in a given span of time; the number of compatible policy conditions; the degree of interdependency between *n* given organizations; the number and significance of interlocking communications systems or structures; and the extent to which membership overlaps.

Such conceptualizations of political integration as a *condition* have been criticized on the grounds that they permit only a general discussion of the environmental factors influencing integration, and that they fail to provide us with the tools needed to make a clear distinction between the situation prior to integration and the situation prevailing during the process, thus obscuring the role of social change. For these reasons, Haas insists that we should look at political integration as a *process:* "Political integration is the process whereby political actors in several distinct national settings are persuaded to shift their loyalties, expectations and political activities toward a new center, whose institutions possess or demand jurisdiction over the preexisting national states. The end result of a process of political integration is a new political community, superimposed over the preexisting ones."

In Haas's work, this definition is rigorously tied to an ideal-type analysis in which the institutions of the ECSC are compared to those of an ideal federal-type system. This kind of heuristic device is certainly above reproach and did in fact yield extremely valuable results. My own investigations, however, have led me to adopt a more cautious conception of political integration, one limited to the development of devices and processes for arriving at collective decisions by means other than autonomous action by national governments. It seems to me that it is logically and empirically possible that collective decision-making procedures involving a significant amount of political integration can be achieved without moving toward a "political community" as defined by Haas. In fact, use of this type of ideal, or model, analysis may well direct the researcher to a different set of questions and a different interpretation of the data collected:

> European integration is developing, and may continue so for a long time, in the direction of different units. . . . We can only speculate about the outcome, but a forecast of the emergence of a pluralistic political structure, hitherto unknown, might not be wholly erroneous. Such a structure might very well permit to a great extent the participating nations to retain their identity while yet joined in the organizations that transcend nationality.

For the purpose of this study, political integration will be defined as a *process*, but without reference to an end point. In specific terms, political integration is (1) the process whereby nations forgo the desire and ability to conduct foreign and key domestic policies independently of each other, seeking instead to make *joint decisions* or to *delegate* the decision-making process to new central organs; and (2) the process whereby political actors in several distinct settings are persuaded to shift their expectations and political activities to a new center.

Although this dual definition lacks the analytical clarity and precision of model analysis, it is, I believe, appropriate to the problem at hand. Not only does it provide us with a set of interrelated indicators by means of which to judge the experience of the EEC, but it specifies what I take to be the process of political integration. The first part of the definition refers to two modes of decisionmaking which are, in my opinion, intimately related, the existence of delegated decisionmaking being a basic precondition for progress in shared decisionmaking. The processes of *sharing* and of *delegating* decisionmaking are likely to affect the governmental structure in each state involved, creating new internal problems of coordination and policy direction, especially between Ministries of Foreign Affairs and such specialized ministries as Economic Affairs, Agriculture, and Labor that are accustomed to regarding their spheres as wholly or primarily of domestic concern. States with traditions of representative and parliamentary government are also faced with the problem created by the development of decision-making centers whose authority derives from an international, rather than a national, consensus.

The second part of the definition refers to the patterns of behavior shown by high policy makers, civil servants, parliamentarians, interest-group leaders, and other elites. Here our attention is directed to the perceptions and resulting behavior of the political actors in each of the states involved. The relationship between this set of indicators and those referring to governmental decisionmaking is very close. By the nature of the process, government policy-makers and civil servants are involved increasingly in the new system of decisionmaking: they attend meetings of experts, draft plans, and participate in an over-all joint decision-making pattern. Similarly, as the locus of decisionmaking changes, so will the tactics of groups and individuals seeking to influence the decision-making process. They may oppose the change, but once made they will have to adjust to it by changing their tactics, or their organization, or both, to accommodate to the new situation. In Haas's words: "Conceived not as a condition but as a *process*, the conceptualization [of political integration] relies on the perception of interests . . . by the actors participating in the process. Integration takes place when these perceptions fall into a certain pattern and fails to take place when they do not." Moreover, "as the process of integration proceeds, it is assumed . . . that interests will be redefined in terms of regional rather than a purely national orientation."

So much for defining the concept of political integration. The problem now is to try to spell out how it can be made to occur in actual life. Since there have been numerous efforts at transnational organization and cooperation that have not had political results of this kind, political scientists have tried to identify constant background, or environmental, factors or conditions upon which political integration is contingent. Thus Deutsch isolates the following conditions as essential or helpful for a pluralistic or amalgamated security-community: initially compatible value systems, mutually responsive elites, adequate communications channels, a commitment to a "new way of life," and the existence of a "core area." Similarly, Haas calls for a pluralistic social structure, a high level of economic and industrial development, and a modicum of ideological homogeneity.

But the examination of background factors or conditions does not help us account completely for the *process* of political integration, nor does it permit differentiation between the situation prior to integration and the situation prevailing during the process. Accordingly, it is necessary to try to identify some additional variable factors to specify *how* political integration occurs. On the basis of Haas's researches and my own experiences in Western Europe, I suggest that the process of political integration requires the following conditions: (1) Central institutions and central policies must develop. (2) The tasks assigned to these institutions must be important enough and specific enough to activate socioeconomic processes to which conventional international organizations have no access. (3) These tasks must be inherently expansive. (4) The member states must continue to see their interests as consistent with the enterprise.

## ■ CENTRAL INSTITUTIONAL DEVELOPMENT

Central institutions are required in order to *represent* the common interests which have brought the member states together, and in order to *accommodate* such conflicts of interest as will inevitably arise. In discussing the institutions of the EEC, I prefer to avoid the concept of "supranationality" and to focus instead on the extent to which the Community institutions are enabled to deal directly with fields of activity, rather than merely influencing the actions of individual governments in respect of these fields. There are four main aspects to be considered:

1. North, Koch, and Zinnes seek to distinguish between compromise and "true integration," both seen as ways of dealing with conflict. Both depend upon *reducing the intensity* of the conflict by uncovering its sources, and by taking the demands of both sides and breaking them into their constituent parts. Each party to the conflict is forced to reexamine and reevaluate its own desires against those of the other party and against the implications of the total situation. True integration is achieved when a solution has been found in which "both desires have found a place," in which the interests of the parties "fit into each other." I suggest that the central institutions of the EEC, by isolating issues and identifying common interests, may play a crucial role here in "precipitating unity."

2. The integrative impact of the central institutions will depend in part upon the *competencies* and *roles* assigned to them. Much, however, depends upon whether or not the institutions make full use of their competencies and upon *how they define their role*. The literature on organizational decisionmaking suggests some relevant questions in this context. What formal and informal decisionmaking and relational patterns will develop? What patterns of commitment will be enforced by organizational imperatives, by the social character of the personnel, by "institutionalization," by the social and cultural environment, and by centers of interest generated in the course of action and decision? I suggest that the early years of the existence of these institutions will be significant in determining their long-range competence, that patterns of internal differentiation and conflicting values will develop, that organizational behavior will be conditioned by the necessity of adjusting to the environment, and that cooptation will be used as a tactic to head off opposition.

3. Central institutions lacking real competency to affect policymaking directly may develop a *consensus* that will influence those national or international decision makers who do determine policy.

4. Finally, the patterns of interaction engendered by the central institutions may affect *the overall system* in which they operate; in other words, these institutions may have latent effects that contribute to political integration. Participants in the activities of central institu-

tions may develop multiple perspectives, personal friendships, a camaraderie of expertise, all of which may reflect back upon the national governments and affect future national policymaking. Such latent effects, however, are significant only if the individuals concerned are influential at the national level, *and* if their activities in the central institutions involve significant policymaking.

## ELITE ACTIVATION

Thanks to the efforts of the so-called "group theorists," political scientists today know that any analysis of the political process must give a central place to the phenomena of group conflict, to the beliefs, attitudes, and ideologies of groups participating in the process of policy formation. If political integration, as we have defined it, is going on, then we would expect to find a change in the behavior of the participants. Consequently we must identify the aims and motives of the relevant political groups, the conditions of their emergence, and the means by which they seek and attain access to centers of political power.

One of the main obstacles to political integration has been the fact that international organizations lack direct access to individuals and groups in the national communities involved. "Short of such access, the organization continues to be no more than a forum of intergovernmental consultation and cooperation."

Actors with political power in the national community will restructure their expectations and activities only if the tasks granted to the new institutions are of immediate concern to them, and only if they involve a significant change in the conditions of the actors' environment. Several patterns of reaction may be expected:

1. Individual firms may undertake measures of self-protection or adjustment in the form of cartels to limit competition, the conclusion of agreements, and so on.
2. Groups may change their political organization and tactics in order to gain access to, and to influence, such new central decision-making centers as may be developing.
3. These activities may act back upon the central institutions and the member states by creating situations that cannot be dealt with except by further central institutional development and new central policies. An example would be a developing need for antitrust legislation in response to an evolving network of agreements between firms in several countries.

4. Such activities may also have latent effects of the kind already described, operative under the same conditions.

## ■ INHERENTLY EXPANSIVE TASKS

Here is a problem of central importance because changes in the policy needs of the member states create definite phases in the life of international organizations. To remedy this, the task assigned to the institutions must be inherently expansive and thus capable of overcoming what Haas calls "the built-in autonomy of functional contexts."

> Lessons about integrative processes associated with one phase do not generally carry over into the next because the specific policy context . . . determines what is desired by governments and tolerated by them in terms of integrative accommodations. . . . There is no dependable, cumulative process of precedent formation leading to ever more community-oriented organizational behavior, unless the task assigned to the institutions is inherently expansive, thus capable of overcoming the built-in autonomy of functional contexts and of surviving changes in the policy aims of member states.

This is the principle involved in the concept of "spillover." In its most general formulation, "spillover" refers to a situation in which a given action, related to a specific goal, creates a situation in which the original goal can be assured only by taking further actions, which in turn create a further condition and a need for more action, and so forth. The concept has been used by Haas to show that integrating one sector of the economy—for example, coal and steel—will inevitably lead to the integration of other economic and political activities. We shall formulate it as follows: the initial task and grant of power to the central institutions creates a situation or series of situations that can be dealt with only by further expanding the task and the grant of power. Spillover implies that a situation has developed in which the ability of a member state to achieve a policy goal may depend upon the attainment by another member state of one of its policy goals. The situation may show various features:

1. The dynamics of spillover are dependent upon the fact that support for any given step in integration is the result of a convergence of goals and expectations. These often competing goals give rise to competing activities and demands, which may be the basis of further convergence leading to further integration.

2. Lack of agreement between governments may lead to an expanded role for the central institutions; in other words, member states may delegate difficult problems.
3. At the level of elite groupings, demands and expectations for further actions may be expressed as a result of partial actions taken by the central institutions.
4. The activities of the central institutions and nonofficial elites may *create situations* that cannot be dealt with except by further central institutional development and new central policies.
5. Far-reaching economic integration, involving all sectors of the economy, as in the EEC, may offer great scope for spillover *between* sectors. Conflicts over further integration in a given sector, involving disparate national interests, may be resolved by bargains between such sectors (e.g., agriculture and energy).
6. Participation in a customs union will probably elicit reactions from nonmember states, a situation which may create problems that can be resolved only by further integration or by expanding the role of the central institutions.

## ■ CONTINUITY OF NATIONAL POLICY AIMS

"Spillover" assumes the continued commitment of the member states to the undertaking. The Treaty of Rome was the result of a creative compromise, a convergence of national aspirations. Political and economic integration cannot be expected to succeed in the absence of a will to proceed on the part of the member states. Granted that it would be difficult for a state to withdraw from the EEC, it must be stressed that little could be done to move beyond minimal obligations if one or several states were to maintain a determined resistance. It seems likely, however, that with the operation of the other integrative factors, the alternatives open to any member state will gradually be limited so as to reduce dependence upon this factor. For the will to proceed need not have a positive content. Given only a general reluctance to be charged with obstruction, or to see the enterprise fail, the stimulus to action can be provided by the central institutions or by other member states.

The way in which decisions are made, in which conflicts of interest among the member states are resolved, will be of definitive importance for political integration, because the kind of accommodation that prevails will indicate the nature of the positive convergence of pro-integration aims, and of the extent to which the alternatives open to national decision makers may have been limited by participation in the enterprise. In this connection we may ask the question, under what conditions does conflict produce a stronger bond between the parties than that which existed before? Moreover, as already mentioned, the mode of accommodation is directly correlated to the developmental potential of the central institutions.

Conflicts between states may be resolved on the basis of "the minimum common denominator," by "splitting the difference," or by "upgrading common interests." The "minimum common denominator" type, characteristic of classical diplomatic negotiations, involves relatively equal bargainers who exchange equal concessions while never going beyond what the least cooperative among them is willing to concede. Accommodation by "splitting the difference" involves a similar exchange of concessions, but conflicts are ultimately resolved somewhere between the final bargaining positions, usually because of the mediatory role performed by a secretariat or expert study groups, or out of deference to third-party pressure such as might be institutionalized in "parliamentary diplomacy." This implies "the existence of a continuing organization with a broad frame of reference, public debate, rules of procedure governing the debate, and the statement of conclusions arrived at by some kind of majority vote." Although such mediating organs may not be able to define the terms of agreement, they do participate in setting limits within which the ultimate accommodation is reached. Accommodation on the basis of "upgrading common interests," whether deliberately or inadvertently, depends on the participation of institutions or individuals with an autonomous role that permits them to participate in actually defining the terms of the agreement. It implies greater progress toward political integration, for it shows that

> the parties succeeded in so redefining their conflict so as to work out a solution at a higher level, which almost invariably implies the expansion of the mandate or task of an international or national governmental agency. In terms of results, this mode of accommodation maximizes . . . the "spillover" effect of international decisions: policies made pursuant to an initial task and grant of power can be made real only if the task itself is expanded, as reflected in the compromises among the states interested in the task.

This last type comes closest to what North, Koch, and Zinnes call "true integration."

We now have a set of definitions, variable factors, indicators, and hypotheses with which to assess the extent to which the EEC is contributing to the process of political integration. We are concerned above all with determining the impact of the EEC on official and nonofficial decision-making patterns in the "Europe of the Six," and with analyzing the structure and content of such central decision-making as may develop.

. . .

# 18 Obstinate or Obsolete? The Fate of the Nation-State and the Case of Western Europe

STANLEY HOFFMANN

*The early 1960s were optimistic years for students of integration. The European Economic Community was pressing integration forward at a rapid pace and neofunctionalists seemed to have discovered the means by which advanced industrialized nations could push the international community beyond the sovereign state and dramatically reduce the possibility of war. But was this, in fact, the end of the nation-state? De Gaulle's precipitation of the "empty chair crisis" in 1965 indicated to many international observers that the nation-state was alive and well. One of them was Stanley Hoffmann of Harvard University.*

*Hoffmann—who was born in Vienna and raised in wartime France—argued in this very long 1966* Daedalus *article (which bears close reading in its entirety) that the states of Europe were still self-interested entities with clear interests, despite their willingness to engage in closer cooperation in areas of "low politics," such as agriculture and trade. The members of the European Communities stubbornly hung on to the sovereignty that counts—control over foreign policy, national security, and the use of force ("high politics")—while only reluctantly bargaining away control over important aspects of their economies in exchange for clear material benefits. Thus func-*

Reprinted with permission from *Daedalus*, Journal of the American Academy of Arts and Sciences, from the issue entitled "Tradition and Change," Summer 1966, vol. 95, no. 3. Notes omitted.

*tional integration, Hoffmann argued, reached its limits very quickly, failing to take Europe "beyond the nation-state."*

*Hoffmann's approach to international relations does not fit neatly into any single category.[1] At one level he is a "realist" who sees international politics as the interaction of self-interested states who protect their sovereignty in an anarchic world. At the same time, he admits the possibility of cooperation among sovereign states, the development of norms governing international behavior, and the impact of domestic politics on state interests. In this sense he is more of a "liberal." These two perspectives come together in his view of European integration. Cooperation among European states has changed the system of state interaction, but it has not eliminated state sovereignty. Integration occurs, according to Hoffmann, when sovereign states, pursuing their national interests, negotiate cooperative agreements—a view often labeled "intergovernmentalism." Intergovernmental bargaining can result in significant cooperation when the interests of the negotiating states coincide. But when states disagree over the best course of action, cooperation stalls, as it did in Europe in the 1960s.*

*Intergovernmentalism, with its emphasis on the strength of the nation-state, provides a theoretical counter to neofunctionalism (Chapters 16 and 17) with its accent on the erosion of sovereignty by supranational actors. Hoffmann, as one of the first intergovernmentalists to challenge the core assumptions of the neofunctionalists, laid the foundation for the great theoretical debate of the early 1990s.*

The critical issue for every student of world order is the fate of the nation-state. In the nuclear age, the fragmentation of the world into countless units, each of which has a claim to independence, is obviously dangerous for peace and illogical for welfare. The dynamism which animates those units, when they are not merely city-states of limited expanse or dynastic states manipulated by the Prince's calculations, but nation-states that pour into their foreign policy the collective pride, ambitions, fears, prejudices, and images of large masses of people, is particularly formidable. An abstract theorist could argue that any system of autonomous units follows the same basic rules, whatever the nature of those units. But in practice, that is, in history, their substance matters as much as their form; the story of world affairs since the French Revolution is not merely one more sequence in the ballet of sovereign states; it is the story of the fires and upheavals propagated by nationalism. A claim to sovereignty based on historical tradition and dynastic legitimacy alone has never had the fervor, the self-righteous assertiveness which a similar claim based on the idea and feelings of nationhood presents: in world politics, the dynastic function of nationalism is the constitution of nation-states by amalgamation or by splintering, and its emotional function is the supplying of a formidable good conscience to leaders who see their task as the achievement of nationhood, the defense of the nation, or the expansion of a national mission.

This is where the drama lies. The nation-state is at the same time a form of social organization and—in practice if not in every brand of theory—a factor of international non-integration; but those who argue in favor of a more integrated world, either under more centralized power or through various networks of regional or functional agencies, tend to forget Auguste Comte's old maxim that *on ne détruit que ce qu'on remplace*: the new "formula" will have to provide not only world order, but also the kind of social organization in which leaders, élites, and citizens feel at home. There is currently no agreement on what such a formula will be; as a result, nation-states—often inchoate, economically absurd, administratively ramshackle, and impotent yet dangerous in international politics—remain the basic units in spite of all the remonstrations and exhortations. They go on *faute de mieux* despite their alleged obsolescence; indeed, not only do they profit from man's incapacity to bring about a better order, but their very existence is a formidable obstacle to their replacement.

If there was one part of the world in which men of goodwill thought that the nation-state could be superseded, it was Western Europe. One of France's most subtle commentators on international politics has recently reminded us of E. H. Carr's bold prediction of 1945: "we shall not see again a Europe of twenty, and a world of more than sixty independent sovereign states." Statesmen have invented original schemes for moving Western Europe "beyond the nation-state," and political scientists have studied their efforts with a care from which emotional involvement was not missing. The conditions seemed ideal. On the one hand, nationalism seemed at its lowest ebb; on the other, an adequate formula and method for building a substitute had apparently been devised. Twenty years after the end of World War II—a period as long as the whole interwar era—observers have had to revise their judgments. The most optimistic put their hope in the chances the future may still harbor, rather than in the propelling power of the present; the less optimistic ones, like myself, try simply to understand what went wrong.

My own conclusion is sad and simple. The nation-state is still here, and the new Jerusalem has been postponed because the nations in Western Europe have not been able to stop time and to fragment space. Political unification could have succeeded if, on the one hand, these nations had not been caught in the whirlpool of different concerns, as a result both of profoundly different internal circumstances and of outside legacies, and if, on the other hand, they had been able or obliged to concentrate on "community-building" to the exclusion of all problems situated either outside their area or within each one of them. Domestic differences and different world views obviously mean diverging foreign policies; the involvement of the policy-makers in issues among which "community-building" is merely one has meant a deepening, not a decrease, of those divergencies. The reasons follow: the unification movement has been the victim, and the survival of nation-states the outcome, of three factors, one of which characterizes every international system, and the other two only the present system. Every international system owes its inner logic and its unfolding to the diversity of domestic determinants, geo-historical situations, and outside aims among its units; any international system based on fragmentation tends, through the dynamics of unevenness (so well understood, if applied only to economic unevenness, by Lenin) to reproduce diversity. However, there is no inherent reason that the model of the fragmented international system should rule out by itself two developments in which the critics of the nation-state have put their bets or their hopes. Why must it be a diversity of nations? Could it not be a diversity of regions, of "federating" blocs, superseding the nation-state just as the dynastic state had replaced the feudal puzzle? Or else, why does the very logic of conflagrations fed by hostility not lead to the kind of catastrophic unification of exhausted yet interdependent nations, sketched out by Kant? Let us remember that the unity movement in Europe was precisely an attempt at creating a regional entity, and that its origins and its springs resembled, on the reduced scale of a half-continent, the process dreamed up by Kant in his *Idea of Universal History*.

The answers are not entirely provided by the two factors that come to mind immediately. One is the legitimacy of national self-determination, the only principle which transcends all blocs and ideologies, since all pay lip service to it, and provides the foundation for the only "universal actor" of the international system: the United Nations. The other is the newness of many of the states, which have wrested their independence by a nationalist upsurge and are therefore unlikely to throw or give away what they have obtained only too recently. However, the legitimacy of the nation-state does not by itself guarantee the nation-state's survival in the international state of nature, and the appeal of nationalism as an emancipating passion does not assure that the nation-state must everywhere remain the basic form of social organization, in a world in which many nations are old and settled and the shortcomings of the nation-state are obvious. The real answers are provided by two unique features of the present international system. One, it is the first truly global international system: the regional subsystems have only a reduced autonomy; the "relationships of major tension" blanket the whole planet; the domestic polities are dominated not so much by the region's problems as by purely local and purely global ones, which conspire to divert the region's members from the internal affairs of their area, and indeed would make an isolated treatment of those affairs impossible. As a result, each nation, new or old, finds itself placed in an orbit of its own, from which it is quite difficult to move away: for the attraction of the regional forces is offset by the pull of all the other forces. Or, to change the metaphor, those nations that coexist in the same apparently separate "home" of a geographical region find themselves both exposed to the smells and noises that come from outside through all their windows and doors, and looking at the outlying houses from which the interference issues. Coming from diverse pasts, moved by diverse tempers, living in different parts of the house, inescapably yet differently subjected and attracted to the outside world, those cohabitants react unevenly to their exposure and calculate conflictingly how they could either reduce the disturbance or affect in turn all those who live elsewhere. The adjustment of their own relations within the house becomes subordinated to their divergences about the outside world; the "regional subsystem" becomes a stake in the rivalry of its members about the system as a whole.

However, the coziness of the common home could still prevail if the inhabitants were forced to come to terms, either by one of them, or by the fear of a threatening neighbor. This is precisely where the second unique feature of the present situation intervenes. What tends to perpetuate the nation-states decisively in a system whose universality seems to sharpen rather than shrink their diversity is the new set of conditions that govern and restrict the rule of force: Damocles' sword has become a boomerang, the ideological legitimacy of the nation-state is protected by the relative and forced tameness of the world jungle. Force in the nuclear age is still the "midwife of societies" insofar as revolutionary war either breeds new nations or shapes regimes in existing nations; but the use of force along traditional lines, for conquest and expansion—the very use that made the "permeable" feudal units not only obsolete but collapse and replaced them with modem states often built on "blood and iron"—has become too dangerous. The legitimacy of the feudal unit could be undermined in two ways: brutally, by the rule of force—the big fish swallowing small fish by national might; subtly or legitimately, so to speak, through self-undermining—the logic of dynastic weddings or acquisitions that consolidated larger units. A system based on national self-determination rules out the latter; a system in which nations, once established, find force a much blunted weapon rules out the former. Thus agglomeration by conquest or out of a fear of conquest fails to take place. The new conditions of violence tend even to pay to national borders the tribute of vice to virtue: violence which dons the cloak of revolution rather than of interstate wars, or persists in the form of such wars only when they accompany revolutions or conflicts in divided countries, perversely respects borders by infiltrating under them rather than by crossing them overtly. Thus all that is left for unification is what one might call "national self-abdication" or self-abnegation, the eventual willingness of nations to try something else; but precisely global involvement hinders rather than helps, and the atrophy of war removes the most pressing incentive. What a nation-state cannot provide alone—in economics, or defense—it can still provide through means far less drastic than hara-kiri.

These two features give its solidity to the principle of national self-determination, as well as its resilience to the U.N. They also give its present, and quite unique, shape to the "relationship of major tension": the conflict between East and West. This conflict is both muted and universal—and both aspects contribute to the survival of the nation-state. As the superpowers find that what makes their power overwhelming also makes it less usable, or rather usable only to deter one another and to deny each other gains, the lesser states discover under the umbrella of the nuclear stalemate that they are not condemned to death, and that indeed their nuisance power is impressive—especially when the kind of violence that prevails in present circumstances favors the porcupine over the elephant. The superpowers experience in their own camps the backlash of a rebellion against domination that enjoys broad impunity, and cannot easily coax or coerce third parties into agglomeration under their tutelage. Yet they retain the means to prevent other powers from agglomerating away from their clutches. Thus, as the superpowers compete, with filed nails, all over the globe, the nation-state becomes the universal point of salience, to use the new language of strategy—the lowest common denominator in the competition.

Other international systems were merely conservative of diversity; the present system is profoundly conservative of the diversity of nation-states, despite all its revolutionary features. The dream of Rousseau, concerned both about the prevalence of the general will—

that is, the nation-state—and about peace, was the creation of communities insulated from one another. In history, where "the essence and drama of nationalism is not to be alone in the world," the clash of non-insulated states has tended to breed both nation-states and wars. Today, Rousseau's ideals come closer to reality, but in the most un-Rousseauean way: the nation-states prevail in peace, they remain unsuperseded because a fragile peace keeps the Kantian doctor away, they are unreplaced because their very involvement in the world, their very inability to insulate themselves from one another, preserves their separateness. The "new Europe" dreamed by the Europeans could not be established by force. Left to the wills and calculations of its members, the new formula has not jelled because they could not agree on its role in the world. The failure (so far) of an experiment tried in apparently ideal conditions tells us a great deal about contemporary world politics, and about the functional approach to unification. For it shows that the movement can fail not only when there is a surge of nationalism in one important part but also when there are differences in assessments of the national interest that rule out agreement on the shape and on the world role of the new, supranational whole.

. . .

Since it is the process of European integration that is its [Western Europe's] most original feature, we must examine it also. We have been witnessing a kind of race, between the logic of integration set up by Monnet and analyzed by Haas, and the logic of diversity, analyzed above. According to the former, the double pressure of necessity (the interdependence of the social fabric, which will oblige statesmen to integrate even sectors originally left uncoordinated) and of men (the action of the supranational agents) will gradually restrict the freedom of movement of the national governments by turning the national situations into one of total enmeshing. In such a milieu, nationalism will be a futile exercise in anachronism, and the national consciousness itself will, so to speak, be impregnated by an awareness of the higher interest in union. The logic of diversity, by contrast, sets limits to the degree to which the "spill-over process" can limit the freedom of action of the governments; it restricts the domain in which the logic of functional integration operates to the area of welfare; indeed, to the extent that discrepancies over the other areas begin to prevail over the laborious harmonization in welfare, even issues belonging to the latter sphere may become infected by the disharmony which reigns in those other areas. The logic of integration is that of a blender which crunches the most diverse products, overcomes their different tastes and perfumes, and replaces them with one, presumably delicious juice. One lets each item be ground because one expects a finer synthesis: that is, ambiguity helps rather than hinders because each "ingredient" can hope that its taste will prevail at the end. The logic of diversity is the opposite: it suggests that, in areas of key importance to the national interest, nations prefer the certainty, or the self-controlled uncertainty, of national self-reliance, to the uncontrolled uncertainty of the untested blender; ambiguity carries one only a part of the way. The logic of integration assumes that it is possible to fool each one of the associates some of the time because his over-all gain will still exceed his occasional losses, even if his calculations turn out wrong here or there. The logic of diversity implies that, on a vital issue, losses are not compensated by gains on other (and especially not on other less vital) issues: nobody wants to be fooled. The logic of integration deems the uncertainties of the supranational function process creative; the logic of diversity sees them as destructive past a certain threshold; Russian roulette is fine only as long as the gun is filled with blanks. Ambiguity lures and lulls the national consciousness into integration as long as the benefits are high, the costs low, the expectations considerable. Ambiguity may arouse and stiffen national consciousness into nationalism if the benefits are slow, the losses high, the hopes dashed or deferred. Functional integration's gamble could be won only if the method had sufficient potency to promise a permanent excess of gains over losses, and of hopes over frustrations. Theoretically, this may be true of economic integration. It is not true of political integration (in the sense of "high politics").

The success of the approach symbolized by Jean Monnet depended, and depends still, on his winning a triple gamble: on goals, on methods, on results. As for goals, it is a gamble on the possibility of substituting motion as an end in itself, for agreement on ends. It is a fact that the transnational integrationist élites did not agree on whether the object of the community-building enterprise ought to be the construction of a new super-state—that is, a federal potential nation, *à la* U.S.A., more able because of its size and resources to play the traditional game of power than the dwarfed nations of Western Europe—or whether the object was to demonstrate that power politics could be overcome through cooperation and compromise, to build the first example of a radically new kind of unit, to achieve a change in the nature and not merely in the scale of the game. Monnet himself has been ambiguous on this score; Hallstein has been leaning in the first direction, many of Monnet's public relations men in the second. Nor did the integrationists agree on whether the main goal was the creation of a regional "security-community," that is, the pacification of a former hotbed of wars, or whether the main goal was the creation of an entity whose position and might could decisively affect the course of the cold war in particular, of international relations in general. Now, it is perfectly possible for a movement to feed on its harboring continental nationalists as well as anti-power idealists, inward-looking politicians and outward-looking politicians—but only as long as there is no need to make a choice. Decisions on tariffs did not require such choices. Decisions on agriculture already raise basic problems of orientation. Decisions on foreign policy and membership and defense cannot be reached unless the goals are clarified. One cannot be all things to all people all of the time.

As for methods, there was a gamble on the irresistible rise of supranational functionalism. It assumed, first, that national sovereignty, already devalued by events, could be chewed up leaf by leaf like an artichoke. It assumed, second, that the dilemma of governments having to choose between pursuing an integration that ties their hands and stopping a movement that benefits their people could be exploited in favor of integration by men representing the common good, endowed with the advantages of superior expertise, initiating proposals, propped against a set of deadlines, and using for their cause the technique of package deals. Finally, it was assumed that this approach would both take into account the interests of the greater powers and prevent the crushing of the smaller ones. The troubles with this gamble have been numerous. One, even an artichoke has a heart, which remains intact after the leaves have been eaten. It is of course true that a successful economic and social integration would considerably limit the freedom governments would still enjoy in theory for their diplomacy and strategy; but why should one assume that they would not be aware of it? As the artichoke's heart gets more and more denuded, the governments' vigilance gets more and more alerted. To be sure, the second assumption implies that the logic of the movement would prevent them from doing anything about it: they would be powerless to save the heart. But, two, this would be true only if governments never put what they consider essential interests of the nation above the particular interests of certain categories of national, if superior expertise were always either the Commission's monopoly or the solution of the issue at hand, if package deals were effective in every argument, and, above all, if the governments' representatives were always determined to behave as a "community organ" rather than as the agents of states that are not willing to accept a community under any conditions. Finally, functional integration may indeed give lasting satisfaction to the smaller powers, precisely because it is for them that the ratio of "welfare politics" to high politics is highest, and that the chance of gaining benefits through intergovernmental methods that reflect rather than correct the power differential between the big and the small is poorest; but this is also why the method is not likely *à la longue* to satisfy the bigger powers as much: facing them, the supranational civil servants, for all their skill and legal powers, are a bit like Jonases trying to turn whales into jellyfish. Of course, the idea—ultimately—is to move from an essentially administrative procedure in which supranational civil servants enter a dialogue with national ministers, to a truly federal one in which a federal cabinet is responsible to a federal parliament; but what is thus presented as linear progress may turn out to be a vicious circle, since the ministers hold the key to the transformation, and may refuse it unless the goals are defined and the results already achieved are satisfactory.

There was a gamble about results as well. The experience of integration would entail net benefits for all, and bring about clear progress toward community formation. Such progress could be measured by the following yardsticks: in the realm of interstate relations, an increasing transfer of power to the new common agencies, and the prevalence of solutions "upgrading the common interest" over other kinds of compromises; in the realm of transnational society, an increasing flow of communications; in the area of national consciousness—which is important both for interstate relations, because (as seen above) it may set limits to the statesmen's discretion, and for transnational society, because it affects the scope and meaning of communication flows—progress would be measured by increasing compatibility of views about external issues. The results achieved so far are mixed: negative on the last count (see below), limited on the second, and marked on the first by features that the enthusiasts of integration did not expect. On the one hand, there has been some strengthening of authority of the Commission, and in various areas there has been some "upgrading of common interests." On the other hand, the Commission's unfortunate attempt to consolidate those gains at de Gaulle's expense, in the spring of 1965, has brought about a startling setback for the whole enterprise; moreover, in their negotiations, the members have conspicuously failed to find a common interest in some vital areas (energy, England's entry), and sometimes succeed in reaching apparently "integrating" decisions only after the most ungainly, traditional kinds of bargaining, in such uncommunity-like methods as threats, ultimatums and retaliatory moves, were used. In other words, either the ideal was not reached, or it was reached in a way that was both the opposite of the ideal and ultimately its destroyer. If we look at the institutions of the Common Market as an incipient political system in Europe, we find that its authority remains limited, its structure weak, its popular base restricted and distant.

. . .

There are two important general lessons one can draw from a study of the process of integration. The first concerns the limits of the functional method: its very (if relative) success in the relatively painless area in which it works relatively well lifts the participants to the level of issues to which it does not apply well anymore—like swimmers whose skills at moving quickly away from the shore suddenly brings them to the point where the waters are stormiest and deepest, at a time when fatigue is setting in, and none of the questions about the ultimate goal, direction, and length of swim has been answered. The functional process was used in order to "make Europe"; once Europe began being made, the process collided with the question: "making Europe, what for?" The process is like a grinding machine that can work only if someone keeps giving it something to grind. When the users start quarreling and stop providing, the machine stops. For a while, the machine worked because the governments poured into it a common determination to integrate their economies in order to maximize wealth; but with their wealth increasing, the question of what to do with it was going to arise: a technique capable of supplying means does not *ipso facto* provide the ends, and it is about those ends that quarrels have broken out. They might have been avoided if the situation had been more compelling—if the Six had been so cooped up that each one's horizon would have been nothing other than his five partners. But this has never been their outlook, nor is it any more their necessity. Each one is willing to live with the others, but not on terms too different from his own; and the Six are not in the position of the three miserable prisoners of *No Exit*. Transforming a dependent "subsystem" proved to be one thing; defining its relations to all other subsystems and to the international system in general has turned out to be quite another—indeed, so formidable a matter as to keep the transformation of the subsystem in abeyance until those relations can be defined.

The model of functional integration, a substitute for the kind of instant federation which governments had not been prepared to accept, shows its origins in important respects. One, it is essentially an administrative model, which relies on bureaucratic expertise for the promotion of a policy defined by the policy authorities, and for the definition of a policy that political decision-makers are technically incapable of shaping—something like French planning under the Fourth Republic. The hope was that in the interstices of political bickering the administrators could build up a consensus; but the mistake was to believe that a formula that works well within certain limits is a panacea—and that even within the limits of "welfare politics" administrative skill can always overcome the disastrous effects of political paralysis or mismanagement (cf. the impact of inflation, or balance of payment troubles, on planning). Two, the model assumes that the basic political decisions, to be prepared and pursued by the civil servants but formally made by the governments, would be reached through the process of short-term bargaining, by politicians whose mode of operation is empirical muddling through, of the kind that puts immediate advantages above long-term pursuits: this model corresponds well to the nature of parliamentary politics with a weak Executive, for example, the politics of the Fourth Republic, but the mistake was to believe that all political regimes would conform to this rather sorry image, and also to ignore the disastrous results which the original example produced whenever conflicts over values and fundamental choices made mere empirical groping useless or worse than useless (cf. decolonization).

The second lesson is even more discouraging for the advocates of functionalism. To revert to the analogy of the grinder, what has happened is that the machine, piqued by the slowing down of supply, suddenly suggested to its users that in the future the supplying of grinding material be taken out of their hands and left to the machine. The institutional machinery tends to become an actor with a stake in its own survival and expansion. But here we deal not with one but with six political systems, and the reason for the ineffectiveness of the Council of Ministers of the Six may be the excessive toughness, not the weakness, of the national political systems involved. In other words, by trying to be a force, the bureaucracy here, inevitably, makes itself even more of a stake that the nations try to control or at least to affect. A new complication is thus added to all the substantive issues that divide the participants.

. . .

What are the prospects in Western Europe? What generalizations can one draw from the whole experience?

. . .

It has become possible for scholars to argue both that integration is proceeding and that the nation-state is more than ever the basic unit, without contradicting each other, for recent definitions of integration "beyond the nation-state" point not toward the emergence of a new kind of political community, but merely toward "an obscur[ing of] the boundaries between the system of international organizations and the environment provided by member states." There are two important implications.

The first one is, not so paradoxically, a vindication of the nation-state as the basic unit. So far, anything that is "beyond" is "less": that is, there are cooperative arrangements with a varying degree of autonomy, power, and legitimacy, but there has been no transfer of allegiance toward their institutions, and their authority remains limited, conditional, dependent, and reversible. There is more than a kernel of truth in the Federalist critique of functional integration: functionalism tends to become, at best, like a spiral that coils *ad infinitum*. So far, the "transferring [of] exclusive expectations of benefits from the nation-state to some larger entity" leaves the nation-state both as the main focus of expectations, and as the initiator, pace-setter, supervisor, and often destroyer of the larger entity: for in the international arena the state is still the highest possessor of power, and while not every state is a political community there is as yet no political community more inclusive than the state. To be sure, the military function of the nation-state is in crisis; but, insofar as the whole world is "permeable" to nuclear weapons, any new type of unit would face the same horror, and, insofar as the prospect of such horror makes war more subdued and conquest less likely, the decline of the state's capacity to defend its citizens is neither total nor sufficient to force the nation-state itself into decline. The resistance of the nation-state is proven not only by the frustrations of functionalism but also by both the promise and the failure of Federalism. On the one hand, Federalism offers a way of going "beyond the nation-state," but it consists in building a new and larger nation-state. The scale is new, not the story, the gauge not the game. Indeed, the Federalist model applies to the "making of Europe" the Rousseauistic scheme for the creation of a nation: it aims at establishing a unit marked by central power and based on the general will of a European people. The Federalists are right in insisting that Western Europe's best chance of being an effective entity would be not to go "beyond the nation-state," but to become a larger nation-state in the process of formation and in the business of world politics: that is, to become a sovereign political community in the formal sense at least. The success of Federalism would be a tribute to the durability of the nation-state; its failure so far is due to the irrelevance of the model. Not only is there no general will of a European people because there is as of now no European people, but the institutions that could gradually (and theoretically) shape the separate nations into one people are not the most likely to do so. For the domestic problems of Europe are matters for technical decisions by civil servants and minsters rather than for general wills and assemblies (a general will to prosperity is not very operational). The external problems of Europe are matters for executives and diplomats. As for the common organs set up by the national governments, when they try to act as a European executive and parliament, they are both condemned to operate in the fog maintained around them by the governments and slapped down if they try to dispel the fog and reach the people themselves. In other words, Europe cannot be what some nations have been: a people that creates its state; nor can it be what some of the oldest states are and many of the new ones aspire to be: a people created by the state. It has to wait until the separate states decide that their peoples are close enough to justify a European state whose task will be the welding of the many into one; and we have just examined why such a joint decision has been missing. The very obstacles which make the Federalist model irrelevant to nations too diverse and divided also make all forms of union short of Federalism precarious. Functionalism is too unstable for the task of complete political unification. It may integrate economies, but either the nations will then proceed to a full political merger (which economic integration does not guarantee)—in that case the federal model will be vindicated at the end, the new unit will be a state forging its own people by consent and through the abdication of the previous separate states, but the conditions for success described above will have to be met—or else the national situations will remain too divergent, and functionalism will be merely a way of tying together the preexisting nations in areas deemed of common interest. Between the cooperation of existing nations and the breaking in of a new one there is no stable middle ground. A federation that succeeds becomes a nation; one that fails leads to secession; half-way attempts like supranational functionalism must either snowball or roll back.

But the nation-state, preserved as the basic unit, survives transformed. Among the men who see in "national sovereignty" the Nemesis of mankind, those who put their hopes in the development of regional superstates are illogical, those who put their hopes in the establishment of a world state are utopian, those who put their hopes in the growth of functional political communities more inclusive than the nation-state are too optimistic. What has to be understood and studied now—far more than has been done, and certainly far more than this essay was able to do—is, rather than the creation of rival communities, the transformation of "national sovereignty": it has not been superseded, but to a large extent it has been emptied of its former sting; there is no supershrew, and yet the shrew has been somewhat tamed. The model of the nation-state derived from the international law and relations of the past, when there was a limited number of players on a stage that was less crowded and in which violence was less risky, applies only fitfully to the situation of today. The basic unit, having proliferated, has also become much more heterogeneous; the stage has shrunk, and is occupied by players whose very number forces each one to strut, but its combustibility nevertheless scares them from pushing their luck too hard. The nation-state today is a new wine in old bottles, or in bottles that are sometimes only a mediocre imitation of the old; it is not the same old wine. What must be examined is not just the legal capacity of the sovereign state, but the *de facto* capacity at its disposal; granted the scope of its authority, how much of it can be used, and with what results? There are many ways of going "beyond the nation-state," and some modify the substance without altering the form or creating new forms. To be sure, as long as the old form is there, as long as the nation-state is the supreme authority, there is a danger for peace and for welfare; Gullivers tied by Lilliputians rather than crushed by Titans can wake up and break their ties. But Gullivers tied are not the same as Gullivers untied. Wrestlers who slug it out with fists and knives, prisoners in a chain gang, are all men; yet their freedom of action is not the same. An examination of the international implications of "nation-statehood" today and yesterday is at least as important as the ritual attack on the nation-state.

. . .

## ■ NOTE

1. We have altered our view of Hoffmann in this edition based on his autobiographical article "A Retrospective," in *Journeys Through World Politics: Autobiographical Reflections of Thirty-four Academic Travelers*, ed. Joseph J. Kruzel and James N. Rosenau (Lexington, Mass.: Lexington Books, 1989), pp. 263–278.

# 19 The Theory of Economic Integration: An Introduction

BELA BALASSA

*Federalists, functionalists, and neofunctionalists in the postwar period were largely concerned with the political results of integration, even if some of them (i.e., most federalists and functionalists) paid little attention to the political dimension of the integration process. They were, after all, chiefly interested in the peaceful resolution of international conflict. Postwar economists were also interested in the integration process in Europe but for different reasons. They were engaged in describing the process of economic integration and its impact on welfare. As war among West European nations became unthinkable in the years immediately following World War II, the economic gains of integration became the chief motive for continuing the process. Thus, the work of the economists took on added importance.*

*Bela Balassa (1928–1991), a professor of political economy at The Johns Hopkins University, was one of the most productive students of economic integration. Drawing on the work of Jacob Viner and others, Balassa made a major contribution to our understanding of the effects of integration on trade and other economic activities in the 1960s and 1970s. In this introductory chapter to his important work,* The Theory of Economic Integration *(1961), Balassa defines economic integration, identifies its stages, discusses political and ideological aspects of the integration process, and specifies what he means by "economic welfare." Finally, Balassa argues that functional*

---

*integration, while perhaps politically expedient, is not as economically defensible as "the simultaneous integration of all sectors."*

## ■ THE CONCEPT AND FORMS OF INTEGRATION

In everyday usage the word "integration" denotes the bringing together of parts into a whole. In the economic literature the term "economic integration" does not have such a clear-cut meaning. Some authors include social integration in the concept, others subsume different forms of international cooperation under this heading, and the argument has also been advanced that the mere existence of trade relations between independent national economies is a sign of integration. We propose to define economic integration as a process and as a state of affairs. Regarded as a process, it encompasses measures designed to abolish discrimination between economic units belonging to different national states; viewed as a state of affairs, it can be represented by the absence of various forms of discrimination between national economies.

In interpreting our definition, distinction should be made between integration and cooperation. The difference is qualitative as well as quantitative. Whereas cooperation includes actions aimed at lessening discrimination, the process of economic integration comprises measures that entail the suppression of some forms of discrimination. For example international agreements on trade policies belong to the area of international cooperation, while the removal of trade barriers is an act of economic integration. Distinguishing between cooperation and integration, we put the main characteristics of the latter—the abolition of discrimination within an area—into clearer focus and give the concept definite meaning without unnecessarily diluting it by the inclusion of diverse actions in the field of international cooperation.

Economic integration, as defined here, can take several forms that represent varying degrees of integration. These are a free-trade area, a customs union, a common market, an economic union, and complete economic integration. In a free-trade area, tariffs (and quantitative restrictions) between the participating countries are abolished, but each country retains its own tariffs against nonmembers. Establishing a customs union involves, besides the suppression of discrimination in the field of commodity movements within the union, the equalization of tariffs in trade with nonmember countries. A higher form of economic integration is attained in a common market, where not only trade restrictions but also restrictions on factor movements are abolished. An economic union, as distinct from a common market, combines the suppression of restrictions on commodity and factor policies, in order to remove discrimination that was due to disparities in these policies. Finally, total economic integration presupposes the unification of monetary, fiscal, social, and countercyclical policies and requires the setting-up of a supra-national authority whose decisions are binding for the member states.

Adopting the definition given above, the theory of economic integration will be concerned with the economic effects of integration in its various forms and with problems that arise from divergences in national monetary, fiscal, and other policies. The theory of economic integration can be regarded as a part of international economics, but it also enlarges the field of international trade theory by exploring the impact of a fusion of national markets on growth and examining the need for the coordination of economic policies in a union. Finally, the theory of economic integration should incorporate elements of location theory, too. The integration of adjacent countries amounts to the removal of artificial barriers that obstruct continuous economic activity through national frontiers, and the ensuing relocation of production and regional agglomerative and deglomerative tendencies cannot be adequately discussed without making use of the tools of locational analysis.

## ■ THE RECENT INTEREST IN ECONOMIC INTEGRATION

In the twentieth century no significant customs unions were formed until the end of the Second World War, although several attempts had been made to integrate the economies of various European countries. Without going into a detailed analysis, political obstacles can be singled out as the main causes for the failure of these projects to materialize. A certain degree of integration was achieved during the Second World War via a different route, when—as part of the German *Grossraum* policy—the Hitlerites endeavored to integrate economically the satellite countries and the occupied territories with Germany. In the latter case, economic integration appeared as a form of imperialist expansion.

The post–Second World War period has seen an enormous increase in the interest in problems of economic integration. In Europe the customs union and later the economic union of the Benelux countries, the European Coal and Steel Community, the European Economic Community (Common Market), and the European Free Trade Association (the "Outer Seven") are manifestations of this movement. Plans have also been made for the establishment of a free-trade area encompassing the countries of the Common Market and the Outer Seven, but negotiations in the years 1957–60 did not meet with success. However, concessions offered in early 1961 by the United Kingdom with regard to the harmonization of tariffs on nonagricultural commodities give promise for the future enlargement of the Common Market in some modified form.

. . .

The interwar period has witnessed a considerable degree of disintegration of the European and the world economy. On the European scene the mounting trade-and-payments restrictions since 1913 deserve attention. Ingvar Svennilson has shown that, as a result of the increase in trade impediments, the import trade of the advanced industrial countries of Europe shifted from the developed to the less developed economies of this area, which did not specialize in manufactured products. This shift implies a decline in competition between the industrial products of the more advanced economies and a decrease in specialization among these countries. But lessening of specialization was characteristic not only among the more advanced European economies but also of the European economy as a whole. This development can be demonstrated by trade and production figures for the period of 1913–38. While the volume of commodity production in Europe increased by 32 per cent during those years, intra-European trade increased by 10 per cent. The formation of a European union can be regarded, then, as a possible solution for the reintegration of European economies.

Another factor responsible for the disintegration of the European economy has been the stepping-up of state intervention in economic affairs in order to counteract cyclical fluctuations, sustain full employment, correct income distribution, and influence growth. Plans for economic integration are designed partly to counteract the element of discrimination inherent in the increased scope of state intervention.

A related argument regards the establishment of customs unions as desirable for mitigating cyclical fluctuations transmitted through foreign-trade relations. The foreign-trade dependence of the European Common Market countries decreases, for example, by about 35 per cent if trade among the six countries is regarded as internal trade. The memory of the depression in the 1930s gives added weight to this argument. Note, however, that for this proposition to be valid, there is need for some degree of coordination in countercyclical policies among the participating countries.

Last but not least, it is expected that integration will foster the growth of the European economies. This outcome is assumed to be the result of various dynamic factors, such as large-scale economies on a wider market, lessening of uncertainty in intra-area trade, and a faster rate of technological change. In this regard, the increased interest in economic growth has further contributed to the attention given to possibilities of economic integration.

. . .

To summarize, economic integration in Europe serves to avoid discrimination caused by trade-and-payments restrictions and increased state intervention, and it is designed to mitigate cyclical fluctuations and to increase the growth of national income.

. . .

## ■ INTEGRATION AND POLITICS

In examining the recent interest in economic integration, we have yet to comment on the role of political factors. There is no doubt that—especially in the case of Europe—political objectives are of great consequence. The avoidance of future wars between France and Germany, the creation of a third force in world politics, and the re-establishment of Western Europe as a world power are frequently mentioned as political goals that would be served by economic integration. Many regard these as primary objectives and relegate economic considerations to second place. No attempt will be made here to evaluate the relative importance of political economic considerations. This position is taken, partly because this relationship is not quantifiable, partly because a considerable degree of interdependence exists between these factors. Political motives may prompt the first step in economic integration, but economic integration also reacts on the political sphere; similarly, if the initial motives are economic, the need for political unity can arise at a later stage.

From the economic point of view, the basic question is not whether economic or political considerations gave the first impetus to the integration movement, but what the economic effects of integration are likely to be. In some political circles the economic aspects are deliberately minimized and the plan for economic integration is regarded merely as a pawn in the play of political forces. Such a view unduly neglects the economic expediency of the proposal. Even if political motives did have primary importance, this would not mean that the economist could not examine the relevant economic problems without investigating elusive political issues. By way of comparison, although the formation of the United States was primarily the result of political considerations, nobody would deny the economic importance of its establishment.

We shall not disregard the political factors, however. Political *ends* will not be considered, but at certain points of the argument we shall examine various economic problems the solution of which is connected with political *means* and political processes. We shall explore, for example, how the objective of exploiting the potential benefits of economic integration affects the decision-making process. Changes in the decision-making process, on the other hand, become a political problem. Nevertheless, we shall go no further than to state the need for coordinated action in certain fields and will leave it for the political scientist to determine the political implications of such developments.

## THE "LIBERALIST" AND THE "DIRIGIST" IDEAL OF ECONOMIC INTEGRATION

The recent interest in economic integration has prompted various proposals concerning the means and objectives of integration. Two extreme views—an all-out liberalist and a dirigist solution—will be contrasted here. The champions of economic liberalism regard regional integration as a return to the free-trade ideals of the pre–First World War period within the area in question and anticipate the relegation of national economic policy to its pre-1914 dimensions. If this approach is followed, integration simply means the abolition of impediments to commodity movements. At the other extreme, integration could also be achieved through state trading and through the coordination of national economic plans without the lifting of trade barriers. This alternative discards the use of market methods and relies solely on administrative, nonmarket means. It can be found in the integration projects of Soviet-type economies; the operation of the Council of Mutual Economic Assistance, comprising the Soviet Union and her European satellites, is based on the coordination of long-range plans and bilateral trade agreements. A similar method, but one which put more reliance on market means, was used by Germany during the last war. In this study we shall examine problems of economic integration in market economies and shall not deal with Nazi Germany and Soviet-type economies. Nevertheless, we shall see that dirigistic tendencies appear in the writings of some Western authors, too.

Among the proponents of the liberalist solution, Allais, Röpke, and Heilperin may be cited. They regard economic integration as identical with trade (and payments) liberalization. Allais asserts that "practically, the only mutually acceptable rule for close economic cooperation between democratic societies is the rule of the free market." Röpke is of the opinion that European economic integration is nothing else than an attempt to remedy the disintegration of the post-1914 period that destroyed the previous integration of national economies. A less extreme position is taken by Heilperin, who rejects the consideration of regional development plans and subsidies to industries for reconversion purposes but accepts state responsibility for investment decisions in certain areas. To the majority of observers, however, the liberalist ideal of integration is a relic from the past, and its application to present-day economic life appears rather anachronistic. As Jean Weiller put it, "It would be a great error to believe that the decision to create a regional union would re-establish the conditions of an economic liberalism, extirpating with one stroke all so-called dirigistic policies."

It can rightly be said that considerations such as the avoidance of depressions, the maintenance of full employment, the problems of regional development, the regulation of cartels and monopolies, and so forth, require state intervention in economic life, and any attempts to integrate national economies would necessarily lead to harmonization in various policy areas. This idea is not new. The need for the coordination of fiscal, monetary, social, and countercyclical policies was stressed in the League of Nations study on customs unions published immediately after the end of the Second World War. In fact, the question is not whether government intervention is needed or not in an integrated area, but whether economic integration results in a more intensive participation of the state in economic affairs or in a more intensive reliance on market methods.

Some authors advocate an intensification of state intervention in economic affairs. The need for economic planning in a union is emphasized, for example, by André Philip and by other French Socialists. In Philip's opinion, "there is no alternative to a directed economy," since "the market can be extended not by liberalizing but by organizing." Although not an advocate of centralized planning, the stepping-up of state intervention is also recommended by Maurice Bye, who contrasts his "integration theory" with Heilperin's "market theory." Considering the pronouncements of French economists and industrialists, it can be said that, by and large, the French view of economic integration contains more dirigistic elements than, for example, that of most German economists and entrepreneurs.

The defenders of dirigistic tendencies fail to consider, however, the lessening of planning and government intervention—and the beneficial effects thereof—in Europe since the end of the Second World War. Although this change does not indicate a return to the pre-1914 situation, it brought about an increased use of the market mechanism and contributed to the spectacular growth of the European economy during the 1950's. It appears, then, that a reintroduction of dirigistic methods would slow down, rather than accelerate, future growth. State intervention may be stepped up in some areas, such as regional development planning, and will also be required to deal with transitional problems, but it is expected that an enlargement of the economic area will intensify competition and lead to less interference with productive activities at the firm level. Therefore, those who regard the European Common Market as a *marché institué* err in the opposite direction from the holders of old-fashioned liberalist views.

. . .

## ▪ ECONOMIC INTEGRATION AND WELFARE

It can be said that the ultimate objective of economic activity is an increase in welfare. Thus, in order to assess the desirability of integration, its contribution to welfare needs to be considered. But the concept of welfare is fraught with much obscurity. First, the noneconomic aspects present some ambiguity; second, even restricting the meaning of the concept to "economic welfare" in the Pigovian tradition, we are confronted with the well-known difficulties of interpersonal comparisons if we try to say anything over and above the Pareto condition: an increase in one man's welfare leads to an increase in social welfare only if there is no reduction in the welfare of any other members of the group. In the case of integration, economic welfare will be affected by (a) a change in the quantity of commodities produced, (b) a change in the degree of discrimination between domestic and foreign goods, (c) a redistribution of income between the nationals of different countries, and (d) income redistribution within individual countries. Accordingly, distinction is made between a real-income component and a distributional component of economic welfare. The former denotes a change in potential welfare (efficiency); the latter refers to the welfare effects of income redistribution (equity).

With regard to potential welfare, separate treatment is allotted to changes in the quantity of goods produced and changes in their distribution. First, there is an increase (decrease) in potential welfare if—owing to the reallocation of resources consequent upon integration—the quantity of goods and services produced with given inputs increases (decreases) or, alternatively, if the production of the same quantity of goods and services requires a smaller (larger) quantity of inputs. If we regard inputs as negative outputs, we may say that a rise in net output leads to an increase in potential welfare. A higher net output entails an increase in potential welfare in the sense that a larger quantity of goods and services can now be distributed among individuals so as to make some people better off without making others worse off. Second, potential welfare is also affected through the impact of economic integration on consumers' choice. Restrictions on commodity movements imply discrimination between domestic and foreign commodities; a tariff causes consumers to buy more of lower-valued domestic and less of higher-valued foreign goods. The removal of intra-union tariffs will do away with discrimination between the commodities of the member countries but will discriminate against foreign goods in favor of the commodities of partner countries. In short, economic efficiency means efficiency in production and efficiency in exchange, and an improvement in one or both constitutes an increase in potential welfare.

Given a change in potential welfare (the real-income component), we also have to consider the distributional component in order to determine changes in economic welfare. It can easily be seen that an evaluation of changes in income distribution would require interpersonal comparisons of welfare. The new welfare economics, however, does not admit the possibility of making interpersonal comparisons. As a possible solution, it has then been suggested that changes in welfare could be determined in terms of potential welfare; that is, the *possibility* of making everybody better off (or, at least, no one worse off) would be taken as equivalent to an increase in economic welfare. This proposition can be criticized primarily on the grounds that the hypothetical situation *after* compensation is irrelevant if compensation actually does not take place. Nevertheless, changes in the real-income component give a good approximation of changes in welfare *within a country,* since compensation is politically feasible, and in case of integration this would actually be carried out to some degree in the form of assistance to relocating workers or reconverting firms. In addition, a nation can be regarded as an entity, where a redistribution of income accompanying an increase in real income can be accepted—provided that the redistribution does not run counter to generally accepted ideals of equity.

The distribution component cannot be neglected if economic integration redistributes income between countries, especially between the member states of a union, on the one hand, and the non-participating economies, on the other. It is not possible to claim an increase in world welfare in every case when the increase in real income in the participating countries will be greater than the loss to third countries. This proposition would hold true only if international comparisons of welfare could be made or if we disregarded differences in the marginal utility of income between countries. The first possibility was ruled out above, and the equality of the marginal utility of income is no less implausible. According to some, the marginal utility of income in an underdeveloped economy might be two or three times as high as in the rest of the world. If such a view were accepted, a union of developed economies which would register gains in the real-income component might still reduce world welfare by redistributing income from "poor" to "rich" countries.

In the preceding discussion we have followed the customary exposition of welfare economics in using the concept of potential welfare in a static sense. Thus an increase in potential welfare was taken as equivalent to an improvement in the allocation of resources at a point of time. Static efficiency, however, is only one of the possible success criteria that can be used to appraise the effects of economic integration. Instead of limiting our investigation to a discussion of efficiency in resource allocation under static assumptions, greater attention should be paid to the impact of integration on dynamic efficiency. I have elsewhere defined dynamic efficiency as the hypothetical growth rate of national income achievable with given resource use and saving ratio. In technical terms, whereas static efficiency would require that the economy operate on its production-possibility frontier, dynamic efficiency can be represented by the movement of this frontier in the northeast direction. The concept of dynamic efficiency can be used in intercountry comparisons to indicate which economy is capable of faster growth under identical conditions with regard to resources and saving, or, alternatively, it can be applied for comparing the growth potentialities of an economy at different points of time. In the present context, we wish to compare the hypothetical growth rate attainable *before* and *after* integration, under the assumption of given initial resources and saving ratio.

Given the static efficiency of an economy, the main factors affecting its dynamic efficiency are technological progress, the allocation of investment, dynamic interindustry relationships in production and investment, and uncertainty and inconsistency in economic decisions. In addition to these factors, the actual growth of national income would also be affected by an increase in the proportion of national income saved and/or by interference with the individual's choice between work and leisure. Changes in the latter variables will be disregarded here, partly because we assume that they are but rarely affected by economic integration, partly because their effects cannot be evaluated in welfare terms, given the disutility of increased saving and/or work. Under these assumptions an increase in the rate of growth can be considered as equivalent to an improvement in dynamic efficiency and represents a rise in potential welfare.

In evaluating the effects of economic integration, we shall use dynamic efficiency as the primary success indicator, taking into account both changes in the efficiency of resource allocation in the static sense and the dynamic effects of integration. In addition, attention will be paid to the impact of integration on income distribution, on the regional pattern of production and income, and on the stability of the participating economies.

. . .

## THE SECTORAL APPROACH TO INTEGRATION

In this chapter, distinction has been made between various forms of economic integration. All these forms require concerted action in the entire field of economic activity, be it the abolition of customs barriers or the coordination of fiscal policies. Another approach to economic integration would be to move from sector to sector, integrating various industries successively. The application of this method had already been commended in the interwar period, and it found many champions in the period following the Second World War. Proposals were made to integrate various sectors such as the iron and steel industry, transportation, and agriculture. The Stikker Plan advocated the integration of national economies by removing barriers, industry by industry. Supporters of this view contended that national governments were more inclined to make limited commitments with reasonably clear implications than to integrate all sectors at the same time. The flexibility of this method was also extolled, and it was hoped that integration in one sector would encourage integration on a larger scale.

From the theoretical point of view, various objections can be raised against the sectoral approach. Whereas the simultaneous integration of all sectors allows for compensating changes, integration in one sector will lead to readjustment in this sector alone, the reallocation of resources in other sectors being impeded by the continued existence of tariffs and other trade barriers—hence the losses suffered by countries whose productive activity in the newly integrated sector contracts will not be compensated for until the next phase. More generally, under the sectoral approach every step in integration results in a new and temporary equilibrium of prices, costs, and resource allocation, and this "equilibrium" is disturbed at every further step. Production decisions will then be made on the basis of prices that are relevant only in a certain phase of integration, and shifts in resource allocation will take place which may later prove to be inappropriate. On the other hand, the adjustment of relative prices and the reallocation of resources proceed more smoothly if all sectors are integrated at the same time, since some industries are expanding, others contracting, and unnecessary resource shifts do not take place.

Integration sector by sector puts an additional burden on the external balance also. At various steps, pressures will be imposed on the balance of payments of countries where the newly integrated sector is a high-cost producer. In the absence of exchange-rate flexibility, this process unnecessarily burdens exchange reserves in some, and inflates reserves in other, participating countries. If, on the other hand, exchange rates are left to fluctuate freely, temporary variations in rates of exchange will bring about transitional and unnecessary changes in the international division of labor.

In addition, lack of coordination in monetary, fiscal, and other policies is likely to cause difficulties under the sectoral approach, since differences in economic policies can lead to perverse movements of commodities and factors. For example, if inflationary policies are followed in one country while deflationary policies are pursued in another, an overadjustment will take place in the integrated sector (or sectors), while trade barriers restrict adjustments in other industries. Finally, any joint decisions made with respect to the integrated sector will affect all other branches of the participating economies.

A noneconomic objection of considerable importance should also be mentioned here. The sectoral approach is bound to bring about a conflict between producer and user interests in individual countries. In countries with relatively high production costs, for example, users will welcome integration because of its price-reducing effect; high-cost producers, however, will object to it. Experience suggests that producer interests have greater influence on governmental decisionmaking; hence these pressures are likely to have a restrictive effect on integration if the sectoral approach is followed. The interests of exporting and importing countries being opposed, there can be no "give and take"—the necessary pre-condition for intercountry agreements in most practical instances.

These theoretical objections suggest the inadvisability of integration sector by sector. This conclusion does not mean, however, that integration in one sector may not be beneficial if political obstacles hinder integration in all areas. The European Coal and Steel Community is a case in point. At the time of its inception, the realization of a European Common Market was not yet possible, but the governments of the participating countries were prepared to accept a limited measure of integration. The establishment of the Coal and Steel Community has been conducive to the expansion of production and trade in the partaking industries, and the Community demonstrated the possibility of integration in Europe, thereby contributing to the establishment of the Common Market.

It has also been argued that the difficulties of adjustment in production and trade in the Coal and Steel Community have been less than expected because the considerable increase in the national incomes of every participating country has made adjustment easier. This does not, however, rule out the possibility of maladjustments in other industries which will not be corrected until trade barriers are removed in all sectors. In addition, the Coal and Steel Community has encountered serious difficulties with respect to transportation policies, fiscal and social problems, etc., which have been due—to a great degree—to the fact that integration extends over only one sector.

# PART 3

# Current Debates in Integration Theory

# 20 The Political Theory of Federalism: The Relevance of Classical Approaches

MURRAY FORSYTH

*The apparent stagnation of the European Community (EC) in the 1970s and early 1980s and the consequent abandonment of neofunctionalism after 1975 had a chilling effect on integration theory. Most scholars (at least in the United States) migrated to other areas; those who remained interested in the EC (primarily Europeans) focused on how the Community actually worked, steering far clear of grand theory. The exception to this rule was the federalist school. Most federalists in the 1970s and 1980s lamented the painfully slow, undemocratic, functionalist approach to integration taken by European leaders and held out the promise of true European unity through a federal constitution. In true federalist fashion they were not as interested in a scientific description of the integration process as they were in prescribing a course of action. They were often the idealistic "true believers" in a United States of Europe.*

*The "relaunch" of Europe in the late 1980s and the resulting revival of grand integration theory encouraged the idealists, but also inspired new or revived thinking among academics about the formation and operation of federations. Constitutional law scholars, political theorists, and students of comparative politics, both in Europe and the United States, have recently been exploring the nature of European federalism in comparison with other federations. Most see an emerg-*

Reprinted with permission from Jochim Jens Hesse and Vincent Wright (eds.), *Federalizing Europe? The Costs, Benefits, and Preconditions of Federal Political Systems* (Oxford: Oxford University Press, 1996). Notes omitted.

*ing European federal constitution; many see the need—as do some European political leaders (Chapter 12)—to make this constitution more explicit and more democratic.*

*Murray Forsyth represents well this new wave of federalist thinking. In this widely cited article, Forsyth seeks to employ older "doctrines of federalism" to highlight the differences between classical federalism and the current "technical-functional approach" to integration (essentially Mitrany's functionalism—see Chapter 14) while also identifying "the less obvious federal component in the present system." He fears that functional integration has unwittingly created a "rudimentary federal structure" that coexists uneasily with the technical policymaking of the European Union (EU). The defects of the functional approach are now acute: "a dense and opaque mass of structures and policies" separates the Union from its citizens; the EU technical apparatus continues to "extend its activities unnecessarily"; the open-ended nature of the enterprise makes it difficult to determine what, if any, powers are "retained by the member states"; and the emphasis on economics risks a cultural backlash. Forsyth thus suggests that the EU engage in a constitutional process to "create a genuine and explicit union in the place of the confused and incoherent one that has so far emerged."*

European integration is a concept that embraces a very wide span of developments and institutions. The central core of the integration process, however, is usually, and with some justification, seen as running from the Schuman Plan through to the Rome treaty, and from there to the Single European Act and the Maastricht Treaty on European Union. The degree to which this long, uneven process can or ought to be termed a federal one, and the relationship and relevance of federal ideas and practices to it, are matters which have been debated since its very beginning. In this chapter I wish to address certain aspects of this problem again. I wish to argue in particular that the older doctrines of federalism, while in no sense providing a blueprint for integration, do help us to understand what integration is, and to clarify the key issues that confront it now and in the future.

In order to make plain the relevance of the classical federal approach, I shall begin by considering the prevailing philosophy of integration, or, in simpler terms, the general assumptions that have predominated in the way in which integration has been prosecuted up till now. I shall then confront these assumptions with the characteristic and traditional concepts of federalism, showing how these serve to bring out certain less obvious features of integration. Central to the argument will be the tension between the technical-functional ideas that permeate so much of the structure and process of integration, and the federal-constitutional reality which has simultaneously grown up in—or been precipitated by—that process. The technical-functional approach, it will be concluded, has begun to show serious limitations, and a more explicit and determined recourse to federal-constitutional principles could help to rectify the lack of coherence and balance that has arisen.

## ■ THE UNDERLYING TECHNICITY OF EUROPEAN INTEGRATION

In the early years of integration, when the Schuman Plan had been launched and ambitious plans for a European Defense Community and a European Political Community were being debated, there seems to have been a widespread sense that integration was federalism in action, and that federal theory and practice were highly relevant to what was taking place. The impressive book *Federalism: Mature and Emergent*, edited by A. W. Macmahon, and published in 1955, stands as perhaps the best academic monument to this period and attitude. Largely the work of American scholars, it sought to bring the historical experience of federalism to bear on the events taking place in Europe. William Diebold's statement "at the basis of the Schuman Plan is a series of truly federal equations" expressed the prevailing assumption of the authors.

With the collapse of the plans for the European Defense and Political Communities, the signing of the Rome Treaty, and the development of the European Economic Community, the prevailing assumption changed. There was still a strong and widely held belief that the Community was the preliminary to a federal system, but far less conviction that it was itself a species of federalism. The prevailing assumption of those who analyzed and wrote about the Community, and indeed of those who worked in its institutions, was that it was an unprecedented form of organization, working according to a unique "Community method," which involved the interaction of "supranational" and "intergovernmental" institutions, and that older theories of federalism had very little to tell one about this kind of body. "On one point," wrote the British Commissioner, Christopher Tugendhat, "all could agree. The Community represented a unique structure which could not be related to any known models of government, nor to any conventional theory of international relations."

As has been emphasized, there have always been many who believe that the Community, with its unique structures, is the preliminary to the creation of a federal system, and who urge that the transition to the federal end-point should be made as quickly as possible. An attempt was made to incorporate this idea of a federal end-point into the founding treaty of the Community at the Maastricht Summit in 1991, though it is worth noting how tentatively the aspiration was worded. Thus the Treaty establishing a European Union, as it was originally drafted by the Dutch Presidency of the European Council, prior to the Maastricht meeting, stated that "This Treaty marks a new stage in the process leading gradually to a Union with a federal goal." In other words, the Community was to be transformed forthwith into a "Union," which was later to be developed into a "Union with a federal goal." Even this tentative proposal failed, chiefly because of the strenuous opposition of the British Government. The final text reads: "This Treaty marks a new stage in the process creating an ever closer union among the peoples of Europe, where decisions are taken as closely as possible to the people."

If the attitude of those for whom the existing process of integration is the preliminary to a federal system is reasonably clear, a word is needed about the perspective of those who are not convinced of the need to posit a federal end-point. For them integration remains simply a "process," or as Andrew Schonfield put it, "a journey to an unknown destination." The Community is regarded as a pragmatic "going concern" that not only does not require to be seen as a means to a federal end, but does not require to be seen as being itself federal. It is simply "there," a unique and flexible mechanism, more tightly organized than a typical international organization, that accumulates new functions from time to time, when this is judged to be necessary by its members.

For most analysts and commentators, then, the development of European integration since 1957 does not represent a federal phenomenon, but rather a unique and unprecedented process, that for some is the preliminary to the creation of a federal structure, and for others is a cumulative functional phenomenon with no precise or definable end. This is not to say that there have not been those who have regarded and defined the Community as a federal or confederal body—and this view will be examined and expounded later in the chapter—but the predominant view has been a different one.

Let us turn now from the way integration has been viewed in public debate to the assumptions that are embedded in the actual process itself. What is the political philosophy underlying the Schuman Plan, the Spaak Report, that provided the basis of the Rome Treaty, the Rome Treaty itself, and its two major amendments, the Single European Act, and the Maastricht Treaty on European Union? The most obvious characteristic common to all these texts is a determination to avoid overall constitutional matters, wherever possible, and to concentrate instead on the elaboration of concrete programmes of joint action by the signatory states in specific economic and social areas. Foreign policy and security objectives have, it is true, been added in the two most recent texts, but they are still secondary, in terms of the extent of the common action envisaged, to the economic and social ones.

Robert Schuman's words in his famous declaration of 9 May 1950 provide the leitmotiv of the whole approach: "L'Europe ne se fera pas d'un coup, ni dans une construction d'ensemble: elle se fera par des réalisations concrètes, créant d'abord une solidarité de fait. . . . Le gouvernement français propose de porter immédiatement l'action sur un point limité mais décisif" [Europe will not be made all at once, or according to a single plan. It will be built through concrete achievements, which first create a *de facto* solidarity. . . . The French government proposes that action be taken immediately on one limited but decisive point]. The Spaak Report, it is true, moved from a *point* to an *ensemble* in the sense that it went beyond the sectoral approach to that of a common market, and we shall return to this important shift later. But it too was expressly "un plan concret d'action" involving "réalisations qui sont immenses, qui predront du temps, mais qui peuvent commencer toute de suite" ["a concrete action plan" involving "great changes, which will take time, but can begin immediately"]. The Rome Treaty, in keeping with this emphasis, was a special form of treaty, a *traité-cadre* or "framework treaty," and its later amendments also have this framework character. In other words, the Treaty and the amendments do not define completely and finally the obligations agreed by the signatories. Rather they set out a series of programmes for the future, involving the progressive elaboration of common policies, increasing cooperation, harmonization, and a whole host of other measures. The formulation of the various programmes in the Treaty and amendments is sometimes very precise and detailed, with stages and timetables and objectives clearly defined, and sometimes surprisingly general.

In keeping with this action-plan philosophy, the institutional framework established by the Treaty and amendments is emphatically a means, a mechanism, an instrument, for the elaboration and implementation of outline programmes. The Commission, to use the conventional terminology, is intended as the motor or propellant of integration, and the guardian of the Treaty. Created and appointed by the member states, its prime task is to ensure that the programmes that they have mapped out and agreed to follow, are in fact implemented. It is, to use another metaphor, the artificially created conscience of the states, constantly reminding them of the promises they have made in their various treaties, but all too aware that, like the individual conscience, it only possesses a relative independence from the beings it tries to guide. Around the central push-and-pull interaction between the Commission and the Council, or between what are conventionally termed the supranational and the intergovernmental organs, are arranged the other major institutions of the Community—the Court, to ensure the legality of the process, and the Parliament, to ensure that it is in some sense democratically supervised. The latter are, as it were, the constitutional penumbra of something that at heart is not conceived of in a constitutional way at all. Finally, out of the continuous process of programme implementation emerges a steadily growing European administrative structure, centered, though by no means wholly concentrated on the Commission. What is being produced by integration is the regulatory or managerial framework of a European economy or society.

What one is confronted with, then, is a dynamic organization, which is technical in the sense that it is conceived primarily as a machinery or apparatus for implementing a set of action programmes. David Mitrany's concept of "functionalism," conceived before the integration process began, still provides perhaps the best theoretical framework (better even than the neo-functional theories of his American followers) for understanding its technical nature. It is true that for Mitrany the function—that is, the concrete problem to be solved—determined the region of the organization established to solve it, and that he was therefore strongly critical of organizations that began, so to speak, from the wrong end, starting with a region—Europe, for example—and defining the problems to be solved in terms of the region. Mitrany was a true cosmopolitan, who sought via functionalism to transcend all territorial frontiers, rather than to create new ones. Having made this important reservation, however, it is possible to see in his doctrine of the functional organization of international relations a peculiarly apposite summary of the assumptions behind the integration process.

Mitrany's central contention was that economic and social developments in the twentieth century had made it imperative to move beyond the classical liberal notions of the nineteenth century. The latter were essentially static, formal, and constitutional, laying down hard and fast rules not only for sharply delimited national areas, but also for the separation of state and society, for the distinction between public and private, for the protection of individual—and in federal systems, of state—rights, and for the provision of such negative functions as law, order, and security. The modern economy, and modern society, by contrast, had given birth to a mass of ceaselessly changing and frequently convergent positive needs which cut across, and rendered largely irrelevant, these hard and fast distinctions. They called instead for a pragmatic, flexible and problem-orientated functional type of government, focused at those points within and beyond national or state boundaries where needs converged.

The whole modern trend, wrote Mitrany, "is to organize government along the lines of specific ends and needs, and according to the conditions of their time and place, in lieu of the traditional organization on the basis of a set constitutional division of rights and powers." Further:

> The function . . . determines the executive instrument suitable for its proper activity, and by the same process provides a need for the reform of that instrument at every stage. . . . Not only is there in all this no need for any fixed constitutional division of authority and power, prescribed in advance, but anything beyond the most general formal rules would embarrass the working of these arrangements.

And again: "Functionalism knows only one logic, the logic of the problem, and of a problem apt to be always in flux in its elements, its spread and its effects. Function is never still." Finally: "The functional way is action itself."

Here it is worth pointing out that Mitrany's vision of the development of functionalism was as strongly influenced by what he had observed happening within particular states as it was by his observation of the international scene. He had witnessed at first hand the Great Depression and the New Deal in America and he had noted how, in the face of imperative social needs the constitutional division of powers between the federal government and the states had been largely bypassed, and concrete action had been taken which had created new types of administrative organs, such as the Tennessee Valley Authority, whose sphere of responsibility cut across state boundaries. "The significant point in that emergency action was that each and every problem was tackled as a practical issue in itself. No attempt was made to relate it to a general theory or system of government." For Mitrany the hard and fast constitutional boundaries implied by federalism were as outmoded as a means of dealing with social and economic demands within the state as they were as a means of dealing with such demands across state boundaries.

Mitrany's ideas have been cited here at some length because they articulate so succinctly many of the unspoken assumptions lying behind the integration process in Europe, and because they bring out so sharply the antithesis between these assumptions and the idea of constitution-making, particularly federal constitution-making. The modern, no nonsense, down to earth, technical, activist, and programmatic approach to politics here finds full expression, and starkly confronts the "old-fashioned" constitutional approach. His words compel one to ask not only whether federal theory and practice has any relevance to the process of integration that has so far taken place, but also whether it can or should have any relevance in the future. Is it indeed outdated? It is to these questions that we must now turn.

## ■ THE FEDERAL COMPONENT OF THE INTEGRATION PROCESS

Federalism has a long, rich, and diverse history and encompasses a wide variety of political forms. This is worth stressing at the outset because it is all too easy to move from the correct assumption that federal structures are more than international or technical structures, and inevitably have a constitutional aspect, to the false conclusion that there is only one model of a federal constitution. As Henry Higgins, one of the speakers in the debates leading up to the constitution of the Australian Federation, rightly said:

> [T]he hon. Gentleman treats federation as if it were an Athena sprung ready armed from the head of Jupiter—that it was something absolutely defined from its first inception. But I take it that "federation" is a word used to indicate a number of devices which have, as their general object the relegating of certain subjects to the central government, and the leaving of other subjects to the state governments.

Higgins's words cannot be too frequently recalled in the European context.

A historical survey of federal institutions immediately reveals contrasting types, and a brief account of some of these types will help to create a realistic way into the subject. First, let it be said that every federal system establishes or incorporates a union, and that the concept of union is a federal one through and through. But while all federal systems embody a union, there is considerable variation between federal systems in terms of the depth and strength of the union. The distinction between confederation and federation was invented in the nineteenth century to try to discriminate precisely between strong and weak forms of union, and is still used widely today. Unfortunately this distinction, which began as a useful instrument, has tended to become frozen into a rigid antithesis, and it is widely assumed that with the help of a few simple criteria all federal systems can be popped into two separate pigeonholes. In practice it is not as simple as this, and preoccupation with the antithesis has the unfortunate effect of deflecting the eye from the common union element in federal systems, and also from the more subtle gradations in the strength and weakness of unions.

Walter Hallstein, the first President of the Commission, demonstrated how a rigid adherence to the confederation-federation antithesis caused the Community to disappear from the federal map. If, he argued, a confederation was defined, in the customary way, as a body which does not possess legislative powers that directly affect the individual members of the union, then the EEC was more than a confederation. On the other hand, the EEC was clearly not a state, and hence was also not a federation, according to the customary definition of the term. What was the Community then? Hallstein was wary of calling it a federal body, and preferred to refer to it simply as a "Community," but he also interestingly termed it a "union of states."

Rather than dwell on the distinction between confederation and federation, it is probably better to focus on a few concrete turning points in the history of federal unions, which illuminate their differing levels of intensity. Thus the change represented by the drafting of the American Constitution in 1787 is real and profound. For the first time, as both the protagonists and opponents of the new Constitution argued, a fully articulated and firmly based government was created at the center of a federal union, alongside the governments of the member units. This feature, as John C. Calhoun wrote, was "new, peculiar, and unprecedented." The American Civil War provides another illuminating turning point: here a trial of strength determined that in the last resort the power and right of the central government of a federal union was superior to that of the members. Already we can distinguish at least three levels of intensity of a federal union: one in which the central organs have not been deliberately welded into a fully fledged government; one in which they have been so welded, but remain co-equal rather than superior to the member governments; and one in which the central government has a status and power superior to the members. All these systems remain federal, but there are plainly wide differences between them.

Another profound difference between federal systems relates to the degree to which the people forming the member units of the union are ethnically and/or linguistically homogeneous. All the early federal unions in Europe and America were homogeneous in one or both of these senses. Not until the nineteenth century do federal systems emerge in which the constituent member units are ethnically and linguistically diverse—namely the renovated Swiss Confederation and the Canadian, or British North America Confederation. This heterogeneity plainly has an impact upon the division of powers and the development of the union. There will always be, in any genuine federal system, a push and pull between the member units and the center, between nation-building at the center and providence-building at the periphery, but in a heterogeneous federal system there will be an additional, natural, built-in limit on the nation-building capacity of the center, whereas in a homogeneous system the sense of being one people can conceivably develop to the point where the federal system itself is seen as an unnecessary restraint on the expression of national unity. The Netherlands, after all, was a federal union for two centuries, but then became, and remains today, a unitary nation-state.

Finally, there is a marked difference between federal unions between states in which the executive branch of government is traditionally powerful, whether because of its accepted role as the legislative pacemaker within a parliamentary system, or because of strong monarchial, princely, or bureaucratic traditions, and between unions between states in which the legislative power is seen as being coequal with or even superior to the executive. It is natural and inevitable that federalism will be more executive in structure in the former than in the latter, though it is by no means inevitable that executive federalism will always manifest itself in the same way or that it will not appear in some form in systems with a more legislative bias. The profound difference between the history and development of the American Senate and the German *Bundesrat* is a sufficient example of this contrast.

These differences not only illustrate the variations within federalism, but are clearly relevant to European integration when viewed from a federal perspective. Not only is Europe highly diverse, ethnically and linguistically, but the position of the executive (or the government) *vis-à-vis* the legislature, in most of the leading European states, is an exceptionally strong one. It is very unlikely, therefore, that a federal system in Europe would resemble that of the United States of America, which is so often taken as the exclusive model for such a system.

The theory of federalism requires to be treated with the same discrimination as federal unions. It is possible to distinguish at least three streams of federal thought that can be dignified with the name of theory. The first may be identified with Kant's doctrine of a gradually expanding federation contained in his famous essay on *Perpetual Peace*. It is founded on the idea that war is the greatest evil, and that the possibility of war is inherent in the co-existence of independent states. It therefore advocates the construction of an ever-widening federation between states, as the most appropriate means of abolishing this evil throughout the world. It is not unfair to call this a moral rather than an authentically political theory of federalism, and Kant defined its starting point succinctly when he wrote: "Now, moral-practical reason within us pronounces the following irresistible veto: *There shall be no war*, either between individual human beings in the state of nature, or between separate states . . . For war is not the way in which anyone should pursue his rights."

A second stream of federal theory sees federal arrangements as the correlate or superstructure of the idea of popular self-government, or of democracy in the classical, participatory sense. This vision has historically had a great variety of exponents, including Rousseau, Proudhon, the so-called "integral federalists" of the twentieth century, the advocates of subsidiarity, and even those who, in America, opposed the tighter union of 1787 (the so-called Anti-Federalists, who actually saw themselves as being loyal to the federal idea). Expressed somewhat crudely, the fundamental argument common to these diverse groups is that those forms of power and authority that are closest to the people, or in which the people participate most directly, are *ipso facto* the most legitimate. It follows that only as little power as is necessary should be delegated upwards to higher levels, which are by definition less participatory, and that the higher levels themselves should be organized as loose federal unions of the lower units, which are by definition more participatory. The word "loose" needs to be stressed here. This form of federalism cannot logically allow a strong federal center to emerge; it must insist on the dependence of the center on the democratic parts. If confederation is taken to mean a loose federal union, then this theory is essentially a theory of confederation. Its ethos was well summed up by the American "states righter" James Jackson Kilpatrick when he wrote in 1957: "I hold this truth to be self-evident: That government is least evil when it is closest to the people. I submit that when effective control of government moves away from the people, it becomes a greater evil, a greater restraint upon liberty." This approach is, of course, reflected in the Maastricht Treaty's stipulation that in the new European Union decisions are to be taken "as closely as possible to the citizen."

The third theory of federalism may be called the classical political theory of federalism. It is concerned with federalism, not as the path to world peace, nor as the correlate of participatory democracy, but in itself, as a phenomenon produced by the pulls and pressures of the political world, with its own logic distinct from that of the unitary state or the world of international relations. Here, federalism is the ensemble of structures and processes whereby a union of states or a union of polities is created and sustained, whether such a union results from a unitary system disaggregating itself, or from a number of political units coming together, or from a simultaneous movement in both directions. Classical federal theory is typically concerned with expounding the nature of such unions, explaining why they are established, and examining their strengths and weaknesses.

Such a classical tradition may be said to have started with *The Federalist*, the series of papers produced by Alexander Hamilton, James Madison, and John Jay, to promote the adoption of the Constitution drafted at Philadelphia in 1787. Though not purporting to be theory, the skill and sophistication with which these papers expounded and justified the principles of the new Constitution make it appropriate to see them as such. To be sure, there had been some speculation about the nature of federal systems before this, but nothing so sustained. Alexis de Tocqueville, in his *Democracy in America*, published in 1835, introduced the ideas of *The Federalist* into European political thought, adding some insights of his own.

. . .

. . . [W]e may now ask how far the kind of analysis characteristic of [the classical tradition] assists our understanding of European integration. It does so, I believe, in two ways. First it enables one to see how far the technical, programmatic process of integration has—almost in spite of itself—precipitated or deposited a rudimentary federal structure. In other words, it enables one to detect the fundamental, constitutional changes that have been brought about by a movement which has, as we have seen, focused resolutely on the nonconstitutional. Secondly, it enables one to understand why, and to some extent also how, the rudimentary, implicit constitutional structures of integration should be rendered coherent and explicit.

To substantiate this contention, it is necessary to develop a little further the notion of "union." It has already been emphasized that the concept of union is a federal one through and through—the very use of the word in bold capitals in the first paper of *The Federalist* is perhaps sufficient proof of this. All federal systems are unions. What then is the classical notion of union?

A union signifies above all that a certain threshold of intensity has been reached in the relationships between states. In a provocative essay, Carl Schmitt argued that the political aspect of any human grouping or arrangement related not to its ostensible ends or objectives (religious, economic, ideological, etc.), but to the intensity of the tie between the members. The closer the bond came to a friend-enemy relationship, the more it was political. A federal union is a political body in this sense. It means an arrangement in which a firm line has been drawn between "us" and "them," between insiders and outsiders. At the minimum—in a union whose content is economic—it means a body in which systematic preference is given by insiders to insiders within an enclosed economic space. At the maximum, it means a body capable of conducting war—the most intense form of the friend-enemy relationship. It always signifies a spatial entity with a boundary, and not a point in the Mitrany sense. It also implies permanence. A temporary arrangement is not a union; it has no distinct political existence. Hence a union goes beyond a co-operative arrangement, or an alliance, or a common arrangement to resolve a particular problem.

A union is represented—in the old classical sense of "made present"—by a set of institutions, which enable it to act as one within the boundaries of the union, and as one *vis-à-vis* outsiders. This classic concept of institutions representing the union can be made clearer by contrasting it with the provisions of the Maastricht Treaty which say merely that the European Union will be "served by a common institutional framework." There is a world of difference embodied in such terminology.

The establishment of these representative institutions, and their endowment with the right and power to act internally and externally, is the constitution of the union. Hence constitution does not mean the creation of a technical agency capable of carrying out certain joint tasks, it is an act by which reality is given to a common political will, the creation of a distinct political personality. It is an act emphatically in the present tense, which changes the status of the partners. The basis of a union is thus always more than a conventional treaty; it is a constituent treaty.

The union does not abolish the constituent members, but rather exists alongside them. In other words, the right and power of the constituent members to act internally (and often externally too) is retained in certain spheres. There must always be, as Calhoun stated with particular clarity, "reserved" powers in a union. The "right and power to act internally," to which reference has been made, means essentially the right and power to make law, or to act, at discretion, in a directly binding manner within the boundaries of the union. A union implies the co-existence of two such discretionary legislative powers, one at the center, one in the parts. It necessarily implies the supremacy of the laws of the center in those spheres in which it is entitled to act. The right and power of lawmaking (which may fairly be referred to as sovereignty), assigned to the union's representative institutions, is the core of a union when viewed internally. The delimitation of the spheres in which this discretionary right and power may be exercised is a secondary thing, a matter of circumstance, though still, of course, of great importance.

This sketch of the key features of a federal union, according to the classical concept, helps us to understand the federal elements which exist within the present European Union as well as those that as yet do not. As regards the former, a resumé may be helpful. The decision made in 1957 to go beyond the sectoral approach and to create a common market, subsequently defined more precisely as an "internal market" or an "area without internal frontiers," is clearly in keeping with the idea of union, and makes the European Community a political entity in the sense outlined above. It draws a boundary between insiders and outsiders, and establishes a far-reaching form of internal preference. The distinction between inner and outer has been deepened by subsequent amendments to the Rome Treaty, such as the programme for monetary union, and the creation of a common citizenship for the individual members of the Community—one of the few genuinely constitutional ingredients of the Maastricht Treaty.

Secondly, the Community is intended as a permanent body; the Rome Treaty was concluded "for an unlimited period." Thirdly, the community's institutions possess the power to make directly binding laws within the spatial boundary of the Community, over a wide range of matters. These laws take precedence over the laws and constitutions of the member states, and national judges are obliged not to apply a state law which conflicts with a directly effective Community law. The Community's Court of Justice has played a most important role in drawing out the full "federal" implications of the Community's law-making power, most notably in the three cases of *van Gend en Loos* (1963), *Costa* v. *ENEL* (1964), and *Simmenthal* (1978).

At the same time, the European Court, while emphasizing the real, direct, sovereign powers possessed by the Community's institutions, has conspicuously refrained from saying expressly that this marks the Community out as a federal body. With understandable caution it has restricted itself to saying that the Community is not "an ordinary international agreement" but has involved the creation of "a new legal order" coexisting with the legal systems of the member states. The German Federal Constitutional Court has gone slightly further. In the late 1960s it stated:

> The institutions of the EEC exercise sovereign rights which the member states have renounced in favor of the Community they have founded. This Community itself is not a State, nor is it a Federal State. It is a Community of a special kind . . . to which the Federal Republic of Germany—like the other Member States—has transferred certain sovereign rights. By this fact a new public authority has been born, which is autonomous and independent in relation to the public authority of the individual Member States. Its acts do not, therefore, need to be ratified by the Member States, nor can they be repealed by them.

The political theorist, however, has no need to be restrained by the caution of the legal profession. To the student of federalism the features of the Community expounded by the European and the German Courts are quintessentially federal. It may be true that the Community is not a "state" or a "federal state" but this does not prevent it from being a federal union, that is to say a permanent linking together of states to form a corporate entity with a distinct boundary *vis-à-vis* the outside world, and possessed of two coexistent structures of government, one at the center, and one at the level of the member states.

Viewing the Community through the lens of classical federalism hence enables us to see the federal structure encased in the technical-functional apparatus. It also permits us to view the institutions in a different light. The conventional approach is to see supranational organs confronting intergovernmental ones, the former being the motor and guardian, the latter, for example the Council of Ministers, being a kind of resistant mass, requiring to be cajoled and pushed forward. In the federal perspective this is a misleading categorization. Intergovernmental bodies such as the Council should not be seen as secondary bodies, or as a regrettable brake on progress. Rather they express an authentic federal principle, which is realized in all federal unions, whether in the form of diets, congresses, senates, or even conferences of premiers, namely the representation of the member units at the center of the union.

## ■ EMPHASIZING THE FEDERAL-CONSTITUTIONAL SIDE OF THE INTEGRATION PROCESS

Our thesis may be summarized by saying that two souls or spirits dwell within the European integration process, as it has developed so far. The most immediately apparent, indeed the dominant one up to now, has been the technical-functional, or the programmatic. Alongside this is the federal-constitutional spirit, manifesting itself less directly, often masked by the technical-functional language of the official texts, but none the less there, and not a mere fiction of aspiration for the future. Familiarity with the classical tradition of federal thought is valuable precisely because it enables one to identify the less obvious federal component in the present system.

The juxtaposition of the two approaches, the tension between them, and the curious ambiguities that can emerge when the attempt is made to express them both simultaneously, can be seen very clearly in the Maastricht Treaty on European Union. On the one hand, the very title suggests a fundamental constituent act, of the kind that was described earlier. The first sentence of Article A of the Treaty does not disappoint this expectation: "By this Treaty, the High Contracting Parties establish among themselves a European Union." This has the true ring of a constitutional decision. So has the wording of the later Article 8 of the amended EEC Treaty, which states: "Citizenship of the Union is hereby established." Unfortunately the clauses and articles in between, and many of the subsequent ones, lack any such constitutional character, and the nature of the Union itself quickly becomes blurred and obscure.

Thus the second sentence of Article A (cited earlier) weakens the definitive nature of the act, by stating that the Treaty marks a new stage in the process of creating an ever closer union. Then the third (the nearest to a definition) states: "The Union shall be founded on the European Communities, supplemented by the policies and forms of cooperation established by this Treaty. Its task shall be to organize, in a manner demonstrating consistency and solidarity, relations between the member states and between their peoples." The first sentence introduces ambiguity: Is the Union founded by the Treaty of Maastricht? Is the Union already in existence? Or does Union consist of an accretion of policies and co-operation? The second sentence could scarcely be more general and insubstantial. In the next Article we are told that the Union "shall set itself" certain objectives, including the establishment of economic and monetary union, and, more remarkably, the assertion of its identity on the international scene. Then it is stated that the Union shall be "served by a single institutional framework" and that the European Council will provide the Union with "its necessary impetus for development." The great bulk of the succeeding articles elaborate new "policies" and "forms of cooperation" to be added to the tasks of the existing EEC, renamed the "European Community." We are back in the world of programmes.

Faced with this curious mixture, one must inevitably ask whether the existing structures have been genuinely reconstituted so that a new political entity has come into existence, a union in the classical sense of the term. Or does the resounding opening phrase merely paper over an organizational adjustment, an extension of the technical and programmatic functions of the existing apparatus? On balance the second alternative seems the most accurate.

It may be objected here that there is no need to make a choice between the technical-functional and the federal-constitutional, and that the two impulses can go on coexisting in the work of integration in the future, as they have coexisted hitherto. A little of one, and a little of the other, as time and circumstances dictate—is that the way forward? This is the question which finally has to be addressed.

There can be no question of denying the achievements of the technical-functional approach, nor of retrospectively arguing that some other course should have been chosen in the 1950s. It is one of the lessons of history that few, if any, federal unions have been constituted *ex nihilo*; the states or polities concerned have always been linked together by some pre-existent bond. The technical approach has created a whole host of bonds, and in this sense has not contradicted but prepared the ground for a European federal union. At the same time the technical approach, as it progresses, reveals defects which cannot be ignored.

The first and most obvious defect is that its persistent application eventually creates a dense and opaque mass of structures and policies, embracing a plethora of different procedures for dealing with specific areas of economic and social life, with which the citizens of the nation-states find it virtually impossible to identify. Not only this, but the treaty base of the whole technical edifice gradually expands into an immense tract not unlike a legal code, that mixes the fundamental with the secondary, the general with the highly specific, and which is as such incapable of attracting the loyalty of those whose destinies it so markedly affects. In place of the general discretionary powers, within broad circumscriptions, which a genuine constitution contents itself with allocating, we have endlessly repeated formulae for dealing with a multitude of specifics. Moreover attempts to insert some form of democratic control into this mass of procedures only seem to make the system even more complex and impenetrable.

Secondly, the very nature of the technical apparatus at the center makes it almost inevitable that it will seek to extend its activities unnecessarily. In other words, the Commission, the motor of the Community, whose authority rests on relatively shallow foundations, has a vested interest in expanding its activities into every area, however trivial, to which the wording of the Treaties and their amendments offers the excuse of opportunity.

Thirdly, the open-ended, programmatic character of the Community and the lack of a comprehensive and definitive allocation of powers to the center make it simultaneously difficult to make a clear definition of the powers retained by the member states. In the beginning, to be sure, this was scarcely seen as a problem; the imperative was to effect a derogation of power by the states, not to guarantee them. However, as the manifold programmes have been put into action, and the in-built tendency of the center to expand its activities has begun to accelerate, so the need to differentiate reserved and delegated—and concurrent—powers inevitably becomes more acute. The steps taken in the Maastricht Treaty to reassure some kind of brake on the expanding powers of the Community's institutions—namely the express declaration of the principle of subsidiarity, and the various provisions stating that the Union and the Community must respect the identity and the cultural diversity of the member states—are indicators of a growing anxiety, but such statements of principle and intent seem feeble indeed when compared with the differentiation of powers typical of an authentic federal constitution.

Finally, and linked to this, it may be argued that the technical spirit of the integration process produces a tendency to underestimate the importance of factors which are not susceptible to a precise, quantitative calculation, namely cultural factors. By this one does not mean, of course, the production or preservation of works of art, but the attachment of the citizens of the European states to their own ways of life. The emphasis that has been placed by the Community on the establishment of a single market with no internal frontiers has been unusually intense when compared with the priorities of other federal systems around the world, and is perhaps ironic when the exceptional cultural diversity of the European continent is borne in mind. It is admittedly difficult to guarantee the individuality of member states in a federal constitution (as the Canadian experience has illustrated), but without some form of guarantee there is a real danger that the single-minded pursuit of economic homogenization will produce some kind of ethnic or nationalist backlash.

In view of these problems and dangers, therefore, there is good reason at this moment, and in the coming years, to place a much greater emphasis on the federal-constitutional approach to integration, and to apply it more openly and thoroughly than has been done in the past. It is not a question of establishing centralization but of establishing a just balance. More precisely, the task is to create a genuine and explicit union in place of the confused and incoherent one that has so far emerged, and to replace proliferating technical mechanisms and programmes with organs clearly constituted to represent a body politic, and capable of acting with discretion within delimited spheres of competence. To adapt Robert Schuman's words, the task is to concentrate on the *ensemble* as much as, if not more than, the specific. As I have tried to indicate the classical tradition of federal thought is by no means irrelevant to this task.

# 21 Integration, Supranational Governance, and the Institutionalization of the European Polity

ALEC STONE SWEET AND WAYNE SANDHOLTZ

*The adoption of the 1992 program to create a single market in Europe (1985) and the passage of the Single European Act (1986) revitalized the European Community (EC) and marked a new stage in the integration process. The new enthusiasm in the Community awoke grand integration theory from a long slumber as scholars—some new, some veterans of former debates—attempted once again to explain what was happening in Europe. Wayne Sandholtz and John Zysman are often credited with relaunching the theoretical debate with a 1989* World Politics *(vol. 41, no. 1) article that explained the 1992 program as the product of a new bargain among business elites, member state politicians, and EC officials. Their explanation emphasized the role played by transnational business interests and supranational institutions and thus resembled neofunctionalism (Chapters 16 and 17), but was often termed "supranationalism" by scholars in the field who wished to differentiate it from state-centered "intergovernmentalism."*

*Sandholtz (University of California, Irvine) and Alec Stone Sweet (Nuffield College, Oxford), in the selection below, have moved beyond a vague supranationalism and explicitly developed a modern neofunctionalist account of the institutional development of the EC. In their view, integration is caused by the increase in cross-border exchange that creates political pressures on governments to regulate in-*

Reprinted with permission from *European Integration and Supranational Governance*, Wayne Sandholtz and Alec Stone Sweet, eds. (Oxford: Oxford University Press, 1998), pp. 1–26. Notes omitted.

*ternational transactions. Governments respond by creating supranational institutions that meet some needs but reveal others, which are met by granting the supranational institutions even more authority in a classic spillover process. Thus, according to Sweet and Sandholtz, by examining the rate of transaction in various sectors—in a direct application of Deutsch (Chapter 15)—one should be able to account for the development and speed of integration in corresponding policy areas.*

*This "transaction-based" theory of integration is simple and testable. It has much in common with the new institutionalism of Pollack (Chapter 23) and the governance approach of Hooghe and Marks (Chapter 24). But as Sweet and Sandholtz make clear, the theory stands in sharp contrast to the intergovernmentalism of Andrew Moravcsik (Chapter 22).*

Six governments, moved by a hope for enduring peace in a prosperous Europe, in 1957 signed the Treaty of Rome establishing the European Community.[1] The EC thus began its life as an agreement among independent nation-states. Forty years later, the European Community has developed into something more than a pact among governments. In fact, it is now commonplace to compare the Treaty of Rome to a constitution, and to refer to the European Community in terms that imply an analogy with nation-states. In this [chapter] we theorize, and assess empirically, the institutionalization of the European Community, that is, its remarkable transformation from an interstate bargain into a multidimensional, quasi-federal polity. We propose a theory of European integration, focusing on the process through which supranational governance—the competence of the European Community to make binding rules in any given policy domain—has developed.

We therefore confront some of the most puzzling questions posed by the evolution of the Community. Why does policymaking sometimes migrate from the nation-state level to the European Community? Why has integration proceeded more rapidly in some policy domains than it has in others? To what extent is the Community governed by "intergovernmental" or "supranational" modes of decision-making? What accounts for the relative dominance of the neoliberal project, and for the relative failure of social democratic visions of Europe to gain influence? We do not claim to have definitively settled all controversies. But our theory yields responses to these questions in the form of testable propositions. . . .

We do not explain the founding of the EC, but rather its institutional development. Our starting point, therefore, is the Treaty of

Rome. The Treaty established a cluster of organizations (Council, Commission, Court, and Parliament) and a set of rules whose central purpose was to promote exchange across national borders. The founders of the European Community reasoned that a "common market," linking their diverse national economies, would both accelerate the generation of wealth and make war among the member states unthinkable. The Treaty of Rome thus created a social and political space that intentionally privileged transnational economic interests. That is, the point of the EC was to facilitate exchange among its member countries. Because the Community was designed to promote intra-EC exchange, its rules and organizations have favored economic actors with a stake in cross-border transactions (trade, investment, production, distribution). Rising levels of transnational exchange trigger processes that generate movement toward increased supranational governance. We do not claim to explain policy processes, or their substantive outcomes, in terms of increasing cross-border exchange; specific policies are the product of complex political interactions. Rather, increasing exchange provokes behaviors and processes that are decisively shaped by the institutional context of the EC, and these processes tend to produce or reinforce supranational rule-making.

In other words, we emphasize the role of transnational exchange (e.g. trade, investment, the development of Euro-groups, networks, and associations) in pushing the EC's organizations to construct new policy and new arenas for policy-relevant behavior. Once constituted, these arenas sustain integration in predictable ways, not least, by promoting additional transnational exchange. . . .

Our analytical goals, and thus our theory, differentiate us from existing approaches. "Intergovernmentalism" [Chapter 22] denies the significance of supranational governance, arguing instead that the member states control policy processes and outcomes. Institutionalization is not an issue because the EC remains as it began, a set of bargains among independent nation-states. Scholars who analyze the EC in terms of "multilevel governance" [Chapter 24] or "policy networks" [Chapter 25] focus on the processes by which the contemporary EC produces policy outcomes. That is, they take a certain amount of supranational governance for granted. But the policy-centered approaches do not take as part of their task the explanation of how the EC developed from an interstate treaty to a system of governance, or why some policy domains have become more integrated than others.

This chapter proceeds as follows. In Section 1, we briefly contrast our theory with the main features of neofunctionalism and intergovernmentalism. Some urge that the neofunctionalist-intergovernmentalist debate be abandoned. We would respond that there has been no genuine debate; since the mid-1970s, very few have claimed the neofunctionalist banner, much less offered a systematic, full-fledged neofunctionalist argument on European integration. Instead, theoretical discussions tend to involve a ritual dismissal of neofunctionalism followed by either a critique or an endorsement of intergovernmentalism. That hardly constitutes a debate. Sometimes the impatience with the neofunctionalist-intergovernmentalist debate simply amounts to the claim that no general theory of European integration is possible (often tied to a preference for analyses of individual policies or sectors). In reply, we are placing on the table a general theory along with supportive empirical evidence. . . . The onus is on those who reject the possibility of broad theories to show why our results should not be taken seriously.

In Sections 2 and 3 of this chapter, we elaborate a theory that offers a positive alternative to intergovernmentalism. We define key concepts, discuss causal relationships between variables, and derive hypotheses about how European integration proceeds. In the concluding section we clarify our differences with intergovernmentalist theories of integration.

## ■ THEORETICAL CONTEXT

The primary theoretical divide in EC studies has been between intergovernmentalism and neofunctionalism. Endless nuance and distinction exist within each approach, but in the end most theorizing on integration endorses either the following statement or its opposite: the distribution of preferences and the conduct of bargaining among the governments of the member states broadly explain the nature, pace, and scope of integration, and neither supranational organization nor transnational actors generate political processes or outcomes of seminal importance. In recent decades, intergovernmentalists have worked to refine their framework, and some have aggressively proclaimed its superiority. At the same time, neofunctionalism has gradually been abandoned. Its original adherents have moved away from integration studies, and critics of intergovernmentalism have not developed their own general theory, least of all by refining neofunctionalism.

We set ourselves the task of developing and testing a theory of how supranational governance evolves over time. What we are seeking to explain, the nature and extent of supranational governance, varies along a number of dimensions. In some sectors, the competence to govern is held exclusively by the Community; in others, national institutions are the primary sites of policymaking; and in many domains, the transfer of power from the national to the supranational level has been only partial. Within the same policy sector, the answer to the question, "who governs?" has changed over time. And in those areas in which EC institutions have become sites of policy innovation and change, one finds variation in the relative capacity of the member-state governments, acting in summits and in the Council of Ministers, to control that policy. In specifying the research problem in this way, we commit ourselves to theorizing integration as a dynamic process that yields divergent outcomes. We therefore problematize the notion, strongly implied by neofunctionalist theories, that integration is the process by which the EC gradually but comprehensively replaces the nation-state in all of its functions. And we reject the comparative statics of intergovernmentalists as a mode of analysis incapable of capturing crucial temporal elements of European integration.

Our theory, set out in Sections 2 and 3 below, privileges the expansion of transnational exchange, the capacities of supranational organizations to respond to the needs of those who exchange, and the role of supranational rules in shaping subsequent integration. We argue that supranational governance serves the interests of 1) those individuals, groups, and firms who transact across borders, and 2) those who are advantaged by European rules, and disadvantaged by national rules, in specific policy domains. The expansion of transnational exchange, and the associated push to substitute supranational for national rules, generates pressure on the EC's organizations to act. Generally, EC organizations, such as the Commission and the Court, respond to this pressure by working to extend the domain of supranational rules, in order to achieve collective (transnational) gains and to accomplish the purposes of the Treaties, broadly interpreted. A first hypothesis, then, is that the relative intensity of transnational activity, measured across time and policy sectors, broadly determines variation on the dependent variable (supranational governance).

We claim that transnational activity has been the catalyst of European integration; but transnational exchange can not, in and of itself, determine the specific details, or the precise timing, of Community rule-making. Instead it provokes, or activates, the Community's decision-making bodies, including the Council of Ministers. Member-state governments often possess (but not always) the means to facilitate or to obstruct rule-making, and they use these powers frequently. Nevertheless, we argue, among other things, that as transnational exchange rises in any specific domain (or cluster of related domains), so do the costs, for governments, of maintaining disparate national rules. As these costs rise, so do incentives for governments to adjust their policy positions in ways that favor the expansion of supranational governance. Once fixed in a given domain, European rules—such as relevant treaty provisions, secondary legislation, and the ECJ's case law—generate a self sustaining dynamic, that leads to the gradual deepening of integration in that sector and, not uncommonly, to spillovers into other sectors. Thus, we view intergovernmental bargaining and decision-making as embedded in processes that are provoked and sustained by the expansion of transnational society, the pro-integrative activities of supranational organizations, and the growing density of supranational rules. And, we will argue, these processes gradually, but inevitably, reduce the capacity of the member states to control outcomes.

Our theory has important affinities with neofunctionalism. We acknowledge the insights of two of the founders of integration theory, Karl Deutsch [Chapter 15] and Ernst Haas [Chapter 16]. On crucial questions, we believe, they got it right. What we find complementary are Deutsch's emphasis on social exchange, communication, and transactions, and Haas's attention to the relationship between global interdependence, political choice, and the development of supranational institutions.

Deutsch and his collaborators held that increasing density of social exchange among individuals over prolonged periods of time would lead to the development of new communities (shared identity) and, ultimately, to the creation of a super-state with centralized institutions. We agree that social exchange across borders drives integration processes, generating social demands for supranational rules, and for higher levels of organizational capacity to respond to further demands. If this demand is not supplied, the development of higher levels of exchange will be stunted. We set aside Deutsch's concern with the formation of communities and identities per se, and the issue of whether or not identity formation precedes state-building. Our dependent variable remains mode of governance, not the construction of a pan-European identity or of a super-state.

Haas conceived of integration as the product of growing international interdependence and pluralist, interest-driven politics. Mitrany [Chapter 14] had theorized what would happen in a world increasingly beset by policy problems that transcended national borders: governmental functions would steadily migrate from national governments, who would act on the basis of "politics," to global technocrats, who would act on the basis of expertise. Haas recognized that the transfer of functions to supranational bodies would always be intensely contested, as some groups foresaw gains while others feared losses. He consequently saw the initial construction of supranational authority as the crucial political hurdle. Stripped down, Haas's neofunctionalist argument runs something like this. Some elite groups (leadership of political parties, industry associations, and labor federations) begin to recognize that problems of substantial interest cannot be solved at the national level. These groups push for the transfer of policy competence to a supranational body, finding each other and establishing cross-national coalitions along the way. If the problem is important enough and pro-integration elites are able to mount sufficient political leverage, governments establish supranational institutions.

Once supranational institutions are born, a new dynamic emerges. Haas pioneered in theorizing the logic of institutionalization at the supranational level. He suggested a dynamic process. The creation of supranational authority leads to changes in social expectations and behavior, which feed back onto supranational policymaking, and so on. As supranational bodies begin to deliver the coordinative solutions that pro-integrationists hoped for, they become the locus of a new kind of politics. Groups increasingly seek influence over supranational policies, opening up new political channels, but also helping supranational organizations acquire expertise, information, and legitimacy, thus bolstering their authority. The dynamic is reinforced by the potential, inherent in integration processes, for functional "spillover." Spillover is achieved when it becomes evident that initial policy objectives can not be adequately attained without such an extension. Neofunctionalists—especially Philippe Schmitter—also attended to the role of bargaining among member governments. But they at least implicitly argued (and we argue explicitly) that, as integration proceeds, member-state governments become less and less proactive, and more and more reactive to changes in the supranational environment to which they belong.

The three constituent elements of our theory are prefigured in neofunctionalism: the development of transnational society, the role of supranational organizations with meaningful autonomous capacity to pursue integrative agendas, and the focus on European rulemaking to resolve international policy externalities. Further, we appreciate Haas's insight that supranational policy-making (governance) generates a dynamic process of institutionalization. We do not, however, embrace all of Haas's neofunctionalism. Haas defined integration as "the process whereby political actors . . . are persuaded to shift their national loyalties, expectations, and political activities to a new and larger center." Again, we leave as an open question the extent to which the loyalties and identities of actors will shift from the national to the European level. There is substantial room for supranational governance without an ultimate shift in identification. And we will specify somewhat differently the causal mechanisms by which integration is provoked and sustained, tying both to the development of transnational society and to contemporary theories of institutions and institutionalization.

Intergovernmentalists conceptualize EC politics as a subset of international relations, namely as an example of interstate cooperation sustained by an international regime. Successful regimes facilitate the ongoing coordination of policy among member states, by reducing the costs of information, policy innovation, and negotiation. In Andrew Moravcsik's "liberal intergovernmentalism," regime theory has been supplemented to take account of domestic politics. At times, Moravcsik conceives European politics as a two-level game. The crucial actors are national executives, who continuously mediate between domestic interests and the activities of the international regime. At other times, Moravcsik sequences, for analytical purposes, national preference formation (domestic politics) and intergovernmental bargaining (regime politics). National executives are constrained by, but also aggregate, domestic interests as national preferences; once fixed, the distribution of preferences among, and the "relative bargaining power" of member-state governments determine outcomes.

European integration is a product of these outcomes. As Moravcsik puts it: "the EC has developed through a series of celebrated intergovernmental bargains, each of which sets the agenda for an intervening period of consolidation." In order to consolidate these bargains efficiently, member-state governments establish and delegate powers to the EC's organizations, like the Commission and the Court of Justice (ECJ). Although intergovernmentalists rarely focus empirical attention on the process of consolidation, they claim that the EC's organizations broadly pursue goals previously determined by the member-state governments, or are called to order if they pursue divergent agendas.

National executives construct the EC's capacity to govern, Moravcsik argues, for two main reasons. First, for electoral reasons executives may find it in their interest to respond to international policy externalities by pooling their sovereignty at the supranational level. Such externalities are generated by international interdependence. Second, in order to enhance their own autonomy *vis-à-vis* domestic actors, national executives may shift competence to govern to an arena (such as the Council of Ministers) that operates with fewer constraints on executive authority than national arenas. Why executives do so in some policy domains, but not in others, appears to be indeterminate.

For Moravcsik, the following sequence encompasses virtually all that is important: rising interdependence > delegation to supranational authorities > intergovernmental bargaining > delegation to supranational authorities > consolidation. Integration proceeds, but the sequence never varies in any meaningful way. In this imagery, transnational actors and society do not exist; instead, he notices domestic groups impact integration processes in autonomous and decisive ways; instead, in accordance with their place in the sequence, they behave as rather faithful agents of intergovernmental bargains. By our reading, rising interdependence constitutes the only important causal factor that both provokes integration and is not decisively determined by intergovernmental bargaining. On this point, intergovernmentalism hardly displaces neofunctionalism, but rather relies on a causal argument developed by the neofunctionalists.

We will return to our differences with intergovernmentalists in the concluding section.

## ■ A TRANSACTION-BASED THEORY OF INTEGRATION

As most students of EC policymaking have observed, simple characterizations of the Community, as either "intergovernmental" or "supranational," will not do. The brute fact is that integration has proceeded unevenly, and theories of integration have failed to explain this unevenness. Most recent research on EC politics has focused either on the grand bargains (the Single European Act or the Maastricht Treaty, for instance), or on how day-to-day policy is made in specific sectors. Neither emphasis has provided an adequate basis for theorizing the dynamic nature of integration over time across policy domains. . . .

### □ *From Intergovernmental to Supranational Politics*

We thus propose a continuum [Figure 21.1] that stretches between two ideal-typical modes of governance: the intergovernmental (the left-hand pole), and the supranational (the right-hand pole). One pole is constituted by intergovernmental politics. The central players in intergovernmental politics are the national executives of the member states, who bargain with each other to produce common policies. Bargaining is shaped by the relative powers of the member states, but

**Figure 21.1 Governance in the European Union**

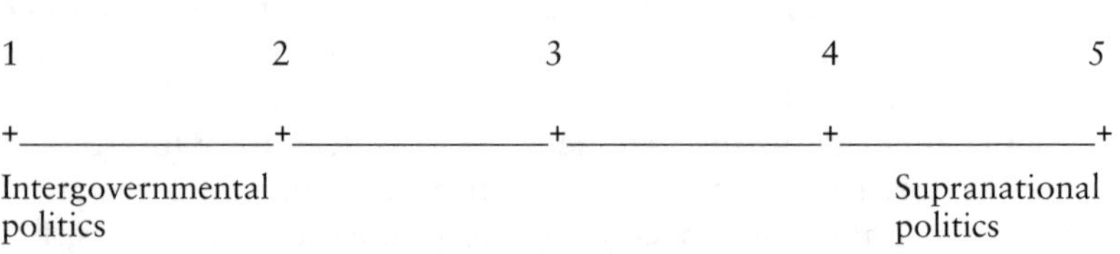


*Note:* From left to right, the continuum measures the increasing influence of three factors on policymaking processes and outcomes within any given policy sector. These factors are: (1) supranational organizations, (2) supranational rules, and (3) transnational society.

also by state preferences, which emerge from the pulling and hauling among domestic groups. These preferences are then given agency, as negotiating positions, by national executives in EC organizations such as the Council of Ministers. The EC level of governance operates as an international regime in the functional, transaction-costs mode: it is a "passive structure" that enhances the efficiency of interstate bargaining.

The other pole is constituted by supranational politics. A "supranational" mode of governance is one in which centralized governmental structures (those organizations constituted at the supranational level) possess jurisdiction over specific policy domains within the territory comprised by the member states. In exercising jurisdiction, supranational organizations are capable of constraining the behavior of all actors, including the member states, within those domains. Many would argue that "federal politics" would be the appropriate label. We use the term "supranational" to emphasize that the EC is an international organization, and that EC politics is a form of international politics. And we have avoided using the term "federal" here in order to avoid an argument about the precise nature of the EC polity and how it compares with other federal polities. Movement from left to right along the continuum indicates that a shift away from intergovernmentalism, and toward supranationalism, has taken place.

In principle, the continuum is capable of situating—and therefore of characterizing—all international regime forms as sites (more or less) of intergovernmental or sites (more or less) of supranational politics. Unlike most regimes, which tend to organize interstate cooperation in one or a few closely related sectors, the EC possesses differing degrees of competence across a diverse range of policy areas. In principle, one could use the continuum to characterize the development of the EC as a whole, in terms of the composite picture of all policy areas. One could also use the continuum to chart the comparative development or lack of development of different policy sectors comparatively. Thus, policy sector A may be located at point 2, shading toward intergovernmental politics, while policy sector B may be located at point 4, exhibiting strong features of supranationalism. Used in this way, the continuum asserts that there are potentially many ECs. As discussed in the next section, we hope that by disaggregating EC governing processes by policy sector, we will be able to learn more about the nature of European integration than we can by working to characterize, in a blanket fashion, the EC as an "intergovernmental" or "supranational" regime.

### □ *Dimensions of Institutionalization*

The continuum measures the movement from intergovernmental to supranational governance in three interrelated dimensions:

- *EC rules*: the legal, and less informal, constraints on behavior produced by interactions among political actors operating at the European level;
- *EC organizations*: those governmental structures, operating at the European level, that produce, execute, and interpret EC rules; and
- *transnational society*: those non-governmental actors who engage in intra-EC exchanges—social, economic, political—and thereby influence, directly or indirectly, policymaking processes and outcomes at the European level.

For any given policy area or process, movement from left to right along the continuum therefore measures the growing presence and intensity of each of these factors.

We understand these dimensions to be crucial indicators of levels of integration in the EC. By "integration," we mean the process by which the horizontal and vertical linkages between social, economic, and political actors emerge and evolve. Vertical linkages are the stable relationships, or patterned interaction, between actors organized at the EC level and actors organized at or below the member-state level. Horizontal linkages are the stable relationships, or patterned interaction, between actors organized in one member-state with actors organized in another. We understand these linkages to be "institutionalized" to the extent that they are constructed and sustained by EC rules.

The three dimensions are analytically distinct, although we expect them to covary, as integration proceeds, in predictable ways. As we move from left to right along the continuum the influence of EC (or supranational) organizations on policymaking processes and outcomes increases. Supranational EC organizations include the Commission, the Court of Justice, the Parliament, and even at times the Council of Ministers. At the left-hand pole, the regime's organizations exhibit little if any meaningful autonomy from the most powerful member states. By autonomy, we mean an organization's capacity to define and pursue, on an ongoing basis, a politically relevant agenda. In intergovernmental politics, organizations facilitate intergovernmental bargaining and logistical coordination (they lower the transaction costs for governments). At point 3 on the continuum, supranational organizations may often be the source of successful policy innovation, a form of "relative"—but meaningful—autonomy. At the supranational pole, institutions may exercise substantial autonomy, as when they are able to innovate, in policy-relevant ways, at times even in the face of member-state indifference or hostility.

The second dimension built into the continuum is legal-normative. As we move from left to right along the continuum, EC rules achieve higher degrees of clarity and formalization. Consider those rules that govern the production, application, and interpretation of all other rules, such as secondary legislation, within the Community. At the far left of the continuum, rules are few and weak; they do not trump individual governmental interests that conflict with them. As we move along the continuum, rules stabilize state bargaining, delegitimize exit, and—at the level of law—lay down binding standards of conduct enforceable by courts. Many of the rules governing EC policymaking are behavioral, that is, they have resulted from many years of constant interaction between state and supranational officials in a myriad of settings. But many of these rules are also highly formal, codified in treaty law, secondary legislation, and the ECJ's jurisprudence. Within any given policy domain, as we move leftward the rules governing the interactions of all actors, public and private, grow more dense and elaborate.

The third dimension captured by the continuum is the presence and influence of transnational actors—interest groups, business, knowledge-based elites—on policy processes and outcomes. In intergovernmental politics, national executives mediate between domestic actors and supranational organizations and rules. In supranational politics, transnational actors have a choice of fora in which to exert their influence. They may target national governmental structures—

executive, legislative, or judicial—as well as supranational bodies, and they may play one level off against the other.

Taken together, these dimensions are constitutive of supranational politics. If this is so . . . these three factors must move together, and the disjunctures that do occur in movement are short-lived. Organizations, rules, and social exchange are closely linked in the development of society and systems of governance; they are similarly connected in supranational politics. Organizations produce and transmit the rules that guide social interaction. They structure access to policy processes, defining political power and privileging some parts of society more than others. As supranational organizations acquire and wield autonomy, they are able to shape not only specific policy outcomes but also the rules that channel policymaking behaviors. As supranational organizations and rules emerge and solidify, they constitute transnational society by establishing bases for interaction and access points for influencing policy. As transnational society endures and expands, the organizations and rules that structure behaviors become more deeply rooted as "givens," taken for granted as defining political life. Growth in one element of the supranational trio (organizations, rules, transnational society) creates conditions that favor growth in the other two. An expansion of the tasks or autonomy of supranational organizations creates opportunities for political action, which actors and groups will seek to exploit, thus expanding transnational society. As societal actors adjust their behaviors in response to new supranational rules, these rules can gradually be locked in. If broader, global trends promote the growth of transnational society, there will be a corresponding demand for increased organizational capacity and rules to coordinate and to guide interactions.

### □ *Why Movement Occurs*

The continuum gives us tools with which to describe EC governance. We have also offered a proposition that would account for some of the dynamics of integration, namely that movement in any one of the dimensions will tend to produce movement in the other two. In other words, there is an internal dynamic of institutionalization. But important questions remain to be theorized. Why does movement on any of the dimensions occur in the first place? Why do some policy domains move farther and faster toward the supranational pole than others? In this section we offer a theoretical account that can generate answers to such questions.

Our starting point is society, in particular, non-state actors who engage in transactions and communications across national borders, within Europe. These are the people who need European standards, rules, and dispute resolution mechanisms—who need supranational governance. In the beginning, the causal mechanism is quite simple: increasing levels of cross-border transactions and communications by societal actors will increase the perceived need for European-level rules coordination, and regulation. In fact, the absence of European rules will come to be seen as an obstacle to the generation of wealth and the achievement of other collective gains. Separate national legal regimes constitute the crucial source of transaction costs for those who wish to engage in exchanges across borders: customs and other border controls, differing technical standards, divergent health and environmental regulations, distinct systems of commercial law, diverse national currencies, and so on. Further, the costs of transacting across borders are higher than those involved in contracting within a single member-state, to the extent that there exists no secure common legal framework at the supranational level, comparable in its efficacy to that of national legal systems. As transnational exchanges rise, so does the societal demand for supranational rules and organizational capacity to regulate. Transactors can exert pro-integration pressure on their own governments, but when these are reticent, transactors can access supranational arenas dominated by the Commission and the European Court of Justice.

Governmental actors clearly have their own interests, which may include maximizing their autonomy and control over resources. They may resist the shift toward supranational policymaking. But as they do so, they inhibit the generation of wealth within their territory by those actors that depend on European transactions. Such resistance is therefore sustainable only at a cost in prosperity. They can also attempt to slow integration or push it in directions favorable to their perceived interests, but they do not drive the process or fully control it. In a fundamental sense, governments are reactive, constantly adjusting to the integration that is going on all around them.

On this point, the contrast between our theory and intergovernmental approaches to the EC could hardly be greater, but we have not written national governments out of the story. In fact, intergovernmental decision-making is ubiquitous in the EC, present even at the far right-hand pole of our continuum (as it is in Canada and other federal systems). EC summits, intergovernmental conferences, and meetings of the Council of Ministers are practically defined by tough, interest-driven negotiation. But that is part of the problem with intergovernmental approaches to integration. Adherents of these approaches always begin by announcing that the "grand bargains" are the defining moments of European integration, and then these historic agreements become the object of empirical research. But the grand bargains are, by definition, intergovernmental. The research results are quite predictable when one looks to intergovernmental bargains for evidence of intergovernmental bargaining. Thus the observation that bargaining among governments is ubiquitous in the EC does not settle theoretical controversy. Put differently, the term "intergovernmental" is useful as a description of a specific mode of decision-making within the EC policy process. But to attend to what is intergovernmental about the construction of supranational governance does not require us to adopt, or to accept the validity of, "intergovernmentalism-as-theory."

Indeed, we argue that intergovernmental bargaining in the EC more often than not is responsive to the interests of a nascent, always developing, transnational society. Indeed, the demand for EC rules and regulation provides the subject matter for the bargaining. With very few exceptions, EC legislation concerns, directly or indirectly, the creation of rules that facilitate or regulate intra-EC exchange and communications. The configuration of social interests that will be affected by European policy innovation may vary from state to state, which creates the differences over which governments must negotiate. But rather than being the generator of integration, intergovernmental bargaining is more often its product.

The exclusive focus on grand intergovernmental bargains can also lead to serious distortions of the historical record. The 1970s have generally been regarded as disconfirmation of neofunctionalism; intergovernmentalists typically note that member-state preferences diverged during those years and that few of the EC's ambitious plans at the beginning of the decade bore fruit. We do not read the story of European integration as one of stop-and-go, at least not in any general or comprehensive sense. At the height of de Gaulle's power in the 1960s, the ECJ moved aggressively to "constitutionalize" the treaties. In the worst days of "Eurosclerosis" in the 1970s, levels of intra-EC trade and other forms of exchange soared. And, as we would expect, both the amount of legislation and the number of organized EC pressure groups grew steadily through the 1970s. Integration always proceeded, in some sectors and from some vantage points, despite the Luxembourg compromise and despite the divergence of state preferences.

. . .

The transactions-based theory implies a coherent answer to the question, why does integration proceed faster or farther in some policy areas than in others? We would look to variation in the levels of cross-border interactions and in the consequent need for supranational coordination and rules. In sectors where the intensity and value of cross-national transactions are relatively low, the demand for EC-level coordination of rules and dispute resolution will be correspondingly low. Conversely, in domains where the number and value of cross-border transactions are rising, there will be increasing demand on the part of the transactors for EC-level rules and dispute-resolution mechanisms. It makes sense, then, that the EC has moved farthest toward the supranational pole with respect to managing the internal market. Intra-EC trade and investment have grown steadily since the founding of the EEC [European Economic Community], creating the need for greater degrees of supranational governance in issue areas closely linked to expanding the common market. Naturally, the EC rules for the single market have in turn encouraged increases in the cross-border transactions they were meant to facilitate. In contrast, there are few societal transactions that are impeded by the absence of a common foreign and security policy. Or, put differently, though some argue for the political benefits that CFSP [Common Foreign and Security Policy] would bring, few societal transactors find its absence costly. There is therefore minimal social demand for integration in that policy domain.

Furthermore, the capacity of supranational organizations to make rules in a given policy domain appears to vary as a function of the level of transnational activity. . . . [L]itigation of free movement of goods disputes dominates the work of the European Court of Justice, and legal principles developed by the ECJ in the domain have animated the Court's decision-making in other areas. Mark Pollack [Chapter 23] finds that the Commission exercises greater autonomy in some policy sectors than in others. The Commission's authority is greatest when it is supported by EC rules, pro-integrative Court decisions, and transnational interests. We would argue that variation in these factors is not random: higher levels of transactions push the EC to legislate, the Court to clarify the rules, and interests to organize. It is therefore not surprising that . . . the Commission's powers are greater in competition policy than in structural funds or external trade. Even within competition policy, the Commission acts with greater authority where transaction levels are high (telecommunications) relative to where they are low (electricity).

The theory also allows us to explain the general direction of integration in the common market. Business is likely to be the segment for which the material stake in cross-border transactions is greatest and most obvious. Indeed, the Treaty of Rome created rules whose purpose was to promote cross-national economic activities. Companies with an interest in cross-national sales or investment will press for the reduction of national barriers, and for the establishment of regional rules and standards. By the same token, the consequences of integration for people in their roles as workers and consumers are less transparent. This would explain why European companies have had a greater impact on integration than have labor or consumers. We can thus account for the decisively neo-liberal (pro-market) character of recent events like the 1992 program and the Maastricht provisions on EMU. If integration is driven fundamentally by private transactors, and if capital is the group with the clearest immediate stake in intra-EC transactions (not to mention the resources required for political influence), it is not surprising that the major steps in integration should be congenial to those segments of business.

We can now also respecify the spillover mechanism. As the most obvious hindrances to cross-national exchange are removed, or their effects reduced by the transaction-cost-reducing behavior of supranational organizations and rules, new obstacles to such transactions are revealed and become salient. With the removal of tariffs and quotas, for example, differences in national compatibility, and so on—become more apparent as obstacles to exchange. Economic actors seeking to benefit from intra-Community exchange will then target these obstacles, both by attacking regulatory barriers through litigation and by pressuring EC legislative institutions to widen the jurisdiction of the EC into new domains. Transactors will always prefer, other things being equal, to live under (or adapt to) one set of rules rather than six, or twelve, or fifteen. As governments and EC institutions respond, spillover occurs.

Globalization, which is integration of a broader geographic scope, can also stimulate movement toward increased supranational governance within Europe. The integration of national markets (for goods, services, and capital) and multilateral approaches to global problems (ozone, climate change, weapons proliferation) can create pressures for integration from above the nation-state. Transnational actors are sometimes the conduit through which globalization stimulates advances in European integration. For instance, with the goal of increasing their competitiveness in world markets, European multinationals pressed for active EC high-technology programs (ESPRIT, RACE) as well as the creation of a genuine internal market. But globalization can also exert pressure directly on EC organizations. For example, the involvement of the EC in global environmental negotiations has strengthened Commission competencies and roles.

## ■ INSTITUTIONALIZATION

Once movement toward the supranational pole begins, European rules generate a dynamic of [their] own, which we call institutionalization. In laying out the continuum, the objective was to establish analytic categories for conceptualizing and identifying movement toward supranational politics. In a subsequent section, we offered a theory as to why policy domains move toward the supranational pole. Our transaction-based theory of movement leads us, when we observe rising levels of transnational exchange, to expect more EC rules. We can thus explain why some policy domains move more quickly toward supranational governance than others. The theory does not tell us what specific rules and policies will emerge, nor what organizational form supranational governance will acquire.

In this section, we propose a theoretical account for why shifts toward supranational governance tend to generate additional movement in the same direction, or at least make it difficult to reverse the shifts that have already occurred. In other words, the EC is not at any given moment simply the organizational instantiation of state interests, combined through negotiation into a lowest common-denominator agreement. The supranational content of the EC does not fluctuate up and down to reflect the interstate bargain *du jour*. Rather, because of institutionalization, EC policy domains can become more supranational without some, or at times a majority of, governments wanting it or being able to reverse it.

Like Haas, we argue that there is a logic of institutionalization. Rules and rule-making are at the heart of this logic. Rules define roles (who is an actor) and establish the social context in which actors' interests and strategies take shape. Rules define the game, establishing for players both the objectives and the range of appropriate tactics or moves. Actors behave in self-interested ways, but both the interests and the behaviors take form in a social setting defined by rules. Actors will try to exploit the rules for selfish advantage, or to change the rules to favor achievement of their objectives. But at any given moment, they take the rules as given. Institutions are systems of rules, and institutionalization is the process by which rules are created, applied, and interpreted by those who live under them.

Institutions, contrary to the image of fixity frequently associated with them, are in constant evolution. People acting within a rule context inevitably encounter the limits of the rules, that is, situations in which their content is unclear or disputed. Rules may not provide clear guidance for new kinds of transactions or behaviors. Or two actors may disagree as to what the rules require in a specific instance. In either case, actors will then make demands on the dispute resolution processes. They may push for the creation of new rules (legislation). Or they may seek reinterpretation of the existing rules (adjudication). As they interpret and apply the rules, courts, legislators, and administrators necessarily modify the rules by establishing their effective meaning. The new or changed rules then guide subsequent interactions, as people adapt their behaviors to the rules. The disputes that arise thereafter take shape in an altered rule structure and initiate the processes that will again reinterpret and modify the rules. The new rules guide actor behaviors, and so on.

The logic of institutionalization is at work in the European Community and is crucial to understanding integration as a process. As European rules emerge and are clarified and as European organizations become arenas for politics, what is specifically supranational shapes the context for subsequent interactions: how actors define their interests, what avenues are available to pursue them, how disputes are to be resolved. This creates the "loop" of institutionalization. Developments in EC rules delineate the contours of future policy debates as well as the normative and organizational terms in which they will be decided. Since rules are central to institutionalization, the Treaty of Rome is the crucial starting point for subsequent integration. The Treaty established EC rules and rule-making procedures, and constituted EC organizations like the Commission and the ECJ.

We would expect that, in general, integration would occur most readily in policy domains included in the Treaty. Policy domains mentioned in the Treaty have the advantage of a legal basis in the Union's fundamental rules. Treaty-based policy domains should move more quickly toward supranational governance, other things being equal, than polity areas for which a competence or legal basis would have to be constructed from scratch. Fligstein and McNichol show that "most of the arenas in which the EC built competencies were laid down in the Treaty of Rome and the original language and definitions gave rise to organizational structures oriented towards producing legislation in those domains."

Integration, however, is not limited to those domains specifically called out in the Treaty. Where cross-border activities are of increasing importance, we expect to find the creation and growth of supranational governance. When there is no Treaty-based competence for such a development, the relevant actors will create one. (Conversely, policy domains mentioned in the Treaty but lacking cross-border transactions are not likely to move toward supranational governance.) Rising levels of cross-border transactions generate demand for EC rules and dispute resolution. Member governments can respond by amending the Treaty, or stretching Treaty clauses to cover new legislation. Art. 236, for instance, permits the EC to establish supranational governance to achieve the general objectives of the Community. This provision has served as the legal basis for EC action in policy domains not specifically mentioned in the Treaty. Perhaps more important in practice, the ECJ has interpreted the Treaty so as to permit the expansion of supranational policy domains. Again: the Court does not choose its questions; it responds to the cases brought, frequently, by transactors seeking clearer EC rules or enforcement of existing rules. The landmark Dassonville line of case law, which underpinned immensely consequential Commission initiatives and intergovernmental bargaining in the move to complete the common market, was sustained by private actors desiring the elimination of national practices that limited intra-EC trade.

. . .

Thus, though the Treaty is the indispensable starting point, over time supranational rules and rule-making processes evolve in ways that are not predictable from the *ex ante* perspective of those who establish them. The new rules create legal rights and open new arenas for politics; in this fashion they structure political processes thereafter. Actors—including governments, private entities, and EC bodies—adapt to the new rules and arenas. This dynamic is wholly absent in the intergovernmentalist account. Intergovernmentalists see governments as the sole mediators between non-state actors and EC policymaking. In contrast, our theory leads us to expect (and we do observe) private actors successfully employing the EC judicial process against member governments and pursuing political strategies directly at the Commission. Intergovernmentalists depict governments as directing the process of integration and establishing its limits. Our approach, in contrast, views governments as powerful actors that cannot always impose their preferred outcomes on other players in the EC political system (transnational actors, the Commission and the ECJ), who also possess substantial legal and political powers.

Finally, governments are ultimately constrained by rules whose production they do not control. National courts, guided by ECJ decisions, can compel their governments to comply with EC rules they have opposed. For example, though the UK has taken the most anti-integration position in the Council with respect to social provisions, British courts responding to private litigants and ECJ rulings have forced the government to change domestic policies so that they align with EC laws that Britain opposed. Similarly, though member governments bargained with each other with respect to telecommunications liberalization, that bargaining took place during the crucial phase under the shadow of the Commission's newfound capacity, affirmed by the Court, to enact its preferred policies via Art. 90 directives.

The rule-centered logic of institutionalization also suggests why it is difficult, and sometimes impossible, for governments to reverse the shifts toward supranational governance that have occurred. The Treaty—the constitution of the European polity—fixes the rule-making processes of the EC and the ECJ is authoritative interpreter of this constitution. As substantive rules, such as secondary legislation, evolve, actors (including governments, as well as EC bodies and non-state entities) adjust their behaviors. The rules, since the impetus behind them is to facilitate cross-border transactions and communications, lead to new kinds and higher levels of transactions. The new transactions entrench interests. The result is a high degree of "stickiness" in movement along the continuum.

Two logics, or languages, capture the essence of that stickiness. The first has to do with path dependence, the second with principal-agent relations. Paul Pierson makes two interrelated points: first, that significant gaps emerge between member-state preferences and the functioning of EC policies and institutions; and second, that once such gaps develop states cannot simply close them. The latter point is the crucial one with respect to the difficulty of reversing shifts toward supranational governance. Pierson argues that institutional change is a "path-dependent" process; once institutional and policy changes are in place, social actors adapt to those changes, frequently making substantial investments in the process. A policy turnabout would entail the loss of these sunk costs, thus raising the costs for governments seeking to unwind supranational governance. Furthermore, decision rules often constitute major obstacles to reversing course. The process of adaptation to change in complex social settings also produces unintended consequences that are difficult to unwind. Thus institutional and policy outcomes become "locked in," channeling politics down specific paths and closing previously plausible alternatives.

Mark Pollack assesses the conditions under which the EC Commission can act autonomously, recognizing that the Commission is the most constrained of the EC's supranational bodies (as compared to the Parliament and the ECJ). He employs principal-agent imagery to argue that the administrative and oversight mechanisms that principals (member governments) use to rein in agents (the Commission) can be costly and of limited effectiveness. Furthermore, agents can exploit divergent preferences among multiple principals, especially under more demanding decision rules, like unanimity.

The path-dependence and principal-agent logics reinforce our argument that institutionalization in the EC is not reducible to the preferences of, or bargaining among, member governments. The expansion of transnational society pushes for supranational governance, which is exercised to facilitate and regulate that society. Once in place, supranational rules alter the context for subsequent transactions and policymaking. Actors—governments, supranational organizations, and non-state entities alike—adapt their preferences, strategies, and behaviors to the new rules. These adaptations, plus the importance of rules in shaping preferences and behaviors, are what make shifts toward supranational governance sticky and difficult to undo. Finally, because specific policies and organizational forms emerge through a path-dependent process, in which numerous social systems interact in quite contingent ways, those outcomes can only be analyzed through historical, process-tracing case studies. Thus, whereas broad aggregate data reflect the casual link between cross-border transactions and EC rule-making, case studies are essential for explaining the specific content and form of EC rules and policies.

## ■ CONCLUSION

We have proposed a theory of integration that relies on three casual factors: exchange, organization, and rules. Transnational exchange provokes supranational organizations to make rules designed to facilitate and to regulate the development of transnational society. To the extent that supranational organizations are successful at doing so, specific causal connections between our three factors will be constructed. These connections sustain an inherently expansionary process, not least, by means of policy feedback. As the structure of European rules becomes more dense and articulated, this structure itself will encourage private and public actors at all levels of the Community to forge new, or intensify existing, linkages (vertical and horizontal). Member-state governments are important actors in this process. Nevertheless, we argue that the integration-relevant behavior of governments, whether acting individually or collectively, is best explained in terms of the embeddedness of governments in integration processes, that is, in terms of the development of transnational society and its system of governance.

We do not want to be misunderstood on this last point. No one denies that certain elements, or stages, of the European policy-making process are intergovernmental. Governments are repositories of immense resources, both material (e.g. financial) and non-material (e.g. legitimacy). In the EC, national executives pursue what they take to be their own interests, which they express as constituting the national interest. And in the bargaining process, executives from the larger states command greater resources and tend to wield greater influence on EC policy outcomes than those from the smaller states. But noticing governments and power does not entail accepting intergovernmentalism as a body of casual propositions about how integration has proceeded. Although we dismiss as untenable Moravcsik's proclamation that his version of intergovernmentalism is the "indispensable and fundamental point of departure for any general explanation of regional integration," we have no trouble recognizing that intergovernmental bargaining is an ubiquitous feature of supranational governance (as it is in many federal polities). Indeed, in our research we constantly attend to the question of whether and how integration shapes the preferences of governments over time, and the extent to which it casts (and recasts) the nature and content of intergovernmental bargaining. In our opinion, Moravcsik has developed a theory of intergovernmental bargaining within a specific institutional context, that of the EC, but not a satisfying general theory of integration.

Our theory accounts for causal relationships between variables that are systematically downplayed or de-emphasized by intergovernmentalism and, we argue, these relationships will regularly produce outcomes that significantly impact the trajectory of integration. Intergovernmentalism is rigid; integration proceeds, but nothing essential in European politics ever changes. In contrast, we expect that integration produces new political arenas; that the politics in these arenas will qualitatively differ from purely intergovernmental politics; and that this difference will have an impact downstream, on subsequent policy processes and outcomes. In Moravcsik's view, supranational organizations, like the Commission, are virtually always "perfectly reactive agents," responding only to the "delegation" of tasks pursuant to the "pooling" of state sovereignty. In contrast, we expect supranational bodies to work to enhance their own autonomy and influence within the European polity, so as to promote the interests of transnational society and the construction of supranational governance. In Moravcsik's view, "Only where the action of supranational leaders *systematically* bias outcomes away from the long term self-interest of member states can we speak of a serious challenge to an intergovernmentalist view" (emphasis in original). In response, we expect what intergovernmentalism is not capable of explaining, namely that, as integration proceeds, the Court and the Commission will routinely produce rules (policy outcomes) that would not have been adopted by governments in the Council of Ministers, or in summitry. And we argue that the long-term interests of member-state governments will be increasingly biased toward the long-term interest of transnational society, those who have the most to gain from supranational governments.

## ■ NOTE

1. We recognize the important distinctions between "European Community" and "European Union." However, since most of the activities we refer to in this chapter occur under the aegis of the European Community, in this chapter we consistently use "EC" and "European Community."

# 22 The Choice for Europe

ANDREW MORAVCSIK

*The revival of neofunctionalism in the 1990s did not go unchallenged. Andrew Moravcsik (Harvard University)—a former student of Stanley Hoffmann's and undoubtedly the most controversial theorist of the contemporary period—wrote a series of closely argued, sometimes polemical articles in the early part of the decade that forced students of the European Union (EU) to take seriously the intergovernmentalist perspective. While most scholars in the field assumed member states were losing sovereignty to increasingly independent supranational institutions, Moravcsik argued that, on the contrary, European governments were still very much in charge of the integration process. Thus many of the theoretical debates in the 1990s took an "us-versus-them" tone: supranationalists v. intergovernmentalists—or more often than not, the world v. Andrew Moravcsik.*

*In reality, Moravcsik and the rest of the field were not worlds apart. Moravcsik, like most of his opponents, was a rationalist and an institutionalist, meaning that he believed human beings generally acted rationally to further their material interests and that the institutions they established had real effects on behavior. But his view of international relations was more like Hoffmann's than Haas's: cooperation was possible among sovereign states, but only when it was in their interest; member states were quick to halt or reverse integration when it no longer met their needs. Moravcsik's basic argument with the field was that most theorists failed to rigorously test their supranational view against the obvious alternative that the EU serves the interests of its member states.*

---

Reprinted with permission from Cornell University Press and Taylor and Francis from *The Choice for Europe: Social Purpose and State Power* by Andrew Moravcsik (Ithaca, New York: Cornell University Press, 1998), pp. 1–17.  Notes omitted.

The Choice for Europe, *of which the introduction is reprinted here, is Moravcsik's monumental attempt "to explain why sovereign governments in Europe have chosen repeatedly to coordinate their core economic policies and surrender sovereign prerogatives within an international institution." His focus is not on the day-to-day operations of the EU, but on the major turning points—the big bargains—in the history of European integration. He argues that European countries in establishing the Community have not engaged in extraordinary behavior, but have, in fact, responded rationally to their changing economic and technological environment. The cooperative agreements they have reached, he argues, reflect their drive for commercial advantage, the distribution of power among them, and their decision to rely on supranational institutions to enforce their commitments. Each of these explanatory factors rests on additional theories of political economy, interdependence, bargaining, international regimes, and so on. In the end, Moravcsik claims not to be articulating a grand theory (contrary to what his critics claim), but rather a multicausal explanation of one aspect of integration, the big bargain. His emphasis on the decisions of national governments, however, continues to set him apart from the majority of EU scholars who prefer to highlight the independence of supranational actors.*

> The study of regional integration should be both included in and subordinated to the study of changing patterns of interdependence.
>
> —*Ernst Haas,* The Obsolescence of Regional Integration Theory, *1975*

The construction of the European Community (EC) ranks among the most extraordinary achievements in modern world politics, yet there is little agreement about its causes.[1] EC rules influence most aspects of European political life, from the regulation of the habitat of wild birds to voting within the World Trade Organization. The EC's complex institutions include a semi-autonomous legal system, parliament, and bureaucracy as well as detailed norms, principles, rules, and practices governing direct relations among national governments. These institutions resemble those of a modern nation-state as much as those of a conventional international regime. Today the EC is a unique, multileveled, transnational political system.

## ■ THE QUESTION: EXPLAINING MAJOR TURNING POINTS

This book addresses the most fundamental puzzle confronting those who seek to understand European integration, namely to explain why sovereign governments in Europe have chosen repeatedly to coordinate their core economic policies and surrender sovereign prerogatives within an international institution. In the history of the EC, the most important such choices are five treaty-amending sets of agreements that propelled integration forward[: the Treaty of Rome, the consolidation of the Common Market in the 1960s, the European Monetary System, the Single European Act, and the Treaty on European Union]. Variously termed constitutive, constitutional, history-making, or grand bargains, they punctuate EC history at a rate of roughly once per decade. Each grand bargain, three aimed at trade liberalization and two at monetary cooperation, set the agenda for a period of consolidation, helping to define the focus and pace of subsequent decision-making. The EC has evolved, as some have said of global economic institutions more generally, as a "sequence of irregular big bangs." At the core of this book is a series of structured narratives of these decisions or, more properly, bundles of decisions. The account focuses primarily on German, French, and British policies.

. . .

## ■ THE ARGUMENT: ECONOMIC INTEREST, RELATIVE POWER, CREDIBLE COMMITMENTS

My central claim is that the broad lines of European integration since 1955 reflect three factors: patterns of commercial advantage, the relative bargaining power of important governments, and the incentives to enhance the credibility of interstate commitments. Most fundamental of these was commercial interest. European integration resulted from a series of rational choices made by national leaders who consistently pursued economic interests—primarily the commercial interests of powerful economic producers and secondarily the macroeconomic preferences of ruling governmental coalitions—that evolved slowly in response to structural incentives in the global economy.

When such interests converged, integration advanced. The fact that economic interests did consistently converge reflected fundamental trends in post-war international political economy—in particular, a fifty-year boom in trade and investment among industrialized countries. The resulting expansion of intra-industry trade both predated the EC and induced policy changes regardless of whether the countries in question were EC members. Similarly, rising capital mobility undermined the autonomy of national macroeconomic policies, creating greater pressures for monetary cooperation. At its core, I argue, European integration has been dictated by the need to adapt through policy coordination to these trends in technology and in economic policy.

This explanation of national preferences for integration is grounded in political economy, not economics. Despite the importance of economic benefits, economists themselves were skeptical of, if not outright opposed to, many of the major steps in European integration. Construction of a customs union, a common agricultural policy, monetary union—almost all were, from the perspective of an economist, "second best" policies. Preferences for such policies emerged from a process of domestic political conflict in which specific sectoral interests, adjustment costs and, sometimes, geopolitical concerns played an important role. Consistent with modern theories of foreign economic policy, I argue that the specific conditions under which governments were willing to liberalize trade reflected their international economic competitiveness; the conditions under which they accepted monetary integration reflected prevailing macroeconomic policies and preferences.

Yet the EC was shaped by more than the convergence of national preferences in the face of economic change. There were important distributional conflicts not just within states but among them. These interstate conflicts were resolved only through hard interstate bargaining, in which credible threats to veto proposals, to withhold financial side-payments, and to form alternative alliances excluding recalcitrant governments carried the day. The outcomes reflected relative power of states—more precisely, patterns of asymmetrical interdependence. Those who gained the most economically from integration compromised the most on the margin to realize it, whereas those who gained the least or for whom the costs of adaptation were highest imposed conditions. To secure the substantive bargains they had made, finally, governments delegated and pooled sovereignty in international institutions for the express purpose of committing one another to cooperate. Where joint gains were large, but each government faced a strong temptation to defect from agreements—as was the case for the Common Agricultural Policy and for Economic and Monetary Union—governments tended to establish qualified majority voting and delegate tasks to the Commission.

In short, I argue that a tripartite explanation of integration—economic interest, relative power, credible commitments—accounts for the form, substance, and timing of major steps toward European integration. . . .

This explanation of integration breaks with the bulk of existing scholarship on the EC. It rejects the view that integration has been driven primarily—as Jean Monnet [Chapter 5] and his social-scientific counterparts, the neofunctionalists, long maintained—by a technocratic process reflecting the imperatives of modern economic planning, the unintended consequences of previous decisions, and the entrepreneurship of disinterested supranational experts. The integration process did not supercede or circumvent the political will of national leaders; it reflected their will. Nor—as the most prominent critics of neofunctionalism contend—can we account for integration primarily as the result of a coincidental postwar link between the "low politics" of foreign economic policy and geopolitical "high politics." The primary motivation of those who chose to integrate was not to prevent another Franco-German war, bolster global prestige and power, or balance against the superpowers. Nor—as numerous historians, political scientists, and members of the European movement continue to maintain—does integration represent a victory over nationalistic opposition by proponents of a widely shared, idealistic vision of a united Europe, an interpretation known in the classical lexicon as the "federalist" theory of integration. To be sure, technocratic imperatives, geopolitical concerns, and European idealism each played a role at the margin, but none has consistently been the decisive force behind major decisions. Nor, finally—although this book shares much with recent studies of European integration in the 1950's by economic historians such as Alan Milward—was integration primarily an effort to preserve a system of social welfare provision unique to postwar Western Europe or any of its member-states.

All such explanations treat the EC as unique, an exception in world politics that requires a *sui generis* theory. This assumption led the study of regional integration to develop over the past forty years as a discipline apart, one divorced from general studies of international cooperation. The paradoxical result: today no claim appears more radical than the claim that the behavior of EC member governments is *normal*. The revisionist quality of the argument in this book lies precisely in its effort to normalize the actions of European governments—to treat them as a subset of general tendencies among democratic states in modern world politics. Governments cooperated when induced or constrained to do so by economic self-interest, relative power, and strategically imposed commitments. Far from demonstrating the triumph of technocracy, the power of idealism, and the impotence or irrelevance of the modern nation-state, European integration exemplifies a distinctly modern form of power politics, peacefully pursued by democratic states for largely economic reasons through the exploitation of asymmetrical interdependence and the manipulation of institutional commitments. If the motivations of postwar European leaders were distinctive, it was because their countries were touched more intensely by economic trends common to all advanced industrial democracies, most notably the rapidly increasing potential for industrial trade among industrialized nations since World War II, disorder in the international monetary system after 1970, and widespread pressures for liberalization and disinflation in recent decades.

Through an analysis of EC history, this book also seeks to advance a distinctive theoretical position in current debates in international relations theory. The explanation of European integration sketched above is formulated as a distinct series of answers to three questions central to modern theories of comparative and international political economy. In a world in which governments are, broadly speaking, rational and instrumental, integration can be seen as a process in which they define a series of underlying objectives or preferences, bargain to substantive agreements concerning cooperation, and finally select appropriate international institutions in which to embed them. Any explanation of rational state choices to coordinate policy through international institutions must therefore address three questions. First, what best explains national preferences, the fundamental motivations underlying support for or opposition to economic integration? Second, given a set of national preferences, what best explains outcomes of interstate bargaining within the EC? Third, given a set of substantive bargains, what best explains state choices to construct European institutions and transfer sovereignty to them? This book suggests a distinct answer to each question. Let us consider each in turn.

Patterns of national preferences, the focus of the first stage, vary greatly over EC history. France, Germany, and Britain promoted and opposed integration in different substantive areas and to different ends. Their respective positions also shifted, if usually only in incremental fashion, over time. In explaining foreign economic policy, international relations theorists concerned with national preference formation have long debated the relative weight of security and political economic motivations.

One theory holds that world politics contains a hierarchy of issues headed by security concerns. Foreign economic policy is driven, therefore, not by its direct economic consequences but by its indirect consequences for national security, termed "security externalities." This is the dominant view in the study of the EC where diplomatic historians, European foreign policy specialists, and those who study the role of ideas in foreign policy have long argued that European economic integration has been pursued not primarily for its own sake but to counter geopolitical threats and realize geopolitical goals. Postwar European leaders who constructed and extended the EC sought to tie down the Germans, balance the Russians, establish a third force against the Americans, overcome right-wing and Communist extremism at home, or suppress nationalism to realize a distinctive vision of European federalism. Geopolitical interest and ideology explain traditional British semi-detachment from Europe, German federalist sympathies, and French vacillation between the two poles.

I conclude instead in favor of an alternative theory of foreign economic policy that holds that there is no hierarchy of interests; national interests tend instead to reflect direct, issue-specific consequences. National preferences concerning international trade and monetary policy can therefore be understood as a reflection of the economic incentives generated by patterns of international economic interdependence—the core of so-called "endogenous" theories of tariff and exchange-rate policy. The dominant motivations of governments in the EC decisions studied here reflected not geopolitical threats or ideals but pressures to coordinate policy responses to rising opportunities for profitable economic exchange, in particular growing intra-industry trade and capital movements. While more strictly commercial in its focus, this view is consistent with those of economic historians who have studied EC history. Trade liberalization followed export opportunities. In monetary policy, preferences for integration reflected the relative macroeconomic performance and preference of national governments alongside commercial considerations.

The primacy of economic interests does not relegate geopolitical ideology to insignificance. Taken by themselves, naked economic preferences would probably have led to a highly institutionalized pan-European free trade area with flanking policies of regulatory harmonization and monetary stabilization—somewhat more intensive arrangements than those pursued by the European Free Trade Area (EFTA) and European Monetary System (EMS). These activities would have been embedded in weaker, less overtly constitutional, but still autonomous international institutions, such as those found in EFTA, the World Trade Organization (WTO), and the North Atlantic Free Trade Area (NAFTA). Explaining the emergence and expansion of a geographically more limited, institutionally more developed, and substantively more diverse institution required attention to geopolitical ideology.

Yet economic interests remained primary. Pressures from economic interest groups generally imposed tighter constraints on policy than did security concerns and the ideological visions of politicians and public opinion. When one factor had to give way, it tended to be geopolitics. Economic interests, moreover, determined the circumstances under which geopolitical ideology could influence policy. Only where economic interests were weak, diffuse, or indeterminate could national politicians indulge the temptation to consider geopolitical goals. Political economic interests predominated even where we would least expect them to. For example, the vital interest behind General de Gaulle's opposition to British membership in the EC, I argue, was not the pursuit of French *grandeur* but the price of French wheat.

The second question concerns the outcomes of interstate bargaining. Of particular theoretical interest are the extent to which negotiated outcomes are efficient, exploiting all possible joint gains, and the extent to which resolution of distributive conflict over the division of gains in specific cases has favored one or another country. EC bargaining, I argue, is generally Pareto-efficient, but its distributive outcomes vary greatly. Some bargains, such as the one struck over the institutions governing a single currency, favored Germany; others, such as the creation of the Common Agricultural Policy, favored France; and still others, such as the establishment of regional policy, favored Britain. How is this variation best explained?

International relations theorists have long debated the relative importance of various factors for the outcomes of noncoercive interstate bargaining. Theoretical debates divide those who hold that international institutions—in particular, autonomous supranational officials empowered by them—decisively influence interstate bargaining from those who believe that bargaining outcomes reflect the relative power of states.

The first theory, as applied to the EC, focuses on the essential role of "supra-national" entrepreneurs in overcoming the high transaction costs of interstate bargaining, which prevent governments from negotiating efficiently. This view, which dominates the study of the EC to this day, follows from neofunctionalist theory, which views the EC as a novel institutionalized realm, but it is also consistent with distinct theoretical approaches to the study of international regimes, negotiation, and law. Many scholars stress the role of international officials, who initiate, mediate, and mobilize societal groups around international agreements. The EC Commission, Court, and Parliament are said to have empowered a particular breed of supranational political entrepreneurs, from Jean Monnet in the 1950s to Jacques Delors in the 1990s. Their interventions, it is argued, have repeatedly increased the efficiency of negotiations and shifted the distributional outcomes in directions favored by international technocrats. I conclude, by contrast, in favor of a second theory, which maintains that interstate bargaining outcomes are decisively shaped by the relative power of nation-states. This view termed "intergovernmental" in the EC literature, draws on general theories of bargaining and negotiation to argue that relative power among states is shaped above all by asymmetrical interdependence, which dictates the relative value of agreement to different governments. These distributive results can be predicted to a first approximation through the use of Nash bargaining theory: the governments that benefit most from the core agreement, relative to their best unilateral and coalitional alternatives to agreement, tend to offer greater compromises in order to achieve it. Where the threat to form an alternative coalition is credible, governments have exploited threats to exclude one another. Bargaining tends to be issue-specific with cross-issue linkages restricted to balancing out benefits among governments and generally taking the form of cash payments or institutional concessions.

The entrepreneurship of supranational officials, by contrast, tends to be futile and redundant, even sometimes counterproductive. Governments generally find it easy to act as their own entrepreneurs and to impose distributional bargains through the use of traditional nonmilitary instruments of power politics, including credible unilateral vetoes, threats of exclusion, and financial side-payments. The distributive outcomes of negotiations have reflected not the preferences of supranational actors but the pattern of asymmetrical interdependence among policy preferences. This is not to deny the influence of supranational entrepreneurs altogether, but their influence has been limited to helping improve the efficiency of one of five agreements, namely the Single European Act (SEA) of 1986. This account reverses the focus of recent EC scholarship. While most analysts generalize from a single case, namely the Commission under Jacques Delors in the mid-1980s, and ask why the Commission was so effective, a comparative analysis invites us to pose the opposite puzzle: Why is the SEA the only major EC bargain about which a serious empirical debate about supranational entrepreneurship can be conducted?

The final step is to explain the choices of governments to delegate and pool sovereignty in international institutions. While the formal powers of supranational officials and qualified majority voting do not extend to major treaty-amending negotiations—hence the skepticism about their influence over the bargains studied in this book [*The Choice for Europe*]—the everyday legislative process *within* the Treaty involves pooling of sovereignty in majority voting arrangements and substantial delegation directly to supranational officials. Here there is much variation. In some areas extensive powers of implementation and proposal have been delegated to central authorities. In others, qualified majority voting governs interstate decision-making. In still others, national vetoes and unanimity voting have been retained. How are the varied choices of governments to delegate and pool sovereignty to be explained?

General theories of international relations and institutional delegation suggest three reasons why governments might pool and delegate sovereignty. First is commitment to the ideology of European federalism. Recent writings on international cooperation stress the independent role of ideas in shaping institutional preferences. Numerous historians and social scientists attribute the EC's quasi-constitutional institutions to pressure from federalists, particularly in Germany and the Benelux countries, who favored them for ideological reasons.

Second is the need to economize on the generation and analysis of information by centralizing technocratic functions in an international organization. Some international lawyers, regime theorists, and economists maintain that international institutions are often more efficient than decentralized governments at processing information; the need for centralized economic planning was a central element in the neofunctionalist conception of integration. The historical record suggests that the role of ideological commitment to Europe was limited to cases where little *de facto* sovereignty was pooled or delegated, or where the substantive implications of doing so remained unclear and relatively modest, such as transfers of agenda setting power from the Commission to the European Parliament. The role of technocratic information was negligible.

I conclude, therefore, in favor of a third explanation. Choices to pool and delegate sovereignty to international institutions are best explained as efforts by governments to constrain and control one another—in game-theoretical language, by their effort to enhance the credibility of commitments. Governments transfer sovereignty to international institutions where potential joint gains are large, but efforts to secure compliance by foreign governments through decentralized or domestic means are likely to be ineffective. This general explanation lies at the heart of functional theories of international regimes, the central strand of which views international institutions as devices to manipulate information in order to promote compliance with common rules. Significant pooling and delegation tend to occur, I find, not where ideological conceptions of Europe converge or where governments agree on the need to centralize policy-making in the hands of technocratic planners, but where governments seek to compel compliance by foreign governments (or, in some cases, future domestic governments) with a strong temptation to defect. It was in fact often the countries least committed in principle to supranational institutions, such as Gaullist France, that imposed them on purportedly federalist governments.

Viewed, then, from the perspective of modern theories of international political economy, this explanation of integration is distinctive in two ways. First, rather than assess competing unicausal explanations or present an amalgam of factors as necessary conditions, this explanation distinguishes clearly between theories that are complements and theories that are substitutes—thereby grounding a multicausal explanation in an explicit framework consistent with rational state behavior. Such a framework must contain distinct explanations of national preferences, substantive bargaining outcomes, and decisions to delegate and pool sovereignty in international institutions. This framework stresses the priority of state preferences, which define not only the goals states seek but to a very substantial degree—via asymmetries in the intensity of preferences—their relative power. This framework is generalizable to any international negotiation. Second, within this framework, the explanation weighs in on the side of economic interests rather than security externalities as fundamental sources of state preferences, the structure of asymmetrical interdependence rather than the process-level intervention of institutional entrepreneurs as a determinant of bargaining outcomes, and the desire for more credible commitments, rather than ideology or technocratic information management, as a motivation to delegate and pool sovereignty. . . .

. . .

## ■ THE LITERATURE BEYOND "GRAND THEORY"

. . . [L]et us take a final moment to consider the relationship of this [theoretical perspective] to existing theory. In doing so, one turns inevitably to "classical" theories of regional integration, the most influential of which is neofunctionalism [Chapters 16, 17 and 21]. Developed by Ernst Haas and others in the 1950s and 1960s, neofunctionalism remains a touchstone for scholarship on European integration. Neofunctionalists initially maintained that the unintended consequences of integration, once launched, would be self-reinforcing. This, they argued, assures the continuance of integration—though this teleology was later heavily qualified. Such feedback takes two forms. Initial steps toward cooperation bolster a technocratic consensus in favor of further integration by expanding, empowering, and encouraging societal groups supportive of further state intervention in the economy. The establishment of international institutions also centralizes power in the hands of supranational officials whose political entrepreneurship promotes further integration.

[*The Choice for Europe*] should not be read as an evaluation of—let alone a wholesale rejection of—neofunctionalism or any other classical theory. To be sure, this book tests (and for the most part disconfirms) some narrower propositions advanced by neofunctionalists—the claims, for example, that national interests are technocratic rather than reflect fundamental domestic conflict, that supranational entrepreneurship decisively alters interstate bargaining outcomes, and that delegation to international institutions reflects the need for centralized, expert planners. In other ways, such as its recognition of the primacy of economic interests, the book supports traditional neofunctionalist claims. In still other ways, such as the extent to which some national preferences for integration may be endogenous to a path-dependent process of prior integration, it does not directly address neofunctionalist concerns. . . .

This book is thus not yet another confrontation with neofunctionalism but an acknowledgement and response to criticisms of the style of "grand theory" neofunctionalism represents—criticisms that emerged in large part from the neofunctionalists themselves. By the early 1970s it was evident even to its creators that neofunctionalism required fundamental revision.

At one level the failure of neofunctionalism was empirical. European integration had not expanded steadily but by stops and starts. Significant domestic conflict remained. Integration had focused not on areas of state intervention and planning, such as atomic energy and public transport, but on areas of market liberalization, such as tariff policy. It had not generated uniformly stronger centralized institutions but a curious hybrid still heavily dependent on unanimous consensus among governments. And governments did not always privilege regional over global multilateral cooperation. These events seemed to disconfirm early, teleological variants of neofunctionalism.

Yet the most important weakness of neofunctionalism was not empirical but theoretical. For once the simple teleology toward integration was abandoned, neofunctionalism and other grand theories lacked the resources to construct a positive response. Neofunctionalism proved at once too ambitious, too vague and too incoherent to generate precise predictions suitable for empirical evaluation. To see why, we need only turn to theoretical lessons neofunctionalists themselves drew from these failures. Three stand out.

The neofunctionalists concluded that an explanation of integration must be imbedded in a multi-causal framework comprised of numerous narrower theories. Scholars came to realize in the 1970s that any single unified theory of American or comparative politics—say, "structural-functionalism"—was too abstract and undifferentiated to permit concrete theory testing and development. Most neofunctionalists concluded that no single theory could satisfactorily account for a phenomenon as complex as European integration; more concrete theories were required. However, their response, namely to construct amalgams of variables, failed to overcome, as Haas observed, the "non-additive character of theories [that] coexist on different levels of abstraction." In an influential critique, Donald Puchala invoked the metaphor of the blind men and the elephant: different theories seemed to explain different aspects of the (elephantine) integration process. It follows that any general explanation of integration cannot rest on a single theory, neofunctionalist or otherwise, but must rest on a multi-causal framework that orders a series of more narrowly focused theories—a conclusion echoed to the present day.

Variables in the multi-causal framework must each be grounded in a general theory of political behavior. Theories that treat regional integration as a *sui generis* phenomenon, Haas argued, could be little better than "pre-theories." They breed theoretical insularity. With the EC as the sole major success, regional integration theory in practice became an ideal-typical summary of factors that appear to have influenced the European case. This focus on a *sui generis* Europe-centered theory cut the study of European integration off from revolutionary theoretical currents in comparative and international political economy over the three decades that followed. Sensing this, Haas proposed that "the study of regional integration should be both included in and subordinated to the study of changing patterns of interdependence." Consistent with this analysis, Stanley Hoffmann, Robert Keohane, Joseph Nye, Henry Nau, and many others drew the conclusion that the EC should be viewed as an international regime designed to manage interdependence.

Finally, each theory should be actor-oriented, that is, it should highlight the purposive choices of states and social actors within constraints rather than the unintended dynamics of broad structural processes. A fundamental weakness of neofunctionalism lay in its aspiration to trace dynamic endogenous effects (incremental feedback, unintended consequences, and the resulting change over time) without a baseline theory of exogenous constraints (state economic interests, political constraints, and delegation) through which dynamic change must take place. For example, neofunctionalists maintained (as I do . . . ) that the pursuit of economic interest is the fundamental force underlying integration, but they offered only a vague understanding of precisely what those interests are, how conflicts among them are resolved, by what means they are translated into policy, and when they require political integration. This in turn reflected the lack of a generalizable micro-foundational basis necessary to support predictions about variation in support for integration across issues, countries, and time.

Without such micro-foundations, the predictions of neofunctionalism were indeterminate. Feedback, Haas conceded in his later self-criticism, "may transform the system" but need not do so. An entire taxonomy of alternative outcomes consistent with the underlying theory arose: "spillover," "spillback," "spill-around," "encapsulation." Once neofunctionalism dropped the optimistic notion that integration was automatically self-reinforcing and would evolve smoothly to federal union without triggering fundamental distributive or ideological conflicts, it could say "little about *basic causes*" of national demands for integration or interstate agreements to achieve it. . . . More concretely, neofunctionalism lacked explicit theories of interest-group politics, interstate bargaining, and international institutions. With few outcomes theoretically excluded, a rule of thumb emerged in the literature on the European Community: when integration stagnated, scholars criticized neofunctionalism; when integration progressed, they rediscovered it.

By the mid-1970s these three criticisms had inspired a degree of consensus concerning the proper theoretical direction forward. Unintended consequences and feedback, the initial core of neofunctionalism, should take a role secondary to the concrete beliefs, preferences, and strategies of political actors. As Haas said, "all political action is purposively linked with individual and group perception of interest." Greater attention should be focused on purposive behavior and strategic interaction: "the type of demands that are made, the variety of concessions . . . exchanged, and the degree of delegation of authority to new central institutions." Hoffmann, Keohane, and even, if to a lesser degree, Haas himself proposed studying the EC as an international regime constructed through a series of purposive decisions by governments with varying preferences and power. Hoffmann proposed a synthetic approach that examined first "the domestic priorities and foreign policy goals of the member states, then . . . the impact of the environment [and] finally the institutional interplay between the states and the Community." Keohane and Hoffmann concluded that spillover and unintended consequences required a prior intergovernmental bargain among member-states, thereby refocusing our attention on the exogenous determinants of major decisions.

Yet most scholarship on European integration over the past two decades has ignored these self-criticisms. Few scholars test general theories or employ a multi-causal framework. Nearly all continue instead either to structure research around a single variable (e.g., supranational influence, domestic politics, public opinion), often linked to an ideal-typical "grand theory" of integration or international relations, or to invoke a theoretically unstructured amalgam of causes. As a result, decades of analysis of the EC have multiplied conjectures about integration but generated few reliable empirical conclusions about the relative importance of forces that have made the EC what it is today. "Confirmed" determinants of integration and "necessary" conditions for its success proliferate unchecked. Some scholars go further, defending this tendency on the ground that integration is the result of an indeterminate, path-dependent process.

The proper measure of our understanding of integration is not the multiplication of intuitively plausible claims; it is the development, evaluation, and ultimately rejection of testable hypotheses. Where hypotheses are rarely discarded, they are rarely confirmed. Thus the basic thrust of this book runs contrary to the current literature on European integration. Rather than employ neofunctionalism and other grand theories as interpretive lenses, it seeks to move beyond them by employing narrower and concrete hypotheses drawn from general theories of economic interest, interstate bargaining, and international regimes to support rigorous testing. . . .

## ■ NOTE

1. Since the ratification of the Maastricht Treaty, the organization has been referred to as the European Union (EU). This [chapter] deals with major interstate bargains up to and including Maastricht, so the older term European Community is used throughout.

# 23 Delegation and Agency in the European Community

MARK A. POLLACK

*The supranationalists and intergovernmentalists hold in common a respect for institutions as shapers of human behavior. They may disagree on what exactly constitutes an "institution," and which ones have the greatest impact on European politics, but they all agree that institutions matter. Several theorists—frequently dubbed "new institutionalists"—have recently focused their attention on EU institutions to determine whether they are independent of member government control. A definitive answer to this question would go a long way to settling the supranationalist-intergovernmentalist debate.*

*Taking their cues from theories developed elsewhere in the social sciences, three "schools" of institutionalism have emerged in EU studies.* Historical *institutionalists explore the period after institutions are created to determine if new institutions force unintended consequences that erode national sovereignty.* Sociological *institutionalists examine the social norms that develop within institutions to determine their impact on decisionmaking. And finally,* rational choice *institutionalists—drawing on economic theories of rational decisionmaking and studies of institutions mainly in the United States—seek to understand why member states create supranational institutions, how they seek to control them, and under what conditions they succeed.*

*In the article below, Mark Pollack (University of Wisconsin–Madison), who studied with both Stanley Hoffmann and Andrew Moravcsik at Harvard, takes a rational choice approach to EU institutions when exploring the relationship between the member states—the "principals" in rational choice terminology—and their supranational*

---

From "Delegation, Agency, and Agenda Setting in the European Community," *International Organization* 51(1)(1997): 99–134. Notes omitted. Reprinted with permission from Cambridge University Press, IO Foundation, and MIT Press.

*"agents." His method is largely deductive. He identifies the tasks ("functions") the principals assign agents to perform and the control mechanisms they employ to keep agents in line. As he proceeds, he examines data from the EU to see if states and EU institutions, in fact, behave as predicted. Pollack argues that EU institutions perform the tasks largely expected of agents, but also demonstrate an independence not accounted for by a "functionalist model." To account for the independence of supranational institutions, Pollack argues that the mechanisms used by member states to control their agents are effective but often too "expensive" to employ. Thus, EU institutions are never totally controlled by national governments, nor are they completely free of member state control. The question is, what determines the relative autonomy of supranational institutions over time and between policy areas? Pollack suggests four factors: (1) "the distribution of preferences among member state principals and supranational agents"; (2) "the institutional decision rules established for applying sanctions, overruling legislation, and changing agents' mandates"; (3) the presence of "incomplete information or uncertainty"; and (4) the influence of transnational interests.*

*Rational choice institutionalism shares much in common with Andrew Moravcsik's intergovernmentalism (Chapter 22). Although Moravcsik differs with Pollack over the independence of supranational institutions, he accepts the assumptions of rational choice theory and employs principal-agent analysis (which is well-known in international relations) to generate hypotheses. The new institutionalism, including its rational choice variant, is also used by a growing number of scholars who see the EU not as a system of international relations, but as a new-style polity (see Chapter 24).*

Do supranational institutions matter—do they deserve the status of an independent causal variable—in the politics of the European Community (EC)?[1] Does the Commission of the European Communities matter? Does the European Court of Justice (ECJ) or the European Parliament? Is the EC characterized by continued member state dominance or by a runaway Commission and an activist Court progressively chipping away at this dominance? These are some of the more important questions for our understanding of the EC and of European integration. They have divided the two traditional schools of thought in regional integration, with neofunctionalists generally asserting, and intergovernmentalists generally denying, any important causal role for supranational institutions in the integration process. By and large, however, neither neofunctionalism nor intergovernmentalism has generated testable hypotheses regarding the conditions under which, and the ways in which, supranational institutions exert an independent causal influence on either EC governance or the process of European integration.

This article presents a unified theoretical approach to the problem of supranational influence, based largely on the new institutionalism in rational choice theory. Simplifying only slightly, this new literature is traceable to Kenneth Shepsle's pioneering work on the role of institutions in the U.S. Congress. . . .

. . .

In this article I join the growing number of scholars who have applied the insights of rational choice institutionalism to the study of the EC. . . . I aim here to build on the insights of these works to construct an institutionalist account of European integration and European governance, and more specifically to generate a series of hypotheses about the conditions under which supranational institutions will be delegated authority and will enjoy autonomy from and exert influence on the member governments of the Community. The primary virtue of the new institutionalism in rational choice theory is that it allows us to transcend the intergovernmentalist-neofunctionalist debate by acknowledging the initial primacy of the member states and, proceeding from this point, to generate a series of hypotheses about supranational autonomy and influence more precise than those generated by either neofunctionalist or intergovernmentalist theory.

For the purposes of analysis, I divide the problem of supranational autonomy and influence into three subsets of questions. First, I ask about types of functions that member states might agree to delegate to supranational institutions. The analysis here is fairly conventional, drawing on functional theories of institutional design under conditions of imperfect information, which generally emphasize the importance of monitoring compliance, interpreting incomplete contracts, issuing secondary regulation, and formal agenda setting. Such functional theories, I argue, provide an excellent initial understanding of the powers of some EC institutions but not of others.

Second, I examine the extent to which supranational institutions are able to carry out their functions independent of the influence of the member states. In so doing, I survey principal-agent theory for various mechanisms of member state control over the agents they create. I argue that the "agency" or autonomy of a given supranational institution depends crucially on the efficacy and credibility of control mechanisms established by member state principals, and that these vary from institution to institution—as well as from issue-area to issue-area and over time—leading to varying patterns of supranational autonomy. More specifically, I argue that both monitoring and sanctioning are costly to member state principals as well as to their supranational agents, and that supranational agents can and do therefore exploit conflicting preferences among the member states to avoid the imposition of sanctions. In empirical terms, I focus primarily on the Commission of the European Communities and on the member states' capacity to control it. Among their control mechanisms are the comitology oversight procedures by the Council of Ministers, the possibility of judicial review by the ECJ, the periodic reauthorization of Council legislation, and the threat to amend the EC's constitutive treaties (the 1957 Treaty of Rome, the 1985 Single European Act, and the 1992 Maastricht Treaty on European Union). By contrast, I argue, EC member governments have fewer mechanisms available to control the ECJ or the European Parliament, which therefore enjoy greater autonomy from the member governments than does the Commission.

. . .

## ■ WHY DELEGATE?

### □ *The Functionalist Approach to Delegation*

Generally speaking, delegation of authority by one or more principals (such as a group of domestic legislators or a group of member states) to one or more agents (such as a regulatory agency or a supranational institution) is a special case of the more general problem of institutional choice or institutional design: Why does a group of actors collectively decide upon one specific set of institutions rather than another to govern their subsequent interactions? The basic approach of rational choice theory to the question of institutional choice is functionalist. That is to say, rational choice theory explains institutional choices in terms of the functions a given institution is expected to perform and the effects on policy outcomes it is expected to produce, subject to the uncertainty inherent in any institutional design. . . . Similarly, in the case of institutional design, the rationally anticipated effects of given institutions, subject to uncertainty, explain actor preferences for certain types of institutions, and the institutions ultimately adopted should reflect these preferences.

. . .

Delegation of authority to an agent—whether a regulatory bureau (as students of U.S. politics have considered) or an international organization (as international relations theorists have)—is considered one particular aspect of the institutional design process. In general terms, principal-agent models of delegation have identified a number of functions for which principals might choose to delegate authority. For the sake of brevity, I focus here on four such functions emphasized in the literature. First, supranational agents may monitor member state compliance with or transgressions of their international treaty obligations. In a context of collective action under imperfect information, institutions can monitor compliance and can provide such information to all participants, in effect "painting scarlet letters" on transgressors. In such cases, institutional actors such as medieval law merchants or international secretariats might monitor the behavior of each actor, making this information available to all the actors, thereby reducing transaction costs and encouraging mutually beneficial cooperation. Furthermore, these institutions need not have power to enforce agreements through sanctions but need only provide information about compliance to facilitate decentralized sanctioning by participants.

Second, supranational agents may solve problems of incomplete contracting. We can conceive of any institutional agreement—whether it be a log-rolling trade of votes among legislators, the establishment of a common market among member states, or an agreement between two firms regarding the future delivery of a product—as a contract. In such a contract, the various parties to the agreement pledge to behave in certain ways (vote, allow free trade, or deliver a product) in the future. However, as Oliver Williamson points out, all but the simplest contracts are invariably incomplete, since it would be impossible (or at least prohibitively costly) to spell out in explicit detail the precise obligations of all the parties throughout the life of the contract. Hence, as Paul Milgrom and John Roberts describe, rather than attempting to write a complete contract that endeavors to anticipate all possible contingencies, "the contracting parties content themselves with an agreement that *frames* their relationship—that is, one that fixes general performance expectations, provides procedures to govern decision making in situations where the contract is not explicit, and outlines how to adjudicate disputes where they arise." These various procedures may, but need not, involve the creation of an agent. If uncertainty is not too great, for example, the parties may simply choose to lay down rules governing future decision making and dispute arbitration. Alternatively, where uncertainty is great and future decision making is expected to be time consuming and complex, the parties may choose to delegate these activities to an agent, such as an executive or a court, that can fill in the details of an incomplete contract and adjudicate future disputes.

Third, supranational institutions, like U.S. regulatory bureaucracies, may be delegated authority to adopt regulations that are either too complex to be considered and debated in detail by the principals or that require the credibility of a genuinely independent regulator who, unlike the governments of the states in question, would have little incentive to be lenient with firms in a given member state.

Fourth and finally, principals may have an incentive to delegate to an agent the power of formal agenda setting, that is, the ability of a given actor to initiate policy proposals for consideration among a group of legislators (or, in the case of the EC, among the member governments in the Council of Ministers). As McKelvey, Riker, and others have noted, any majoritarian system in which each and every legislator had the right to initiate proposals would encourage an endless series of proposals from disgruntled legislators who had been in the minority in a previous vote. In such a system, no decision would be an equilibrium, and the result would be endless cycling among alternative policy proposals. Thus any legislature would have a rational incentive to develop rules regarding which actors can initiate proposals, and when.

Given the technical responsibilities of policy initiation, however, as well as the power of an agenda setter over policy choices, the choice of which actor is chosen as the agenda setter matters. In the U.S. Congress, this power is given largely to congressional committees. This procedure has two distinct benefits. First, it gives representatives disproportionate clout in areas of interest to their constituents, and, second, it provides groups of representatives with incentives to become "experts" in a given field and to make this information available to all representatives. As we shall see presently, however, the formation of such committees within the Council of Ministers has proven impractical, leading the member states to delegate agenda-setting powers to a supranational agency, the Commission of the European Communities.

## □ *Delegation to Supranational Institutions in the EC*

. . .

To what extent do the four functions emphasized in the rational choice literature accurately describe the powers delegated to EC supranational institutions? Let us consider each of the four in turn.

First, with regard to monitoring compliance with EC legal obligations, both the Commission and the ECJ play important roles. The Commission, for example, performs a central monitoring function as guardian of the treaties, monitoring member state compliance with EC law, and, under Article 169 of the Treaty of Rome, initiating legal proceedings against member states found to be in noncompliance with their legal obligations. In addition to these treaty responsibilities, member states also have charged the Commission, in various pieces of secondary legislation, such as the various structural fund regulations, to monitor the implementation of specific EC programs in the member states. The ECJ, by contrast, does not actively monitor the behavior of member states, but it does, in response to Commission proceedings (Article 169) or "fire-alarm" complaints from private citizens (Article 177), play a crucial role in identifying and painting scarlet letters on transgressors, thereby allowing for decentralized enforcement of treaty provisions.

Second, EC institutions provide a solution to problems of incomplete contracting. The ECJ, for example, has been delegated the authority to interpret the rather vague treaty language prohibiting "quantitative restrictions on imports and all measures having equivalent effect," which are defined only vaguely in Articles 30–36 of the Treaty of Rome. Similarly, where national regulations in areas such as the environment act as nontariff barriers to trade, the treaty does not provide a detailed remedy, but rather specifies a process of "harmonization" of national regulations, to be undertaken by the Council of Ministers on a proposal from the Commission, which may in certain circumstances adopt such harmonized regulations on its own authority.

In this sense, the Commission can be considered a regulatory bureaucracy—the third function emphasized in the literature on delegation. More specifically, the Commission plays a crucial role in setting down the basic lines of EC competition policy and engages in considerable implementing regulation and day-to-day management in areas such as agriculture and the internal market. Simplifying only slightly, the Commission's competition policy competencies are laid down in Treaty of Rome Articles 85–94 and in the Merger Control Regulation of 1989. By contrast, the Commission's regulatory role in agriculture and the internal market is not spelled out explicitly in the treaties, which provide the Council with the obligation to "confer on the Commission, in the acts which the Council adopts, powers for the implementation of the rules which the Council lays down." These implementing powers, however, may be subject to "certain requirements" laid down by the Council, which are discussed in some detail below.

Fourth and finally, EC member states have, in many but not all areas of policymaking, delegated formal agenda-setting authority, or the "exclusive right of initiative" to the Commission. As we shall see, this has provided the Commission with an important agenda-setting power in the Council of Ministers, especially where voting takes place by qualified majority, but it has the advantage to the member states of providing a series of relatively unbiased and well-informed policy proposals to the Council, which would otherwise have to rely on the rather unevenly distributed resources of the member states themselves. The Commission's power of initiative, however, has been limited by the member states in a number of areas, including the second and third pillars of the European Union and the process of amending the EC's constitutive treaties. In addition, the Single European Act and the Maastricht Treaty allocated the European Parliament significant new legislative powers, including a conditional right to set the Council's agenda with the consent of the Commission.

### □ *The Virtues and Limits of the Functional Approach*

Even this cursory examination of delegation in the EC yields a striking dichotomy between the functions of the Commission and the ECJ, on the one hand, and those of the European Parliament, on the other. Despite its simplicity, the functionalist model of delegation yields surprisingly accurate predictions regarding the functions delegated to the Commission and the Court, whose primary tasks do indeed concern monitoring, interpreting, and elaborating incomplete contracts, credible regulation, and agenda setting. It also calls our attention to the hybrid nature of the European Commission, which combines the agenda-setting power of congressional committees with the monitoring, incomplete contracting, and regulatory functions of U.S. regulatory bureaucracies—thereby allowing us to draw on both sets of literatures to model the Commission.

However, despite the accuracy of functionalist predictions regarding the Commission and the Court, the functionalist approach fails almost completely at predicting the functions delegated to the European Parliament, including both its budgetary and its legislative powers. Clearly, the functionalist model fails to account for the ideological concern for democratic legitimacy that has led member governments to assign increasingly significant powers to the Parliament in successive treaty amendments. The Parliament, moreover, is not strictly speaking the agent of the member governments. Although member governments created, assigned powers to, and may collectively decrease or increase the power of the Parliament, the individual members of the European Parliament (MEPs) ultimately are selected not by member governments (as are EC commissioners and ECJ judges) but by their national parties and national electorates. Nevertheless, despite the unusual nature of the Parliament by comparison with standard principal-agent models, I will argue below that institutionalist analyses offer important insights into the autonomy of MEPs from member governments, as well as the nature of Parliament's agenda-setting powers under the EC's cooperation and codecision procedures.

A second and more fundamental weakness of the functional approach to delegation is its assumptions that the institutions adopted are those that most efficiently perform the tasks set out for them by their creators and are chosen for that reason. As Keohane points out, the fact that an institution performs certain functions does not necessarily mean that the institution was designed with that purpose in mind; rather, institutions such as the Commission and the ECJ might gradually take on new roles that were not foreseen at the time of their creation. Indeed, as Paul Pierson points out, and as neofunctionalists have long asserted, the institutions in existence at any point in time may reflect the "unintended consequences" of earlier institutional decisions made by actors with imperfect information and short time horizons. Perhaps most important, the functions of supranational institutions may reflect not so much the preferences and intentions of their member state principals but rather the preferences, and the autonomous agency, of the supranational institutions themselves. It is to this problem of supranational agency that we now turn.

## ■ AGENCY AND ACCOUNTABILITY: THE MECHANISMS OF MEMBER STATE CONTROL

### □ *Agency Losses, Agency Costs, and Control Mechanisms*

Under certain circumstances, therefore, member government principals might be expected to delegate authority to a supranational agent such as the Commission of the European Communities or the ECJ. However, this initial delegation immediately raises another problem: What if the agent, say the Commission, has preferences systematically distinct from those of the member governments and uses its delegated powers to pursue its own preferences at the expense of the preferences of the principals? As D. Roderick Kiewiet and Mathew McCubbins summarize the problem, "Delegation . . . entails side effects that are known, in the parlance of economic theory, as agency losses. There is almost always some conflict between the interests of those who delegate authority (principals) and the agents to whom they delegate it. Agents behave opportunistically, pursuing their own interests subject only to the constraints imposed by their relationship with the principal." This "shirking," or bureaucratic drift, thus emerges as the primary source of agency losses and the central problem of principal-agent analysis. In addition, a second process, known as "slippage," occurs when the structure of delegation itself provides perverse incentives for the agent to behave in ways inimical to the preferences of the principals.

The importance in this context of information, and of asymmetrically distributed information in particular, can scarcely be overstated. In any principal-agent relationship, the agent is likely to have more information about itself than others have, making control or even evaluation by the principal difficult. Without some means of acquiring the necessary information to evaluate the agent's performance, the principal seems to be at a permanent disadvantage, and the likelihood of agency losses seems large.

The principal, however, is not helpless in the face of these advantages. Rather, when delegating authority to an agent, principals can adopt various administrative and oversight procedures to limit the scope of agency activity and the possibility of agency shirking. *Administrative procedures* define *ex ante* the scope of agency activity, the legal instruments available to the agency, and the procedures it must follow. Such administrative procedures may be more or less restrictive, and they may be altered in response to shirking or slippage, but only at a cost to the flexibility and comprehensiveness of the agent's activities. In the case of the EC, both the Commission and the ECJ generally have been given a broad mandate, while prior to the Single European Act, the European Parliament was restricted to a limited institutional role.

*Oversight procedures,* on the other hand, allow principals *ex post* to 1) monitor agency behavior, thereby mitigating the inherently asymmetrical distribution of information in favor of the agent, and 2) influence agency behavior through the application of positive and negative sanctions. Among the formidable array of sanctions at the disposal of legislative principals are budgetary control; control over appointments; and power to override agency behavior through new legislation and to revise the administrative procedures laid down in the agent's mandate.

If these control mechanisms were costless, we would expect principals to adopt a full range of administrative and oversight procedures to minimize or eliminate agency losses. These mechanisms, however, are not costless. As Kiewiet and McCubbins succinctly state: "Agency losses can be contained, but only by undertaking measures that are themselves costly." Strict oversight procedures, for example, consume considerable resources, and sanctions may impose costs upon principals as well as agents, as we shall see. Hence, principals will adopt a given control mechanism only if its cost is less than the sum of the agency losses that it reduces.

In the pages that follow, I consider the various control mechanisms available to member state principals, in terms of both their costs and their ability to constrain supranational agents and thereby reduce agency losses. Throughout the discussion, I reject two extreme formulations of the principal-agent problem. In the first extreme position, dubbed "the abdication hypothesis" or the "runaway-bureaucracy thesis," the principal abdicates its policymaking role to an agent, which then becomes the central figure in policymaking, entirely unconstrained by the principal. In this view, regulatory bureaus and other agents possess an incontrovertible informational advantage over their legislative principals, whose oversight procedures are lax and ineffective, leaving agents free to "run amok" in pursuit of their own policy preferences. The runaway-bureaucracy thesis has had a number of advocates among students of the U.S. regulatory bureaucracy, and among both advocates and critics of European integration, who typically attribute considerable independence to both the Commission and the ECJ.

Largely in response to the runaway-bureaucracy school, a "congressional dominance" school has more recently argued that, rather than abdicating control to runaway bureaucracies, principals (be it the U.S. Congress or EC member states) retain total or near-total control over the actions of their agents. Weingast and Mark Moran, for example, argue forcefully that regulatory bureaus such as the Federal Trade Commission do not run amok but are instead clearly responsive to the preferences of congressional oversight committees, even in the absence of any overt intervention by these committees. In his study of the EC, Garrett makes a similar claim about the ECJ, arguing that "the principles governing decisions of the European court and hence governing those of domestic courts following its rulings are consistent with the preferences of France and Germany."

In the view of the congressional dominance and intergovernmentalist schools, therefore, agency independence may often be more apparent than real. More specifically, because principals often opt to use unobtrusive forms of political oversight (see below), and because agents may rationally anticipate the reactions of principals to certain types of behavior, agency behavior that at first glance seems autonomous may in fact be subtly influenced by the preferences of principals, making genuine agency autonomy exceedingly difficult to measure. Indeed, as Weingast and Moran point out, the more effective the control mechanisms employed by the principal, the less overt sanctioning we should see, since agents rationally anticipate the preferences of the principals—and the sanctions likely to be applied by them—and incorporate these preferences into their behavior.

We should therefore be cautious about attributing autonomy to supranational agents without carefully examining the less obtrusive forms of control available to member states. However, as Terry Moe points out in an important critique of the congressional dominance view, theorists in this school tend to presuppose the complete efficacy of agency control mechanisms without theorizing explicitly how these mechanisms might work, their costliness to principals as well as agents, and the ability of agents to exercise some degree of autonomy within the constraints of imperfect control mechanisms. Moe therefore argues for a theory that explicitly models the control relationship, including the costs and difficulties of employing the control mechanisms whose efficacy is simply assumed in the congressional dominance literature.

In the pages that follow, I take up Moe's challenge, discussing both the control mechanisms available to principals and the costs and difficulties associated with their use, which might limit the extent of principals' control over their agents. In contrast to both the runaway-bureaucracy and the congressional dominance schools, I hypothesize that agency autonomy is not constant but varies primarily with the efficacy and credibility of the control mechanisms (both administrative and oversight procedures) available to principals. Next, I examine the actual control mechanisms used by member state principals to supervise and control EC institutions and provide a preliminary assessment of the costs and credibility of these mechanisms in "reining-in" supranational agents such as the Commission and the ECJ. EC institutions, I suggest, neither run amok nor blindly follow the wishes of member governments but rather pursue their own preferences within the confines of member state control mechanisms whose efficacy and credibility vary from issue to issue and over time.

## □ *The Variety of Oversight Procedures*

The essence of oversight procedures is that they allow principals to 1) *monitor* the activity of their agents to determine the extent of agency losses and 2) *sanction* their agents in light of the information thus provided. The first part of this definition refers to the (partial) correction of informational asymmetries in favor of the agent, while the latter allows principals to apply positive or negative sanctions and thus to reward agents' appropriate behavior and punish shirking. Both aspects present principals with considerable challenges.

In a seminal article, McCubbins and Thomas Schwartz argue that oversight mechanisms are of two types. The first type, which they call "police-patrol oversight," comprises (a congressional committee in their example) active monitoring of some sample of the agent's behavior by the principal "with the aim of detecting and remedying any violations of legislative goals and, by its surveillance, discouraging such violations." Such procedures might include public hearings, field observations, and the examination of regular agency reports. Police-patrol procedures, they argue, can be effective in assessing agency conformity with legislative intent in at least a cross-section of agency activities, but only at a high cost to the principal. In the case of multiple principals, moreover, police-patrol oversight can be thought of as a public good (in the sense that a single principal, having expended resources in oversight activities, cannot exclude the other principals from the benefit of those activities) and is thus likely to be undersupplied. Police-patrol oversight, therefore, if effective, is at best a costly and problematic option for principals.

By contrast, a second type of oversight, which McCubbins and Schwartz call "fire-alarm oversight," requires less direct centralized involvement by the principals, who instead rely on third parties (citizens, organized interest groups) to monitor agency activity and, if necessary, seek redress through appeal to the agent, to the principals, or through judicial review. Such fire-alarm oversight mechanisms, they concede, are likely to produce patterns of oversight biased in favor of alert and well-organized groups, but from the perspective of the principals they have the double advantage of focusing on violations of importance to their political constituency and of externalizing the costs of monitoring to third parties. As Moe points out, however, fire-alarm oversight covers only a subset of agency behavior, namely, those activities that are likely to mobilize politically powerful groups to protest. Outside of this subset, which may indeed be quite small, agency behavior may be essentially uncontrolled.

Finally, in a variation on third-party oversight, Kiewiet and McCubbins argue that principals can efficiently monitor their agents through the use of institutional checks, in which a number of agencies are established with conflicting sets of incentives or organizational goals. In such a system, one agent, for example a comptroller, may be charged with monitoring the activities of another and reporting this information to the principals; or it may be given the power to veto or block the activities of another agent, limiting the ability of that agent to pursue its private interests at the expense of the interests of the principals.

### Costs of Sanctioning

The foregoing analysis assumes not only the efficacy of monitoring procedures but also the ability of principals to apply negative sanctions against the agent in the event of shirking. As McCubbins, Roger Noll, and Weingast point out for the U.S. case, however, the costs to principals of sanctioning agents can also be quite high. . . . The costs of sanctions to the principals may in turn limit the credibility of principals' threats to apply these sanctions against the agent, and thus increase the discretion available to agents.

In a later contribution, McCubbins, Noll, and Weingast elaborate on the problem of sanctioning by multiple principals, such as the President, the House of Representatives, and the Senate in the American political system, arguing that clashes of interest among these principals can be exploited by an agent to avoid sanctions and maintain a considerable degree of autonomy. That is to say, any effort by the principals to sanction their agent must enjoy the unanimous support of all three actors. If any one of the three principals is made better off by the agent's shirking, then that principal will block the application of sanctions—allowing the agent to pursue its own preferences without the risk of sanction.

Applying McCubbins, Noll, and Weingast's analysis beyond the U.S. case suggests three more general points about the ability of multiple principals to apply sanctions *ex post,* and the implications of this ability for agency autonomy. First, and most obviously, the model draws our attention to the conflicting preferences among multiple principals and the ability of an agent to exploit these conflicts, as long as the agent's activities remain within the set of Pareto-optimal outcomes.

Second, the ability of an agent to exploit conflicting preferences among the principals also depends crucially on the decision rules governing the application of sanctions (or overruling legislation or changing an administrative procedure) against the principal. In McCubbins, Noll, and Weingast's model, the decision rule governing the application of sanctions is unanimity among the three institutional actors (Senate, House, President), since any of the three can veto any application of sanctions. Put differently, it is not only the conflict of interest but also the relatively demanding decision rule of unanimity that the agent is able to exploit in order to shirk successfully within its legislative mandate.

Third, the ability of principals to sanction a shirking agent depends on what Fritz Scharpf calls the "default condition" in the event of no agreement among the principals. If the default condition is the status quo—the continuation of existing institutions and policies—Scharpf argues that these institutions and policies will persist indefinitely, rigidly unchanging in the face of an ever-changing policy environment, a phenomenon he calls the "joint-decision trap." Extending Scharpf's argument to principal-agent relations, we can argue that a status quo default condition makes any revision of the agent's mandate more difficult, since it privileges the existing delegation of authority to the agent, thereby increasing the agent's autonomy. By contrast, a default condition under which the agent's mandate expires and must be reauthorized privileges would-be reformers among the principals, who may demand amendment of the agent's mandate as the cost of their support for such reauthorization; this should, *ceteris paribus*, limit the autonomy of the agent.

For all of these reasons, principals concerned with limiting bureaucratic drift might be expected to adopt legislation featuring strict administrative procedures, low institutional thresholds to the use of sanctions, and periodic reauthorization of the agent's mandate in order to minimize the risk of agency shirking. Once again, however, such decision rules are not without costs: the first two of these options would risk governmental paralysis, and the third could entail reopening a Pandora's box of delicate institutional bargains. The ultimate choice of decision rules should therefore reflect some trade-off among these considerations by member state principals. Whatever institutional rules finally are chosen, they should matter a great deal for the autonomy of an agent from its principals.

## □ *Mechanisms of Member State Control in the EC*

Although agency control mechanisms can reduce agency losses, they are often costly (and therefore noncredible) and are never perfectly effective. Furthermore, the difficulties that principals encounter in threatening and imposing sanctions on an agent are compounded in settings like the EC, where the institutional hurdles to the imposition of sanctions—typically a unanimous or qualified majority vote of the member states—are particularly high. This section examines the administrative and oversight procedures established by EC member states. As will be seen, these procedures encompass everything from intrusive police patrols to decentralized fire alarms, differing considerably from one supranational agent to another, from one issue-area to another, and over time. I focus in particular on the Commission of the European Communities and the various oversight mechanisms available to the member governments in attempting to control its behavior: 1) the primary police-patrol method of oversight, namely, the comitology system of member state oversight committees; 2) various methods of fire-alarm oversight, most notably the EC legal system and the pivotal role of the ECJ; 3) the costs and credibility of overruling or sanctioning agency shirking; and 4) the costs and credibility of revising an agent's mandate in response to persistent shirking.

*Comitology as police patrols.* The most intrusive—and expensive—form of oversight, according to McCubbins and Schwartz's scheme, is police-patrol oversight. EC member states utilize such oversight in a number of issue-areas (such as agricultural and internal market policy) under the general rubric of comitology. As noted above, most of the Commission's executive powers are not laid down explicitly in the treaties but rather are specified in secondary Council of Ministers legislation. In practice, since the early delegation of executive powers to the Commission in the area of agricultural policy in the 1960s, the Council generally has made the exercise of these powers subject to oversight by one of several varieties of oversight committees, the nature of which is typically specified in the enabling legislation. After the ratification of the Single European Act in 1987, this system of committees was codified and rationalized in the famous Comitology Decision of 13 July 1987, which specified three types of oversight committees: advisory, management, and regulatory. In schematic form, the various procedures are as follows.

First, under the advisory committee procedure, the Commission must refer its proposed actions to the committee, which may "if necessary" proceed to a vote by simple majority on the Commission's proposals. The Commission is then obligated to take the "utmost account" of the committee's opinion but may nevertheless act as it sees fit. Of the three procedures, the advisory committee procedure provides the Commission with the greatest autonomy and member states with the weakest influence; it is used most commonly in the area of competition policy.

Second, under the management committee procedure, which originated and still predominates in EC agricultural policy, the Commission refers its implementing measures to the committee. The committee may initiate a vote by qualified majority within a deadline laid down by the Commission. If the committee delivers a favorable opinion or fails to deliver any opinion before the deadline, the Commission may adopt the measure with immediate effect. If, however, the committee adopts an unfavorable opinion by qualified majority vote, the Commission must communicate the proposal to the EC Council, which can take a different decision by qualified majority. The management committee procedure, therefore, is clearly more restrictive than the advisory committee procedure, yet even here a qualified majority vote is required to secure a referral to the Council, and a second such vote is required within the Council in order to overrule the Commission's decision. Failing this double qualified majority, the Commission proposal stands. To wit, the Commission can exploit differences among the member states to avoid any reference to the Council; hence it can ensure the implementation of its proposals in much the same way that McCubbins, Noll, and Weingast's regulatory agencies exploit differences among the three branches of government to avoid sanctions.

Third and finally, under the regulatory committee procedure, which was explicitly designed to control the Commission more closely than the management procedure, the Commission may adopt only those measures that are approved by a qualified majority vote within the committee. In contrast to the management committee procedure, which requires a qualified majority to secure a reference to the Council, here a minority can secure such a reference. Council member states can then take a different decision by qualified majority vote, or, in some instances, block the Commission's proposal by vote of a simple majority.

To what extent do these comitology procedures allow the member states to control the actions of the Commission? At first glance, the remarkably low rate of committee referrals to the Council—typically less than 1 percent of all Commission decisions—seems to suggest that committee oversight is perfunctory and that the Commission is largely independent in its actions. However, as the congressional dominance school points out with regard to regulatory bureaucracies, and as Gerus argues with specific reference to the EC's comitology procedures, rational anticipation of committee action by the Commission may mean that the Commission is effectively controlled by the member states, despite the startling rarity of sanctions against it. As one Commission official explained, having one's proposal referred from a committee to the Council can cast a long shadow over the career prospects of a young *fonctionnaire*—a powerful incentive to rationally anticipate a proposal's reception in the relevant committee.

The story, however, does not end there, for two reasons. First, as the thumbnail sketches above suggest, the procedures impose varying requirements on the Commission—and varying thresholds to overruling actions by the committee and the Council. Commission discretion, in other words, is not entirely eliminated by oversight procedures, but it is constrained to different degrees depending on the type of committee procedure selected. Indeed, this is why member states and the Commission often disagree on the choice of procedures, and it is why member states sometimes "tighten" committee procedures in response to Commission shirking.

Second, although regulatory committee procedures clearly provide the member states with the most effective control over the Commission, this control imposes costs on the principals as well as their agent, and more specifically presents the member states with a clear and explicit trade-off between member state control, on the one hand, and speed and efficiency of decision making, on the other. This trade-off between efficiency and control is reflected, for example, in the Council's procedural choices for various types of legislation: an advisory committee procedure is used for competition policy; a management committee procedure for agriculture; and a regulatory committee procedure for legislation regarding customs, veterinary and plant health, and food. Although the latter procedure applies to a number of issue-areas, member states' willingness—in the interests of speed and efficiency—to afford the Commission the greater discretion associated with the advisory and management procedures in areas such as agriculture, competition policy, and regional policy is striking.

*Institutional checks, judicial review, and fire alarms.* In addition to active police-patrol oversight, member states also employ both institutional checks and fire-alarm oversight of the Commission. Indeed, almost every EC institution besides the Commission plays a role in monitoring and checking the Commission's behavior. The European Parliament, for example, enjoys the power to approve and to dismiss the Commission as a whole, although it may not sanction individual commissioners; the Court of Auditors monitors and reports on the Commission's implementation of EC policies; and the ECJ may, under Articles 173 and 174, review the legality of Commission acts, which may be declared void "on grounds of lack of competence, infringement of an essential procedural requirement, infringement of this Treaty or any rule of law relating to its application, or misuse of powers." In addition, under Article 175, the Court may also rule on the Commission's failure to act on its responsibilities under the treaties.

In terms of the principal-agent model sketched above, the provisions of Articles 173–75 create an effective system of fire-alarm oversight by allowing complaints to be brought not only by member states and EC institutions but also by any natural or legal person who can demonstrate that the Commission action is of "direct and individual concern" to him- or herself. Although the ECJ has interpreted the latter requirement narrowly, individuals nevertheless constitute the large majority of plaintiffs in Article 173 cases, and their ability to bring such cases has indeed created a system of fire-alarm oversight similar to that described by McCubbins and Schwartz.

*The costs and credibility of* ex post *sanctions.* Member state principals, therefore, possess ample means of both police-patrol and fire-alarm oversight to monitor the behavior of their agents. However, as we have seen, such information is useful only if the principals can credibly threaten the agent with sanctions in the event of noncompliance; and such sanctions can be more or less costly to the principals as well as the agent. In addition, as we have seen, agents can exploit conflicting interests among the principals, as well as decision rules governing the application of sanctions, allowing them to shirk without incurring sanctions from the principals. Given these considerations, how "usable," or credible, are the possible sanctions available to member state principals? Simplifying slightly, the literature points to four possible avenues open to principals: cutting the agency's budget, dismissing or reappointing agency personnel, adopting new legislation that overrules agency action, and unilaterally refusing to comply with an agency decision. Let us briefly consider each in turn.

The first option, that of cutting agencies' budgets as a sanction, is widely cited in the congressional dominance literature, which argues that, through its power of the purse, Congress determines the very existence of an agency and therefore has considerable leverage over its behavior. As Moe points out, however, the use of budgetary cuts as a means of sanctioning is a blunt instrument:

> A fundamental problem here is that budgets play two roles—one that shapes the incentives of bureaucrats, one that provides a financial foundation for programmatic behavior—and these may often work at crosspurposes. Suppose, for example, that a committee wants substantially higher levels of regulatory enforcement but the agency refuses. . . . If the committee slashes the agency's budget as punishment, . . . it is simultaneously denying the agency the very resources it needs to comply with the committee's wishes. There is no clear solution. The budget is simply not a very dependable control mechanism.

These difficulties apply equally to the EC where cuts in the Commission budget for, say, agriculture, could have adverse programmatic consequences for member governments' domestic constituencies.

A second option would be for the principals to dismiss or refuse to reappoint agency personnel perceived to be drifting from the preferences of the principals. A number of institutional obstacles that apply to all three EC supranational institutions stand in the way of using appointments as a sanction. In the case of the Commission, for example, each member state nominates one or two commissioners, and the member states collectively name a president of the Commission (by unanimity). Under the treaties, however, the Commission may not be dismissed during its five-year term of office, and in practice, member states have a say only over the reappointment of commissioner(s) they had nominated and of the president. ECJ judges hold longer terms than do commissioners (six years), but as in the case of commissioners, member states may not dismiss them during their tenure. Furthermore, judges are protected by the Court's tradition of unanimous rulings, which makes it difficult for member states to single out the views of individual judges for sanctioning. Finally, members of the European Parliament (MEPs) are no longer appointed by national parliaments but since 1979 have been directly elected and thus are responsible not to member governments but rather to their political parties and national electorates. (As Simon Hix and Christopher Lord point out, this provides member government with influence on MEPs from their own political parties but not on those from opposition parties.)

A third option . . . consists of overruling a Commission or ECJ decision through new Council legislation. Here once again, however, a member state unhappy with a Commission or Court action would need to assemble the necessary majority, or even a unanimous vote, in favor of such new legislation. Furthermore, the Commission may, through use of its sole right of initiative in many areas, complicate this task by proposing its own preferred legislation, which under Article 149(1) can be amended only by a unanimous vote of the member states. This is not to say that overruling is impossible, since a unanimous coalition can be put together through log-rolling in the Council; but the institutional barriers to new legislation are high and, once again, allow supranational agents to exploit differences among the member state principals.

Finally, a fourth and more drastic option is unilateral noncompliance with a decision of the Commission or the ECJ. This is indeed one of the central claims both of Kilroy and of Garrett and Weingast, who argue that the ECJ should be aware of the preferences of the larger member states in particular, since noncompliance by such a state could damage the reputation of the Court and render its rulings a dead letter. Here again, however, unilateral noncompliance has significant costs in terms of a member state's reputation among its partners. Furthermore, as a number of scholars have pointed out, the ECJ has a partner in its efforts to ensure national compliance: because national courts generally have accepted the supremacy of EC law over national laws, member governments seeking to avoid compliance would have to defy not only the ECJ but their own national court as well, thereby raising the costs of noncompliance even higher. This is not to say that noncompliance is impossible—indeed, in the case of de Gaulle's "empty chair policy" it proved exceedingly effective—but it is costly, and awareness of these costs by all actors may limit the credibility of a member state's threat of unilateral noncompliance.

*Revising the agent's mandate.* Perhaps the most effective sanction against a shirking agent is the revision of its mandate by amending the treaty or regulation that delegates authority to it. Once again, the ability of member states to control supranational institutions by reforming the administrative procedures in their mandate or its mix of oversight procedures depends crucially on the voting rules for institutional change and the default condition in the event that member states fail to agree on such a change.

The threat of treaty revision is, in some ways, the ultimate threat, but the institutional barriers to carrying the threat through—calling of an intergovernmental conference, agreement by unanimity, ratification by member states—are high. In addition, as noted above, the default condition for treaty provisions is the *status quo*, meaning that in the absence of a unanimous agreement on revision, the powers of the Commission, the ECJ, or the European Parliament stand. Indeed, in Scharpf's terms, the powers of EC institutions under the treaties constitute a model joint-decision trap, in that a single member state can indefinitely block any reform, reduction, or expansion of the powers of EC institutions. For this reason, the threat of treaty revision is essentially the "nuclear option"—exceedingly effective, but difficult to use—and is therefore a relatively ineffective and noncredible means of member state control.

Some of the Commission's executive powers, however, are established not by treaty provisions but by Council regulations with fixed expiration dates. Examples include the structural fund regulations and the European Strategic Program for Research and Development (ESPRIT). In these cases, the relevant regulations require periodic revision and readoption by the Council, meaning that the default condition is not the status quo but expiration of the program, and with it, the Commission's executive powers. The practical result of this need for Council revision, then, is that member states are periodically given the opportunity to "clip the Commission's wings" if it acts in a way that diverges from their interests. Just as important, the requirement of unanimity even for renewal of such regulations means that member states with grievances against the Commission can threaten to veto readoption of the regulation unless their concerns are addressed. Stated another way, where the default condition is expiration of the regulation, the decision rule of unanimity favors those member states who would cut back the executive powers of the Commission, not those who would seek to protect them. Such periodic revisions of the Commission's mandate are relatively commonplace in EC policymaking and are found in programs such as the ESPRIT, the Measures to Encourage Development of the Audiovisual Industry (MEDIA), and the Commission's management of the Community's structural funds.

*Supranational autonomy and member state control.* I have thus far hypothesized that supranational autonomy is primarily a function of the control mechanisms established by member states to control their international agents—and that the costs and credibility of these control mechanisms vary considerably from agent to agent and from one issue-area to another for a given agent. If this hypothesis is correct, the implications for the autonomy of EC institutions are twofold.

First, the analysis presented above suggests that the autonomy and influence of the Commission should vary considerably across issue-areas and over time as a function of the varying administrative procedures, oversight mechanisms, and possibilities for sanctioning available to the member governments. . . . A second implication of principal-agent analysis is that, *ceteris paribus*, the European Parliament and the ECJ should both be less constrained by the member governments than is the Commission. The reason for this is simple: while the Commission enjoys a large number of substantive responsibilities in areas ranging from trade and competition policy to agriculture and structural policy, it is also subject to a large number of oversight procedures (including the EC's comitology oversight committees, judicial review, and monitoring by the European Parliament and the Court of Auditors) and is in many cases relatively easy to sanction or overrule through a qualified majority vote of the member governments. By contrast, the Parliament, although granted a more restricted range of legislative and budgetary powers, is seldom subject to explicit oversight and can be sanctioned only through the relatively difficult expedient of treaty amendment, requiring unanimous agreement among the member governments and ratification by national parliaments and electorates. Individual members of the European Parliament, moreover, are not appointed by the member governments, as are European commissioners, but are directly elected by their electorates, thus granting them an additional degree of independence from their national governments.

Similarly, the relatively weak control mechanisms available to the member governments would lead us to expect—and allow us to explain—the apparent autonomy of the ECJ in influencing the course of European integration.

. . .

## CONCLUSIONS

In this article, I have attempted to model the principal-agent relationship between member government principals, on the one hand, and supranational agents such as the Commission of the European Communities, the ECJ, and the European Parliament, on the other. I argued, first, that a functionalist model of delegation does a remarkably good job of explaining the functions delegated to the European Commission and the ECJ but that such a model fails in explaining the powers of the European Parliament and almost certainly underestimates the importance of unintended consequences and supranational agency. In the second section, I examined this problem of supranational agency, theorizing that the autonomy of institutions such as the Commission and the Court can be seen as a function of the efficacy and credibility of the control mechanisms established by the member states' monitor and sanction agency activity. Third and finally, I examined the conditions under which a supranational agent such as the Commission might enjoy formal and informal agenda-setting powers.

Throughout the discussion, four factors merged as the most important determinants of supranational autonomy. The first of these factors, familiar from Moravcsik's intergovernmentalism and from various rational choice analyses, is the distribution of preferences among member state principals and supranational agents. In all of their activities, I have argued, supranational institutions act within the constraints of member state preferences, which must be taken into account during all supranational executive, judicial, and legislative or agenda-setting functions. However, I have also argued that supranational agents may exploit differing preferences among the member states to avoid the imposition of sanctions against shirking.

. . . Thus, as we saw in the article's second section, agents like the Commission and the ECJ can exploit member state differences to shirk within certain limits, exploiting cleavages among the member states to avoid sanctions, Council overruling of decisions, or alteration of the agent's mandate. . . . In short, while supranational institutions cannot act without regard to the preferences of the member governments, they can operate creatively within the constraints of those preferences to act autonomously, avoiding sanctions from . . . the member governments in the Council.

Second, as we have also seen, the ability of agents to exploit differing preferences among the member states depends in turn on the institutional decision rules for applying sanctions, overruling legislation, and changing agents' mandate. These rules vary over time and across issue-areas, and with them, the autonomy of agents. Thus, for example, the administrative and oversight procedures established for the EC's supranational institutions vary considerably across the institutions, across issue-areas for a given institution, and over time, making supranational institutions more or less difficult to discipline and thereby leading to very different degrees of supranational autonomy. . . . Once again, therefore, institutions matter, which is why member states and EC institutions argue about them.

Third, the role of incomplete information or uncertainty in principal-agent relationships can hardly be overstated. As we have seen, incomplete information influences the initial member state decision to delegate powers of monitoring and contract interpretation to supranational agents. Similarly, the autonomy of a supranational institution is greatest when it has more information about itself than do others and when member states have difficulty monitoring its activities. . . .

Fourth, and finally, the literature on supranational entrepreneurship emphasizes that the influence of supranational institutions is greatest in situations where those institutions possess clear transnational constituencies of subnational institutions, interest groups, or individuals within the member states, which can act to bypass the member governments and/or to place pressure directly on them. Indeed, I would argue, all three EC supranational institutions possess such transnational constituencies: interest groups and multinational firms in the case of the EC Commission, national courts in the case of the ECJ, and national electorates in the case of the European Parliament. In all three cases, national constituencies act both as a constraint on the freedom of action of the supranational institutions and as a counterbalance to the influence of the member governments. To take only one example, the ECJ is unquestionably constrained by the need to secure the voluntary acceptance by national courts of EC law; however once such acceptance is secured, the costs of noncompliance to the member governments rise, and the autonomy of the Court *vis-à-vis* the member governments increases correspondingly. In other words, all three supranational institutions navigate constantly between two sets of constituents: the member government principals that created them and may still alter their mandates and the transnational constituencies that act both as constraint and resource in the institutions' efforts to establish their autonomy.

Taken together, these hypotheses suggest a fruitful agenda for empirical research, which has only begun to address systematically the questions raised by the rational choice literature on institutions and agency. As we have seen, such hypotheses about delegation and agency can be exceedingly difficult to test, in part because supranational institutions may rationally anticipate the preferences of the member states, giving their behavior the appearance of independence while in fact demonstrating the efficiency of member state control. In methodological terms, rational choice theorists have relied largely on statistical analyses of agency behavior to test their principal-agent models in the U.S. context. As Moe and as Donald Green and Ian Shapiro have pointed out, however, many of these studies suffer from inadequate specification and operationalization of hypotheses and poor empirical testing of cases, which are typically selected precisely in order to confirm, rather than test, rational choice models.

These criticisms suggest both theoretical and methodological cautions for future research. In theoretical terms, the hypotheses generated above must be further specified and operationalized so as to focus on measurable variables such as decision rules. We should be careful not to manipulate assumptions about principal and agent preferences, since testing hypotheses can in practice become an exercise in "curve-fitting." In methodological terms, statistical analyses should be supplemented by case studies in order to allow better specification of actor preferences (both principals and agents), and a more nuanced and empirically accurate picture of the nature of the relationship between these actors. Only if we apply both methods can we reveal the fine-grained details of supranational delegation [and] agency. . . .

## ■ NOTE

1. . . . In this article, the focus is on the first pillar (the EC) [of the European Union] and the roles of the supranational institutions within it. I therefore refer to the EC throughout.

# 24 Multi-Level Governance in the European Union

LIESBET HOOGHE AND GARY MARKS

*For some in the late 1990s, the world of "grand integration theory" was growing intellectually stale. Furthermore, the European Union (EU) at the end of the century looked less and less like a system of cooperating nation-states and more and more like a "domestic" political system, albeit with some rather unique characteristics. As a result of these developments, many students of the EU began to speak of European "governance" as a special political phenomenon that demanded explanation. Many of these scholars were trained in comparative politics rather than international relations and thus brought to their studies theories of politics and decisionmaking that were usually applied to European nation-states.*

*Those who took a governance approach to EU politics did not wholly abandon the supranational-intergovernmental debate because to proceed they had to first prove that the EU was not the result of normal international relations (as Moravcsik maintained—see Chapter 22) but rather a new domestic polity. We see this most clearly in the work of Liesbet Hooghe and Gary Marks (both of the University of North Carolina at Chapel Hill), two early advocates of a governance approach, who draw a very stark contrast between "state-centric" (intergovernmentalist) and "multilevel governance" models of EU decisionmaking. They marshal considerable evidence to demonstrate that member states have lost individual and collective control over the European decisionmaking process. Other supranationalists have, of course, covered much of this ground, but the unique contribution made by Hooghe and Marks is their* description *of what has taken the*

---

Used with permission from *Multi-Level Governance and European Integration* by Liesbet Hooghe and Gary Marks (Lanham, Maryland: Rowman and Littlefield Publishers, 2001), pp. 1–32. Notes omitted.

*place of state-centric decisionmaking. In their view, European governance is now dominated by a complex web of interconnected institutions at the supranational, national, and subnational levels of government. National governments no longer automatically get their way; they can now be outvoted in the Council of Ministers, stymied by their electorates, or bypassed by their own local governments, interest groups, and executive bureaucracies. "Multilevel governance" has opened up opportunities for public and private interests of all kinds to enter the policymaking process, thus gently, almost imperceptibly, undermining state sovereignty.*

*The multilevel governance approach is more descriptive than theoretical. It changes the way we look at the EU and encourages us to search for theories of domestic rather than international politics that might help explain policy outcomes.*

Developments in the European Union (EU) over the last two decades have revived debate about the consequences of European integration for the autonomy and authority of the state in Europe. The scope and depth of policy making at the EU level have increased immensely. The European Union completed the internal market on schedule in 1993, and eleven of the fifteen member states formed an economic and monetary union (EMU) in 1999, with a European central bank and a single currency, the euro. These policy-making reforms have been accompanied by basic changes in European decision making. The Single European Act (1986), which reduced nontariff barriers, also established qualified majority voting in the Council of Ministers and significantly increased the power of the European Parliament. The Maastricht Treaty (1993) increased the scope of qualified majority voting in the Council and introduced a codecision procedure giving the European Parliament a veto on certain types of legislation. The Treaty of Amsterdam (1999) extended codecision to most areas of policy making in the European Community, except for EMU.

Our aim in this chapter is to take stock of these developments. What do they mean for the political architecture of Europe? Do these developments consolidate national states or do they weaken them? If they weaken them, what kind of political order is emerging? These are large and complex questions, and we do not imagine that we can settle them once and for all. Our strategy is to pose two basic alternative conceptions—state-centric governance and multi-level governance—as distinctly as possible and then evaluate their validity by examining the European policy process.

The core presumption of state-centric governance is that European integration does not challenge the autonomy of national states. State-centrists contend that state sovereignty is preserved or even strengthened through EU governments. No government has to integrate more than it wishes because bargains rest on the lowest common denominator of the participating member states. In this model, supranational actors exist to aid member states, to facilitate agreements by providing information that would not otherwise be so readily available. Policy outcomes reflect the interests and relative power of national governments. Supranational actors exercise little independent effect.

An alternative view is that European integration is a polity-creating process in which authority and policy making influence are shared across multiple levels of government—subnational, national, and supranational. While national governments are formidable participants in EU policy making, control has slipped away from them to supranational institutions. States have lost some of their former authoritative control over individuals in their respective territories. In short, the locus of political control has changed. Individual state sovereignty is diluted in the EU by collective decision making among national governments and by the autonomous role of the European Parliament, the European Commission, the European Court of Justice, and the European Central Bank.

We make this argument in this chapter along two tracks. First, we analyze the variety of conditions under which national governments will voluntarily or involuntarily lose their grip on power. Second, we examine policy making in the EU across its different stages, evaluating the validity of contending state-centric and multi-level models of European governance.

## ■ TWO MODELS OF THE EUROPEAN UNION

The models that we outline below are drawn from a large and diverse body of work on the European Union, though they are elaborated in different ways by different authors. Our aim here is not to replicate the ideas of any particular writer, but to set out the basic elements that underlie contending views of the EU so that we may evaluate their validity.

The core ideas of the *state-centric model* are put forward by several authors, most of whom call themselves intergovernmentalists [Chapter 22]. This model poses states (or, more precisely, national governments) as ultimate decision makers, devolving limited authority to supranational institutions to achieve specific policy goals. Decision making in the EU is determined by bargaining among national governments. To the extent that supranational institutions arise, they serve the ultimate goals of national governments. The state-centric model does not maintain that policy making is determined by national governments in every detail, only that the overall direction of policy making is consistent with state control. States may be well served by creating a judiciary, for example, that allows them to enforce collective agreements, or a bureaucracy that implements those agreements, but such institutions are not autonomous supranational agents. Rather, they have limited powers to achieve state-oriented collective goods.

EU decisions, according to the state-centric model, reflect the lowest common denominator among national government positions. Although national governments decide jointly, they are not compelled to swallow policies they find unacceptable because decision making on important issues operates on the basis of unanimity. This allows states to maintain individual as well as collective control over outcomes. While some governments are not able to integrate as much as they would wish, none is forced into deeper collaboration than it really wants.

State decision making in this model does not exist in a political vacuum. In this respect, the state-centric model takes issue with realist conceptions of international relations, which focus on relations among unitary state actors. National governments are located in the domestic political arena, and their negotiating positions are influenced by domestic political interests. But—and this is an important assumption—those arenas are discrete. That is to say, national decision makers respond to political pressures that are *nested* within each state. The fifteen national governments bargaining in the European arena are complemented by fifteen separate national arenas that provide the sole channel for domestic political interests at the European level. The core claim of the state-centric model is that policy making in the EU is determined primarily by national governments constrained by political interests nested within autonomous national arenas.

One can envision several alternative models to this one. The one we present here, which we describe as *multi-level governance*, is drawn from several sources. Once again, our aim is not to reiterate any one scholar's perspective, but to elaborate essential elements of a model drawn from several strands of writing, which makes the case that European integration has weakened the state.

The multi-level governance model does not reject the view that national governments and national arenas are important, or that these remain the most important pieces of the European puzzle. However, when one asserts that the state no longer monopolizes European-level policy making or the aggregation of domestic interests, a very different polity comes into focus. First, according to the multilevel governance model, decision-making competencies are shared by actors at different levels rather than monopolized by national governments. That is to say, supranational institutions—above all, the European Parliament, the European Commission, and the European Court—have independent influence in policy making that cannot be derived from their role as agents of national executives. National governments play an important role but, according to the multi-level governance model, one must analyze the independent role of European-level actors to explain European policy making.

Second, collective decision making among states involves a significant loss of control for individual national governments. Lowest common denominator outcomes are available only on a subset of EU decisions, mainly those concerning the scope of integration. Decisions concerning rules to be enforced across the EU (e.g., harmonizing regulation of product standards, labor conditions, etc.) have a zero-sum character and necessarily involve gains or losses for individual states.

Third, political arenas are interconnected rather than nested. While national arenas remain important arenas for the formation of national government preferences, the multi-level governance model rejects the view that subnational actors are nested exclusively within them. Instead, subnational actors operate in both national and supranational arenas, creating transnational associations in the process. National governments do not monopolize links between domestic and European actors. In this perspective, complex interrelationships in domestic politics do not stop at the national state but extend to the European level. The separation between domestic and international politics, which lies at the heart of the state-centric model, is rejected by the multi-level governance model. National governments are an integral and powerful part of the EU, but they no longer provide the sole interface between supranational and subnational arenas, and they share, rather than monopolize, control over many activities that take place in their respective territories.

## ■ FROM STATE-CENTRIC TO MULTI-LEVEL GOVERNANCE

Has national government control over EU decision making been compromised by European integration? In this section we argue that state sovereignty has been diminished by restrictions on the ability of individual governments to veto EU decisions and by the erosion of collective government control through the Council of Ministers.

### □ *Limits on Individual National Government Control*

The most obvious constraint on the capacity of a national government to determine outcomes in the EU is the decision rule of qualified majority voting in the Council of Ministers for a range of issues from the internal market to trade, research policy, and the environment. In this respect, the European Union is clearly different from international regimes, such as the UN or World Trade Organization, in which majoritarian principles of decision making are confined to symbolic issues.

State-centrists have sought to blunt the theoretical implications of collective decision making in the Council of Ministers by making two arguments.

The first is that while national governments sacrifice some independent control by participating in collective decision making, they more than compensate for this by their increased ability to achieve the policy outcomes they want. Andrew Moravcsik has argued that collective decision making actually enhances state control because national governments will only agree to participate insofar as "policy coordination increases their control over domestic policy outcomes, permitting them to achieve goals that would not otherwise be possible." By participating in the European Union, national governments are able to provide policy outcomes, such as a cleaner environment, higher levels of economic growth, and so forth, that they could not provide on their own. But two entirely different conceptions of power are involved here, and it would be well to keep them separate.

On the one hand, power or political control may be conceptualized as control over persons. *A* has power over *B* to the extent that she can get *B* to do something he would not otherwise do. This is a zero-sum conception: if one actor gains power, another loses it. By contrast, power conceived as the ability to achieve desired outcomes entails power over nature in the broadest sense. According to this conception, I have power to the extent that I can do what I wish to do. A government that can achieve its goal of low inflation and high economic growth is, from this standpoint, more "powerful" than one that cannot.

The latter way of conceiving power is not "wrong," for concepts can be used in any way one wishes to use them. But it does confuse two things that are sensibly regarded as separate: who controls whom, and the ability of actors to achieve their goals. . . .

A second line of argument adopted by state-centrists is that majoritarianism in the Council of Ministers camouflages, rather than undermines, state sovereignty. They argue that treaty revisions and new policy initiatives remain subject to unanimity, and that the Luxembourg compromise gives national governments the power to veto any policy that contravenes their vital national interests. Ultimately, they emphasize a national government could pull out of the EU if it so wished.

However, the Luxembourg veto is available to national governments only under limited conditions, and even then, it is a relatively blunt weapon. As we detail below, the Luxembourg veto is restricted by the willingness of other national governments to tolerate its use.

From the standpoint of physical force, member states retain ultimate sovereignty by virtue of their continuing monopoly of the means of legitimate coercion within their respective territories. If a national government breaks its treaty commitments and pulls out of the EU, the EU itself has no armed forces with which to contest that decision. In this respect, the contrast between the European Union and federal system, such as the United States, seems perfectly clear. In the last analysis, national states retain ultimate coercive control over their populations.

But monopoly of legitimate coercion tells us less and less about the realities of political, legal, and normative control in contemporary capitalist societies. A Weberian approach, focusing on the extent to which states are able to monopolize legitimate coercion, appears more useful for conceptualizing the emergence and consolidation of states from the twelfth century than for understanding changes in state sovereignty from the second half of the twentieth century. Although the EU does not possess supranational armed forces, a member state is constrained by the economic and political sanctions—and consequent political/economic dislocation—that it would almost certainly face if it revoked its treaty commitments and pulled out of the European Union.

### □ *Limits on Collective National Government Control*

We have argued that national governments do not exert individual control over decision making in the Council of Ministers. State-centrists may counter that states still retain collective control over EU decision making through the Council of Ministers and the treaties.

In this section, we argue that neither the Council of Ministers nor the treaties give national governments full control over EU decision making. The Council is the most powerful institution in EU decision making, but it exists alongside a directly elected European Parliament (EP) that has a veto on legislation relating to a third of all treaty provisions. The power of the EP in the European political process has grown by leaps and bounds over the past twenty years, and collective national control of decision making has declined as a result.

The treaties are the main expression of national authority in the process of European integration. Because representatives of national governments are the only legally recognized signatories of the treaties, one may argue that state authority is enhanced in the process of treaty making. If a domestic group wishes to influence a clause of a formal EU treaty, it must adopt a state-centric strategy and focus its pressure on its national government.

To evaluate treaties as a vehicle for national government control, one needs to ask two questions: first, to what extent do national governments control the process of treaty negotiation and ratification; and second, to what extent do treaties determine European policy making.

National governments are the key actors in negotiating treaties, but since the tumultuous reception of the Maastricht Treaty in 1993, they have had to contend with the participation of many kinds of domestic actors. In Britain, opposition and back-bench Members of Parliament almost derailed the Treaty in the House of Commons. Just at a time when some observers were claiming that treaty making was strengthening national governments at the expense of parliaments, events in the United Kingdom were proving exactly the opposite. A Conservative government was held ransom by back-benchers, and a split developed within the party on the issue of European integration that fatally weakened the government during the remainder of its term and in the subsequent general election of 1997. In Germany, ratification of the Maastricht Treaty mobilized German regional governments who tried to block the Treaty in the constitutional court. In France, ratification was fought out in a popular referendum in September 1992, and the result was a hair's-breadth win for the government (51 percent in favor; 49 percent opposed). In each of these countries, and across the EU, public opinion was mobilized in ways that placed national governments on the defensive.

Tensions, and sometime outright splits, have arisen within major parties. The British Conservative party is deeply divided on the question of European monetary integration, as revealed in public squabbles and in a survey of MPs. In France, the Gaullist party split into two independent factions in the European election of 1999. In Germany, fissures are evident within the Christian Democratic party, and between the Christian Democrats and their Bavarian sister party, the Christian Social Union. These tensions are not random, but can be explained systematically in reference to party ideologies. . . .

So while it is true that national governments have a formal monopoly in making treaties, it is not at all clear that treaty making, or the process of European integration in general, has strengthened national governments against parliaments, regional governments, or public pressures.

To what extent do treaties allow national governments to determine institution building? The treaties are the ultimate legal documents of the European Union, so it may seem strange to pose the question. But a moment's thought suggests that the question is worth asking after all. To what extent are American, French, or German political institutions determined by their respective constitutions? Treaties, like constitutions, are frameworks that constrain, but do not determine, institutional outcomes. We would regard a study of American politics that focused exclusively on the development of the U.S. Constitution as strangely skewed. Treaties, like constitutions, are sensibly regarded as points of departure, not final destinations, in understanding the workings of a regime because they do not capture the way in which actors adapt to—and exploit—formal rules.

EU treaties have been reformed more frequently than most constitutions, and they lie closer to the ground of policy making. However, national government control is, to some extent, handcuffed by unanimity. Treaties have to surmount the highest conceivable decisional barrier: unanimous agreement among the principals. This not only makes innovation difficult but also makes it difficult for national governments to rein in institutions, as we discuss below.

The extent to which treaties constrain EU institutions is diminished because the treaties themselves tend to be vaguely written. The treaty-making process is heavily biased towards diffuse agreements that avoid contentious issues and allow politicians from all countries and of all ideological stripes to claim success at the bargaining table. The principals in treaty negotiations are not simply representatives of national preferences but are flesh and blood politicians who have private preferences that include a desire to perform well at the next general election. In this respect, the principals sitting around the European bargaining table, no matter how zero-sum their preferences, have a collective desire to agree to something so that the negotiation itself is not perceived as a failure. Ambiguity can serve rational political purposes. When individual or collective national control bumps up against electoral considerations, we expect that electoral considerations will usually emerge the winner.

These considerations suggest that the control of national governments over EU policies and institutions is highly imperfect. National governments no longer monopolize EU decision making, partly because the European Parliament has become a co-legislator over much EU policy; increased public scrutiny of EU decision making increases the weight of public opinion on government policy; and national governments have limited control over supranational agents, such as the European Commission and the European Court of Justice. We examine these in turn.

*European Parliament.* The empowerment of an autonomous and directly elected Parliament over the past two decades presents a fundamental problem for accounts that conceive authority as delegated or pooled by member states. It seems forced to conceive the Parliament as an agent designed by national governments to realize their preferences. The EP increases, rather than reduces, transaction costs of decision making in the EU. The development of the EP cannot be explained as a functional response on the part of national governments to problems of intergovernmental bargaining. On the contrary, the EP is better explained in terms of the response of national governments to domestic pressures for greater democratic accountability in the European Union.

The EP does not fit well into an intergovernmental account of European integration. One line of response is that while Parliament has been strengthened, this has not been at the expense of other institutions. Andrew Moravcsik writes that the cooperation procedure "increased the participation of the Parliament without infringing on the formal powers of either the Commission or the Council." As we have noted above, the notion that power can be supplied as a normal good, so some people can have a bit more without anyone having less, confuses political power with ability. The rules comprising the basic governing institutions of the EU are interwoven, as we explain in the following section, so that a reform of one involves change for all. In the case of the cooperation procedure adopted in 1986, the increase in the formal power of the European Parliament came mainly at the expense of the Council of Ministers. The EP could offer amendments to certain legislation that could only be rejected by the Council if it did so unanimously. Formal theorists of EU rules agree with almost all participants and observers that this was an important increase in the EP's authority. While there has been disagreement about the relative consequences of cooperation and codecision (adopted in 1993), it is plain that the combined effect of these reforms has been to significantly strengthen the Parliament.

It is true that the European Parliament is elected nationally and can be conceived as a forum "in which national representatives, generally organized in political parties, can influence the legislative process." Members of the European Parliament, like those in the United States and most other democracies, represent those living in particular territories, but they do not represent the governments of those territories. Most members have interests and ideologies that may or may not lead them to preserve the authority of central governments, and these preferences are usually consistent with the political party to which they owe their election. Party membership is often a more powerful influence on parliamentarians' behavior and attitudes than country of origin.

The emergence of the European Parliament as a powerful European player has altered the institutional balance in the European Union, as we argue in detail below. The authoritative competences of the European Parliament are more narrowly circumscribed than those of the Council, but the Parliament is nonetheless a weighty player. As a result, national governments cannot impose their collective will in many areas of policy making.

*Public scrutiny.* EU decision making has come under greater public scrutiny. Prior to the Single European Act, European integration was essentially a technocratic process in which national governments coordinated around limited policy goals. European integration was pragmatically oriented, rather than politicized, and national governments dominated decision making to the virtual exclusion of other domestic actors. On the occasions when conflict did flare up—usually in the form of collective protest by farmers, coal miners, or steelworkers—national governments sought to buy off opposition through sectorial deals. EU bargaining was largely insulated from public pressures.

This changed with the introduction of the single market in the mid-1980s. As the reach of European policy making broadened, and as the stakes in most issue areas grew, so domestic groups were drawn directly into the European arena. Such mobilization has created new linkages between supranational institutions and subnational groups, and it has induced citizens with similar interests or ideological convictions to organize transnationally. EU decision making is no longer insulated from the kind of political competition that has characterized democratic politics in the member states.

In the pre-Maastricht era, treaty ratification was dominated by national governments through party control of their national legislatures. Not only did they determine the content of treaties but they could be reasonably confident that those treaties would be accepted in their respective domestic arenas. The Maastricht Treaty would change all that. The rejection of the Maastricht Treaty in June 1992 by Danish citizens sent a shock wave through European elites, and their anxiety was enhanced by a near-replay in the French referendum of September 1992. Moreover, public opinion polls indicated that German and British voters too might have rejected the Treaty if they had been given the opportunity. The fact that the Danes reversed their decision a year later did not put to rest fears that the process was out of control. Public scrutiny has changed the rules of the game of treaty negotiation. The action has shifted from national governments and technocrats in semi-isolation to domestic politics in the broad and usual sense: party programs, electoral competition, parliamentary debates and votes, public opinion polls, and public referenda.

*Principal-agent dynamics.* Even if national governments operated in a world without a European Parliament and without public pressures, it is likely that EU decisions would only imperfectly reflect the preferences of national governments. As governments have agreed to collaborate on more and more issues in the EU arena, so they have turned to supranational agents, particularly the European Commission and the European Court of Justice, to make collaboration work, and by so doing they risk diluting their control over decision making.

Principal-agent theory builds on the insight that principals—national governments, in this case—are not able to plan for all possible future ambiguities and sources of contention, and so they create agents—such as the European Commission and the European Court of Justice—to ensure compliance to interstate agreements and adapt them to changing circumstances. According to this line of theorizing principals exert control over agents by creating the necessary incentives. If a principal discovers that an agent is not acting in the desired way, the principal can fire the agent or change the incentives.

Scholars who have applied principal-agent theory to American political institutions have found that the incentives available to principals are often ineffective. There are grounds for believing that limits on principal control in the EU are particularly severe.

*Multiple principals.* In the European Union there are as many principals as there are member states. Each has a veto over basic institutional change. This vastly complicates principal control. The more hands there are on the steering wheel, the less control any driver will have. The consequences of this in the EU are particularly severe because national governments have had widely different preferences concerning supranational agents.

As noted earlier, one consequence of multiple contending principals in the EU is that the treaties provide ample room for interpretation. The treaties are hammered out in interstate negotiations, in which there is a powerful incentive to allow ambiguity on points of contention so that each government can claim success in representing national interests.

The basic treaties of the EU have legitimated Commission initiatives in several policy areas, yet they are vague enough to give the Commission wide latitude in designing institutions. This has been described as a "treaty base game" in which the Commission legitimates its preferences by referring to a prior treaty commitment. This was the case in structural (or cohesion) policy, which, in the wake of the Single European Act, was transformed by the Commission from a straightforward side payment transferring money from richer to poorer countries to an interventionist instrument of regional policy.

The European Court of Justice (ECJ) does not merely act as an agent in adapting member state agreements to new contingencies. Through its rulings, it has engineered institutional changes that escape, and transcend, treaty norms. Supranational authority in the ECJ deepened from the 1960s, with the establishment of principles of supremacy and direct effect, as a result of Court rulings, not because of treaty language. The constitutionalization of EU treaties is the product of Court activism, not of national government preferences.

*Hurdles to change.* Unanimity is a double-edged sword for supranational institutions in the EU. It raises the bar for any kind of major institutional change in the EU, whether it empowers supranational institutions or reins them in. A supranational actor need only dent a united front of national governments in order to block change. For example, the Commission sidestepped an attempt by a powerful coalition of national governments, including the U.K., Germany, and France, to renationalize cohesion policy in 1993 because it managed to gain the support of just three small member states: Ireland, Portugal, and Belgium.

*Informational symmetries.* Principal control may be weakened if an agent has access to information or skills that are not available to the principal. As a small and thinly staffed organization, the Commission has only a fraction of the financial and human resources available to national governments, but its position at the center of a wide-ranging network including national governments, subnational governments, and interest groups gives it a unique informational base for independent influence on policy making.

*Mutual distrust.* It is the collective interest of national governments to enact certain common regulations, but each may be better off if others adhere to them while it defects. One response is to establish a court that can contain defection. Another is to have very detailed legislation. The reverse side of ambiguity in the treaties has been a willingness on the part of national governments to allow the Commission to formulate precise regulations on specific policies so as to straitjacket principals and reduce their scope for evasion. The Commission likes to legitimate its role in technocratic terms, as the hub of numerous specialized policy networks of technical experts designing detailed regulations.

## ■ POLICY MAKING IN THE EUROPEAN UNION

Who are the key actors in European Union policy making? If the state-centric model is valid, one would expect to find that national governments dominate. This entails three conditions. First, each state should maintain its sovereignty in the process of collective decision making. Second, national governments, by the virtue of the European Council and the Council of Ministers, should be able to impose their preferences collectively on other European institutions, i.e., the European Parliament, the European Commission, and the European Court of Justice. Third, national governments should control the access of subnational groups in the European arena. If, however, the multi-level governance model is valid, we should find that state sovereignty is compromised in collective national decision making, that collective national decision making does not determine policy outcomes, and that subnational interests mobilize beyond the reach of national governments directly in the European arena.

To make headway with this issue, it makes sense to disaggregate policy making. We divide the policy-making process into four sequential phases: policy initiation, decision making, implementation, and adjudication. We lean on analyses of formal rules where they bear on these phases, but we also pay attention to informal practices that shape the way actors interpret and exploit formal rules.

### □ *Policy Initiation: Commission as Conditional Agenda Setter*

In political systems that involve many actors, complex procedures, and multiple veto points, the power to set the agenda is extremely important. The European Commission alone has the formal power to initiate and draft legislation, which includes the right to amend or withdraw its proposal at any stage in the process, and it is the think tank for new policies. In this capacity, it annually produces two to three hundred reports, white papers, green papers, and other studies and communications. Some are highly technical studies about, say, the administration of milk surpluses. Others are influential policy programs, such as the 1985 white paper on the internal market; the 1990 reform proposals for the common agricultural policy, which laid the basis for the European position in the GATT negotiations; the 1993 white paper *Growth, Competitiveness, and Employment*, which argued for labor market flexibility; or the 1997 *Agenda 2000*, which shaped the debate on enlargement to Central and Eastern Europe.

To be able to play its policy-initiation role, the Commission needs access to information. It has superior in-house knowledge concerning agriculture, where one fifth of its staff is concentrated, and it has formidable expertise in external trade and competition, the two other areas where Commission competence is firmly established. In other fields, the Commission relies upon member state submissions, its extensive advisory system of public and private actors, and paid consultants.

Does the European Commission make a real difference? Does it exert significant autonomous influence over the agents, as a multilevel governance perspective would suggest? Or is it largely a decorative institution that draws up legislation primarily to meet the demands of national governments, as a state-centrist might suggest?

In recent years, the Commission itself has understandably stressed its lack of autonomy from more democratically accountable institutions. In an internal accounting exercise in 1998, the Commission estimated that only 5 to 10 percent of legislative proposals arose spontaneously within the Commission itself. The rest were a response to international obligations (35 percent), amendments to or codification of existing law (25 to 30 percent), requests from other EU institutions, national governments, or interest groups (20 percent), or required by prior treaty (10 percent).

The proportions are revealing, but not quite in the way the Commission intended. Within each of these categories, except perhaps for treaties, the Commission has a measure of influence. With respect to international obligations, the Commission itself negotiates on behalf of the EU on trade and, since the 1990s, the environment. So, for example, the Commission represents the EU in the World Trade Organization, and while it must be in close contact with national governments on sensitive trade issues, it plays a central role in negotiations. The Commission also takes the lead in negotiating with countries that wish to join the EU and with countries seeking economic or cultural cooperation with the EU. The second and third categories listed here—amendments and codification of existing law, and Commission response to other actors—encompass widely varying situations. In some, the Commission merely codifies agreements worked out among national governments, as is the norm in transport, energy, and fisheries policies. In others, such as the annual renegotiation of agricultural production quotas and prices or the renegotiation of cohesion funding every five to seven years, the Commission has significant agenda setting power. Finally, Commission proposals reflect treaty commitments, but even here the Commission is by no means passive, for reasons noted above. To the extent that treaty commitments are vague, the Commission has leeway in pressing them into institutional form. The great reform of EU cohesion policy was, for example, mandated by treaty in 1986 but was hammered into innovative institutional form by the Commission. According to the Commission, which has no reason to belittle national governments, treaties generate only one-tenth of its legislative proposals.

The picture that emerges is one where the Commission holds the pen but is subject to pressures from many actors. Policy initiation in the European Union is a multi-actor activity. It includes, in addition to the Commission, the European Council, the European Parliament, the Council of Ministers, and interest groups alongside individual member states.

*European Council.* A potentially powerful principal with respect to the Commission is the European Council, the summit of the political leaders of the member states (plus the president of the Commission), which is held three or four times a year. The European Council has immense prestige and legitimacy and a quasi-legal status as the body that defines "general political guidelines." However, its control of the European agenda is limited because it meets rarely and it provides the Commission with general policy mandates rather than specific policy proposals. European Council mandates have proven to be a flexible basis for the Commission to build legislative programs.

. . .

*European Parliament and Council of Ministers.* More direct constraints on the Commission originate from the European Parliament and the Council of Ministers. Indeed, the power of initiative has increasingly become a shared competence, permanently subject to contestation, among the three institutions. The European Parliament and the Council can request the Commission to produce proposals, although they cannot draft proposals themselves. So far, the European Parliament has made relatively little use of its recently gained competence in Article 192, which enables it, by an absolute majority of its members, to request the Commission to act. By 1999 only a handful of such requests had been made.

The Council of Ministers, and particularly the presidency of the Council, began to exploit this window in the legal texts from the mid-1980s. Governments often bring detailed proposals with them to Brussels when they take over the Council presidency. The Council can also circumvent the Commission's formal monopoly of legislative proposal by making soft law, i.e., by ratifying common opinions, resolutions, agreements, and recommendations. More often, though, national representatives and Commission officials work hand in hand to push a new issue up (or down) the agenda. Most initiatives germinate in the machinery of advisory committees and working groups that the Commission has set up for consultation and pre-negotiation. Many committees are made up of national government nominees (usually civil servants), but others consist of interest group representatives or experts. As it is the Commission that organizes and pays for these committees, it is well placed to shape their agenda. National representatives wishing to raise an issue need to cultivate the Commission officials in charge, for they must be persuaded that an initiative is important enough to go on the agenda.

*Interest groups.* Diffusion of control over the EU's agenda does not stop here. Interest groups have mobilized intensively in the European arena and, while their power is difficult to pinpoint, it is clear that the Commission takes their input seriously. The passage of the Single European Act precipitated a sharp increase in interest group representation in Europe. National and regional organizations of every kind have mobilized in Brussels, and these are flanked by a large and growing number of European peak organizations and individual companies from across Europe. According to a Commission report, some 3,000 interest groups and lobbies employing about 10,000 people were based in Brussels in 1992. Among these are 500 "Eurogroups," which aggregate interests at the European level and some 150 offices in Brussels representing regional and local authorities. Most groups target their lobbying activity at the European Commission and the European Parliament, for these are perceived to be more accessible than the secretive Council.

The Commission's ability to create new advisory committees has helped it reach out to new constituencies, and these include many subnational groups. An example of this strategy was the creation of the Advisory Council for Local and Regional Authorities in 1988 to advise the Commission on initiatives in cohesion policy. The Commission hoped to mobilize support from below for a "partnership" approach to structural programming in which the Commission, national, and subnational governments would jointly design, finance, and implement economic development programs. One of the Commission's longer-term goals was to institutionalize regional participation, and a step was taken in this direction with the establishment of a Committee of the Regions in 1993. While the Commission alone was not responsible for this outcome—pressure by the German *Lander* and the Belgian regions on their respective governments was pivotal—the Advisory Council laid the groundwork. The purview of the Committee of the Regions was extended in the Amsterdam Treaty of 1999.

European institutions compete for control over agenda setting. Interest groups and subnational governments vie to influence the process. One consequence is that it is difficult to assign responsibility for particular initiatives. . . .

Policy initiation engages a wide range of participants, but the Commission is the critical actor in this phase, whether one looks at formal rules or political practice. The Commission's leverage on setting the agenda depends on its ability to anticipate and mediate demands, and its capacity to employ expertise derived from its role as the think tank of the European Union. While the Commission uses its formal powers of initiative from time to time to shape the agenda autonomously, it is usually responsive to the wishes of the European Council, the Council of Ministers, the European Parliament, or interest groups. It is inaccurate to claim that the Commission's role is merely an agent of national governments. A balanced reading of the evidence suggests instead that the Commission operates in a system of multi-level governance involving competition and interdependence among it and the European Council, Council of Ministers, and European Parliament. These institutions share authority in the intricate game of policy initiation.

## □ *Decision Making: State Sovereignty in Retreat*

The thrust of the state-centric argument is to give great weight to the legislative powers of national governments in the decision-making stage. In this view, national governments adjust policies to their collective preferences, define the limits of European collaboration, and determine the role of the European Commission and the ECJ and, if need be, curtail their activities. If previous decisions have unintended consequences, the Council can correct them. National governments may then be said to be in complete control.

According to the EU treaties, the main legislative body is the Council of Ministers, composed of national governments. Before the Single European Act of 1986, the chief legislative weapon of the Parliament was to slow down legislation by withholding its opinion. Such actions were rare, and the Council was effectively the sole legislative authority. This is no longer the case, however. In the first place, individual governments have operated under serious constraints since the Single European Act. Second, even collectively, national governments exert, at most, conditional control. National government control has been eroded by the legislative power of the European Parliament, the role of the European Commission in overcoming transaction problems, and the efforts of interest groups to influence outcomes in the European arena.

*Limits on individual control.* The most transparent blow to individual sovereignty has come from the progressive extension of qualified majority voting in the Council. . . . Two broad observations can be made. First, treaty negotiators never intended unanimity to be the default rule for the Council of Ministers. From the start, there were at least as many treaty provisions with majority rule as with unanimity. And second, the proportion of rules stipulating unanimity in the Council has steadily declined from 49 percent under the Treaty of Rome (1958–1987), to less than 45 percent under the Single European Act (1987–1993), to 35 percent under the Maastricht Treaty (1993–1999), with a slight increase to almost 37 percent under the Amsterdam Treaty (from 1999). Qualified majority voting is now the rule for decisions under the first pillar for Community policies, such as the single market, competition policy, economic and monetary union, regional policy, trade, environment, research and development, transport, employment, immigration and visa policy, social policy, and education. Qualified majority voting also applies to some provisions under the second pillar for Common Foreign and Security Policy (CFSP pillar), namely to "proposed actions related to agreed strategies," and to a handful of decisions under the third pillar for Justice and Home Affairs (JHA pillar). The decision rules are complex, but the bottom line is clear: over broad areas of EU competencies, individual governments may be outvoted.

One might point out that these formal rules do not necessarily determine behavior. Under the informal Luxembourg compromise of 1966, a national government can veto a decision subject to majority voting if it claims that its "vital national interests" are at stake. This gentlemen's agreement, one may argue, is proof of the ultimate sovereignty of member states. However, the Luxembourg compromise has always featured more strongly in academic debates than in the practice of European politics. It was invoked less than a dozen times between 1966 and 1981, and it has been used only a handful of times since.

The real impact of the compromise was to reinforce a veto culture, which inhibited majority voting if a national government expressed serious objections. During the 1970s, this paralyzed hundreds of Commission proposals, but the very existence of this veto culture was its undoing. It eroded during the 1980s as the European Parliament and many national leaders became intolerant of deadlock. A turning point was the inability of the British government in 1982 to veto a decision on agricultural prices to extract a larger British budgetary rebate. Prime Minister Margaret Thatcher's veto was ruled inadmissible, and a qualified majority vote was taken in the Council of Ministers over British objections. Thereafter, national governments became more reluctant to invoke the compromise or tolerate its use by others. The last successful use of the Luxembourg veto was in June 1985. As Neill Nugent has observed, the Luxembourg compromise "is in the deepest of sleeps and is subject only to occasional and largely ineffective awakenings."

It has become much more difficult for national governments to justify the veto so that others will accept its use on a particular issue normally determined by qualified majority. Every government will find itself in a minority from time to time. Why should a particular government be able to escape the consequences of this? Unless that government forces its will on others by threatening to shut down decision making—a strategy as rare as it is risky—it must gain acquiescence within the Council for its veto. In practice, the conditions are restrictive: the issue must be clearly linked to vital national interests, and the government concerned must convincingly claim that it risks severe domestic political damage (e.g., mass demonstrations or a cabinet crisis). An individual government can sustain a veto only if other governments approve. This is a far cry from the original intention of the Luxembourg compromise, which legitimized unconditional defense of national sovereignty—French President Charles de Gaulle vetoed the EU budgetary reform of 1965 on the grounds that it was too supranational. The notion of vital national interest has evolved to justify defense of substantive interests, not defense of national sovereignty itself.

The Luxembourg veto is, in any case, a dull weapon. It cannot block alternative courses of action, as the German federal government learned in 1985 after it had vetoed a Council regulation on lower prices for cereal and colza. The Commission responded by invoking its emergency powers and achieving virtually the same result unilaterally.

There are other ways for national governments to defend individual interests, but they depend on the consent of the other governments. For example, special safeguards can be built into the treaties, a practice that has proliferated since the Maastricht Treaty. Particular states have been granted derogations, that is, special exemptions. The United Kingdom and Denmark each have derogation from European monetary union. Several derogations have been granted in the areas of state aid, environmental policy, and energy policy. Sometimes they are written into special protocols, such as those attached to the Amsterdam Treaty that meet concerns of Denmark, Ireland, and the U.K. on border controls and EU immigration and visa policy. The Amsterdam Treaty also inserted a new decision rule—constructive abstention—that allows a member state to abstain from voting on an issue and to formally declare that it will not implement a decision that nonetheless commits other EU member states. Constructive abstention is, however, restricted to certain issues under the CFSP pillar. In addition, the treaties preserve unanimity for the most sensitive and contested policy areas, particularly major foreign policy decisions, nearly all decisions on justice and home affairs, and much of fiscal policy. And finally, there is the norm within the Council of Ministers that it should operate consensually on delicate political issues. The norm appears to be weakening, however. A recent count found that the Council overrules one or more national governments on around one-quarter of all decisions. The weekly *European Voice* estimated that between January 1995 and January 1998, Germany was most often outvoted in the Council, followed by Britain and, at some distance, Italy.

Derogations, constructive abstention, Council norms, and the continued vitality of unanimity soften the blow of European integration for national sovereignty. But qualified majority voting has been extended, the Luxembourg veto has retreated, and decision making in the Council has become more contentious. There is evidence that larger, as well as smaller, countries find themselves outvoted. Authority over broad areas of policy has shifted from individual national states to collective decision making in the Council of Ministers.

*Collective national control.* The Council of Ministers shares decision-making authority with other European institutions. Over the last three decades, the European Parliament has been transformed from a decorative institution to a directly elected co-legislator. Direct election of representatives to the Parliament was mandated in 1976 (followed by the first EU-wide elections in 1979); parliamentary consultation was strengthened in the early 1980s; a cooperation procedure, giving the Parliament significant agenda-setting powers, and an assent procedure were part of the Single European Act of 1986; and codecision, giving the Parliament a veto over many areas of legislation, was introduced under the Maastricht Treaty of 1993 and extended under the Amsterdam Treaty of 1999. Through the assent procedure, the EP has a veto over enlargement of the EU and over most association agreements and treaties between the European Union and third parties. According to some observers, these changes constitute "a major step towards a bicameral legislative model (with two strong players) at the EC level."

Institutional analysis demonstrates that the Parliament must be taken seriously in explaining legislative outcomes. . . . The Parliament was almost powerless under the Treaty of Rome. It played no role in 73 percent of the provisions and was consulted on the remaining 27 percent. By 1999 and the Amsterdam Treaty, the EP had emerged as a force to be reckoned with. Roughly equal proportions of provisions mandated codecision, consultation, and exclusion. The Council of Ministers is stronger, of course. It votes under all treaty provisions, but the trend seems perfectly clear, as are the implications for the collective capacity of national governments to determine policy making. In place of the original Council-dominated process, Council, Parliament, and Commission now interact in making policy.

The cooperation procedure allowed the Commission to set the agenda. It could decide to take up or drop amendments from either the Council or Parliament, a power that made it a broker—a consensus crafter—between the two institutions. The Council could not decide legislation without the support of either the Commission or the European Parliament unless it was unanimous.

Under the codecision procedure the European Parliament can veto Council legislative proposals. A conciliation committee, consisting of representatives from both institutions with a representative of the Commission as broker, tries to hammer out a compromise if Parliament and Council are deadlocked. To become law, a compromise proposal needs to be approved by a majority in the Parliament and a qualified majority in the Council. The codecisions procedure comes close to putting the European Parliament "on an essentially equal footing with the Council." The Commission retains important agenda-setting powers, though its broker role is weaker than under the cooperation procedure. Under both procedures the Council is locked in a complex relationship of cooperation and contestation with the two other institutions. This is multi-level governance in action and is distinctly different from what one would expect in a state-centric system.

One reason why the collective control of national governments has eroded is because the Council often lacks information, expertise, and the coordination to act quickly and effectively. The Council is an egalitarian institution, and this can complicate coordination, particularly now that there are fifteen member states. The Commission is more coherent because it is more hierarchical. It is far from a unitary organization, and there are often rivalries between its departments, but it is usually more able than the Council to present a united front on a particular proposal. Formal decision rules in the Council of Ministers often help the Commission focus discussion or broker compromise. While national representatives preside at Council meetings, the Commission sits in to clarify, redraft, and finalize the proposal; in short, it holds the pen.

European defense policy illustrates the Commission's capacity to frame decision making. The regulation of defense industry in Europe is debated between those who regard it as a normal industry that does not require special treatment and those who emphasize its special security role. The former favor deregulation in order to exploit economies of scale; the latter wish to preserve national firms or at least organize them on a European-only basis. In the European Commission, the directorate-generals for industry and the internal market favor deregulation and liberalization, while the directorate-general for external relations conceives the issue as one of security in the context of Common Foreign and Security Policy. This tug-of-war made it impossible for the Commission to weigh in on EU decision making until November 1997, when the two protagonists, external relations and industry, found a way to combine their views in a report emphasizing the dual character of the industry. The report, entitled *Implementing European Union Strategy on Defense-Related Industries*, laid out two complementary plans—a European defense equipment policy in the framework of the CFSP and an industrial action plan for defense-related industries in the framework of the EC pillar. By linking Community policies to CFSP measures, the Commission catapulted itself into the heart of decision making on European defense industry, and it provided the Council of Ministers with a focal point in its search for a feasible policy.

The frustrations of intergovernmental cooperation may lead national governments to voluntarily cede authority to supranational agents, as immigration policy illustrates. When in the late 1980s the Commission made a case for an EU-wide immigration policy to give backbone to the free movement of people in the single market, national governments rejected a supranational solution. Cooperation on immigration and border control under Schengen (1985) and on asylum (the 1990 Dublin Convention) were attempts by national governments to overcome regulatory problems among themselves. Intergovernmental problem solving reached its zenith in the Maastricht Treaty, where national governments institutionalized cooperation in immigration policy, visa policy, border control, and police cooperation in the third pillar of Justice and Home Affairs. This arrangement excluded the Commission, the ECJ, and the European Parliament from decision making, but frustrations quickly piled up. The Schengen agreement did not enter into force until 1995, and even then Britain, Ireland, and Denmark decided to stay outside. The Dublin Convention was ratified only in 1997.

In the run-up to the Amsterdam conference, national governments openly conceded that the third pillar did not function properly. The intergovernmental reflection group that prepared the Amsterdam Treaty observed that the voluntary legal framework of Justice and Home Affairs created "uncertainty in legal protection" for citizens because it was not based on transparent principles, and "enforcement problems" because it was difficult for national governments to make binding commitments. The reflection group noted further that unanimity voting exacerbated these problems and recommended that immigration policy be incorporated into the first (EC) pillar of the European Union. In the Amsterdam Treaty, national governments transferred the bulk of immigration policy to the EC pillar, which means that—after a transition period of five years—the Commission will have the sole right of initiative, the European Parliament will codecide, the Council of Ministers will vote on most issues by qualified majority, and the ECJ will adjudicate. "What used to be defined as areas of 'common interest' between member states has now become an objective of the EU."

The Commission's unique resources sometimes enable it to step beyond its role of umpire to become a negotiator. Cohesion policy offers an example. In establishing the framework for structural funds for 1994 to 1999 during the summer of 1993, Commission officials negotiated bilaterally with officials from the relevant states. The Belgian presidency served as umpire. In essence, the Commission became a thirteenth participant around the bargaining table. Something similar has taken place from time to time even in the most intergovernmental forum—treaty bargaining—as revealed in the Maastricht negotiations. When the British government refused the watered-down social provisions at Maastricht, Jacques Delors put his original, more radical, social policy program of 1989 on the table and proposed to attach it as a special protocol to the Treaty, leaving Britain out. Faced with the prospect that the whole negotiation might break down, the other eleven national governments hastily signed up to a more substantial document than they had originally anticipated.

In sum, the Council is the senior actor in the decision-making stage, but the European Parliament and the Commission are indispensable partners. The Commission's power is predominantly soft in that it is exercised by influence rather than sanction. Except for agriculture, external trade, and competition policy, where it has substantial executive autonomy, it can gain little by confrontation. The Commission's influence depends on its ability—and indispensability—in crafting consensus among institutions and among national governments. Extensive reliance on qualified majority voting should in principle enable the Commission to be bolder, as it does not have to court every national government. Nevertheless, ideological convergence in the Council since 1997 and ineffective leadership of the Commission have weakened the Commission's pivotal role at the start of the twenty-first century. It remains to be seen whether the Commission's relative decline will outlive these conjunctional factors.

The European Parliament's position is based more on formal rules. Its track record under cooperation and codecision shows that it does not shy away from confrontation. In return for parliamentary assent to enlargement and the GATT, the Council agreed to allow parliamentary observers in the preparatory negotiations for the intergovernmental conference of 1996–1997, and the Parliament emerged as the main institutional winner in the Amsterdam Treaty. It is intent on making the most of its power, even if it treads on the toes of its long-standing ally, the European Commission. Since the Amsterdam Treaty, the European Parliament's assent is needed for the appointment of the Commission president, as well as for the whole team. "The result of these reforms is a quasi-parliamentary system (i.e., the classic 'indirect' mechanism) for selecting this branch of the EU executive, whereby the commission president is nominated by the member states and ratified by the European Parliament immediately following the EP elections." In spring 1999, a Parliamentary inquiry into fraud, mismanagement, and nepotism in the Commission forced the Santer Commission to resign *en masse* under a cloud of accusations.

Authoritative competencies in Europe are exercised across multiple levels of government. At the European level, national governments and supranational actors share authority, and the institutions in which they operate have intermeshing competencies.

### *Implementation: Breaking the State Mold*

Multi-level governance is prominent in the implementation stage. The formal division of authority between the Commission, which had sole executive power, and member states, which monopolized policy implementation, no longer holds. National governments have come to monitor the executive powers of the Commission, and the Commission has become involved in day-to-day implementation in a number of policy areas, and this brings it into close contact with subnational governments and interest groups. As for agenda setting and decision making, the mutual intrusion of institutions into the other's terrain is contested.

The commission's formal mandate gives it discretion to interpret legislation and issue administrative regulations or decisions for specific cases. It used to announce at least 4,000 administrative regulations annually, and an equal number of decisions, but in the late 1990s this number more than halved. Still, the Commission remains formally responsible for the bulk of EU rules.

From the 1980s the Council of Ministers and individual governments became intimately involved in the executive powers of the Commission. The term for this is *comitology*, which refers to the practice of having a committee of national representatives assist the Commission in its executive work. Many regulations have their own committee attached to them. Rules of operation vary from committee to committee, and they are a source of friction among the Commission, the Parliament, and the Council. Some committees are only advisory; others can prevent the Commission from carrying out a certain action by qualified majority vote; a third category must approve Commission actions by qualified majority. In each case the Commission presides.

At first sight, comitology may seem to give national governments control over the Commission's actions in principal-agent fashion, but this impression is misleading. Comitology is weakest in precisely those areas where the Commission has extensive executive powers, e.g., in competition policy, state aids, agriculture, commercial policy, and the internal market. Here, the Commission has significant space for autonomous action. Comitology does not alter the basic fact that national governments have lost their monopoly of authority in many policy areas: for example, they no longer control competition within their borders, they cannot aid national firms as they deem fit, and they cannot autonomously conduct trade negotiations.

National governments often select people outside the central executive to represent them in comitology. Most participants in comitology are not national civil servants but are subnational officials, interest group representatives (particularly from farming, union, and employer organizations), technical experts, scientists, or academics. Subnational participation in comitology is most common for federal or semi-federal states, though in recent years, more centralized states have followed suit.

Though subnational officials, technical experts, interest group representatives, and private actors are selected by their national government to participate in comitology, they have particular territorial or group interests, as well as the national interest, to defend. Comitology was designed to allow national governments to monitor the Commission, but it has had the additional, and unintended, consequence of deepening subnational and group participation in the European political process.

Commission officials now play a role in day-to-day policy implementation. The Commission was never expected to perform ground-level implementation, except in unusual circumstances (such as competition policy, fraud, etc.). Yet in some areas this has changed. The most prominent example is cohesion policy, which absorbs about one-third of the EU budget. The bulk of the money goes to multi-annual regional development programs in the less developed regions of the EU. The structural funds reform of 1988, followed by revisions in 1993 and 1999, involves regional and local governments as well as social actors in all states of the policy process—the selection of priorities, choice of programs, allocation of funding, monitoring of operations, and evaluation and adjustment of programs. Each region or country receiving funding is required to set up monitoring committees with a general committee on top and a cascade of subcommittees focused on particular programs. Commission officials can and do participate at each level of this tree-like structure. Partnership is implemented unevenly across the EU, but just about everywhere it institutionalizes some form of direct contact between the Commission and subnational governments. Such links break open the mold of the state, so that multi-level governance encompasses actors beneath, as well as above, central states.

### □ *Adjudication: An Activist Court in a Supranational Legal Order*

State-centrists have argued that a European legal order and effective European Court of Justice are essential to state cooperation. Unilateral defection is difficult to detect, and thus it is in the interest of states to delegate authority to a European court to monitor compliance. The ECJ also mitigates problems of incomplete contracting by applying current agreements to future contingencies. From this point of view, the ECJ is an agent of the member states. However, a number of scholars have convincingly argued that the Court has become more than an agent of member states. With the help of the Commission, and in collaboration with national courts, the ECJ has transformed the European legal order in a supranational direction.

The ECJ has laid the foundation for an integrated European polity. The Court has built an impressive body of case law establishing the Treaty of Rome as a document creating legal obligations directly binding on national governments and individual citizens alike. These obligations have legal priority over laws made by member states. Directly binding legal authority and supremacy are core attributes of sovereignty, and their application by the ECJ suggests that the EU is becoming a constitutional regime.

The Court was originally expected to act as an impartial monitor "to ensure that in the interpretation and application of the treaties the law is observed," but from the beginning the Court viewed these interstate treaties as more than narrow international agreements. The Court's expansive role is founded on the failure of the treaties to specify the competencies of major EU institutions. Instead, the treaties set out "tasks" or "purposes" for European cooperation, such as the custom union (Treaty of Rome), the completion of the internal market (Single European Act), or economic and monetary union (Maastricht Treaty). The Court has constitutionalized European law and European authority in other policy areas by stating that these were necessary to achieve these functional goals.

Court rulings have been pivotal in shaping European integration. However, the ECJ depends on other actors to force issues on the European political agenda and condone its interpretations. Legislators (the European Council, Council of Ministers, Commission, and Parliament) may reverse the course set by the Court by changing the law or altering the EU treaties. The ECJ is no different from the Council, Commission, or European Parliament in that it is locked in mutual dependency with other actors.

One outcome of this interlocking is the principle of "mutual recognition," which became the core principle of the internal market program. In the landmark case of *Cassis de Dijon* (1979), the Court stated that a product lawfully produced in one member state must be accepted in another. But it was the Commission that projected the principle of mutual recognition onto a wider agenda, the single market initiative, and it did this as early as July 1980 when it announced to the European Parliament and the Council that the

*Cassis* case was the foundation for a new approach to market harmonization.

National courts have proved willing to apply the doctrine of direct effect by invoking Article 234 of the Treaty of Rome, which stipulates that national courts may seek "authoritative guidance" from the ECJ in cases involving Community law. In such instances, the ECJ provides a preliminary ruling, specifying the proper application of Community law to the issue at hand. While this preliminary ruling does not formally decide the case, in practice the court renders a judgment of the "constitutionality" of a particular statute or administrative action in light of its interpretation of Community law. The court that made the referral cannot be forced to accept the ECJ's interpretation, but if it does, other national courts will usually accept the decision as a precedent. Preliminary rulings expand ECJ influence, and judges at the lowest level gain a *de facto* power of judicial review, which had been reserved for the highest court in the state. Article 234 gives lower national courts strong incentives to circumvent their own national judicial hierarchy. With their support, much of the business of interpreting Community law has been transferred from national high courts to the ECJ and the lower courts.

ECJ decisions have become an accepted part of the legal order in the member states, shifting expectations about decision-making authority from a purely national-based system to one that is multilevel. The doctrines of direct effect and supremacy were constructed over the strong objections of several national governments. Yet, the influence of the ECJ has as much to do with creating opportunities for other actors, including the Commission and lower national courts, to influence European rule making as it does with its enlarged scope for unilateral action.

## ▪ CONCLUSION

Multi-level governance does not confront the sovereignty of states directly. Instead of being explicitly challenged, states in the European Union are being melded into a multi-level polity by their leaders and the actions of numerous subnational and supranational actors. State-centric theorists are right when they argue that national states are extremely powerful institutions that are capable of crushing direct threats to their existence. The institutional form of the state emerged because it proved a particularly effective means of systematically wielding violence, and it is difficult to imagine any generalized challenge along these lines. But this is not the only, or even the most important, issue facing the state. One does not have to argue that states are on the verge of political extinction to believe that their control of those living in their territories has significantly weakened.

It is not necessary to look far beyond the state itself to find reasons that might explain such an outcome. When we disaggregate the state into the people and organizations that shape its diverse institutions, it is clear that key decision makers, above all those directing the national government, may have goals that do not coincide with projecting national sovereignty into the future. The state is a means to a variety of ends, which are structured by party competition and interest group politics in a liberal democratic setting.

Even if national governments want to maintain national sovereignty, they are often not able to do so. A government can be outvoted because most decisions in the Council are now taken by qualified majority. Moreover, the national veto, the ultimate instrument of sovereignty, is constrained by the willingness of other national governments to tolerate its use. But the limits on sovereignty run deeper. Even collectively, national governments do not determine the European agenda because they are unable to control the supranational institutions they have created. The growing diversity of issues on the Council's agenda, the sheer number of national principals, the mistrust that exists among them, and the increased specialization of policy making have made the Council of Ministers reliant upon the Commission to set the agenda, forge compromises, and supervise compliance.

The most obvious blow to Council predominance has been dealt by the European Parliament, which has gained significant legislative power since the Single European Act. Indeed, the Parliament has become a principal in its own right. The Council, Commission, and Parliament interact within a legal order, which has been transformed into a supranational one through the innovative jurisprudence of the European Court of Justice.

Since the 1980s, these changes in EU decision making have crystallized into a multi-level polity. With its dispersed competencies, contending but interlocked institutions, and shifting agendas, multi-level governance opens multiple points of access for interests. In this process of mobilization and counter-mobilization, national governments no longer serve as the exclusive nexus between domestic politics and international relations. Direct connections are being forged among political actors in diverse political arenas.

Multi-level governance may not be a stable equilibrium. There is no explicit constitutional framework. There is little consensus on the goals of integration. As a result, the allocation of competencies between national and supranational actors is contested. It is worth noting that the European polity has made two U-turns in its short history. Overt supranationalist features of the original structure were overshadowed by the imposition of intergovernmental institutions in the 1960s and 1970s. From the 1980s, a system of multi-level governance arose, in which national governmental control became diluted by the activities of supranational and subnational actors. The surreptitious development of a multi-level polity has engendered strong reactions. The EU-wide debates unleashed by the Maastricht Accord have forced the issue of national sovereignty onto the public agenda. Where governing parties themselves have shied away from the issue, opposition parties, particularly those of the extreme right, have raised it. States and state sovereignty have become objects of popular contention—the outcome of which is as yet uncertain.

# 25 Making Sense of EU Decision-Making

JOHN PETERSON AND ELIZABETH BOMBERG

*The study of politics is in large part the study of how governments make decisions. Thus, students of European integration have from the beginning made Community decisions and the decisionmaking process the subject of analysis. These policy studies—if they took a theoretical approach at all—usually attempted to validate one of the two major theoretical perspectives on offer: supranationalism or intergovernmentalism. The governance approach, however, broke with this tradition by treating the European Union (EU) as a unique polity that cannot be explained exclusively in terms of interstate bargaining or supranational entrepreneurship. From this perspective, EU policymaking is extraordinarily complex; understanding it requires a full range of theories drawn from both international relations and comparative politics.*

*John Peterson (University of Glasgow) and Elizabeth Bomberg (University of Edinburgh) focus on the nuts and bolts of European Union decisionmaking, but they are far from atheoretical. In this selection from their book* Decision-Making in the European Union, *they seek to bring order to the theoretical debate by applying different theories to different "levels of analysis." They begin by assuming that the EU is a "unique system of 'multi-level governance'" that can be viewed at one level—the "super-systemic"—as a system of cooperating nation-states, at the "systemic level" as a system of supranational institutions, and at the "sub-systemic level" as a system of policy networks. Each level is served by a set of theoretical perspectives that explain the type of decision made at that level. In short, Peterson and Bomberg refuse to see the various theories of integration as competi-*

Used with permission from *Decision-Making in the European Union* by John Peterson and Elizabeth Bomberg (London: Palgrave, 1999), pp. 4–30. Notes omitted.

*tive; each serves a different level of analysis in complementary fashion. Even neofunctionalism (Chapter 21) and intergovernmentalism (Chapter 22), according to Peterson and Bomberg, complement one another—making the major debate in integration studies no longer necessary.*

Why study decision-making in the European Union (EU)? A deceptively simple answer is: because a large share of public policy affecting 370 million European citizens (and many beyond the EU's borders) is now decided at this level of governance. The accuracy of Jacques Delors' famous prediction that 80 percent of all economic and social legislation would be decided at the EU level by the late 1990s remains disputed. What is clear is that trying to measure how much legislation is decided at different levels of government in Europe is both pointless and beside the point. What makes the EU novel, interesting and worthy of close study is "its unique *combination* of national and supranational rules and institutions."

This [chapter] is about how national and supranational (and sometimes subnational) institutions and actors combine in the making of *decisions*: that is, choices or solutions that end some uncertainty or reduce contention. A decision is not the same as a *policy*: action (or inaction) by public authorities facing choices between alternative courses of public action. When *any* choice is made, the result is a decision. All policies are a product of decisions about what to do, how to do it, and how to decide what to do. Decisions are the building blocks of policies.

Yet some decisions are "bigger" than policies. Decisions to embrace quasi-constitutional change, such as reform of the EU's Treaties, transcend "ordinary" choices about what action (or inaction) should be taken by the EU within its defined areas of competence. "Big" decisions may redefine the EU's competence or alter its institutions in ways that lead to changes in EU policy.

Our strategy for understanding the EU, and all that it does, is to study the lowest common unit of every move it makes: the individual decision. This research strategy particularly befits the European Union because it is a unique system of "multi-level governance." The term *governance* is everywhere in the recent EU literature, but it is rarely defined very clearly. We define governance as the imposition of overall direction or control on the allocation of valued resources. Governance is synthetic: it results from a mix of factors, including political leadership, state-society relations, institutional competition, electoral politics, and so on. The EU's existence as an extra level or layer of governance that has been "fused" onto the nation-state makes the mix unusually eclectic in Europe compared to other parts of the world.

Quite a lot of work on the EU—in fact, much of the best work—is concerned with decision-making. Our own contribution is to supply the "two things" that Caporaso finds missing from existing work. First, we specify a clear continuum of different types of decision in EU governance. Second, we offer "representative cases of major decisions and minor and intermediate decisions."

This chapter introduces our framework for analysis, which specifies three analytical categories or types of EU decision. We begin by introducing decision-making as a general approach to understanding politics, and consider how theory can help us make sense of EU decision-making.

## ▪ DECISION-MAKING AND EU POLITICS

Some of the best-known, classic works of political science have focused on decision-making. A prime example is Graham Allison's *Essence of Decision*, which "mines" competing models of decision-making to explain American policy during the Cuban missile crisis. Allison's is one of the shrewdest works ever in the study of decision-making, yet he admits there are stark limits to our ability to explain what happens in the real political world:

> In attempting to explain a particular event, the analyst cannot simply describe the full state of the world leading up to that event. The logic of explanation requires that he [*sic*] single out the relevant, important determinants of the occurrence.

There have been systematic studies of the key determinants of EU decision-making. Rosenthal's study of decision-making in the early years of the European Economic Community (EEC) is an exception. Following Allison, it tests three competing models of decision-making: intergovernmentalism (with member states controlling decision-making), pressure politics (with decisions determined by "grass-roots, interest group and parliamentary pressures") and what Rosenthal calls "elite networks." During a period (1968–71) when intergovernmentalism appeared to dominate, Rosenthal nonetheless found that "elite networks" offered the most compelling explanations for the outcomes of EEC decision-making. Within elite networks, decision-making was a product of "subtle, behind-the-scenes lobbying and elaborate committee work." Investigating this type of informal, backroom decision-making is not easy, yet Rosenthal's evidence suggests it cannot be ignored.

This type of decision-making *has* been ignored, or dismissed as unimportant, by most international relations (IR) scholars. IR scholars can be relied upon to raise important, basic questions about *power*, including questions about who or what determines which issues are subjected to EU decisions. Most students of IR concede that the European Union's mere existence poses a challenge to "neo-realism," which remains a dominant paradigm in the study of IR. Neo-realism assumes that "states are the key actors in world politics; they are substantively and instrumentally rational; and their preferences and choices are largely shaped by the absence of a centralized international authority, i.e. inter-state anarchy." For neo-realists, EU decision-making is the "practice of ordinary diplomacy" although "under conditions creating unusual opportunities for providing collective goods through highly institutionalized exchange." Thus the European Union is *only* as powerful as its member states wish it to be.

Inspired but not abducted by neo-realism, Milward and Moravcsik both argue that the EU strengthens the nation-state, as opposed to weakening it. EU decision-making, according to them, is primarily *intergovernmental.* It is dominated by national interests and allows governments to "escape" from pesky domestic pressures that limit their room for maneuver at the national level.

For instance, given its neo-liberal policy agenda, the EU may empower national governments by "limiting decision-making to relatively noncontroversial matters." The difficulty of securing agreements at the EU level may "prevent certain grievances from developing into fully-fledged issues which call for decisions": EU commitments (such as the EMU [Economic and Monetary Union] convergence criteria) may effectively preclude measures (such as higher taxes to fund redistribution) that benefit the poor or powerless. The result is a "mobilization of bias," as "some issues are organized into politics while others are organized out." Put another way, the Union may guarantee the sanctity of "non decisions" that lead it to ignore or neglect certain problems: *not* to choose is, in a way, to make a choice.

The problem, of course, is how to organize a research agenda to investigate "non decisions." Moreover, EU decision-making is clearly *not* always limited to non-controversial matters, or issues that all its member states can agree should be on the Union's agenda, as we would expect under conditions of "ordinary diplomacy." Explaining why means engaging in *policy analysis*, or dissecting a choice to act (or not to act) and examining which actors or interests determine the outcome, and why. Policy analysis suggests, contrary to intergovernmentalist assumptions, that the EU may be as much like New Haven, Connecticut as like the United Nations, in that it sometimes features pluralistic competition in "subject matter domains encompassing both routine and nonroutine decisions, conflict and innovation, with a rather heavy emphasis on innovation."

Intergovernmentalists have a counterattack: when the EU becomes a source of innovative public policy it is because one or more member states has managed to "seize" the policy agenda in pursuit of its national interest. Yet because member states are the source of most policy ideas does not mean that they exert tight control over EU decision-making. The Union's institutions, particularly the European Commission, often welcome the initial "push" of a certain member state (or group of them) to put an issue on the agenda. They then may grab control of the decision-making process in a way that is unwelcome to the national initiator.

More generally, the EU has become a polity in its own right, in which decision-making is not a simple matter of intergovernmental bargaining. Important decisions arise from bargaining which is inter*institutional*, involving the Commission, the Council of Ministers, European Parliament (EP) and (sometimes) the European Court of Justice (ECJ). Power is shared at the supranational level, and not *only* between states.

The EU is a powerful level of governance, and in fact is the main regulator of the most highly regulated societies in the world. It must craft policy solutions that surmount conflicts of national interest in a system that features abundant and widely distributed vetoes. Yet it often seems that "the policy-making capacities of the Union have not been strengthened nearly as much as capabilities at the level of member states have declined." The EU itself is resource-poor, spending less than 2 percent of all public money in the Union. It must aggregate an enormous number of interests, in a polity of 370 million EU citizens, without the benefit of strong, Europe-wide political parties, pressure groups or trade unions. The EU has an almost impossible job with few means to do it. Often the only plausible strategy is to encourage the formation of something like Rosenthal's elite networks, or "policy networks," which can "prepare" decisions and build consensus through informal exchange and backroom bargaining.

Policy networks are conceptual tools of public policy analysis. They help describe and explain decision-making which "shapes" policy away from the limelight. The term "policy network" is a metaphor for a cluster of actors, each of which has an interest, or "stake," in a given EU policy sector and the capacity to help determine policy success or failure. EU policy networks usually bring together a diverse variety of institutional actors and other "stakeholders": private and public, national and supranational, political and administrative.

Actors in policy networks are dependent on each other for scarce resources, such as information, expertise or legitimacy. They thus have incentives to share resources, bargain and agree on how to try to "shape" policy in the interests of their sector. Much of what the EU does is highly technical. Policy structures are highly fragmented—between, say, agriculture or environmental or cohesion policy. Thus EU policy networks tend to be technocratic, consensual and policy-specific. Policy networks play an important functional role in EU governance: they aggregate the interests of a variety of different actors in a highly "differentiated polity" marked by "the fragmentation of policies and politics."

Policy network analysis seeks to determine how decisions are negotiated within such networks. It seems apt for a system of governance that is weakly institutionalized, resource-poor and has no "government," yet which often takes a strong lead in governing Europe. In this system, "the capacity of individuals and small groups to influence decisions" remains striking. However, the "big" decisions that determine the pace and direction of European integration preoccupy the highest political levels where power is concentrated, regardless of how "fragmented" or technocratic the EU is. At this level of decision-making, the Union has a firm, intergovernmental backbone. The student of EU decision-making thus must be concerned with explaining a range of different decisions taken at different levels in a multi-level system of governance. Our approach is to draw on a range of theories that are "pitched" at different levels of decision-making (see Table 25.1), on the assumption that "different kinds of theories are appropriate for different parts of the EU puzzle." Otherwise, we run headlong into the classic "level of analysis" problem which has preoccupied international relations scholars. Put simply, a theory which seeks to explain or predict "big decisions," such as the launch of EMU, should not be judged by how well it explains or predicts a decision to change the way that pig carcasses are measured.

Of course, advocates of particular theories often claim (implicitly, at least) that "their" theory can tell us everything we really need to know about EU decision-making. Espousers of a single "metatheory" of EU politics may accuse us of being magpies or engaging in "intellectual ad-hocery." Yet, echoing Hix, we know of "no general theory of American or German government," and thus question the

**Table 25.1 Putting Theory in Its Place**

| Level | Type of Decision | Bargaining Mode | Rationality | "Best" Theory |
|---|---|---|---|---|
| Super-systemic | History-making | Intergovernmental | Political | Liberal intergovernmentalism; neofunctionalism |
| Systemic | Policy-setting | Interinstitutional | Political; technocratic | New institutionalism |
| Sub-systemic | Policy-shaping | Resource exchange | Technocratic; consensual | Policy network analysis |

wisdom of searching for a general theory of the EU. Moreover, we know of no other international organization (IO) which approaches the EU's decision-making power. European integration has produced a distinctive model of "deep regionalism" that resists simple characterizations. EU decision-making is heavily nuanced, constantly changing and even kaleidoscopic.

## ■ THREE TYPES OF DECISION

Our framework for analysis of EU decision-making (see Table 25.1) acknowledges the multi-level character of the Union. It specifies the different actors, modes of bargaining, and rationalities—or criteria for determining what are "good" decisions—which "drive" decision-making at different levels. It categorizes different types of decision by outcome, and specifies which actors tend to dominate choices which produce a specific kind of outcome, and why.

The framework is a heuristic one: that is, one which aids learning, discovery or problem-solving. It is *not* intended to imply that only one type of decision is ever taken at each level of governance, or that these levels are demarcated by neat, dividing lines (like boundaries on a map). Issues often "jump" up and down between levels of decision-making before they are resolved. Our framework's three levels do not always correspond to organizational aggregation (that is national cabinets at the top, the Council in the middle and the Commission at the bottom) or political jurisdiction (as in supranational, national and sub-national). The framework offers analytical categories of different kinds of decision, not explanatory variables which specify which factors will determine outcomes. In that sense, it is theoretically neutral: it does not seek to "referee" debates between competing models so much as it tries to combine the insights of different theories by specifying precisely where they are "pitched." It applies them where they have the most analytical leverage: to the most appropriate "piece of the EU puzzle." In short, our framework is a template for making sense of EU policy episodes, which result from an accumulation of different kinds of decision.

## ■ HIGH POLITICS AND "HISTORY-MAKING" DECISIONS

History-making decisions do precisely what the term implies: they "make history" by changing the EU—altering its procedures, rebalancing the relative powers of its institutions, or adjusting the Union's remit. They are taken at a "super-systemic" level, or one that transcends the EU's policy process. Because they are quasi-constitutional in character, they preoccupy decision-makers at the highest political levels.

Generally, history-making decisions emerge in one of three ways. First, they are taken as a consequence of intergovernmental conferences (IGCs) called to revise the EU's founding treaties. Second, they are taken by the European Council and determine the EU's agenda, priorities or finances. Increasingly, in an enlarged Union, they may determine the sub-group of EU member states that undertakes specific, integrative projects. Third, more rarely, they come in the form of legal decisions taken by the ECJ, which set out the limits of the EU's powers or define principles of governance.

History-making decisions usually come at "high-political junctures, moments when new high-level deals make it possible for specific linkages and interdependencies to become important." For example, a decision was taken in spring 1985 to convene a European Council in Milan to discuss the Dooge Report, a paper on reform of the Community's institutions. Only later did the Commission, sensing that the time was right for a more general relaunch of the EU, decide to table its *White Paper on Completing the Internal Market* at the June 1985 summit. The market liberalization program it promised became linked to institutional reform in a way that, for example, overcame the objections of the United Kingdom to making more decisions by qualified majority voting (QMV) as opposed to unanimous voting.

Budgetary decisions which "make history" now occur in regular cycles when the European Council adopts multi-annual "financial perspectives." The first, agreed in 1988, was truly historic in that it reduced the need for more budgetary wrangling over the next five years and set the precedent for the successor "Delors II" package covering 1993–9. Subsequent financial agreements were adopted as complex package deals that set clear parameters for EU spending. They did not change EU governance in abrupt or dramatic terms, but went far towards determining, in practical terms, the EU's policy remit for years at a time.

Decisions about how much money the EU will spend on what are often the end results of very hard-nosed intergovernmental negotiations about policy details. However, the role of ideas is perhaps more important in the EU than in any other system of governance, given the Union's ambitions to transform and modernize European political economies. Simply put, ideas are "shared causal beliefs": accepted knowledge about which policy measures will cause desirable outcomes to occur. In particular, neo-liberal ideas—inflation and wage control, monetarism, stable interest rates—inspired the decisions to launch the so-called 1992 project to "complete" the internal market. Similarly, the creation of the euro was underpinned by the emergence of "a new consensus opposed to demand management and wedded to the concept of sound money as the single most important goal of economic policy."

More broadly, as Helen Wallace has argued, European integration as a process has always been driven by ideals: in equal measure, by shadows of the past and shadows of the future. The process stagnates when principal decision-makers forget how European integration rescued Europe from the chaos of the 1940s and made possible its post-war political stability and economic prosperity. Equally, European integration stalls when political leaders begin to doubt that closer European unity can bring about a future that is better than the present.

Most theoretical work on the EU is concerned with "history-making" decisions that determine the general pace and direction of European integration. The longest established theory of integration, neofunctionalism, is concerned with how one quasi-constitutional decision to integrate might "spill over" and provoke further, related acts of integration. Neofunctionalism assumes that integration feeds upon itself through two linked processes. The first is societal: social actors demand integration, and the demand is satisfied by using—or, more likely, adjusting—existing rules, institutions and structures in ways that further integration. The second is a technocratic process: leadership is provided by the "power of the expert, the ability of supranational technocrats to structure the agenda, and the variable ability of the Commission to broker deals." The essence of political integration is the gradual emergence of a "collective decision-making system."

The unidirectional logic of neofunctionalism was heavily criticized when European integration appeared to stagnate and even reverse in the late 1960s and 1970s. The theory appeared to make a comeback in the 1980s as the pace of European integration accelerated again, yet dissatisfaction with neofunctionalism, especially amongst IR scholars, led to the development of alternative theoretical models, especially "liberal intergovernmentalism" [Chapter 22].

Liberal intergovernmentalism (LI) focuses firmly on "major decisions in the history of the E[U]." The core assumptions of LI are that "states are rational self-interested actors, that they 'read' the demands of society, that these demands are somehow aggregated . . . and that [states] negotiate over their differences in the international arena." LI is compatible with the insight that the EU may *strengthen* the state, instead of weakening it, by giving European leaders strategic opportunities to make decisions in forums insulated from domestic pressures. The EU also gives them policy tools for managing the complex interdependence that makes Europe's destiny a more or less collective one. Yet, in line with the demands of IR scholarship, LI purports to be a general theory of international co-operation that is not specific to Europe.

LI assumes that "governments first define a set of interests, then bargain amongst themselves to realize those interests." Governments act with more or less autonomy depending on how effectively and with what intensity domestic groups make demands on them. Yet Sandholtz argues that "the national interests of EC states do not have independent existence; they are not formed in a vacuum and then brought to Brussels. Those interests are defined and redefined in an international and institutional context that includes the EC" itself. There is little theoretical room within LI for the shaping of national interests *within* the context of EU bargaining.

In particular, intergovernmentalists who approach the EU from an international relations paradigm have almost naturally tended to miss the importance of the ECJ because "an international organization, almost by definition, does not have a court that exercises judicial review in the sphere of constitutional law as opposed to international law." More generally, the role of the Court in pushing integration forward through history-making legal decisions boosts neofunctionalism. Its advocates "argue that in the march toward European Union, as community building gathered speed, the issues before the court have become more politically salient." The ECJ has taken numerous, highly political decisions, based on ostensibly *legal* rationale, to extend or deepen integration.

Neofunctionalism's most glaring weakness is its implicit assumption that the EU is a uniquely efficient solution to a set of functional problems. In many respects, the Union is highly *inefficient*; it is simply the most readily available means for organizing co-operation. Moreover, neofunctionalism tends to ignore the fundamentally political (as opposed to technocratic) rationality of history-making decisions.

Nevertheless, LI and neofunctionalism are complementary more than they are competitive. Intergovernmentalism is primarily a theory that explains the *process* of bargaining between member states. Neofunctionalism is a theory of how the *context* of EU decision-making evolves. This view is echoed by Pierson, who qualifies LI's image of near-total member state control yet concedes the "strong institutional position" of national actors. Central to Pierson's account are "lags between decisions and long-term consequences." History-making decisions are often "leaps in the dark" with consequences that cannot be foreseen with clarity. The result is "control gaps": national governments lose control over a process created originally to strengthen them, and the EU evolves according to its own integrative logic. An important source of this logic is the ECJ, which is more autonomous than most national courts and all other EU institutions. Another source is the "dense networks of experts" which limit the range of future institutional or policy choices by controlling access to the EU's agenda in specific sectors. The result, paradoxically, is "highly fragmented but increasingly integrated polity."

Intergovernmentalists argue that what is most important about the super-systemic level is that it *exists*: member states can always revise the treaties if they are unhappy with the "increasingly integrated policy" they have created. The ECJ cannot stop them. Yet neo-functionalist logic is visible in many history-making decisions. It may be true to claim that states retain the "ultimate right to decide" in EU governance, but the range of choice open to EU member states is constrained, in important ways, by the logic of the project they themselves have created.

## ■ SETTING POLICY: THE SYSTEMIC LEVEL

Most EU decisions—certainly all important ones—are preceded by bargaining. The character of much of the bargaining is intergovernmental, with member states mobilizing their ministers, officials and even their nationals in EU institutions to press forward their national preferences. Yet "the fact that many (or most) EU decisions look like interstate bargains . . . tells us nothing about how the institutional context shapes preferences and EU decision-making." Even theorists who use "rational choice" models insist that "one can understand the legislative process in Europe only through detailed institutional analysis of the interactions among the Council, the Commission and the EP, and in particular the sequencing of decisions."

"Policy-setting" decisions are taken at the end of the EU's legislative process, or when the EU arrives at a "policy *decision* point." When the EU legislates, it operates as a political system in which powers are shared between institutions (as opposed to an international organization in which power is monopolized by states). Most EU policies are "set" when the terms of a directive are agreed according to the "Community method" of decision-making: the Commission proposes, the Council disposes, the EP amends, and so on. Yet policy is "set" in a variety of ways and it occurs whenever the Union chooses between alternative courses of action in policy sectors where it has legal competence or the will to act. Few policies are set without a good measure of interinstitutional sparring.

A valuable approach for understanding the policy effects of such institutional politics is the so-called "new institutionalism" (NI) [Chapter 23]. Its basic lesson is that institutions *matter*: they are the source of much political behavior and not impartial "black boxes" which simply transform preferences into policies. Like the EU itself, the NI crosses the boundary between international relations and comparative politics: informing the analysis of IR scholars concerned with interdependence and institutionalized cooperation, while also occupying a "central place in comparative political science."

The NI offers powerful diagnostic tools for understanding systemic level EU decision-making. Not only does it shed light on bitterly fought battles for institutional advantage between the Council, EP and Commission. It also reminds us that EU institutions do *not* give equal access to all that wish to influence the policy process. Above all, a new institutionalist analysis of the EU reveals that the Union's common institutions are often more than mere arbiters in the decision-making process, and have become key players in their own right.

What makes the new institutionalism new? Primarily, it is its concern with factors *beyond* the formal roles or legal powers of executives, parliaments, and so on, and its focus on values, norms and informal conventions that govern exchanges between actors. The NI differentiates between "institutions" and "organizations": institutions are "rules" of the game and organizations are "the players." The NI thus highlights how "players" become socialized to the rules of the game in EU decision-making, and its ethos of bargaining towards consensus. For example, member states fight pitched battles to place their own nationals in key posts in the Commission and EP, but Bellier's fascinating anthropological research suggests that most of the EU's officials "go native" and adopt a truly supranational European identity.

When the NI has been applied to national politics, it has shed most light on federal systems. As in federal systems, the EU is the scene of dilemmas associated with shared decision-making. It is thus prone to "least common denominator" solutions, which offend few policy stakeholders or actors with an interest in EU decisions, but may not solve policy problems very effectively. In the EU, as in the United States (USA) or Germany, it remains difficult to form minimum winning coalitions for most policy proposals because decisions are easily blocked and veto points are so plentiful. Regardless of whether QMV applies, informal institutional norms in the Council often dictate that unanimity—or something close to it—is needed for the setting of any important policy. Even when QMV is strictly applied, a relatively small group of states can block decisions. Scharpf argues that the EU combines *de facto* unanimous decision rules, diffused power and a "bargaining" style of decision-making which seeks, above all, a "deal" as opposed to the solution to a problem. The result is a "joint decision trap" which renders the EU a relatively ineffective system of governance. According to this view, the Union is usually incapable of true policy innovation.

Perhaps above all, the NI helps explain why the setting of precedents is so fiercely contested in the EU. At the heart of most NI analyses is the concept of "*path dependency*," or the notion that "once an historical choice is made, it both precludes and facilitates others. Political change follows a branching model. Once a particular fork is chosen, it is very difficult to get back on the rejected path." Path dependency may be viewed as a product of the joint decision trap: the need for agreement between so many different decision-makers—including many beyond Brussels—does not only mean that it is achingly difficult to "set" policy in the first place. It becomes even harder to *change* policy, even when it outlives its usefulness. The "sunk costs" of agreeing a policy in the first place are often considerable, leading to situations where EU policies become analogous to the QWERTY system of organizing letters on a computer keyboard: one solution may prevail over others even though it proves to be far less efficient than discarded alternatives would have been.

Unanimity is almost always required at the super-systemic level for any major institutional change, yet the EU continues to trundle along, even when it appears in danger of falling apart, because unanimity is also needed for decisions which *roll back* integration. More generally, politically institutions are "sticky" and tend to change more slowly than governments or the preferences of policy-makers. Thus institutions become a force for continuity more than change.

In particular, institutionalized arrangements differ markedly between EU policy sectors. Reforms designed to rationalize decision-making or make it simpler and more transparent are difficult to agree on unanimously. Path dependency leads to an "organic accretion" of decision-making procedures: new ones are fastened onto old ones in the same way that lichens attach themselves first to a tree, then to other lichens, adding layer upon layer, overlapping but never shedding. In the EU, the result is enormous procedural differentiation, with the number of different, formal decision-making procedures increasing steadily (the Amsterdam Treaty offered a modest "shedding"). After the Maastricht Treaty, the EU had more than 23 distinct procedures for making binding decisions.

In a system marked less by competition between different political philosophies than by competition between institutions, the new institutionalism highlights how apparently consensual policy-making does not preclude clandestine attempts to shift boundary and decision rules: "the triangular relationship between the Commission, Council and Parliament is a dynamic . . . or unstable one in which the institutions frequently use all political and legal means available to increase their impact on the decision-making process or defend their prerogatives." Attempts to "shift" decision rules are abetted by the proliferation of so many different decision rules.

In particular, the EU's abundance of decision-making procedures acts to empower the Court of Justice. The ECJ must frequently adjudicate in interinstitutional disputes about which procedure should apply to a particular legislative initiative. Most ECJ decisions are relatively undramatic, concerning the application of competition policy or the implementation of directives at the national level. Yet the Court is still a powerful institutional actor at the systemic level, particularly because it must rule on disputes about procedure and act as a "court of appeal" for interests which cannot get a hearing from other institutions.

At the same time, the discretion of national governments and courts in applying Community law is wide. Rates of compliance with EU rules are patchy and uneven between member states. Governments have shown great creative imagination in resisting or subverting the Court's rulings. The ECJ lacks any police force or army to enforce its will and must earn its authority by reputation. Thus new institutionalism stresses both the capacity of the Court to influence Union policy and its inability to enforce its decisions directly. One important reason why nearly everything is negotiable in EU decision-making is that the "EU legal system is not based on a solid institutional foundation."

The new institutionalism is more a set of assumptions, a "method for deriving analytical insights," than a proper theory, which can describe, explain and predict the outcomes of systemic decision-making. The NI's virtues are clear, yet even its staunchest advocates concede that "the EU is not yet a state with a stable institutional system, so the development of a convincing grand-theoretical explanation of its governance seems to be highly unlikely." The EU remains a relatively young and experimental system of governance. As such, "informal political processes have to bear rather more weight than in a long-established polity, with entrenched rules and engrained practices." Yet, if we treat informal processes (particularly at the sub-systemic level) as "institutions," surely we are stretching the concept of institutions to its breaking point.

## ■ SHAPING POLICY: THE SUB-SYSTEMIC LEVEL

Policy shaping decisions do not "decide" EU policy. Rather, they determine policy details or what policy options will be considered "by ruling some policy alternatives as permissible or impermissible." Article 211 of the treaties explicitly mandates that the Commission should "participate in the *shaping* of measures taken by the Council and the European Parliament." Most "policy-shaping" decisions are taken early in the policy process when policies are being formulated and, in fact, before the EU's formal legislative process even begins. These early stages are when most lobbying activity occurs. Once political agreement begins to emerge at the systemic level even an informal deal "often tends to be rather inflexible. Modifying it in any way may mean starting the bargaining process all over again, as once part of it has been unstitched the whole garment starts to unravel."

In particular, the margins for changing the content of EU legislation seem to shrink quite quickly after the Commission has tabled a proposal. After that point, according to a senior Commission official, "scope for changing the proposal exists only at the margins, involving about 20 percent of the total proposal." This allegation may seem to overstate the powers of the Commission, but it is indicative more of *when* crucial decisions are taken in the EU's policy process than who controls decision-making.

When policies are formulated, important decisions may emerge from consultations between the Commission and policy stakeholders in formal, purpose-built forums created to facilitate exchanges of ideas and agendas. "However, at least as pertinent"—usually more so—"are the informally constituted and flexible networks that are so much present." The EU is a "hothouse" for relatively informal policy networks for four basic reasons. First, despite recent attempts to formalize consultation between the Commission and policy stakeholders, the EU continues to lack formal institutions which can adequately "manag[e] the policy dialogue." The EU depends fundamentally on its ability to forge consensus between a wide variety of decision-makers before policies may be "set." It thus requires extensive, informal, "pre-legislative" bargaining over the shape of most proposals before they have any chance of being accepted.

Second, rules of access to EU decision-making are usually unclear. For Wallace, this ambiguity explains why policy networks, "currently amongst the most attractive and rewarding areas of study, have become so important." Informal networking allows the participation of a far larger number and wider range of different stakeholders than could ever be accommodated in formal consultative mechanisms.

Third, both the EU's multi-level character and policy remit encourage a sort of governing by co-ordination. Much EU legislation is decided in the form of directives, which set out a general set of objectives while leaving most details as to how they might be achieved to member states themselves. To a considerable extent, the precise content of directives is determined later at a non-political level by various types of officials, together with interested interest groups and lobbyists, in response to broad policy injunctions. Governments thus have incentives to engage with private actors, who "have to be drawn into the policy networks because they provide necessary expertise and because effective implementation depends on their support."

Fourth, and finally, the EU attracts actors interested in policy change, but it is a consensual system in which opposition is appeased or minimized. Policy networks (in environmental policy) may promote change by facilitating bargaining over the terms and extent of new EU measures. Alternatively, some (in agriculture or external trade policy) consolidate the veto power of vested interests. Above all, policy networks facilitate the detailed bargaining which must precede attempts to satisfy different needs in different member states with the same policy.

Most policy networks provide stability, and often outlast political changes such as the election of new governments. In this context, most interest groups in Europe continue to focus the bulk of their lobbying at the national level, where most of the resources are held that groups want or need. Relationships between interest groups and national administrations are usually more long-standing and routinized than is the case at the EU level. The result is that the national level is more likely to breed stable, tightly integrated networks, or "policy communities," which strictly control access to the policy agenda.

Compared to most national systems of government, the Union seems a relatively open market for influence and access. Such "open competition for scarce resources leads to shifting coalitions . . . [and] few 'frozen' cleavages that lead to permanent coalitions." It is plausible to suggest that most EU policy networks remain relatively unstable "issue networks," or the polar opposites of "policy communities." The memberships of issue networks are not drawn from a stable "community" but rather are fluid and defined by specific issues that arise on the EU's agenda. Compared to their national equivalents, EU policy networks appear to be more complex, crowded and unstable.

Yet actors at the EU level are often dependent on each other and on the functional success of the EU as a successful manager of interdependence. The EU is more a technocracy than a democracy, in that "political hegemony cannot be established by fighting ideological battles in the political market-place" and power is usually a function of resources which help solve problems: "expert knowledge, political insight, and bargaining experience." Thus policy networks spring up around specific EU policy sectors, marshalling technocratic expertise and seeking to shape policy options which are likely to be endorsed by political decision-makers at the systemic level. The Commission usually plays the role of facilitator and "ring-leader": "There are always ministries, groups, and factions in each country which share to some degree the policy goals of the Commission and whose positions are strengthened by virtue of an alliance with it." However, the bargaining mode within policy networks is resource exchange between mutually dependent actors (see Table 25.1) and thus the Commission must negotiate a policy agenda with its "clients."

Given the highly technical nature of EU governance, we can expect policy networks to be dominated by "epistemic communities," or "network[s] of professionals with recognized expertise and competence in a particular domain" who define problems, identify compromises and supply "expert" arguments to justify political choices. Nonetheless, the EU also offers opportunities for political agency, or purposive action in pursuit of political goals. Policy networks may provide access to politically minded "advocacy coalitions" of elected and bureaucratic officials, interest group leaders, journalists and other actors which wish to "steer" the EU's policy agenda. Advocacy coalitions are groups of actors with "core policy beliefs," who are likely to be capable of effective political action when their members interact repeatedly, exchange information easily and unite in support of policies which will treat them fairly, if not all equally. Successful advocacy coalitions may shift the EU's policy agenda from the "bottom-up," as appeared to occur when member states accepted (first) the need for the Social Charter and then the Maastricht Treaty's social protocol to "flank" the 1992 project with EU social policies. Advocacy coalitions are not the same as epistemic communities: the former have political objectives while the latter tend to be motivated more by technocratic considerations. But both types of coalition compete for control of the EU's agenda, and thus seek to "penetrate" policy networks that act as the sentinels of the agenda in specific sectors.

Institutional reforms often provide new openings for advocacy coalitions. The cooperation procedure—introduced by the Single European Act—not only induced considerable internal reform of the Commission (the creation of a new unit in its Secretariat-General for relations with the EP), it also offered MEPs [Members of the European Parliament] "membership cards" to selected policy networks. After the Maastricht Treaty went a step further and mandated "co-decision," the Commission was forced to engage the EP's relevant committees early in the policy process in order to get its legislation accepted, sometimes even helping MEPs to draft mutually acceptable amendments to proposed legislation.

The EP became a far more powerful player in some sectors than in others, in part because co-decision applied to some (the internal market) but not all (agricultural policy). As such, policy network analysis helps us come to grips with how "sectorized" EU decision-making is: there are quite separate and different types of policy networks for, say, environmental and cohesion policy despite overlaps between their memberships.

Because rival sectoral networks compete to control the EU's policy agenda, networks need an effective "sherpa": an agent who can ensure that the sectoral actors have a guardian when an initiative reaches the systemic level of decision-making. The Commissioner with responsibility for a given portfolio is the most obvious candidate. Policy networks are empowered if "their" Commissioner commands the trust of his/her colleagues on the college, as well as national ambassadors and ministers who ultimately set policy. When policy networks lack an effective sherpa, the interests of their members can be trounced by those of competing networks: for example, when a proposed consumer policy measure has implications for agricultural producers.

In this climate, policy networks that show solidarity and can bargain their way to internal consensus enjoy powerful advantages. The Commission thus "goes to extraordinary lengths to establish constituencies of Euro-groups around each Directorate-General—practically 'sponsoring' their formation." The number of "Euro-groups" featuring direct memberships (as opposed to being federations of national groups) that are officially recognized by the Commission has grown significantly. Relatively integrated Euro-groups in pharmaceuticals, information technology and automobiles have emerged as a result of the co-existence of three factors: the strong international orientation of the industries, the clear remit of the EU in these sectors and the domination of the industries by a relatively small number of firms. Relatively tightly knit policy communities exist in all of these sectors.

It is worth recalling that the early neo-functionalists assigned to such interest groups a powerful role as an "engine" of integration. However, the representatives of Euro-groups in Brussels rarely seem to act with much autonomy. In fact, "Real power has shifted away from the representative bodies in Brussels to . . . national member organizations" and many Euro-groups are not much more than the sum of their parts. The broad aggregation of interests in EU decision-making is difficult and rare.

Aspinwall even sees an "advocacy void" arising from lack of strong transnational pressure groups (or EU-wide political parties). The number of interest groups represented in Brussels increased exponentially from around 200 in 1960 to something like 2200 by the mid-1990s. Yet the clear majority remained national or sub-national (as opposed to transnational) in orientation. By the late 1990s, there were about 700 truly transnational groups in Brussels, but—for the sake of comparison—around 1900 organized groups in Denmark. There were something like 23,000 organizations organized nationally in the USA in the non-profit sector alone.

Certainly, Brussels was crawling with more than 10,000 lobbyists by 1990, but most represented single companies or were their organization's only representative (besides secretarial personnel) in Brussels. The estimate that the Commission brought together roughly 30,000 participants annually in its organized meetings seemed slightly less like Euro-pluralism given that more than 80 percent were national civil servants. In fact, recent literature on EU interest representation often concludes that, contrary to what might be expected, multi-level decision-making appears to advantage state actors over private actors compared to centralized, hierarchical decision-making. The effective separation of powers between levels of EU governance has the Madisonian effect of curbing the power of private "factions," which face enormous difficulties in "capturing" all levels and in all sectors. One upshot is that the EU may "strengthen the state" even at the deepest reaches of the sub-systemic level.

Consistent with this thesis is the notion that the EU is a "mobilizer of bias" not only in favor of states, but also in favor of private interests that are most powerful at the state level: producers are advantaged more than consumers by the EU's existence and neo-liberal ethos. Narrow interests are privileged more than diffuse "promotional" or "cause" groups such as women's rights or environmental groups. Traditionally, the EU has tended to validate Olson's theory "that successful collective action is more likely in settings where small groups will be strongly motivated to act." In contrast, "broadly-based interest organizations find it difficult to cope with the EU, because they cannot be as closely linked to issue-specific networks as sectoral interest groups."

Yet, the EU is a system in flux. Recent research suggests that the EU does not always empower the already powerful, particularly as it begins to legislate on broader, "non-economic" questions (social policy, environmental protection, and so on). If "policy determines politics" then it makes sense that more and more diffuse interests have managed to shape decision-making over time. Usually, they have formed alliances with the Commission (environmental groups) and EP (consumer groups), or learned to use the ECJ (women's rights groups). Because the EU's institutions instinctively aim for pan-European solutions to policy problems, broadly based groups learn quickly that they enjoy more influence if they can present themselves as transnational in scope and "pro-European" in ideology.

On balance, however, Euro-representation remains underdeveloped. The Brussels lobbying environment has become far more "crowded," but relative to the Union's enormous scale, a remarkably small number of actors may "capture" the EU's policy agenda. Remarkably few actors can sometimes shape (if not "make") policies for the many in a polity of 370 million EU citizens, which is set to become significantly larger in the early 21st century.

Given these contingencies, policy network analysis may be an "inefficient research strategy" for making sense of EU decision-making. It is often more "efficient," sometimes even plausible, to link policy outcomes to a real or imagined set of national preferences, and then a process of intergovernmental bargaining. Yet we recall Heclo's warning when he first introduced the notion of "issue networks": "Looking for the few who are powerful, we tend to overlook the many whose webs of influence provoke and guide the exercise of power." These "webs of influence" may be opaque and difficult to study, but they clearly exist and shape EU policy in crucial ways.

## ■ CONCLUSION

We have ranged broadly across the existing literature in search of concepts and theory that can help us make sense of EU decision-making. It is clear that, whenever the EU decides, it is after a process of bargaining. As a consequence, we must be sensitive to the bargaining mode that characterized decision-making at different levels of analysis (see Table 25.1). Bargaining on the terms of most "history-making" decisions seems primarily intergovernmental. Yet, neofunctionalism helps explain why and how the context of European integration evolved to the point where such bargaining resulted in the relaunch of European integration in the 1980s or was constrained by the ECJ and the process of legal integration.

When the EU sets policy, bargaining is often as much between institutions—the Commission, Council and EP—as between governments. Despite the EU's intergovernmental backbone, institutional objectives are far more important in the Union's policy process than in most other systems of government. The EU's institutions are often less concerned with substantive policy objectives than with gaining institutional ground.

Finally, most EU policy outcomes are the ultimate products of overtly political choices taken by ministers or MEPs, but choices are shaped in crucial ways by decisions taken in sub-systemic policy networks. Actors who want to penetrate policy networks must have valued resources that they are willing to exchange in pursuit of their goals. Bargaining within EU policy networks is mostly informal, but "sectoral networks, like states, operate within institutionalized rules that both enable and constrain action." Put another way, "Networks will only function if they are embedded in overarching institutions, in a common understanding of the game they are in." Even if nearly everything is negotiable in EU decision-making, formal institutions, decision rules and accepted norms are crucial in determining how the game is played. . . .

# 26 The Governance Approach to European Integration

MARKUS JACHTENFUCHS

*Hooghe and Marks (Chapter 24) and Peterson and Bomberg (Chapter 25) have introduced us to the governance approach to European Union (EU) politics. The "approach" is not a theory, but a perspective that opens the EU to a wide variety of theories of politics. Markus Jachtenfuchs (International University Bremen) in this summary essay attempts to make sense of the governance approach and its implications for the study of the EU.*

*Jachtenfuchs draws a distinction between classical theories of integration and the governance approach, arguing that the former attempts to explain the EU (the EU is the dependent variable) while the latter uses the EU to explain political phenomena (the EU is the independent variable). Thus, while neofunctionalism and intergovernmentalism attempt to identify the causes of European integration, the governance approach explores the ways the EU influences domestic "policies and politics" (Europeanization), explains the rise of the EU as a "regulatory state," and examines the intertwining of institutions and levels of government through network analysis.*

*While Jachtenfuchs is generally positive about the "achievements" of the governance approach, including its openness to other sub-disciplines of political science, he is also aware of its weaknesses. In particular he worries that the approach fails to take adequate account of "political power and rule," that it proliferates case studies, and that—most important—it has no clear theoretical focus. These "shortcomings," however, represent the maturation of the EU and EU scholarship. In Jachtenfuchs's view, a theory of European integration "is neither feasible nor desirable"; its time is past. Instead of*

---

Used with permission from *Journal of Common Market Studies* 39(2)(2001): 245–264. Notes omitted. 

*looking for a theory to explain the EU, scholars should see the EU as "a unique laboratory for enhancing our understanding of politics in the twenty-first century"—and use it appropriately.*

## ▪ INTRODUCTION

In the last decade, the study of European integration has definitely come through the "dark ages" of the 1970s and early 1980s, a term that seems to be justified more with reference to the general mood prevailing at the time but which does not show up in time series of macro-quantitative data on the EU's development. In any case, since that period the quantity of scholarly work has increased considerably, theoretical issues rank high on the agenda of the sub-field and a number of substantive discoveries have been made. Still, the field is in rapid development and has a far from consolidated status with established theories, methods and a broadly consensual corpus of general knowledge and propositions. This article attempts to give an overview of the governance approach that has played an important role in the vitalization of European integration studies. Although it does not seek to discuss the concept of governance itself, governance can be understood as the intentional regulation of social relationships and the underlying conflicts by reliable and durable means and institutions instead of the direct use of power and violence. An even more straightforward definition of governance is to regard it as the ability to make collectively binding decisions, although in this case the definition of governance comes close to that of politics. The article is deliberately one-sided in that it looks only at the efficiency side of governance and for reasons of space entirely excludes the responsibility side, i.e. the question of democratic and legitimate governance. The argument proceeds in three steps. The first part traces the roots of this approach on the basis of sociology of knowledge perspective, the second presents a more general overview and synthesis of the approach, and the third contains a critical evaluation and an outlook for the future.

## ▪ FROM POLITY-MAKING TO GOVERNANCE

### □ *Conceptual Roots*

The early phase of European integration studies was characterized by the search to understand the nature of the Euro-polity and the causes of its development. In this respect, the 1960s saw a lively debate between two theoretical orientations, neofunctionalism and intergovernmentalism. Whereas neofunctionalism saw the main dynamics of European integration in a broad social process of modernization, the rise of technocracy and what we today would call "globalization," intergovernmentalism while not denying the importance of these factors insisted that nation-states would not adapt smoothly to these social changes but that their reactions were shaped first and foremost by the competitive dynamics of the anarchical international system.

After its leading scholar [Haas] had declared its "obsolescence," regional integration theory vanished from scientific discussion. Students of regional integration directed their attention to other fields. The fundamental ideas of neofunctionalism proved to be extremely fruitful for other fields of research, symbolized by figures such as Joseph Nye for interdependence theory, John Gerard Ruggie for regime theory or Philippe Schmitter for neocorporatism. Others, such as Leon Lindberg, left the international realm and directed their attention towards domestic issues, such as the governance of the American economy or value change in western societies.

Hence, European integration studies appeared moribund in the mid-1970s. The emerging polity that had been so exciting both politically and scientifically seemed to have lost its momentum and its transformative power in the European state system. The standard rules of international relations seemed to apply and govern the relations between states in the European Union (EU) as well as elsewhere in the world. From this perspective, European integration was no more than a sub-field of the study of international relations and international organization.

However, research on European integration declined only if seen from the perspective of international relations theory. Scholars who were not interested in the possibility of a fundamental transformation of the international system but simply fascinated by the actual working of the new European institutions increasingly dominated the field. A major work from this perspective is *Policy-Making in the European Community* [by Helen Wallace and William Wallace], now in the fourth edition.

. . .

The 1970s and the 1980s should not easily be dismissed as a lost era in the study of European integration just because grand theories in international relations had reached a dead end, and emphasis had moved to other issues. These two decades were full of empirical discoveries and yielded theoretical insights upon which present scholarship still builds. What may explain the bad reputation of this phase is its lack of theoretical focus—but not necessarily of theoretical interest. It did not have a common question that served as a focal point for competing theories and gave rise to substantive debates. Scholarship became fragmented and remained unconcerned with "big questions."

At the same time, normalization gained ground. Studies of party systems, electoral behavior or policy-making that are part of the established normal science of the study of domestic political systems were increasingly carried out with reference to the European Union. The same questions were asked that were asked elsewhere without ever turning to the fundamental issue of whether the basic categories of the sub-discipline of international relations—the nation-state and the anarchical international system—were still in place.

This started to change in the early 1990s. The internal market programme, launched in 1985, had given new political impetus to the stagnating integration process. This had two effects. On the one hand, it served as a stimulus for the question of classical integration theory and a renewed controversy surrounding the old issue of how the development of the Euro-polity could be explained.

On the other hand, a different question gained ground. As the Euro-polity grew more and more important, it became more interesting for researchers who were not genuinely interested in the European integration process as such, but had very different specializations such as comparative politics or policy analysis. In the latter field in particular, the development of the European Union seemed to abolish the conditions for an established division of labor within political science according to which students of domestic and comparative politics, on the one hand, and students of international relations on the other, dealt with rigidly separated fields of inquiry. Whereas the first had to do with matters within one or more states, the latter were concerned with what happened between states and remained largely unconcerned with domestic affairs.

True, there had been pioneering attempts to bridge the gap between the two camps of political science, raising questions about the impact of the international system on economic policy-making in different states. On the whole, however, they remained in a minority.

This was possible because, despite a growing literature on international interdependence, the assumption was that the external and internal relations of states were neatly separated. In other words, the idea that states were internally and externally sovereign remained at least a useful "as if" assumption on the basis of which a large body of substantive research could be produced. In the European Union after 1985, this assumption could no longer be upheld. The integration process blurred the distinction between domestic politics and international relations, and brought into question the assumption of the internally and externally sovereign nation-state. In the fast-growing literature on the impact of the European Union on domestic affairs of its member states, three major lines of thought emerged. These dealt with the Europeanization of the policies and politics, the rise of regulatory policy-making, and the emergence of a new mode of governance. Whereas the first two developed more or less simultaneously, the third joined in later.

At first sight, these lines of thought and the individual works that are part of them appear to deal with a highly diverging range of issues. They share, however, a common preoccupation which is entirely different from classic integration theory. Instead of asking how and why the Euro-polity came into existence, they take it as a given, and look at the impact of the Euro-polity on national and European policies and politics. To put it differently: in classic integration theory, the Euro-polity is the dependent variable, whereas in the governance literature it is the independent one.

## □ *Europeanization*

The literature on the Europeanization of policies and politics started from the empirical observation that by no stretch of analytical imagination could political processes and policy-making in an EU member state now be adequately understood without taking into account the influence of the EU. From this starting point, a number of paths of inquiry developed that are not mutually exclusive and indeed are partly overlapping.

Two interrelated major concerns are characteristic of this type of literature. The first is an attempt to arrive at a broad empirical assessment of the degree of Europeanization of public policy across time and sectors. In this context, Europeanization is understood as the degree to which public policies are carried out either by the member state alone, jointly by member state and EU, or exclusively by the European Union. Several of these assessments are based on a scale originally developed by Lindberg and Scheingold. This scale ranges from 1 (exclusive domain of member state) to 5 (exclusive Union competence). The overall impression from this literature is, first, that over time and after an initial push of Europeanization most policy fields remain stuck somewhere between 3 and 4. Only in very few areas such as foreign trade policy has the EU achieved exclusive competence (i.e. a value of 5 on the Lindberg-Scheingold scale). This is not an indicator of the partial failure of integration, but on the contrary of its maturation. An average approximating a value of 5 would amount to a centralist state which is neither likely nor desirable. The present level is by and large comparable to that observed in federal systems but with a different distribution of individual scores, most notably in the field of foreign and security policy.

Second, variation between policy sectors is still huge. Hence, there is no uniform trend towards an ever-increasing Europeanization of policy-making as could be inferred from early neofunctionalist theorizing. Instead, we find joint policy-making in most fields with no signs of this being only a transitory stage towards complete Europeanization. On the contrary, joint policy-making seems to be both a general and a fairly stable pattern.

The second concern was with the substance of policies. Although this was often not set out explicitly, this type of literature had a distinct normative concern, namely the fear that national systems of regulation that were perceived as guaranteeing high standards of environmental, social or consumer protection or other valuable achievements were jeopardized by European integration. The reason for this assumption was the functioning of the EU's decision-making process. As most of the decisions were (and still are) taken by unanimity either *de jure* or *de facto,* it was reasonable to assume that outcomes reflected the lowest common denominator or the position of the least advanced member state. This becomes problematic in particular if seen in conjunction with the observation above. If an increasing number of policies are at least partly governed by the EU in addition to the member state *and* EU decisions are taken at the lowest common denominator level, it follows that in high-standard countries an increasing number of policies are in danger of harmonization towards the bottom.

Theoretical arguments and empirical observation lead to a complex picture with no clear tendency yet visible. Empirical studies have shown that the assumption of a *general* trend of harmonization towards the bottom is untenable. In the first place, the Europeanization of policy-making does not even lead to increasing uniformity, as one might perhaps expect. On the contrary, European policies present themselves as a "patchwork," a complex mixture of different policy-making styles, instruments and institutions. The process at work is less one of intentional and detailed harmonization but of "regulatory competition."

Second, if seen together European policies vary in terms of problem-solving capacity and effectiveness. In some fields, the EU was able to adopt policies even beyond those of the most advanced member states. At present, a number of partial theories seek to explain the observable empirical pattern of how the EU was able to escape from deadlock. They deal with negative *v.* positive integration, product *v.* process regulation, regulatory *v.* distributive policies, the availability of a credible exit option or the institutional transformation of conflicts and preferences. Even if one has no fundamental doubts about the possibility of achieving generalizable knowledge about policy processes, the available empirical evidence and the theoretical explanations to hand seem to indicate that there are no simple links between the EU's activity in a given policy area and the quality of policy outcomes.

## □ *The Rise of Regulatory Politics*

This type of research can be traced back to the work of a single author: Giandomenico Majone. Starting in the early 1990s, Majone has systematically put forward theoretical arguments and empirical evidence that the European Union is what he calls a "regulatory state." Although his theory has been perceived largely as positive, it has a number of normative consequences that are probably more important than the analytical implications. In addition, Majone's conceptualization of the EU provided a fresh look at old institutions and opened up new possibilities for comparison.

In the first place, conceiving of the EU as a regulatory institution cuts across the dichotomies of the neofunctionalism *v.* intergovernmentalism debate in classic integration theory. It leaves aside the latter's concern with the driving forces of integration and looks at policy outcomes from a specific perspective. Regarding the EU as an instance of "regulatory federalism" thus provides a solution to the intriguing $n=1$ problem of integration theory by comparing it to other (federal) regulatory systems such as the US. It also adopts the analytical perspective of the governance approach as outlined above by asking how the type of polity impacts on the policy adopted.

Majone's argument is that for a number of reasons, the EU is particularly well suited to regulatory policy-making, whereas at the same time it is ill equipped to deal with distributive or redistributive issues. The first reason is straightforward and simple; as the EU's budget is small compared to a federal state, policy-makers at the center (particularly in the European Commission) will propose regulatory policies out of their institutional self-interest in order to increase their power and influence. Regulatory policies do not require substantial financial commitment from public authorities because they put the financial burden of regulation on the addressees of regulation, i.e. mostly on private firms. Regulatory policy-making is by no means conflict-free because private actors may strongly oppose such regulation by referring to competitive pressures (as in the case of car emission standards). In general, however, the level of conflict to be expected is much lower than in the case of distributive or even redistributive policies where winners and losers are often easily visible and find themselves in a confrontational zero-sum game.

Second, the political goal of creating a European market requires a substantial degree of regulatory activity. In this view, markets are not self-constituting and self-stabilizing, but require constant regulation in order to constitute and maintain them. As a result, the Commission 1985 White Paper was by no means deregulatory in the sense of simply abolishing regulations but amounted to a massive reregulation at the European level. Again, this is no accident but is rooted in the institutional structure of the European Union. In the EU, a unified economy co-exists with a fragmented political system in which each member state has an incentive to defect from European legislation in order to obtain benefits for its own population. In this situation, an institution insulated from political pressures, such as the European Commission, is particularly well suited to implement credible commitments for market preservation.

Third, the type of policy normally required in the European market is characterized by a high degree of specialized technical knowledge (e.g. in the field of medical drugs). Here, markets are best served by an efficiency-oriented policy that is best provided by experts independent of political pressure. Behind this is the idea that only in this case may policies achieve the optimal level of collective welfare, whereas political pressure typical of democratic institutions is likely to favor particular interests. Here, the EU institutions and in particular the Commission, the Court and most notably the newly established regulatory agencies are good examples of an "independent fourth branch of government" or of "non-majoritarian institutions." In addition, the structural problems of democracy at the European level and the somewhat weak legitimacy provided by the European Parliament make the EU an ideal candidate for efficiency-oriented regulatory policies. Efficiency-oriented policies, the argument says, require at best a weak degree of democratic control because they aim at Pareto-efficient solutions that are in the interest of everyone. Redistributive policies, on the other hand, are by definition not Pareto-efficient. As they make some people, groups or states better off at the expense of others, these policies require a high degree of democratic legitimacy that cannot be provided by the EU. Hence, the EU should concentrate on (efficiency-oriented) social regulation and leave (redistributive) social policy to the member states.

By this point at the latest, the normative implications of the theory become clear. The theory of the EU as a regulatory state not only seeks to understand regulatory growth in the European Union as a function of its institutional structure. At the same time it prescribes a particular institutional model for the EU as a response to the functional requirements of transnational markets, solutions to the problems of credible commitments and structural problems of democratic legitimacy. Contrary to most of the Europeanization literature, it does not confine itself to taking stock of the multitude of patterns, structures, ideas, and processes of European policy-making, but provides a yardstick for assessing the development of the Euro-polity beyond the old dichotomies of "federal state" and "intergovernmental organization."

### □ *Network Governance*

In the policy-analytic literature of the last decade, "networks" is one of the most frequently used terms. With its emphasis on informal, loose structures that extend across and beyond hierarchies, the network concept appeared particularly well suited to grasp the essence of multi-level governance in the European Union. The network concept seemed to be the main opponent of intergovernmentalism which stressed clear hierarchies and privileged channels of access. In this respect, the network metaphor became a fruitful heuristic device for empirical analysis that considerably increased empirical knowledge about the actual working of EU policy-making at the micro-level, despite criticisms of its fuzziness.

In the first place, applying network analytic concepts to the study of the EU is another welcome attempt at seeing the EU in a comparative perspective. It appears that, on the whole, the fragmented and fluid institutional structure of the EU and the lack of a strong power center leads to an increase of channels of access and a larger variation of participants in the policy-making process as compared to governance systems in territorial states. But here, as in so many other fields of inquiry on the EU, we lack systematic and quantitative overall evidence.

A second branch of literature does not look at particular patterns of relationships between social actors in the tradition of sociometric analysis, but regards networks as a particular mode of governance between hierarchy and anarchy or markets. Benz in particular has argued that networks are characterized by loose coupling of their constituent elements. Hierarchy, on the one hand, is characterized by rigid links between constituent elements, and markets, on the other hand, by no coupling at all. As a result, networks would be particularly well suited to the highly fragmented and decentralized institutional structure of the EU. As a prediction, it follows that networks should be more characteristic for the EU than for the average member state. In addition, the prevailing mode of network governance in the EU offers an explanation as to why the EU has managed to escape the "joint-decision trap." In essence, this is possible because in network governance, negotiators have relatively flexible mandates from their constituencies, whereas in more hierarchical systems such as German federalism, their negotiating position is much more rigid due to "narrow coupling" with their constituencies.

A variant of this literature has an even broader view of network governance: it is characterized by "consociation" as the organizing principle of political relations on the one hand, and the pursuit of individual interests (as opposed to the common good) as the constitutive logic of the polity. Thus, it is not only an analytical concept but also a political ideology, a kind of micro-constitutionalism of the European Union, because it starts from the assumption developed in modern systems theory that society is constituted by a number of sub-systems which largely function according to their own autonomous logic. For efficiency as well as for normative reasons, the autonomy of these sub-systems should be respected. Hierarchical governance in such a setting is not a very promising endeavor. If one adds territorial sub-systems to this perspective, one has an exact image of the European Union. Although this approach is still at an early stage—as is the case with most of the works reviewed above—it has the great advantage that it moves away from the proliferation of case studies on microscopic policy fields which only complicate our knowledge of the EU rather than simplifying it in order to discern characteristic features.

## ■ CRITICAL EVALUATION

### □ *Achievements*

Much of the new dynamics in the study of European integration in the last decade is due to its governance orientation. This is not to deny that the question of classical integration theory (which forces and actors account for the development of the Euro-polity?) has not also seen a major development, driven notably by the controversy surrounding Andrew Moravcsik's liberal intergovernmentalist analysis of constitutional bargains [Chapter 22]. However, whereas the latter has a narrow focus, the former is much broader in orientation. This is both its strength and its weakness, as the following section claims.

The move in the analytical focus from polity development to governance has two important implications. First, it considerably broadens the field of inquiry and invites contributions from other sub-disciplines of political science, most notably from comparative politics, policy analysis and increasingly from political theory. As a result, the study of European integration diffuses into a number of sub-fields of political science with no particular interest in the EU as such. European integration has become a part of normal politics in a wide variety of issues and hence has to be taken account of by those working on these issues. With European integration becoming such a cross-cutting theme, its study hardly has any analytical core any longer. Political theory, electoral studies, interest group behavior and policy analysis all look at the EU from conceptual angles which are so different that the results are hard to communicate beyond the boundaries of the respective sub-discipline. As a result, European integration as a coherent field of study is disappearing. The old battles of the past between grand theories such as neofunctionalism and intergovernmentalism still continue, but they have lost their structuring force because they are of interest to only a small fraction of those studying the EU.

This is not a bad development. On the contrary, it is a sign of maturation and normalization, just as there is no theory of American, French or German politics and no sub-discipline for the study of one's own political system (at least in the eyes of some). It also alleviates the old $n$=1 problem that has plagued students of European integration for so long. As long as one takes into account the differences in the structure of the polity, there is no problem in comparing, say, patterns of interest intermediation or environmental policy-making in the US and the EU.

The second consequence is a certain disjuncture between American and European scholarship, with the former focusing more on classical integration theory and the latter more on the patterns and transformation of governance. This is easily explained by differing degrees of exposure to the object of inquiry. From a European perspective, the emergence of a supranational system that interferes in almost all aspects of political life is hard to deny. The consequences are also important not only for political scientists but for citizens. What from the outside may look like a rather obscure area interesting only to a handful of policy specialists (such as health and safety measures in the food sector) becomes an issue of public debate with constitutional implications if seen from inside.

To some degree, this is again a normal effect: interest in details decreases with distance from the object of study. Two points are, however, worth mentioning. First, there is no consensus as to whether health and safety measures in the food sector are a minor policy issue or a major constitutional question. Those who think it is such a question and who on the whole believe that the EU has developed into a political system with a constitution of its own are mostly located within Europe—but not all European scholars share this view. The health and safety example is one of a number of similar issues. Thus, it may seem that perhaps the most exciting and most important aspect of European integration—namely the transformation of traditional nation-states into constituent units of a new transnational political system that is not going to become a state—is largely overlooked from the outside. Second, this is not necessarily the sign of a comparative advancement of European scholars. There is also the risk of substantial parochialism.

On the whole, the governance approach to European integration has in the last three decades developed into a strong alternative to classical integration theory, both in terms of quantity and quality. The main growth period has been the 1990s because of the increasing intermingling of European and domestic affairs. Looking at governance in the European Union is not a competing approach to classical integration theory but a complement. Classical integration theory and the governance approach ask two different but complementary questions, the former on the causes and outcomes of polity development, the latter on forms, outcomes, problems and development paths of governance in the Euro-polity.

Like all dichotomies, this is a simplified image. Neofunctionalism, to take a prominent example from classical integration theory, has had a built-in feedback loop between polity development and governance: precisely because, under the conditions of internationalization and industrialization, governance by the EU was supposed to have a superior problem-solving capacity as compared to governance by the nation-states, [and] social actors were supposed to contribute to the further strengthening of the Euro-polity. Still, the basic research questions of the two branches of European integration studies are different. In the first case, the Euro-polity is the *explanandum;* in the second, it is the *explanans*.

The governance perspective considerably enlarges the perspective of looking at the EU as compared to classical integration theory with its strong international relations flavor. Simple as this may be, this is perhaps its most important effect. The fundamental concern of international relations theory is the question whether, to what degree and how international anarchy can be overcome. This is an extremely important question because it concerns the conditions for peaceful, non-violent relationships in a horizontally organized environment with no supreme authority and with no monopoly of the legitimate use of force.

Today, it is all too easily forgotten that classical integration theory began by trying to offer both a political and a scientific alternative to realism: regional integration in general and European integration in particular were seen as processes to overcome the anarchical structure of the international system, at least in limited geographical domains, and were supposed to create durable zones of peace beyond unstable balance-of-power arrangements. But this analytical perspective also has the disadvantage of elevating the question of the future of the sovereign nation-state to a fundamental issue of peace and war against which the problems of the European welfare state are just minor technical questions.

Again, this is a stark statement that does injustice to modern approaches of classical integration theory such as liberal intergovernmentalism or "multi-level governance." But the main issue remains: just because classical integration theory is engaged in a debate about the future of the sovereign state with respect to international institutions, it is less interested in a number of important questions that are at the core of the governance approach.

Most prominent in this respect is the question of the possibilities of democratic and legitimate governance beyond the nation-state (both in its analytical as well as its normative dimension) which has been neglected here because a fair treatment would require a separate paper. Second is the concern with the problem-solving capacity of national systems of governance and their transformation by Europeanization. Third is the question of political conflict as a result of the insertion of national systems of rules and regulations into a European political system.

Finally, by leaving aside the question of the future of the nation-state the governance approach is able to bridge the conceptual gap between the opposing ideal-typical worlds of the anarchical international system and hierarchical domestic systems. Both empirical research and theoretical arguments have pointed out for some time now that the idea of the modern state as externally sovereign and internally hierarchical is more an idealization of nineteenth-century political thought than a useful analytical concept for the reality of the twenty-first century. The state is increasingly faced with largely autonomous functional sub-systems and corporate actors. As a result, negotiating systems proliferate. This implies that the clear-cut distinction between the international system and domestic systems is increasingly blurred. A governance perspective has the potential to avoid a reification of this distinction by looking at the institutional forms of governance in negotiation systems.

## □ *Critique*

The governance approach, however, has a number of shortcomings. Although it considerably broadens the analytical horizon as compared to classical integration theory, it has a strong bias towards effective and efficient problem-solving and almost completely ignores questions of political power and rule. It certainly is not alone in this respect. Apart from the neo-Marxist theory of regulation (not to be confused with Majone's approach), some works of a broadly defined post-modern flavor and some individual authors, these questions are almost completely ignored in the contemporary scientific discussion on the EU. Nevertheless, a perspective that starts from the assumption that the EU has developed into a new type of political system different from traditional nation-states should not ignore these issues.

Second, the strong policy orientation has led to a proliferation of case studies. Case studies are a legitimate method of political science and they are of particular importance in the political system of the European Union where we still lack solid microanalyses about how policy-making in the European Union works concretely. There is, however, a strong tendency to replicate the fragmentation of EU policy-making in research. The tendency of policy specialists to dig deeper and deeper into their field of specialization, leaving the rest of the world out of sight, is a phenomenon not confined to EU studies. But it does appear to be even stronger in the EU than in national settings because the mere complexity of the policy processes at stake considerably increases the workload. This is not only a problem for Ph.D. students. Studies covering more than a single policy and including more than two member states are extremely rare. Here we risk increasing information without increasing knowledge.

Third, this tendency is furthered by the fact that the governance perspective offers a *problematique* but does not constitute a coherent theory. It does not even attempt to become one. This is not bad in itself as theory-driven (or worse, meta-theory-driven) debates tend to be sterile and decoupled from empirical reality. A problem-oriented approach such as the governance perspective offers the potential of innovation by recombining elements of different streams of thinking in the social sciences. To do so, it needs a clear focus. Such a single, overarching thematic focus is not visible—governance as such is too broad an issue. The only eligible candidate to my mind, governance in negotiating systems, is still a largely German enterprise with limited international resonance.

Instead, we can observe several streams of discussion that are more or less autonomous. They may be divided along the classical distinction of polity, politics and policy. The policy-oriented literature is flourishing and taking up elements of both international relations and comparative studies of policy-making. A second stream is the literature on political processes, mainly interest group and party politics, and there is a growing literature on legislative politics, particularly from a rational choice perspective. Finally, a polity-oriented perspective looks at constitutional structures and democracy. The challenge for all three discourses is to avoid an exclusive EU orientation and parochialism by adopting a comparative perspective. In the last resort, such a development would integrate the European Union as one object of inquiry among others into standard middle-range theories such as party politics, legislative behavior, democratic accountability, governmental systems and the like—functional instead of territorial organization.

In the end, there would be no theory of European integration just as there is no theory of Swedish politics. However, international relations theory would not be the only broader theory that is able to say something meaningful about the EU. Donald Puchala's famous metaphor, "Of Blind Men, Elephants and International Integration" in this perspective is not the statement of a problem but of a desirable state of affairs. The multi-faceted nature of the European Union has no particular relevance to it. A "theory of European integration" is neither feasible nor desirable. What is sometimes subsumed under this label are mostly theories of international relations applied to the European Union. The governance approach offers to integrate the European Union in a number of other theories beyond international relations. This is not a trivial exercise. But it is worth pursuing since the EU is the place where fundamental developments that are transforming the possibilities of effective and responsible governance are probably stronger than elsewhere. In this respect, the EU constitutes a unique laboratory for enhancing our understanding of politics in the twenty-first century. To realize this promise is the great challenge of the governance approach.

# 27 Social Construction and European Integration

JEFFREY T. CHECKEL

*Perhaps the most interesting development in integration theory in the late 1990s was the introduction of "constructivism" to the debate. Constructivism, like neofunctionalism and intergovernmentalism, has its roots in international relations theory. Unlike competing perspectives, however, constructivism critiques "rationalist" social science—particularly rational choice theory—as overly individualistic and materialist. Constructivists maintain that political actors—including nation-states—do not always make decisions based on calculations of material benefit. In their view, decision makers formulate their opinions and take actions in a social context—in relationship with other people. These groups operate according to certain norms of behavior; they consider some ideas more acceptable than others; and they agree on certain "facts" about the world. Constructivists, in sum, explore the ways group norms, ideas, and even cultures shape, and sometimes change, the identities and interests of political actors.*

*The European Union (EU), with its levels of government and many formal and informal institutions, provides an ideal arena for constructivist exploration. But constructivists are hardly united in their approach to the EU. Some constructivists take a radical, postmodern perspective, arguing that the EU is a linguistic construct that masks and perpetuates power relations (e.g., capital over labor; men over women) within Europe. Several of these theorists doubt that meaningful knowledge can come from traditional social scientific inquiry. Other constructivists do not reject the scientific method but*

---

Used with permission from *The Social Construction of Europe*, edited by Thomas Christiansen, Knud Erik Jørgensen, and Antje Wiener (London: Sage Publications, 2001), pp. 50–64.

*wish to bring social variables into explanations of integration. Jeffrey Checkel (University of Oslo) takes this latter approach.*

*In Checkel's brand of constructivism, institutions matter deeply. He argues, in fact, that institutions, as social formations, influence behavior profoundly by constructing, "through a process of interaction, the identities and interests of member states and groups within them." This construction process involves "learning," which he defines as a shift in the perceived interests of political actors. As a social scientist, Checkel is most concerned with understanding how learning takes place at the European level, how it influences policy, and how the new European norms influence actors at the national level. In short, Checkel wants to know how new social relations at the European level affect the perception of interests at lower levels.*

*Supranationalists, intergovernmentalists, and governance theorists have managed to unite (no small feat!) in opposition to the constructivist challenge. The new great division in the field seems to be between some form of rational choice theory that leaves little room for social, cultural, or ideological factors and constructivism, which views all of these causal variables as central. Rationalism still predominates, but constructivism has a growing number of adherents.*

## ■ INTRODUCTION

Over forty years after the European project began, it is striking how little we know about its socialization and identity-shaping effects on national agents. Indeed, prominent Europeanists are themselves deeply divided on this question, with some arguing that integration has led to a fundamental shift in actor loyalty and identity, while others claim the opposite. The basic premise of this chapter is that both schools are right: constructing European institutions is a multifaceted process, with both rationalist and sociological toolkits needed to unpack and understand it.

Put differently, much of European integration can be modeled as strategic exchange between autonomous political agents with fixed interests; at the same time, much of it cannot. Constitutive dynamics of social learning, socialization, routinization and normative diffusion, all of which address fundamental issues of agent identity and interests, are not adequately captured by strategic exchange or other models adhering to strict forms of methodological individualism. For these constitutive processes, the dominant institutionalisms in studies of integration—rational choice and historical—need to be supplemented by a more sociological understanding of institutions that stresses their interest- and identity-forming roles.

After briefly addressing definitional issues and the literature on integration, I argue that social construction, a growing literature in contemporary international relations (IR), can help students of integration to theorize and explore empirically these neglected questions of interest and identity. Specifically, the chapter shows how a social constructivist cut at institution-building explains key aspects of Europeanization, social learning and normative diffusion better than its rationalist competitors, with the practical goal being to elaborate the specific methods and data requirements for such work.

Before proceeding, three comments are in order. First, my analytic starting point is that research on integration should be problem, and not method-, driven; the goal is to encourage dialogue and bridge-building between rationalists and social constructivists. By itself, each school explains important elements of the integration process; working together, or at least side-by-side, they will more fully capture the range of institutional dynamics at work in contemporary Europe. Indeed, too many constructivists are themselves method-driven, ignoring the obvious empirical fact that much of everyday social interaction is about strategic exchange and self-interested behavior.

Second, and following on the above, the constructivism favored in this chapter belongs to what has been called its modernist branch. These scholars, who combine an ontological stance critical of methodological individualism with a loosely causal epistemology, are thus well placed, within the integration literature, "to seize the middle ground"—staking out a position between positivist and agent-centered rational choice, on the one hand, and interpretative and structure-centered approaches on the other.

Third, the chapter's central focus is theoretical and methodological, and not empirical. My concern is how one could develop and apply, in a systematic manner, constructivist insights to key puzzles in the study of integration. . . .

## ■ INSTITUTIONS AND EUROPEAN INTEGRATION

Of the many institutionalisms floating around these days in economics, political science and sociology, I need briefly to discuss three: rational choice institutionalism, historical institutionalism, and sociological institutionalism. For rational choice scholars, institutions are thin: at most, they are a constraint on the behavior of self-interested actors—be they interest groups or unitary states in IR. They are a strategic context that provides incentives or information, thus influencing the strategies that agents employ to attain given ends. In this thin conception, institutions are a structure that actors run into, go "ouch," and then recalculate how, in the presence of the structure, to achieve their interests; they are an intervening variable.

For historical institutionalists, institutions get thicker, but only in a long-term historical perspective. In the near-term here and now, they are thin—structuring the game of politics and providing incentives for instrumentally motivated actors to rethink their strategies; they are a constraint on behavior. Over the longer term, however, institutions can have deeper effects on actors as strategies, initially adopted for self-interested reasons, get locked into and institutionalized in politics. Institutions thus can be both intervening and independent variables.

Sociological institutionalists are unabashedly thick institutionalists. Not only in the distant future, but in the near term, institutions constitute actors and their interests. What exactly does it mean for institutions to constitute? It is to suggest that they can provide agents with understandings of their interests and identities. This occurs through interaction between agents and structures—mutual constitution, to IR scholars. The effects of institutions thus reach much deeper; they do not simply constrain behavior. As variables, institutions become independent—and strongly so.

In our research and theorizing about Europe, should one of these institutionalisms be favored, serving as the baseline? The answer here is "no," for ultimately this is an empirical question. No doubt, there are many situations and aspects of integration where agents operate under the means-end logic of consequences favored by rational choice and some historical institutionalists (meetings of the European Council or the hard-headed interstate bargaining that features prominently in intergovernmentalist accounts). At the same time, the less static perspective favored by sociologists reminds us that much social interaction involves dynamics of learning and socialization, where the behavior of individuals and states comes to be governed by certain logics of appropriateness (informal communication in working groups of the Council of Ministers, European-level policy networks centered on the Commission). Unfortunately, these latter logics, while equally compelling and plausible, have received little systematic theoretical attention in studies of Europeanization.

Indeed, to students of international politics well versed in the never-ending neo-realist–neo-liberal controversy, the debates over Europeanization and European integration produce an eerie feeling of *déjà vu*. On the one hand, the discussion has helped advocates of opposing approaches to sharpen their central arguments and claims; similar intellectual clarifications have occurred over the past decade in the debate between neo-realists and neo-liberals in IR.

At the same time and in a more negative sense, the debate over Europeanization, like any academic discourse, has emphasized certain methods and actors at the expense of others. To my reading, much of the discussion has been about institutions—be they encompassing governance or federal structures, historically constructed organizational and policy legacies, or, more narrowly, bodies of the European Union (EU) such as the Commission or European Council. Moreover, in most cases, the analysis is about how such institutions structure the game of politics, provide information, facilitate side payments or create incentives for agents to choose certain strategies.

Such an emphasis, however, comes at a cost. It short-changes the role that institutions can play in politics, or, more to the point, in European integration. In particular, their constitutive role, typically stressed by sociologists, is neglected. If the neo-debate in contemporary IR can be accused of neglecting fundamental issues of identity formation, much of the current discussion about European integration can be accused of bracketing this constitutive dimension of institutions. Put differently, the great majority of contemporary work on European integration views institutions, at best, as intervening variables. Missing is a thick institutional argument, derived from sociology, that demonstrates how European institutions can construct, through a process of interaction, the identities and interests of member states and groups within them.

## ■ SOCIAL CONSTRUCTION AND INTEGRATION

In this section, I develop an approach that addresses the above-noted gaps, and do so by drawing upon a growing and vibrant body of IR scholarship: social constructivism. As presently elaborated, constructivism—at least the modernist branch of concern here—is an argument about institutions, one which builds upon the insights of sociological institutionalism. It is thus well suited, in a conceptual sense, for expanding our repertoire of institutional frameworks for explaining European integration. Moreover, modernist social constructivists remind us that the study of politics or integration is not just about agents with fixed preferences who interact via strategic exchange. Rather, they seek to explain theoretically both the content of actor identities/preferences and the modes of social interaction—so evident in everyday life—where something else aside from strategic exchange is taking place.

So defined, constructivism has the potential to contribute to the study of integration in various areas. Below, I consider two: learning and socialization processes at the European level, and the soft or normative side of Europeanization at the national level. In each case, I explore what a constructivist approach entails, how it could be carried out empirically and its value added compared to existing work on integration. I also address and counter the argument that my results cannot be generalized. The section concludes by noting how a constructivist approach to integration can build upon and systematize theoretical arguments and descriptive insights advanced by a growing number of Europeanists. I also argue that the whole exercise is not one of reinventing the wheel.

### □ *Learning and Socialization*

What does it mean for an agent to learn? Social learning involves a process whereby actors, through interaction with broader institutional contexts (norms or discursive structures), acquire new interests and preferences in the absence of obvious material incentives. Put differently, agent interests and identities are shaped through interaction. Social learning thus involves a break with strict forms of methodological individualism. This type of learning needs to be distinguished, analytically, from the simple sort, where agents acquire new information, alter strategies, but then pursue given, fixed interests. Simple learning, of course, can be captured by methodological individualist/rationalist accounts.

Consider small group settings: it is intuitively obvious that there are times when agents acquire new preferences through interaction in such contexts. This is not to deny periods of strategic exchange, where self-interested actors seek to maximize utility; yet, to emphasize the latter dynamic to the near exclusion of the former is an odd distortion of social reality. Now, the perhaps appropriate response is "so what?" In an abstract sense, it readily can be appreciated that social learning takes place at certain times, but how can one conceptualize and empirically explore whether and when it occurs? Luckily, there is a growing literature in contemporary IR—by constructivists, students of epistemic communities and empirically oriented learning theorists—that performs precisely this theoretical/empirical combination. More specifically, this research suggests four hypotheses on when social learning occurs; these could be translated to empirical work conducted at the European level.

1. Social learning is more likely in groups where individuals share common professional backgrounds—for example, where all/most group members are lawyers or, say, European central bankers.
2. Social learning is more likely where the group feels itself in a crisis or is faced with clear and incontrovertible evidence of policy failure.
3. Social learning is more likely where a group meets repeatedly and there is high density of interaction among participants.
4. Social learning is more likely when a group is insulated from direct political pressure and exposure.

Clearly, these hypotheses require further elaboration. For example, can a crisis situation be specified *a priori* and not in a *post-hoc* fashion as is typically done? When is the density of interaction among group participants sufficiently high for a switch to occur from strategic exchange to interactive learning? These are difficult issues, but they are only being raised because a first round of theoretical/ empirical literature exists. Europeanists could build upon and contribute to this work—for example, by exploring and theorizing the impact, if any, of different EU voting rules (unanimity, qualified majority voting) on these group dynamics.

The deductions also point to a powerful role for communication. However, in keeping with this chapter's attempted bridging function, it is a role between that of the rationalists' cheap talk, where agents (typically) possess complete information and are (always) instrumentally motivated, and the postmodernists' discourse analyses, where agents seem oddly powerless and without motivation. Yet, this role itself requires further unpackaging: underlying my communication/learning arguments are implicit theories of persuasion and argumentation.

On the latter, students of integration can and should exploit a rich literature in social psychology, political socialization and communications research on persuasion/argumentation. At core, persuasion is a cognitive process that involves changing attitudes about cause and effect in the absence of overt coercion; put differently, it is a mechanism through which social learning may occur, thus leading to interest redefinition and identity change. The literature suggests three hypotheses about the settings where agents should be especially conducive to persuasion:

1. When they are in a novel and uncertain environment and thus cognitively motivated to analyze new information;

2. When the persuader is an authoritative member of the in-group to which the persuader belongs or wants to belong; and
3. When the agent has few prior, ingrained beliefs that are inconsistent with the persuader's message.

While these deductions partly overlap with the first set, further work is still needed—for example, how to operationalize "uncertain environments" and integrate political context. On the latter, my strong hunch is that persuasion will be more likely in less politicized and more insulated settings. All the same, both sets of hypotheses do elaborate scope conditions (when, under what conditions persuasion and learning/socialization are likely), which is precisely the promising middle-range theoretical ground that still awaits exploitation by both constructivists and students of European integration.

What are the data requirements for research based on the above hypotheses? Essentially, you need to read things and talk with people. The latter requires structured interviews with group participants; the interviews should all employ a similar protocol, asking questions that tap both individual preferences and motivations, as well as group dynamics. The former, ideally, requires access to informal minutes of meetings or, second best, the diaries or memoirs of participants. As a check on these first two data streams, one can search for local media/TV interviews with group participants. This method of triangulation is fairly standard in qualitative research; it both reduces reliance on any one data source (interviewees, after all, may often dissimulate) and increases confidence in the overall validity of your inferences.

. . .

## □ *Socialization/Diffusion Pathways*

Constructivists view norms as shared, collective understandings that make behavioral claims on actors. When thinking about norms in the EU context, two issues must be addressed: 1) through what process are they constructed at the European level; and 2) how do such norms, once they reach the national level, interact with and socialize agents? Now, the distinction between European and national levels is false, as multiple feedback loops cut across them; at the same time, the dichotomy can be justified analytically as it helps one to unpack and think through different stages in the process of European norm construction. In what follows, I am less interested in formal legal norms developed and promulgated, for example, by the European Court of Justice; a growing body of literature in both law and political science already addresses such understandings and their impact. Rather, the constructivist value added comes from its focus on the less formalized, but pervasive social norms that are always a part of social interaction.

On the first issue—the process of norm development—constructivists have theorized and provided empirical evidence for the importance of three dynamics. First, individual agency is central: well-placed individuals with entrepreneurial skills can often turn their individual beliefs into broader, shared understandings. The importance of this particular factor has been documented in case studies covering nearly a one-hundred year period and a multitude of international organizations and other transnational movements. In the literature, these individuals are typically referred to as moral entrepreneurs; in the language of my earlier discussion, they are the agents actively seeking to persuade others.

Second, such entrepreneurs are especially successful in turning individually held ideas into broader normative beliefs when so-called policy windows are open. This means that the larger group, in which the entrepreneur operates, faces a puzzle/problem that has no clear answer, or is new and unknown. In this situation, fixed preferences often break down as agents engage in cognitive information searches. While the policy window concept was first elaborated by public policy (agenda-setting) and organizational theorists (garbage can models), it was only more recently that constructivists applied its insights in the international realm to explain norm formation.

Third, processes of social learning and socialization (see the previous section) are crucial for furthering the norm creation process first begun by individual agents exploiting open policy windows. The basic point is that individual agency is insufficient to create durable social norms. A brief example clarifies the point. In the mid-1980s, several close advisers to Soviet leader Gorbachev played the part of entrepreneurs seeking to advance new ideas about international politics. In the near term, such individually held beliefs, which were influential in shaping Gorbachev's own preferences, were decisive in bringing the Cold War to a dramatic, peaceful and unexpected end. Yet, once the [Soviet Union] collapsed and Gorbachev was swept from power, these ideas largely vanished, as many analysts of Russian foreign behavior have noted. Put differently, absent social learning among a larger group of actors—that is, the development of norms—the particular ideas held by specific agents had no real staying power.

When and if new European norms emerge, one must still theorize about the mechanisms through which they diffuse to particular national settings and (perhaps) socialize agents. Here, constructivists have identified two dominant diffusion pathways: societal mobilization and social learning. In the first case, non-state actors and policy networks are united in their support for norms; they then mobilize and coerce decision-makers to change state policy. Norms are not necessarily internalized by the elites. The activities of Greenpeace or any number of European non-governmental organizations exemplify this political pressure mechanism.

The second diffusion mechanism identified by constructivists is social learning, where agents—typically elite decision-makers—adopt prescriptions embodied in norms; they then become internalized and constitute a set of shared intersubjective understandings that make behavioral claims. This process is based on notions of complex learning drawn from cognitive and social psychology, where individuals, when exposed to the prescriptions embodied in norms, adopt new interests.

. . .

## ■ CONCLUSIONS

My arguments throughout this chapter were based on an obvious but too often neglected truism about our social world: the most interesting puzzles lie at the nexus where structure and agency intersect. The real action, theoretically and empirically, is where norms, discourses, language and material capabilities interact with motivation, social learning and preferences—be it in international or European regional politics. Research traditions such as rational choice, postmodernism and, more recently, large parts of constructivism, which occupy endpoints in the agent-structure debate, have life easy: they can ignore this messy middle ground. Yet, the true challenge for both rationalists and their opponents is to model and explore this complex interface. . . .

As one scholar recently put it, "regional integration studies could uncharitably be criticized for providing a refuge to homeless ideas." While constructivism is certainly not homeless, Europeanists should resist the temptation simply to pull it off the shelf, giving it a comfortable European home in yet another *n*=1, non-cumulative case study. Rather, these scholars have the opportunity given their immensely rich data set to push forward one of the most exciting debates in contemporary international and political theory.

# Index

# About the Book

Introducing your students to both the concept of a united Europe and integration theory, this popular reader is better than ever. The first section, presenting the visions of the primary shapers of the union, now includes the reflections of current European leaders on a constitution for Europe. The second section introduces the seminal work of early scholars as they struggled to understand postwar European integration: the ideas of federalism, functionalism, neofunctionalism, intergovernmentalism, and other classic integration "isms" are developed here. The completely updated third section explores recent theoretical developments in scholarship on the integration process.

This new edition continues in the tradition begun with the first edition, offering students a chance to be party to the long-running, sometimes heated, always engaging conversation among those dedicated to creating, maintaining, or simply understanding the European Union.

**Brent F. Nelsen** is professor of political science at Furman University. **Alexander Stubb** is adviser to the president of the European Commission and visiting professor at the College of Europe, Bruges.